# Creating Fiscal Space for Poverty Reduction in Ecuador

*A Fiscal Management and Public Expenditure Review*

**Document of the World Bank and the Inter-American Development Bank**

ISBN-10: 0-8213-6256-9        ISBN-13: 987-0-8213-6256-3
eISBN: 0-8213-6257-7
ISSN: 0253-2123              DOI: 10.1596/978-0-8213-6256-3

Cover Art: Eduardo Kingman (Ecuador, 1913-1998), *Lugar Natal*, 1989, oil on canvas, 40 in. x 53 in., Inter-American Development Bank Art Collection, Washington, D.C. Courtesy of the Inter-American Development Bank. Photo of art: IDB Photo Libary Unit.

Library of Congress Cataloging-in-Publication Data has been requested.

# CONTENTS

# LIST OF TABLES

## LIST OF FIGURES

## LIST OF BOXES

## LIST OF ANNEX TABLES

## LIST OF ANNEX FIGURES

# ABSTRACT

The last Public Expenditure Review for Ecuador (PER) was produced in 1993. More than a decade later, the purpose of this report is to provide the Ecuadorian authorities with the World Bank's and Inter-American Development Bank's joint comprehensive account of their diagnoses and recommendations in the area of fiscal management and public expenditure. As the Gutiérrez Administration moves forward in its second year in office, it is hoped that the content of this PER will be useful for Ecuador both to deal with the formidable fiscal challenges it faces and to take advantage of the existing opportunities in its development agenda.

This report consists of two volumes. Volume I examines whether, and how, the core goals of public expenditure management, i.e., balanced fiscal aggregates, resource allocations to strategic sectors, and equity and microeconomic efficiency of public spending are met in Ecuador. Volume II presents sector studies on fiscal sustainability, the fiscal rules, education, health, pensions, the results of a national teachers tracking survey, water and sanitation, electricity, telecommunications and oil.

The report does not provide full coverage of all areas affected by public expenditure. It focuses on the main themes that are critical for Ecuador's fiscal consolidation and poverty reduction following dollarization. In most cases, it does provide choices to key policy questions that are likely to occupy Ecuadorian policymakers over the remaining of the Government, like defining FEIREP proceedings, budget allocations, or social programs prioritization. Thus, it provides an independent analysis of the selected areas where both Banks are specially involved, and a set of possible recommendations to address them. This report reflects policy developments through May 31, 2004.

According to the Ecuadorian Authorities, the PER is "an important contribution from the World Bank and the Interamerican Development Bank to public policy. Volume I, in particular, correctly identifies fiscal vulnerabilities in the new context of dollarization, and proposes an adequate fiscal management that increases expenditure flexibility, develops budget management reform, increases public (social) investment, and brings transparency to public expenditure. All this is supported by an implicit proposal for a Fiscal Pact for Poverty Reduction. For its part, Volume II deals with sectoral policies, and their link to fiscal management. It identifies the most efficient and cost-effective interventions in the social sectors, while making an optimal use of the reduced and available fiscal space. The study also recognizes the importance of political constraints, and the difficulties of setting steady rules in a non-cooperative game among national political actors that are particularly reflected in budget allocations. It correctly emphasizes the need to bring full transparency of information on the management of public accounts among all domestic actors as starting point for sectoral reform. The report has a global view and suggests positive steps. Somehow, it should contribute to align fiscal and institutional policies in the social and basic infrastructure sectors, and to strengthen them in the context of the ongoing negotiations for a Free Trade Agreement with the US., while preserving difficult domestic equilibria on the development agenda."

# ACKNOWLEDGMENTS

This report is a joint effort of the World Bank and the InterAmerican Development Bank. José R. Lopez-Cálix (WB) and Alberto Melo (IDB) are authors, editors and the task managers responsible for completing the whole task. Its initial preparation was coordinated by Sara Calvo (WB) and Carlos Elias (IDB). The report is a collective effort of several authors of chapter sections and background papers presented in two volumes.

Volume I. Chapter 1 was prepared by Alberto Melo, with inputs from Jonas Frank (WB—party politics). Chapter 2 was prepared by Alberto Melo, Elaine Tinsley (WB) and Sara Calvo (WB) including inputs from Jorge Shepherd (consultant—Fiscal Trends), Daniel Artana and Cynthia Moskovits (consultant—Fiscal Policy), Carlos Díaz and Alejandro Izquierdo (IDB—Fiscal Sustainability), Jeffrey Rinne (WB—Civil Servise) and Jonas Frank (WB—Tax Revenues). Chapter 3 was prepared by José R. López-Cálix based on inputs from Michael Geller (WB—Military Expenditures), Rob Vos, Juan Ponce, Mauricio León (consultants—Social sector). Chapter 4 was prepared by José R. López-Cálix with inputs from Elaine Tinsley (WB—Budget Management), Jorge Shepherd (consultant—Social Expenditures), Jonas Frank (WB—Decentralization), and Carolina Sanchez-Páramo (Appendix E—reform of cooking gas subsidy). Vicente Fretes-Cibils (WB), Bruce Fitzgerald (WB) and McDonald Benjamin (WB) provided invaluable oversight and comments on all the chapters. The Statistical Appendix was prepared by Elaine Tinsley with inputs from Jorge Shepherd, Jonas Frank, and Rob Vos. The report also benefited from the useful contributions and complementary analysis on budget management by Diego Mancheno (MEF), Roberto Salazar (MEF), Hugo Muñoz (MEF), Maria de los Angeles Rodriguez (MEF), Lenín Parreño (Banco Central), Fabián Carrillo (MEF), Javier Game (MEF), Roberto Iturralde (MEF), and Paula Suarez (MEF). The draft also benefited from comments collected during a joint IMF/IDB/WB seminar held in Quito on May 20-21, 2004, and another during a joint MEF/IDB/World Bank workshop held in Quito on November 4–5, 2004 on a preliminary version of this report. More in particular, valuable suggestions were received from Patricia McKenzie (WB), Gonzalo Afcha (IDB), Julio Viñuela (IMF), Raju Jan Singh (IMF), Trevor Alleyne (IMF) and Esteban Vesperoni (IMF). Peer reviewers were Yasuhiko Matsuda (WB), Amanda Glassman (IDB), and Carlos Elias (IDB), who provided very helpful comments. Valuable contributions were also received from Francesca Castellani (IDB), Rodrigo Suescun, Carolina Sánchez-Páramo, Emmanuel James, Franz Drees, William Doritinsky, Daniel Dulitzky, Ernesto May and Mauricio Carrizosa (all WB) during all process. This Volume was edited by Diane Stamm and Chris Humphrey (Executive Summary) and assembled under the general production support by Michael Geller.

Volume II. Contributing authors include: Carlos Díaz and Alejandro Izquierdo (Fiscal Sustainability); Daniel Artana and Cynthia Moskovits (Fiscal Rule and Oil Stabilization Fund); Rob Vos, Juan Ponce, Mauricio León (IDB–Health, Education); Rafael Rofman (WB-Pensions); F. Halsey Rogers, José R. López-Cálix, Nancy Córdova, Michael Kremer, Karthik Muralidharan, Jeffrey Hammer, Nazmul Chaudhury (WB, CEDATOS and Harvard University—National Teachers Tracking Survey); Maria Angélica Sotomayor (WB-Water and Sanitation) with support from Franz Drees (WB); Horacio Yépez (Consultant—oil) with support from Eleodoro Mayorga (WB—Oil); Carlos Gómez and Eloy Vidal (WB—Telecom); and Fernando Lecaros (consultant—Electricity) with support from Philippe Durand (WB—Electricity). The Volume was edited by John Moody and María Antonieta Gonzalez and assembled under the general production and editing support by Rosalía Rushton.

The report benefited from the overall guidance and support of Marcelo Giugale (WB—Country Director), Ana Maria Rodríguez (IDB), Vladimir Radovic (IDB), Vicente Fretes-Cibils (WB–Lead Economist), Mauricio Carrizosa (WB–Sector Manager), Ernesto May (WB–LCSPR Director), Javier Game (consultant–IDB), Margarita Andrade and Alexander Shapleigh (SALTO/USAID), and David Yuravlivker (IMF).

This document also benefited from the excellent administrative and production support of Francisco Irias, and Carolina Torres. Alexandra del Castillo, Ana Maria Vicuña, Lucy Vargas, Cynthia Guzmán, Vinicio Valdivieso, and Ana Maria Villaquirán provided critical, timely and qualified operational support to field research in Quito.

The team would also like to express its sincere gratitude and appreciation for the cooperation and contributions of the Ecuadorian authorities throughout the process. We are particularly grateful to Mauricio Pozo, Gilberto Pazmiño, and Messrs. Galo Viteri, Fernando Suárez, Fausto Herrera, Roberto Salazar, Hugo Muñoz, Mauricio Yépez, Leopoldo Báez, Ramiro Galarza, Ivonne Baki, Christian Espinosa, Diego Martínez, Polibio Córdoba, Jenny Guerrero, Paula Suárez, and Liszett Torres. In the same vein, we would like to recognize the valuable inputs provided by the ROSC/CFAA/PER seminar participants held in Quito on May 20–21, 2004. Participants at the first seminar included: Mauricio Pozo, Gilberto Pazmiño, Roberto Salazar, Diego Mancheno, Hugo Muñoz, Fabián Carrillo, Luis Benalcázar, María de los Ángeles Rodríguez, Jorge Recalde, Stalin Nevárez, Eduardo López, Milton Ordóñez, Fausto Solórzano, Estuardo Peñaherrera, Raúl Baca Carbo, Carlos Pólit, Xavier Ledesma, Patricio Acosta, Roberto Passailaigüe, Teófilo Lama, Mauricio León, Genaro Peña, Elsa de Mena, Leonardo Viteri, Juan Abel Echeverría, Jorge Marún, Jaime Estrada, Mauricio Yépez, Leopoldo Báez, José María Borja, Luis Palau, Dora Currea, Mauricio Valdez, David Yuravlivker, Lars Klassen, Julio Viñuela, Gabriel Montalvo, Carlos Pimenta, Javier Game, Paula Suárez, Rick Garland, Maria Lorena Correa, Alexander Shapleigh, Margarita Andrade, Wistano Saez, Rafael Donoso, Victor Acosta, Marco Varea, Esteban Vesperoni, Patricio Rivera, Fausto Herrera, Virginia Velasco, Iván Leiva, Giovanni Coronel, Singh Raju, Alexandra Lastra, Alicia Guzmán, Juan García, Nelly Molina, Ernesto Pérez, José Samaniego, Pablo Lucio Paredes, and Alfredo Arízaga. Participants at the second seminar in Quito on November 4–5, 2004 were: Mauricio Yépez, Javier Game, Ramiro Viteri, Renato Valencia, Roberto Iturralde, Fausto Herrera, Patricio Rivera, Jenny Guerrero, Nelly Molina, Verónica Poveda, Paula Suárez, Verónica Loján, Diego Mancheno, Alfredo Astorga, Nelly Molina, Paúl Carrillo, Nelson Gutiérrez, Alfonso Tique, and Baudouin Duquesne.

The companion volume to this report is referred to as Volume II within the text. To download the background papers and related documents please visit http://www.worldbank.org/laceconomicpolicy and look under "publications." Volume II's condensed Table of Contents is below.

# ECUADOR PUBLIC EXPENDITURE REVIEW VOLUME II TABLE OF CONTENTS (CONDENSED)

# ABBREVIATIONS AND ACRONYMS

| | |
|---|---|
| AIDS | Acquired Immune Deficiency Symdrome |
| AIDIS/AEISA | *Asociación Interamericana de Ingeniería Sanitaria y Ambiental/Asociación Ecuatoriana de Ingeniería Sanitaria y Ambiental* (Pan-american Association of Environmental and Sanitary Engineering/Ecuadorian Association of Environmental and Sanitary Engineering) |
| ANDINATEL | *Empresa Andina Ecuatoriana de Telecomunicaciones* (Andean-Ecuadorian Telecommunications Company) |
| ANEEL | *Agencia Nacional de Energía Eléctrica* (National Agency of Electric Power) |
| APEID | Asia-Pacific Centre of Educational Innovation for Development |
| APRENDO | System of Academic Achievement Tests |
| BCE | Central Bank of Ecuador |
| BCG | Bacille Calmette Geurin Vaccine, Vaccination for Tuberculosis |
| BDH | *Bono de Desarrollo Humano* (Conditional Cash Transfer System) |
| BEDE | *Banco Ecuatoriano de Desarrollo* (Ecuadorian Development Bank) |
| CAE | *Corporación Aduanera Ecuatoriana* (Ecuadorian Customs Corporation) |
| CAF | *Corporación Andina de Fomento* (Andean Corporation of Promotion) |
| CATEG | *Corporación para la Administración Temporal Eléctrica de Guayaquil* (Corporation for the Temporary Electric Administration of Guayaquil) |
| CEDATOS | *Centro de Estudios y* Datos (Center of Studies and Data) |
| CEDEGE | *Centro de Desarrollo de la Cuenca del Guayas* (Center of Development for the Guayas Basin) |
| CELADE | *Centro Latinoamericano y Caribeño de Demografía* (Caribbean and Latin-American Center of Demography) |
| CEM | *Centros Educativos Matrices* (Educational Centers Headquarters) |
| CEMEIN | *Centro Estadal de Medicamentos e Insumos* |
| CENACE | *Corporación Centro Nacional de Control de Energía* (National Central corporation of Energy Control) |
| CEPAR | *Centro de Estudios de Población y Desarrollo Social* (Population Studies and Social Development Center) |
| CFAA | Country Financial and Accountability Assessment |
| CG | Central Government |
| CNRH | *Consejo de Recursos Hídricos* (Council of Water Resources) |
| CONAM | *Consejo Nacional de Modernización del Estado* (Council for Modernization of the State) |
| CONAMU | *Consejo Nacional de las Mujeres* (National Council of Women) |
| CONAREM | *Consejo Nacional de Remuneraciones* (National Council of Remunerations) |
| CONATEL | *Consejo Nacional de Telecomunicaciones* (National Telecommunications Council) |
| CONECEL | *Consorcio Ecuatoriano de Telecomunicaciones* (Ecuadorian Telecommunications Consortium) |
| CONELEC | *Consejo Nacional de Electricidad* (National Electicity Consortium) |
| CONTRATANET | government e-procurement portal |
| CPC | Credible Repayment Commitment |
| CPF | *Comité de Padres de Familia* (Family Parents Committee) |
| CPH | Cox Proportional Hazard (a Survival Model) |
| CREA | *Centro de Reconversión Económica del Azuay* (Center of Economic Reconversion of the Azuay) |

| | |
|---|---|
| CREG | *Comisión Reguladora de Energía y Gas* (Regulating Commission of Energy and Gas) |
| CTC | *Compañía de Teléfonos de Chile* (Chile Telephone Compay) |
| CTI | Technical Investments Commission |
| DFID | Department for International Development |
| DHS | Demographic Health Survey |
| DPT | Vaccination for Diphtheria, Pertussis and Tetanus |
| DSA | Debt Sustainability Analysis |
| EBFs | extra-budgetary funds |
| EBITDA | Earnings Before Interest, Taxes, Depreciation and Amortization |
| ECAPAG | *Empresa Cantonal de Agua Potable y Alcantarillado de Guayaquil* (Cantonal Business of Drinking Water and Sewer System of Guayaquil) |
| ECORAE | *Ecodesarrollo de la Región Amazónica Ecuatoriana* (Amazon Regional Eco-Development Tax) |
| ECV | *Encuesta de Condicionales de Vida* |
| EDAP | *Entidades Depositarias de Ahorro Previsional* |
| EMAAP-Q | *Empresa Metropolitana de Alcantarillado y Agua Potable – Quito* (Quito's Water Utility) |
| EMEDINHO | *Encuesta de Medición de Indicadores sobre la Niñez y los Hogares* (Special Module of Household Survey) |
| EMELEC | *Empresa Eléctrica del Ecuador* (Electric Company of Ecuador) |
| EMELGUR | *Empresa Eléctrica Regional Guayas Los Ríos, S.A.* (Regional Guayas-The Rivers Electric Company, Inc.) |
| EMs | Emerging Market Countries |
| ENDEMAIN | *Encuesta Demográfica y de Salud Materno Infantil* (Demographic Survey of Child-Maternal Health) |
| ENRE | *Ente Nacional Regulador de la Electricidad* (National Regulator Entity for the Electricity) |
| EPC | Engineering, Procurement, and Construction |
| EPS | *Empresas Prestadores de Servicios* |
| ETAPA | *Empresa Pública Municipal de Telecomunicaciones, Agua Potable, Alcantarillado* (Public Company for Telecommunications, Drinking Water, and Sewer System) |
| EUC | Education Unit Center |
| FASBASE | *Fortalecimiento y Ampliación de Servicios Básicos de Salud* (Strengthening and Expansion of Health Services) |
| FEIREP | *Fondo de Estabilización, Inversión Social y Productiva y Reducción de Endeudamiento* (Fund for Stabilization, Productive and Social Investment and Reduction of Indebtedness) |
| FEP | *Fondo de Estatización Petrolera* (Oil Stabilization Fund) |
| FISE | *Fondo de Inversión Social de Emergencia* (Emergency Social Investment Fund) |
| FODESEC | *Fondo de Desarrollo Seccional* (Fund for Sectional Development) |
| FONDETEL | *Fondo para el Desarrollo de la Telefonía Rural* (Telecommunications Development Fund) |
| FS | *Fondo de Solidaridad* (Solidarity Fund) |
| FTSRL | Law on Fiscal Transparency, Stabilization and Responsibility |
| GDP | Gross Domestic Product |
| GOE | Government of Ecuador |
| GTZ | German Technical Cooperation Agency |
| HDI | Human Development Index |

| | |
|---|---|
| HIPC(s) | Highly Indebted Poor Country (ies) |
| ICE | *Impuesto a los Consumos Especiales* (Special Consumption Tax) |
| IDB | Inter-American Development Bank |
| IEOS | *Instituto Ecuatoriano de Obras Sanitarias* (Ecuadorian Institute of Sanitary Works) |
| IESS | *Instituto Ecuatoriano de Seguridad Social* (Ecuadorian Social Security Institute) |
| IM | Infant Mortality |
| IMF | International Monetary Fund |
| INEC | (*El Instituto Nacional de Estadística y Censos* (Integrated System of Household Surveys) |
| INECEL | *Instituto Ecuatoriano de Electrificación* (Ecuadorian Power Authority) |
| INH | *Instituto Nacional de Higiene* (National Institute of Hygiene) |
| IPS | interbank payment system |
| IRS/SRI | Internal Revenue Service/Servicio de Rentas Internas |
| ISR | personal income tax |
| ISSFA | Military Social Security Institute |
| ISSPOL | *Instituto de Seguridad Social de la Policía Nacional* (Institute of Social Security of the National Police) |
| ITT | Oil Fields (*Ishipingo-Tambococha-Tiputini*) |
| ITU | International Telecommunications Union |
| IVM | Internal Value Measurement |
| JASS | *Juntas de Agua y Saneamiento* (Committee for Water and Disinfection) |
| LAC' | Latin America and The Caribbean |
| LMG | *Ley de Maternidad Gratuita y Atención a la Infancia* (Law of Free Maternity and Attention to Infancy) |
| LNG | Liquefied Natural Gas |
| LOAFYC | *Ley Orgánica de Administración Financiera y Control* (Organic Law of Financial Management and Control) |
| LSMS | Living Standards Measurement Study |
| MBS/STFS | *Ministerio de Bienestar Social* (Ministry of Social Affairs) |
| MDGs | Millennium Development Goals |
| MED | Ministry of Education |
| MEF | *Ministerio de Economía y Finanzas* (Finance Ministry) |
| MEM | *Ministerio de Energía y Minas* (Ministry of Energy and Mines) |
| MIDUVI | *Ministerio de Desarrollo Urbano y Vivienda* (Ministry of Urban Development and Housing) |
| MNL | Multinomial Logit Model |
| MO | Mendoza-Oviedo |
| MPH | Ministry of Public Health |
| MYBF | Multiyear Budgeting Framework |
| NBI | *Necesidades Básicas Insatisfechas* (Unmet Basic Needs) |
| NFPS | Non Financial Public Sector |
| NWFP | North West Frontier Province |
| OECD | Organization for Economic Co-operation and Development |
| OLS | Ordinary Least Squares |
| ORDs | Regional Development Organizations |
| OSCIDI | *Oficina de Servicio Civil y Desarrollo Institucional* (Office of Civil Service and Institutional Development) |
| OSINERG | *Organismo Supervisor de la Inversión en Energía* (Supervising Agency for Energy Investment) |

| | |
|---|---|
| OTECEL | Bellsouth, *Empresa Telefónica* |
| PACIFICTEL | Pacific Telephone—Fixed line telecommunications operator in the coastal region |
| PAE | *Programa de Alimentación Escolar* (School Breakfast Program) |
| PAHO | Pan-American Health Organization |
| PAI | *Programa Ampliado de Inmunización en las Américas* (Immunization Program) |
| PANN | *Programa Nacional de Nutrición y Alimentación* (National Nutritional Program for Children) |
| PEM | Public Expenditure Management |
| PER | Public Expenditure Review |
| PGE | *Presupuesto General de Estado* (Central Government Budget) |
| PHRD | Public Human Resource Development |
| PPA | Power Purchasing Agreement |
| PPC | *Programación Periódica de Caja* (cash balance periodic programming) |
| PPS | Project for Public Spaces |
| PRADEC | *Programa de Asistencia y Desarrollo Comunitario* (programs of Aid and Common Development) |
| PRAGUAS | *Programa de Agua y Saneamiento para Comunidades Rurales y Pequeños Municipios* (Project Appraisal Document, Rural and Small Towns Water Supply and Sanitation Project) |
| PROBE | Public Report on Basic Education |
| PROMEC | *Proyecto de Modernización de los Sectores Eléctrico, Telecomunicaciones y Servicios Rurales* (Power and Communications Sectors Modernization and Rural Services Project) |
| PROST | Pension Reform Options Stimulation Toolkit – developed by the World Bank |
| PRS | Poverty Reduction Strategy |
| RER | Real Exchange Rate |
| RGP | Referential Generation Price |
| ROSC | Reports on the Observance of Standards and Codes |
| RUC | *Registro Único de Contribuyentes* (centralized taxpayers registry) |
| SAPYSB | *Subsecretaria de Agua Potable y Saneamiento Básico* (Undersecretary of Drinking Water and Basic Sanitation) |
| SELBEN | *Sistema de Identificación y Selección de Beneficiarios de los Programas Sociales* (Poverty Mapping and Strengthening Database) |
| SENATEL | *Secretaria Nacional de Telecomunicaciones* (National Telecommunications Office) |
| SENRES | *Secretaría Nacional Técnica de Desarrollo de Recursos Humanos y Remuneraciones del Sector Público* (National Technical Office of Human Resources Development and Remunerations of the Public Sector) |
| SIAN | Sistema Integrado de Alimentación y Nutrición |
| SIEH | *Sistema Integrado de Encuestas de Hogares* (Integrated Home Survey System) |
| SIGEF | *Sistema Integrado de Genercia Económica y Financiera* (Integrated Financial Management System) |
| SIGOB | *Sistema de Gestión de Gobierno* (Government Management System) |
| SINEC | *Sistema Nacional de Estadísticas y Censos* (National System of Statistics and Censuses) |
| SNEM | *Servicio de Erradicación de Malaria* (Malaria Eradication Service) |
| SOTE | *Sistema de Oleoducto Transecuatoriano* (Trans-Ecuadorian Pipeline) |

| | |
|---|---|
| SPA | *Subsecretaria de Protección Ambiental* (Undersecretariat on Environmental Protection) |
| SPR | Strategic Policy Research |
| SSC | *Seguro Social Campesino* (rural social security) |
| SSO | *Seguro Social Obligatorio* (obligatory social security) |
| STFS | *Secretaria Técnica del Frente Social* (Technical Secretariat of the Social Front) |
| STFS-SIISE | *Sistema Integrado de Indicatores Sociales del Ecuador* (Integrated System of Social Indicators of the Social Cabinet) |
| SUPTEL | *Superintendencia de Telecomunicaciones* (Super-intendence of Telecommunications) |
| TELECSA | Ecuadorian Telecommunications—South America |
| UBN | Unsatisfied Basic Needs |
| UDENOR | *Unidad de Desarrollo del Norte* (Northern Development office) |
| UNDP | United Nations Development Programme |
| UNE | *Union Nacional de Educadores del Ecuador* (National Teacher's Union) |
| UNESCO | United Nations Educational, Scientific and Cultural Organization |
| UNICEF | United Nations Children's Fund |
| VAT | Value-Added Tax |
| VOIP | Voice-over-IP |
| WFP | World Food Programme |
| WHO | World Health Organization |

REPUBLIC OF ECUADOR – FISCAL YEAR: January 1 – December 31
CURRENCY EQUIVALENTS: (Exchange Rate Effective as of 11/11/2004)

Currency Unit    = US dollar
US$1.00    = US$1.00

WEIGHTS AND MEASURES: Metric System

| IBRD | | IDB | |
|---|---|---|---|
| Vice President: | David de Ferranti | Manager, Regional Operation III: | Ciro de Falco |
| Country Director: | Marcelo M. Giugale | Deputy Manager, Regional Operations Dept. III: | Máximo Jeria |
| Sector Director: | Ernesto May | Chief, Country Division 5: | Vladimir Radovic |
| Sector Leader: | Mauricio Carrizosa | | |
| Lead Economist: | Vicente Fretes-Cibils | | |
| Senior Economist, Co-Task Manager | José R. López-Cálix | Country Economist, Co-Task Manager: | Alberto Melo |

# EXECUTIVE SUMMARY

## Ecuador: Creating Fiscal Space for Poverty Reduction Fiscal Management and Public Expenditure Review

Since Ecuador adopted full dollarization in early 2000, its fiscal performance has significantly improved. The new exchange rate regime is underpinned by sound fiscal policies and structural reforms. Following a difficult transition, the Gutiérrez administration strengthened the dollarization framework with its Program of Economic Restructuring and Human Development. The results achieved thus far are encouraging: Ecuador is one of the best-performing economies in Latin America.

- Growth has resumed and is expected to reach above 5 percent in 2004.
- Inflation fell to single digits in late 2002 and is projected to continue declining below 3 percent in 2004.
- The Non Financial Public Sector (NFPS) primary and overall fiscal surpluses in 2003 are among the highest in the Latin American region (4.7 percent of GDP and 1.7 percent of GDP) and are projected to reach similar levels in 2004, reinforced by the new Fiscal Responsibility, Stabilization, and Transparency Law (FRSTL);
- The current account deficit has halved, most arrears were cleared and public indebtedness was lowered by about 5 percent of GDP in 2003. These outcomes are also projected to further improve in 2004.

The Ecuadorian economy, however, remains vulnerable. External factors, particularly oil prices, have a strong impact on the economy (Figure ES.1), as do shocks such as sudden stops of capital flows, rising interest rates, falling remittances or natural disasters. Shocks cause stress in the fiscal accounts, depreciate the real exchange rate, and threaten fiscal sustainability. The effect of these shocks could be augmented or alleviated by the Government's use of fiscal policy, which is the principal macro-economic policy tool available in a dollarized economy.

Poverty reduction is critical to sustain the country's stability in the medium term. As a result of the triple—banking, debt and exchange—crises of the late 1990s, poverty has increased. The national poverty rate increased from 40 to 45 percent between 1990 and 2001, and the number of poor increased from 3.5 million to 5.2 million, with a marked concentration of new poor in the urban areas. President Gutiérrez has committed to designing and implementing a Poverty Reduction Strategy (PRS) to reduce this high level of poverty and to achieve the Millennium Development Goals (MDGs). Reversing poverty trends and improving living standards is a *sine qua non* for maintaining the country's stability, while mitigating macro volatility.

To strengthen the economy's resistance to shocks, reduce the high rates of poverty, and achieve the MDGs, this report highlights the need for public policy to focus on three main goals: (a) strengthened fiscal sustainability; (b) increased fiscal space for pro-poor efficient and

## FIGURE ES.1: OIL PRICES, GROWTH AND THE NFPS FISCAL DEFICIT

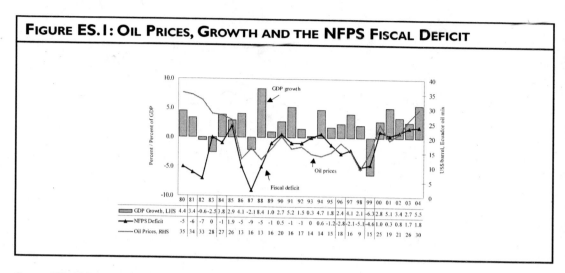

| | 80 | 81 | 82 | 83 | 84 | 85 | 86 | 87 | 88 | 89 | 90 | 91 | 92 | 93 | 94 | 95 | 96 | 97 | 98 | 99 | 00 | 01 | 02 | 03 | 04 |
|---|---|---|---|---|---|---|---|---|---|---|---|---|---|---|---|---|---|---|---|---|---|---|---|---|---|
| GDP Growth, LHS | 4.4 | 3.4 | -0.6 | -2.5 | 3.8 | 2.9 | 4.1 | -2.1 | 8.4 | 1.0 | 2.7 | 5.2 | 1.5 | 0.3 | 4.7 | 1.8 | 2.4 | 4.1 | 2.1 | -6.3 | 2.8 | 5.1 | 3.4 | 2.7 | 5.5 |
| NFPS Deficit | -5 | -6 | -7 | 0 | -1 | 1.9 | -5 | -9 | -5 | -1 | 0.5 | -1 | -1 | 0 | 0.6 | -1.2 | -2.8 | -2.1 | -5.1 | -4.6 | 1.0 | 0.3 | 0.8 | 1.7 | 1.8 |
| Oil Prices, RHS | 35 | 34 | 33 | 28 | 27 | 26 | 13 | 16 | 13 | 16 | 20 | 16 | 17 | 14 | 14 | 15 | 18 | 16 | 9 | 15 | 25 | 19 | 21 | 26 | 30 |

Source: World Bank staff's estimates.

equitable public spending; and (c) improved budget management for results-oriented service delivery. These three objectives are closely interrelated. Given external vulnerability and dollarization, fiscal sustainability is a pre-requisite for poverty reduction, as nothing hurts the poor more than an unstable macroeconomy. However, meaningful poverty reduction also requires fiscal space, understood as the amount of non-wage expenditure devoted to poverty reduction, and resources shifted toward pro-poor priority programs, executed with efficiency and equity considerations. Furthermore, in a context of scarce resources, sound budget management is essential to eliminate waste and rigidities and improve service delivery.

## Fiscal Policy Faces Historical and Structural Constraints

**To consolidate fiscal discipline, Ecuador must overcome the inherited effects of three decades of predominantly misguided fiscal policies before dollarization.** Public sector net worth declined between 1970 and 2000, and it has remained flat since then. Fiscal revenues are volatile and pro-cyclical. Past expansionary spending resulted in high deficits financed with mounting debt. In addition, budget rigidity due to earmarking repeatedly provokes serious liquidity problems for the national Treasury. These shortcomings are compounded by the political economy constraints. In Ecuador, the prevailing political-economy regime was formed in the early 1970s under the influence of the oil boom of those years. Its main features are those common in societies where rent-seeking is pervasive: acute competition for oil rents; conflict-prone social relationships; a fragmented political system where social and political actors face seemingly insurmountable difficulties to reach consensus; a state captured by privileged groups and always on the verge of becoming just the institutional locus where decisions on rent distribution are made and clientelistic favors and privileges are purveyed. As a result, governance and institutions are weak, the efficiency and efficacy of public administration is severely impaired and the opportunities for arbitrariness and corruption in the exercise of power multiply. Throughout the last three decades, the internal connection between this political-economy regime and the practices and institutions that frame the conduct of fiscal policy is particularly visible in four systemic features of fiscal policy and public finance, namely: (i) the large size of Government and its role as a producer and provider of non-public goods and services, frequently at subsidized prices; (ii) the existence of a set of tax expenditures, whose function is to channel (potential) government revenue to the private sector; (iii) the fact that policymakers' incentives tend to be biased toward a short-term horizon; and (iv) the extended use of the deeply flawed institution of earmarking.

To face these shortcomings, Ecuador chose a very demanding institutional framework for the conduct of economic policy. While dollarization eliminates the risk of a currency crisis and the hyperinflation it entails, policy tools for demand management are severely restricted, and the buffer of the nominal exchange rate is no longer available. Moreover, for all its advantages for financial stability, dollarization in the context of an open capital account needs to be supported by a robust, well-regulated financial system.

## Fiscal Trends and Challenges

The first task is to consolidate the current trend toward fiscal sustainability. Fiscal revenue is close to 25 percent of GDP, high by Latin American standards. This implies that while, non-oil tax receipts should be raised, expenditure adjustments rather than revenue increases must be the principal means to achieve a sustainable fiscal path. The current administration must deal with the fact that currently too much is spent on rigid and non-priority goods and services, and too little on pro-poor programs.

The Government is not using high oil prices as an excuse for expansionary fiscal policy, despite the highest oil prices in more than two decades. This restrained fiscal policy recognizes that Ecuador is still in a fragile fiscal position. Structural estimates of the fiscal stance confirm the prudent management of fiscal policy after dollarization. The average fiscal stance (the difference between the actual and "structural" budget balance) was a surplus of about 1 percent of GDP between 2000–03.

Revenue management has improved significantly under the reformed Internal Revenue Service (IRS), but faces difficult structural constraints. Since revamping the IRS in the late 1990s, for the first time in 30 years tax revenue has become roughly equivalent to non-tax revenue as a share of GDP. The IRS has a centralized taxpayers registry with crosschecking systems, and applies sanctions to non-compliers. However, the tax system remains segmented in a myriad of nuisance taxes (84 overall), and is burdened by extensive earmarking and a multiplicity of tax exemptions. Both earmarking and exemptions are costly (each accounting for about 4 percent of GDP in 2004) and increasing. Tax earmarking severely undermines budget management, since it promotes an inefficient and inequitable use of resources, and constrains the authorities' ability to reduce expenditure when needed.

Although fiscal policy has been prudent in macro-economic terms, the existing spending structure is not conducive to poverty reduction: public wages and pensions have increased at the cost of cutbacks in public investment and social outlays. Since 2000, non-financial public sector (NFPS) primary spending has been on an expansionary trend. This is mainly propelled by wages and salaries, and contrasts with the constant trend maintained during the pre-dollarization period. This expansionary pattern indicates that the gains achieved by cutbacks in capital and social outlays, as well as in savings in interest payments, have been used to pay for the growing salaries and pensions.

The rapid increase in payroll spending is not mainly due to the size of the civil service, but to increases in wages. The size of the Ecuadorian civil service is about average when compared to other Latin American countries. However, the rate of growth of the public payroll has been high. In real terms, the payroll grew 21.3 percent in 2001, 35.4 percent in 2002 and 19.5 percent in 2003. Not surprisingly, the share in current expenditure going to wages and salaries almost doubled in the last four years, rising from 25 percent in 2000 to 45 percent in 2003.

The changes in the sectoral composition of government expenditure also constraints social outlays. Social expenditures remain low and have slightly declined in the last two years. In 2004, education and health spending accounts for about 4 percent of GDP, about half the LAC averages of 7.5 percent of GDP. Social assistance, an important element for preserving a safety net on vulnerable sectors, accounts for about 1 percent of GDP. At the same time, military spending, at about 3 percent of GDP, is twice as high as the Latin American average of about 1.5 percent of GDP, and on the rise, following the increased military activity in neighboring Colombia.

**To deepen its fiscal consolidation, Ecuador implemented an oil stabilization fund together with well-defined fiscal rules.** The FRSTL created an oil fund (FEIREP) with the objective of stabilizing fiscal revenues, repurchasing debt and saving some funds for education and health. Quantitative rules were introduced on the growth of the Central Government real primary spending (3.5 percent a year), non-oil deficit reduction (0.2 percent a year), and debt ratio reduction (toward a ceiling 40 percent of GDP in the medium term). The Law also introduces constraints on subnational debt and rules on fiscal transparency. The creation of the fund is positive for preserving government's net worth. However, estimates show that the current rules might force the government to save too much at certain times and not enough at others; that resources allocated to its stabilization (countercyclical) component are less than optimal for providing full insurance; and that if its design were improved, the mandatory reduction of the non-oil deficit at an annual pace of 0.2 percent of GDP might be eliminated once public debt reaches 40 percent. In the short term, however, making the fund comply with its mandated role is critical, and any change to its rules for political reasons would damage its credibility.

**A preliminary assessment indicates that compliance with fiscal rules has been reasonable so far.** In 2004, the rules governing planned real primary spending and the non-oil deficit were met. The scheduled reduction of public debt-to-GDP ratio was also on track in 2003. On the execution side, however, performance was mixed: the executed real primary expenditure, instead of increasing, fell by almost 1 percent of GDP in 2003, and the non-oil deficit reduction was not achieved in 2003, after two consecutive years of reduction. However, the reduction in the public debt-to-GDP ratio of about 5 percent of GDP in 2003 was consistent with high primary surpluses devoted to reach the mandated ceiling target of 40 percent of GDP in 2006 (Figure ES.2).

**Despite this positive performance, debt sustainability remains vulnerable to shocks, as a debt sustainability simulation illustrates.** A 50 percent drop in the price of oil from US$24 to US$12 per barrel would lead to a drop in export proceeds and to a 33 percent depreciation of the real exchange rate. Tradable goods would become more expensive relative to nontradable goods and this will lower the value of output—that has a large nontradable component—thus leading to an increase in the debt-to-GDP ratio. The 50 percent drop in the price of oil would also require an increased primary balance from 4.5 to 5.2 percent of GDP, that is, almost 1 addi-

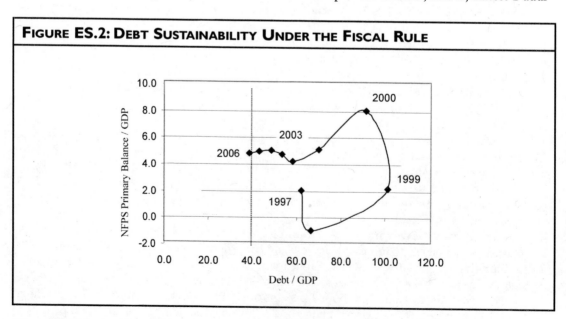

**FIGURE ES.2: DEBT SUSTAINABILITY UNDER THE FISCAL RULE**

Source: World Bank staff's estimates.

tional point of GDP, just to sustain 2003 levels of debt. And if this shock were accompanied by an increase in 200 basis points in interest rates and a fall of 1 percentage point in GDP growth, then the required primary surplus for debt sustainability would rise to about 7 percent of GDP. These numbers illustrate potential risks for the future.

## Pro-Poor Expenditure and the Room for Additional Fiscal Space

The Government recognizes that the present fiscal stance is inconsistent within the framework of a poverty reduction strategy. Its objectives are to take advantage of the process leading to the PRS to improve the amount and quality of public expenditures: level, composition, and targeting. To help assess these objectives, this section addresses the following issues:

- Trends in social outcomes, particularly in education and health
- Trends in pro-poor expenditure
- Finding fiscal space to increase spending for poverty reduction

### Trends in Social Outcomes

Educational outcomes continued to improve during the 1990s and into the new millennium:

- There has been continuous growth in the average level of schooling since the 1970s: in 2001, the average adult had completed 7.3 years of schooling, up from 6.7 years in 1990. This level is above the Latin American mean, and is about the same as East Asia.
- By 2001, the gender gap had practically been closed: 7.5 years for males compared to 7.1 years for females. Educational levels of the female population have risen much faster than that of males, such that, in terms of net enrolment rates, girls already outperform boys at all educational levels.
- Net enrolment in primary education increased from 88.9 to 90.1 percent between 1990 and 2001, approximating the MDG of primary education for all.

**Health indicators have also improved:**

- Life expectancy at birth increased from 48 years to 72 years between 1950 and 2000. This upward trend was sustained during the 1990s, adding another 5 years to life expectancy.
- Parallel declining trends are found in child and infant mortality rates. The overall mortality rate dropped from 13.8 per 100,000 inhabitants in 1960 to 4.5 per 100,000 inhabitants in 2001. This rate did not change much during the 1990s. In contrast, since 1970, the infant mortality rate fell by 70 percent in Ecuador, which is an impressive achievement. The infant (aged 0–1) mortality rate has followed an almost linear trend since 1950, reaching 33 per 1,000 live births during 1995–2000, down from 140 during 1950–55. Child (aged 1–5) mortality rates follow similar trends (WHO 2003).
- The drop in infant mortality coincides with a long-term decline in fertility rates. Fertility dropped from almost 7 per woman in the 1950s and 1960s to 2.8 during 2000–05. During the 1990s, fertility dropped faster in rural than in urban areas, but the rate is still 1.5 times higher for rural women.

**Important concerns, however, remain in the education sector**. The transition rates from primary to secondary education and from secondary to tertiary did not improve in the 1990s. Significant disparities remain, particularly affecting rural, indigenous, and black populations. The average level of schooling of the rural population is less than half the one of the urban population, and the gap is even larger for the indigenous and black populations. This is also the case for illiteracy rates. Overall education quality is poor, with math and language test scores worsening between 1996 and 2000 and starting from an extremely low baseline (Ecuador scores lowest for the Latin America region). Internal efficiency indicators, measured by desertion and repetition rates, have also worsened, with the number of years pupils need to complete primary education increasing from 6.7 years to 6.9 years between 1995 and 2001; and higher dropout by girls in secondary rural schools and by boys in urban schools, seemingly for economic reasons. Finally, retention rates and education quality also appear affected by the high rate (14 percent) of teacher absenteeism and frequent teacher strikes in Ecuador

**Similarly, concerns appear in the health sector that will put pressure for additional financing.** The decline in fertility and the increase in life expectancy are changing Ecuador's demographic profile. The causes of mortality are moving away from traditional child diseases (malnutrition, respiratory and infectious diseases) toward diseases associated with higher levels of economic well-being and urban lifestyle (cardiovascular and cancer health risks). Preventable diseases remain the main causes of child (1 to 5) and infant (0 to 1) mortality. The prevalence of AIDS has increased, with 10 times more cases reported in 2002 than in 1990. Finally, malaria trends remain closely associated with the occurrence of the *El Niño* effect.

**Selected MDGs in education and health are within reach, however, especially if supported by additional social expenditure, well targeted, effective, and financed by low-cost programs explicitly linked to specific outcomes.** Positive educational and health outcomes have been obtained despite low education and health budgets, apparently poorly functioning education and health systems, a significant amount of non-pro-poor spending in both sectors, and a high incidence of malnutrition. Continued overall improvements in education, urbanization, fertility rates, and sanitary conditions explain these seemingly paradoxical outcomes. However, no linear extrapolation guarantees that these trends will continue. This is why a pro-poor shift in social spending is desirable.

*Trends in Pro-Poor Expenditure*

**About half of social spending and all subsidies to basic services are not pro-poor.** In a context of fiscal adjustment, making better use of resources is essential to reduce poverty. Government spending on education and health could be better spent to achieve improved educational and health outcomes and greater equity. In education, while primary education and to a lesser extent secondary education are pro-poor, spending in tertiary education is heavily skewed against the poor. This is all the more worrisome considering that spending in primary and secondary education has had a constant share in the total sector budget since 1995, but higher education has received about a 33 percent increase over the same period.

**Incidence analysis also points out to significant non pro-poor spending in social expenditure.** Taking the difference between the richest and poorest quintiles, it appears that the school breakfast, primary school spending, and the *Bono* cash transfer, in that order, are the most pro-poor programs (Figure ES.3). This happens despite significant targeting problems in their implementation and poor nutritional impact on their beneficiaries, specially in the school breakfast. At the bottom of the classification, university education, IESS health care and the cooking gas appear to be the most non-pro-poor outlays.

**Furthermore, none of the three subsidies to basic services—water, telecom, and electricity—caters to the poor, and they are highly distortionary from an efficiency perspective.** These subsidies represent a big drain for the government resources: about 1.3 percent of GDP. The implicit subsidy for telephone service is the most unequally distributed, followed by the water subsidy. Electricity is the largest subsidy. While tackling the telecom and electricity subsidies is a priority for the central government, dealing with the water subsidy requires collaboration with subnational governments.

**The efficiency of expenditure on basic infrastructure also has significant shortcomings.** There are high losses in the power sector due to theft and inappropriate billing; the water and

## FIGURE ES.3: INCIDENCE OF SOCIAL EXPENDITURE, 1999

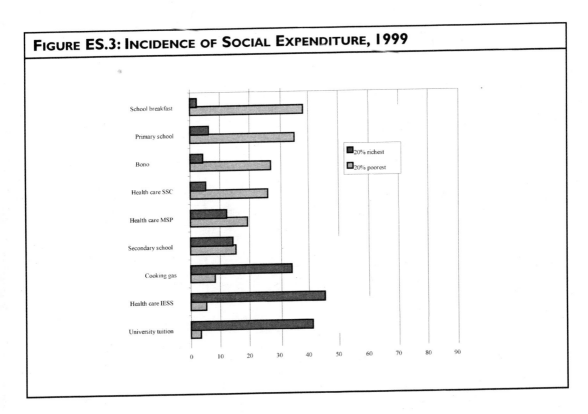

Source: Table 3.1.

sanitation sector has massive shortfalls of resources in non-wage and maintenance expenditures due to significant cuts in transfers to municipal governments, and the telecom sector has low operational surpluses due to low and distortionary rates against the poor. Telephone penetration was almost 10 times lower in the poorest quintile and only 1 out of 20 rural people has telephone service.

*Finding Fiscal Space to Increase Spending for Poverty Reduction*
**Rigid expenditure limits fiscal space for poverty reduction.** Central government expenditure has become increasingly rigid, leaving almost no fiscal space for development needs. In 2004, wages and salaries account for 32 percent of total spending, earmarked transfers, inertial services and investment are 34 percent, and debt service is 30 percent, which adds to 96 percent of the total budget, up from 86 percent in 2001. This means that the non-rigid and non-inertial spending barely represents 4 percent of the total budget, leaving a very small residual fiscal space—no bigger than half a percent of GDP—for freely allocated public investment. **Should this pattern continue, and the residual fiscal space that could potentially be allocated to investment in poverty reduction would fully disappear by 2006.** Reversing this situation points out to the urgent need to explore possible sources for creating additional fiscal space within the fiscal aggregate ceiling allowed by the fiscal rule.

   **The Government could create fiscal space of up to about 6 percent of GDP.** This is a considerable margin, considering that only 1-2 percent of GDP would be needed to achieve selected MDGs in education and health (Table ES.1). These estimates assume that the Government decides to maintain a constant tax burden, curbs expansionary spending in the payroll and pensions, and improves the pro-poor content of expenditure policies. The additional fiscal space would also contribute to a further reduction of non-priority expenditure required to compensate for any revenue loss emanating from a fall in oil prices or another external or domes-

### TABLE ES.1: POTENTIAL SOURCES OF FISCAL SPACE AND ESTIMATED ANNUAL IMPACT

| Measures | Percent of GDP |
|---|---|
| *On-budget* | |
| Curb capital spending ratio toward its "structural" level (budget reallocation) | 0.2 |
| Interest savings from debt repurchase | 0.2 |
| Reduce defense spending to end-1990s level | 1.0 |
| Make optimal use of public spending (Competitive-based Fund) | 0.2 |
| *Off-Budget* | |
| Reduce selected off-budget earmarking of oil revenues | 0.6 |
| Incorporate and cut oil-subsidies to budget (gas, diesel, and electricity) | 2.3 |
| Eliminate 25 percent of overall tax exemptions | 1.0 |
| VAT | 0.7 |
|   Internal | 0.3 |
|   External | 0.4 |
| Income | 0.3 |
|   Firms | 0.2 |
|   Individuals | 0.1 |
| Rationalize spending of ORDs | NA |
| Integrate 10 percent of subnational spending with national priorities | 0.4 |
| Allocate resources from Solidarity Fund to the PRS | 0.1 |
| **TOTAL** | **6.0** |

*Source:* World Bank staff calculations.

tic shock. In addition, the Government could create fiscal space for increased pro-poor spending, especially in the education, health, and social protection sectors, by: (a) revising the current allocations of social expenditure and programs through the development of a competitive-based fund; and (b) making better use of the available targeting instruments, like SELBEN, to unify criteria and consolidate programs. Notice however, that whatever solutions are adopted, they will have to be accomplished within the annual fiscal ceiling mandated by the FRSTL. The existence of this ceiling, and the little room for tax reform implies that the main effort will have to come from expenditure shifting activities.

An input–output model developed as part of this report identifies the main inputs that determine achieving key MDGs. It is possible to identify inputs required for reaching at least the three MDGs of universal primary and secondary education enrolment and reduced infant mortality. These can be achieved with four cost-effective programs: teacher training and the expansion of the *Bono de Desarrollo Humano* for primary and secondary education, and expansion of the coverage of the immunization and Free Maternity programs for infant mortality.

## Public Expenditure Management (PEM) and Other Institutional Issues

Developing an effective poverty reduction strategy for Ecuador requires, as a precondition, an overall reform of the budget process and, more broadly, of all levels of PEM. A sound PEM is the key policy instrument that articulates the country's fiscal ceilings and rules with, on one hand, priorities reflected in the budget and, on the other hand, improvements in public sector performance and service delivery. Hence, PEM reform requires an enhanced performance of the budgeting system, rapid upgrading of its budget and financial management procedures, a complete overhaul of budgeting procedures by social agencies in charge of priority social programs and of provincial and sectional governments receiving transfers, transparent information access at all levels of government to allow results-oriented budgeting in the future, and, only when these reforms have gained ground, a multi-year budgeting framework (MYBF) that would allow aligning expenditure inputs with expected social outcomes. At present, Ecuador is not ready for a MYBF.

**Since 2003, Ecuador has taken steps to improve its overall PEM.**

- The passage of the Fiscal Law in 2002 set quantitative rules for budget formulation, laying the groundwork for multiyear budgeting, and requiring subnational entities to submit monthly revenue and expenditure reports.
- The country has been prudent in its budget formulation and assumptions; while attaining with an acceptable aggregate level of budget under-execution (below 5 percent);
- It has reinitiated the extension and modernization of the coverage of its integrated financial management system (SIGEF) with the goal of producing consolidated balances for 90 percent of the central government by 2005;
- A single database for central government-financed public investment has been built;
- An inter-bank payment system (IPS) of public employees located at the Central Bank has started to develop a central registry database for all government employees at SIGEF; and
- CONTRATANET, an electronic public procurement system, has been set up on a pilot basis, initially as an informational—not yet transactional—system.

**Despite these improvements, a standard global assessment carried out as part of this report shows that the country ranks poorly in all but one of the 16 international PEM benchmarks.** Benchmarks refer to overall budget formulation, monitoring, execution, control and reporting procedures. A survey developed by this study shows that the country ranks in the bottom tier, even when compared to heavily indebted poor countries (HIPCs). The survey findings are confirmed by parallel studies in standard transparency rankings (ROSC) prepared by the IMF, and the Country Financial and accountability Assessment (CFAA) jointly prepared by the World Bank and the Inter-American Development Bank (IADB).

**The most important weaknesses are:** (a) poor and inertial budget planning, with a bias in favor of defense and security forces and against spending in the social sectors; (b) the presence of significant off-budget funds; (c) poor Treasury management, reflected in arrears, cash rationing and long delays in the transfer of resources to social programs; (d) absence of a results-oriented framework; and (e) an outdated integrated financial management system that does not allow timely and reliable reporting on budget execution, which affects monitoring and limits transparency, control and public oversight of fiscal accounts.

**Poor performance of social expenditure in Ecuador is closely linked to PEM shortcomings.** Recent reviews of international experience with poverty reduction strategies have concluded that in many countries, the practice of PEM is an obstacle to the achievement of poverty reduction objectives. Ecuador is no exception. Failures in the budget process and institutional bottlenecks systematically lead to underexecution of social programs. These shortcomings result in underbudgeting or in long interruptions and delays in the channeling of budgeted resources. Perhaps the most important failures are unrealistic budget planning, wide variations in deviations between budgets approved and executed—with a bias in favor of defense and security forces and against spending in the social sectors—a lack of effective interventions resulting from budget fragmentation through a myriad of overlapping social programs and the presence of significant off-budget funds, and delays in the actual transfer of resources, arising from cash rationing and poor execution capacity at the level of line agencies. Arrears have been declining since 2000, but a sizable financial gap of about US$548 million still remained for 2004 by mid-year.

**Weaknesses in the budget processes and institutional bottlenecks play a major role in the poor performance of social programs and municipal spending.** Recent reviews of international experience with poverty reduction strategies have concluded that in many countries, the practice of PEM is an obstacle to achieving poverty reduction objectives. Ecuador is no exception. A review of budgeting procedures in both selected social programs and subnational governments done as part of this report also identifies important shortcomings.

**In the priority social programs, shortcomings are multiple**. A lack of effective interventions and budget under-execution result from budget fragmentation through a myriad of overlapping social programs, which have grown increasingly fragmented and disorganized. There are 45 social programs and some are duplicative. Long interruptions, delays and deviations exist in the channeling of budgeted resources to priority social programs. Cash constraints are particularly acute in the first semester of the year. Excessive bureaucratic controls also play a role in delaying compliance with budget allocations. Most performing social programs are those which have their own budget execution capacity (and financing mechanisms) and little intermediation from ministries.

**In provincial and municipal governments, budget procedures replicate similar weaknesses observed at the central government**. This is the case in terms of inertial budgeting, low predictability of transfers, absence of national directives, and poor reporting. However, this report finds that since 2003, MEF has over-complied with committed transfers to provincial and sectional governments, which reflects that fact that Treasury's cash rationing has been unequally applied in the public sector. Unfortunately, this has not been accompanied by increased accountability and responsibility, thus weakening the framework for fiscal discipline at the subnational level and opening the door for wasted and unreported resources transferred to subnational governments and for irresponsible subnational borrowing.

**Fiscal discipline and implementation of an effective poverty reduction agenda could be facilitated by a reform of all levels of PEM**. Sound PEM is the instrument that articulates the country's fiscal ceilings and rules with, on the one hand, priorities reflected in the budget and, on the other hand, improvements in public sector performance and service delivery. To ensure the fiscal discipline needed to support dollarization, the Government should first set the annual ceiling of fiscal balances. Then, based on such a constraint, a shift to pro-poor allocations of expenditures would be easier to implement with an improved expenditure management process that is strategic in focus, feasible in terms of available fiscal space, and results-oriented with proper monitoring and evaluation mechanisms.

## Conclusion and Policy Recommendations

**Ecuador's impressive fiscal performance of 2003 and 2004 is encouraging, but fragile.** Several structural bottlenecks could impede fiscal discipline and recovery, which is a pre-condition to develop a poverty reduction agenda. Tax earmarkings, multiple exemptions, an expansive payroll and growing pensions bill have reduced to a minimum the available fiscal space for development needs. Reversing poverty trends is critical for the country's stability, and this can only be achieved with well-targeted, effective and efficient pro-poor programs. The *status quo* is not an option for poverty reduction.

**Preserving a sound fiscal position and deepening positive social outcomes is well within reach.** Among the country's many strengths are: a prolonged oil windfall; the existence of and compliance with fiscal rules; substantive progress on social outcomes despite decreasing budgets; and a series of on-going reforms on budget management. Last September an important test was the Government's capacity to successfully resist short-term election-motivated pressures for amending the fiscal rule in order to misuse FEIREP resources. The lessons from international experience on the implementation of poverty reduction strategies suggest three guiding principles

*First*, the GOE needs to articulate the message that its fiscal management reforms are designed to help the poor. If reforms are to succeed, they have to be pro-poor. Ecuador's fiscal stress and poor budget management is deeply rooted in a governance system benefiting rent-seeking elites, be it reflected on pro-rich subsidies, especially on basic infrastructure; off-budget operations that prevent transparency and foster corruption, or regressive transfers to subnational governments explained by party politics. The challenge for the Government is to provide more effective, efficient, sustainable and equitable assistance to the poor.

*Second*, the reform of the fiscal management agenda needs to be designed and implemented with a medium-term view and national consensus. Piecemeal, short-term reforms can only bring short-term, often not long lasting gains. For example, the creation of Contratanet allowed the surge of an informational system about public procurement that has improved its transparency, but the more difficult task to converting it into a transactional system still remains to be undertaken. The establishment of a commission to draft such bill and the commission's decision to consult with civil society on the draft are steps in the right direction.

*Third*, the implementation of the PRS has to be monitored in an transparent way. Sharing reliable and timely information is as critical as the strategy itself. In the absence of transparency, the strategy loses credibility. This requires a combination of several steps including the development of benchmark indicators, not only fiscal, but especially social—inputs, outputs and outcomes. These should be designed in such a way that they can be monitored on a regular basis and reported before the Legislature and civil society. In addition, client surveys could be commissioned to assess the quality of service delivery. All reports should be made public.

## Policy Recommendations

To address the challenges faced by the Government in its fiscal policy, this report recommends an agenda of policy actions that would promote the three key objectives of fiscal stability, pro-poor spending, and budget management. While fiscal reforms face formidable political-economy and institutional obstacles in Ecuador, increasingly large segments of public opinion may be won over to the pro-reform camp if a close connection between the need for fiscal adjustment and the creation of the fiscal space needed for a poverty reduction strategy is spelled out to the citizenry.

**The medium-term objective of fiscal policy in Ecuador remains to strengthen and preserve the sustainability of the fiscal accounts.** This could be supported by an implicit or explicit Fiscal Pact on the following general goals: deal with the public sector's insolvency risk; eliminate the structural bias toward expenditure expansion in the management of public finances; address the issue of the Treasury's short-term liquidity problems; and comply with the fiscal rule requirements in the short tem (thereby building credibility). The fiscal rule could be amended in a few years to make it a sharper, more coherent, and more powerful instrument for fiscal consolidation. More specific recommendations in this area include the following:

- Ecuador needs to lower its insolvency risk by producing and preserving the high primary surpluses needed to gradually reduce the debt-to-GDP ratio to the sustainable levels of 40 percent of GDP in the period 2006-2007. An important caveat is that while the FRSTL sets 40 percent as the goal, and this is a reasonable achievement, an additional 5 percent reduction would be desirable for unexpected contingencies and shocks.
- The Government should persevere in the pursuit of a comprehensive tax reform in the medium term, especially once oil prices start returning to their historic level. This would create additional fiscal space.
- As the adoption of revenue measures is politically constrained in the short-term, curbing the bias towards expenditure expansion, especially on the payroll and pension benefits, should be the top key priorities of fiscal policy.
- Regarding FEIREP, in the short-term strict compliance with the mandatory use of 70 percent of FEIREP funds to repurchase the most expensive debt first (particularly in global bonds), is needed to reduce interest payments. If the country complies with projected debt reduction repurchases, it would save an average 0.2 percent of GDP, which would be available for pro-poor programs. In the medium term, legal amendments to the FEIREP and fiscal rules would improve the fund's effectiveness. Possible amendments include the redefinition of the reference price for crude oil that is included in the budget. Another is

to gradually approach the criterion of the 3.5 percent real growth rate for primary expenditures with reference to the executed budget of the previous year, as opposed to the approved budget. A third is the elimination of the 0.2 percent of GDP mandated non-oil deficit reduction, once the country reaches the 40 percent of GDP ceiling and oil proceeds for stabilization purposes can be increased.

■ Given the large country risk premium on public debt, and findings from the debt sustainable analysis, oil revenues should reduce public debt to 40 percent of the GDP and, later, accumulate financial assets that would eventually allow the country to have a small non-oil deficit, even after oil reserves are depleted. The external debt buyback should be accompanied by additional fiscal space to buffer the impact of future shocks and streamlined expenditures. Debt buyback is no substitute for expenditure rationalization. Besides, by following the proposed debt strategy, it may be more difficult and costlier to borrow internally if Ecuador faces a shock, because developing countries, in contrast to developed countries, cannot borrow commercially when they suffer a shock.

■ The Treasury's short-term liquidity difficulties badly affect the authorities' credibility and the country's reputation. Given the specific composition of the public debt, closing the liquidity gap is critically dependent on the Government's willingness and ability to design programs of substantial structural reforms. This would be the basis for an agreement with the IMF and would enable the country to obtain rapidly disbursing and freely disposable funds. This is also the road to enhanced credibility for the medium-term debt reduction plan.

**Shifting public expenditure toward a pro-poor focus involves actions on several fronts.**

■ *Basic Infrastructure Subsidies:* (a) reduce the total electricity subsidy provided to consumers below a maximum amount of electricity consumption, since the actual ceiling of residential consumers below 300 kilowatt-hours is too high to target the truly poorest households; (b) reduce tariffs for public telephones, which are 10 times higher than tariffs for residential users, and eliminate cross-subsidies through completion of the tariff rebalancing between domestic and international rates approved by CONATEL in 2003; and (c) reduce and make transparent cross-subsidies in the highly decentralized water and sanitation sector, linked to operational performance, while defining the amount of subsidy allocated per connection considering the size and income level of the population.

■ *Expenditure on social services:* (a) freeze or reduce subsidies to university tuition to finance access for poorer groups, for instance, to secondary education; (b) increase the very small budgets of pro-poor programs, like primary education, the school breakfast or the Free maternity Law; and (c) introduce results-oriented budgeting to all pro-poor programs, by defining monitoring indicators, undertaking regular monitoring and evaluation mechanisms, and allowing strong civil society participation.

■ *Link and protect budget support to MDG goals and improve its performance:* (a) provide additional budget resources (for about 0.1–0.2 percent of GDP) to primary education and infant mortality; (b) focus additional resources on secondary education, child malnutrition, basic health, and child care, which would raise additional budget needs to about 0.8 percent of GDP in 2004, 1 percent of GDP in 2005, and almost 2 percent of GDP in 2007; and (c) define a set of performance indicators that would allow their progress monitoring. Indicators should result from a combination of a consensus-building exercise and international expertise. An important conclusion of this approach is that not all sector and program budgets need to be linked to performance indicators, but only the ones that are critical for achieving the goals of the PRS.

**A reform of public expenditure management is essential to accompany poverty reduction.** This includes implementing a budgeting system that reverts inertial expenditure; rapidly upgrades the budget and financial management system (SIGEF); overhauls budgeting procedures by both social agencies in charge of priority social programs and subnational governments receiving transfers; makes information access transparent at all levels of government to promote participation; and, only when previous reforms have gained ground, establishes a multi-year budgeting framework that align expenditure inputs with expected social outputs. More specifically, the following measures are suggested:

- On *overall public expenditure management*: (a) create a Cash Committee at MEF composed of representatives of all offices that manage budget design and execution; (b) revert inertial budgeting through already adopted freezing of the wage payroll; (c) gradually integrate off-budget activities into the Treasury's Single Account (*Cuenta Única*), especially non-constitutional earmarkings and subsidies currently channeled through PetroEcuador; and (d) overhaul SIGEF to promote proper registration and timely information of budget execution. An important step in this direction has been done with their publication in the 2005 budget.
- On *budget management in social programs*: (a) review the overall budget protection policy with an initial assessment of the number of social programs and the amount of resources allocated to them effectively representing government priorities, with programs receiving the minimum amount of resources needed to achieve their goals; (b) merge or eliminate duplicate social programs to reduce resource waste following the example of the nutritional ones under the *Sistema Integrado de Alimentación y Nutrición* (SIAN); (c) eliminate cash constraints in the first half of the year, a recurrent and severe problem in many agencies; (d) rationalize, simplify, and if possible automate, budget procedures and forms for requesting reimbursement of payments; and (e) consider the creation of "virtual" poverty fund. Obvious candidates for elimination are those programs that show a significant degree of low budget execution and/or poor targeting.
- On *budget management in provincial and sectional governments*: (a) design a strong regulatory and institutional framework that clearly assigns expenditure responsibilities in line with subnational governments' administrative capacity; (b) condition delivery of some or all transfers on timely and reliable budget reporting by subnational governments, as mandated by the FRSTL and following up upon recent MEF efforts for building a database on subnational fiscal accounts; and (c) promote responsible subnational borrowing by establishing further norms under which the central government can intervene in local governments when and if they violate the fiscal rules, and clearly excluding the possibility of a bailout.

## A Selection of the Key Policy Recommendations

Based on the analysis done in this report, and among the set of recommendations proposed, the following sub-sct of sequenced priority actions are suggested:

*I. High Priority for the near term (6–12 months)*
**Obtain primary surpluses between 4.5-5 percent of GDP.** This could be achieved in the short term by reducing spending and by complying with the fiscal rule. Current primary spending should be curbed by preserving until 2005 the on-going freeze of the public payroll and maintaining pensions at their 2003 level in real terms.

**Comply with mandated debt reduction** using 70 percent of FEIREP proceedings for repurchasing of external debt.

**Announce a draft budget reform bill** to: (a) integrate off-budget activities, especially subsidies paid by PetroEcuador; (b) freeze or reduce non-constitutional budget earmarkings; and (c) reduce central government 40 percent contribution to IESS.

**Create a Treasury Committee** that manages and makes transparent current cash strapped budget execution.

**Ensure SIGEF overhaul** by: (a) fulfilling its commitment to consolidate fiscal accounts; (b) producing timely disaggregated reports in the MEF website; and (c) completing its re-design for moving to an internet-based system.

**Undertake a comprehensive review of budget protection policy** to: (a) weed-out non-performing priority social programs and select the most performing ones under a "virtual" poverty fund; (b) merge most of the remaining overlapping ones following the example of the nutrition ones under SIAN; (c) guarantee a high level of execution of their budget agreed for 2004 and 2005; (d) commit additional resources required by compliance with selected MDGs in the 2005 budget.

*Priority for the medium term (1–3 years)*
**Amend the Fiscal Transparency, Stabilization and Responsibility Law,** ensuring that: (a) quantitative rules apply to *executed*, not only *approved* spending, (b) resources for the anti-cyclical role of FEIREP are augmented, once the ceiling 40 percent debt-to-GDP ratio is attained; (c) additional rules are introduced for subnational governments; and (d) provincial and municipal governments comply with the transparency requirements contained in the fiscal rule.

**Adopt decisions on policy alternatives proposed for creating fiscal space in the context of an implicit or explicit Fiscal Pact (see Table ES.1).** This implies expenditure shifting activities. Tax reform, in particular, should expand the tax base by reducing tax exemptions, and continue improving tax administration.

**Increase the level of education, health and social protection budgets, while raising their quality and share devoted to pro-poor programs.** This implies to focus additional spending on (a) teachers' training and secondary education, on health provision by the Free Maternity Program, and on the revamped *Bono;* (b) pro-poor programs (possibly supported by a Competitive-based Fund); (c) other priority public investment, especially if it is donor-financed, which would require close coordination through sector approaches.

**Freeze or re-target non pro-poor subsidies and spending on non pro-poor social programs** in nominal terms at their 2003 level, especially for higher education and pensions. Retargeting of the cooking gas, diesel, and electricity subsidy is a priority.

**Develop a strategic vision for electricity, water, sanitation and telecom sectors,** accompanied by a time-bound implementation plan, to: (a) expand coverage; (b) improve service provision; (c) reduce regressive subsidies; and (d) allow for private competition for service provision among suppliers and accountability to users.

# Chapter 1

# FISCAL POLICY IN A DOLLARIZED ECONOMY

On January 9, 2000, Ecuador decided formally to adopt the U.S. dollar as its national currency, thus converting fiscal policy into the centerpiece of its macroeconomic management. This was a major institutional change that created a new context for both government economic policy and private economic activity. The banking, currency and debt crises that precipitated the move to dollarization were triggered by a combination of exogenous (both external and weather-related) shocks. These shocks included: (a) the sudden stop in capital flows into Ecuador, (b) the fall in oil prices, and (c) the supply shock from the *El Niño* phenomenon. These shocks also took place at a moment where expenditures were increasing rapidly in response to shocks. The decision to dollarize stabilized expectations, and economic activity began to turn around.

**Since dollarization the economy has recovered and macroeconomic balances, including the fiscal balance, have improved.** The recovery is due to high oil prices, low international interest rates, a trend toward a recovery in the financial system, growing remittances from expatriated workers, strong private investment (much of it associated to the construction of a new oil pipeline), an increase in real wages, and recent sound fiscal policy leading to the stabilization of expectations. Real gross domestic product (GDP) growth during 2000–03 averaged 3.5 percent; inflation declined from 91 percent in 2000 to 6.1 percent at the end of 2003; the capital account benefited from the foreign direct investment (FDI) flows associated to the construction of a new oil pipeline; and after the surge in imports brought about by the pipeline project came to a halt (because of project completion), the current account deficit of the balance of payments dropped from 4.8 percent of GDP in 2002 to 1.9 percent of GDP in 2003.

**In light of these positive developments, the issue arises as to whether the country has finally taken a path leading to long-term, sustained economic growth and can at last feel assured of its economic viability and future stability.** The short answer is that the country is making progress along the path toward improved stability, but the economy is still fragile, major vulnerabilities remain, and there is still some way to go to reach the goals of sustained growth and durable stability. As a first step to diagnosing the country's vulnerabilities, this chapter discusses historical and structural developments in fiscal policy and public expenditure. The chapter is divided into three sections. The first section reviews the historical background that preceded dollarization; the second section discusses the main challenges the country faces in strengthening the institutional framework for dollarization; and the third section explores the structural features of fiscal policy in Ecuador, emphasizing the political economy determinants of fiscal performance.

In doing this, the chapter claims that the ultimate root of Ecuador's fiscal predicament lies in the political-economy regime that emerged in the aftermath of the oil boom of the seventies.

## A. The Ecuadorian Economy: Some Historical Background

**The discovery of oil and gas in the late 1960s and the oil boom of the early 1970s changed the landscape of Ecuadorian society.**[1] The value of petroleum and natural gas output, which was virtually zero in 1971, jumped to 9.5 percent of GDP in 1973 and 23.0 percent of GDP in 1974, reflecting both the start-up of large-scale production and the fourfold increase in world oil prices. The newly found wealth gave rise to a rent-oriented, conflict-prone, and deeply fragmented political-economy regime that would come to dominate public policy making in the next decades. A major feature of this regime was that fiscal income from oil was used to finance an increase in the size of the State and to subsidize private spending through, among other means, low prices of domestic petroleum products, reduction in the taxation of non-oil activities, and a number of other subsidies. In light of the large amount of resources initially available, this strategy was successful at first. Economic growth in the 1970s was spectacular: the average annual growth rate of real GDP during 1971–80 was 9.1 percent.[2] Average inflation was a moderate 14.0 percent. Growth of manufacturing output was also stimulated by the adoption of import-substitution policies, which shielded a budding but inefficient, domestic-market-oriented, manufacturing sector.

**But, as the economy boomed, the seeds of future crises were planted by the authorities' fiscal behavior.** Despite large revenues from oil, Ecuadorian governments incurred substantial fiscal deficits.[3] Successive fiscal deficits were covered by rapidly increasing external borrowing. External debt more than doubled between 1970 and 1975, then increased ninefold between 1975 and 1980, grew another 74 percent between 1980 and 1985, and still another 25 percent between 1985 and 1988.

**The eighties were a decade of severe external shocks and slow growth.** In 1982, the terms of trade declined sharply, petroleum receipts stagnated and there was a sudden cessation of credit from external sources. The collapse of oil prices in 1986 precipitated a prolonged period of fiscal crisis and macroeconomic instability that peaked in 1988. In January 1987, the country stopped servicing its external debt with commercial banks, and interest arrears climbed to almost US$1.0 billion by the end of the Febres Cordero administration in August 1988. In the meantime, inflation was on the rise and reached 75.8 percent in 1989.

**The period 1988–1991 was marked by initial, but unsuccessful, efforts at stabilization.**[4] The government also undertook significant structural adjustment initiatives, including a partial tax reform, trade liberalization, and progress toward financial sector liberalization. However, in these years, inflation persisted at high levels, and, in the run up to the 1992 elections, government expenditure rose sharply. This was, in sum, a transition period in which some advances toward stabilization and structural reform were made.

**Only in 1992 did the Ecuadorian government launch a relatively successful macroeconomic stabilization program.** On the structural reform front, financial liberalization was basically completed, the foreign exchange market was fully unified, trade liberalization was deepened,

---

1. The outline of developments in the 1970s and 1980s draws on World Bank (1984, 1991, and 1993); and Beckerman (2002).

2. Real GDP growth in 1972 was 14.4 percent, and in 1973 was a staggering 25.3 percent!

3. There was a deficit in the accounts of the non-financial public sector every year from 1975 to 1982. After the fiscal adjustment episode of 1983–85, deficits resumed with a vengeance, and the average deficit during 1986–88 was 6.6 percent of GDP, until a new adjustment effort reduced it to 0.3 percent of GDP in 1989.

4. Real public spending was reduced 5.0 percent in 1988, and was kept relatively constant through 1991. In 1990, the government resisted pressures to expand expenditures when the Gulf crisis generated a large windfall in petroleum prices. Most cuts took place in current expenditures (wages, goods and services, interest, and transfers), and not in public investment. As a result of the stabilization effort, real growth recovered to between 3.0 and 5.0 percent during 1990–92.

most of the smaller public enterprises were privatized, and some progress was made in State modernization through the 1992 Public Budgets Law and the 1993 Modernization of the State Law. The government also made substantial progress in controlling public finances. It reduced non-financial public expenditure, in part through a program that reduced public sector staffing by nearly 10 percent. Inflation was reduced to the 20 to 30 percent range from the 40 to 50 percent range that prevailed in the early 1990s (de la Torre and others 2001). As Beckerman (2002) points out, these were hard-won reforms, secured in the face of broad political opposition.

**In the early nineties, the wave of foreign private capital flows engulfed the Ecuadorian economy.**[5] In late 1992, Ecuador joined other emerging markets as a receiver of important flows of capital, which were largely intermediated through the domestic financial system. Private capital flows surged from an average of US$200 million a year (about 2.0 percent of GDP) during 1989–1992 to US$730 million a year (about 5.0 percent of GDP) in 1994. The inflows led to a lending boom that peaked in the second half of 1994, when bank credit to the private sector was expanding at annual rates of around 60 percent in real terms. The euphoria of the credit boom intensified information asymmetry problems, resulting in a generalized underestimation of the nature and extent of the risks taken by financial intermediaries. With asset prices soaring, the fast expansion of firms' balance sheets during 1993–94 implied much more risk-taking than what was then perceived by bankers. The inflows included a significant component of short-term speculative capital: non-FDI private flows to Ecuador swelled from a cumulative US$12 million (0.1 percent of GDP) in 1991–1992 to US$506 million (3 percent of GDP) in 1993–94. And the stock of registered private-sector debt (much of which was short-term in nature) jumped form US$258 million at end-1992 to US$832 million at end-1994. Because of their volatility, the flows of short-term capital introduced a major factor of vulnerability for the economy.

**The lack of an effective regulatory and supervisory framework deepened the vulnerability to volatile capital flows.** Three Ecuador-specific shocks,[6] compounded by the general slump in confidence brought about by the Mexican crisis of 1995–96, triggered a gigantic reversal in short-term capital flows in the mid-1990s. The accumulated outflow of non-FDI capital in 1995–96 was US$1.5 billion (8 percent of GDP), three times the accumulated non-FDI inflow during 1993–94. Real credit stagnated. Interest rates went up. High interest rates sharply raised firms' debt-service obligations, which caused a large drop in the value of firms and their collateral. Nonperforming loans increased from less than 4.0 percent at end-1994 to 9.0 percent by the end-1996. A medium-intensity banking crisis emerged. Real GDP growth fell from about 6.0 percent in the second half of 1994 to 0.8 percent during July 1995–June 1996.

**The post-1995 crisis period was characterized by worsening macroeconomic imbalances.** This was also a period of policy inaction vis-à-vis the reforms needed in the financial system, high political instability, and a slowdown economic activity. According to Jácome (2004), in spite of a favorable external environment, Ecuadorian governments muddled through in 1996 and 1997, keeping the economy and the financial system in an unstable equilibrium.

**Starting in 1998, a new string of exogenous shocks occurred that led to the end-1990s crises.** El Niño had struck in late 1997, destroying agricultural crops, which impaired the assets of several banks of the coastal region. Oil prices sank below US$10 dollars per barrel. But by far the decisive shock was the sudden stop in capital flows brought about by Russia's partial debt repudiation in August 1998. Ecuador's capital-flow reversal was impressive by any standard. Net inflows of about US$2.2 billion in 1998 changed into net outflows of US$1.3 billion, a reversal of

---

5. The narrative about the 1990s draws on de la Torre and others (2001); Beckerman (2003); Jácome (2004); IMF (2000); and Izquierdo (2002).

6. The three Ecuador-specific shocks were: (a) the war with Peru in early 1995; (b) a prolonged drought that caused a major energy crisis; and (c) the forced resignation of Vice President Dahik, who was considered by market participants at home and abroad as the economic reform leader *par excellence* in the Durán Ballén administration.

US$3.5 billion, equivalent to 20 percent of 1998 GDP, or 56 percent of that year's credit to the private sector. The adjustment in the capital account also affected the current account, which swung from a deficit of 11 percent of GDP in 1998, to a surplus of 6.9 percent of GDP in 1999, as the country was forced to undergo a substantial real exchange rate depreciation.

**The Ecuadorian downturn combined three crises.** The *banking* crisis started in April 1998 with the traumatic closure of a small bank. It gained momentum in August 1998 when a medium-size bank was closed after having been unable to honor its obligations and, subsequently, when the largest bank of the system requested assistance from the Central Bank. The *debt* crisis exploded in August 1999, when Ecuador defaulted on its Brady bonds as the logical result of rising public sector indebtedness. The *currency crisis* started in the aftermath of the decision, in February 1999, to float the exchange rate in order to limit international reserve losses. Over the following weeks, the exchange rate lost 30 percent of its value. Eventually, the different dimensions of the crisis fed on each other. The initial runs against the banks prompted the Central Bank to provide liquidity. Fresh liquidity fueled the attack against the currency, which depreciated in the context of the free float. The nominal devaluation adversely affected balance sheets, eroding the solvency of debtors and, ultimately, that of the banks. This prompted more liquidity assistance and reinitiated the devaluation–insolvency spiral. In the end, a vicious cycle set in of currency depreciation, corporate insolvency, growing bank insolvency, runs against the banks, banks' declining liquidity, and Central Bank assistance that further fueled the run on the currency. The process did not stop endogenously. Rather, it was halted by an exogenous (political and administrative decision), namely, the abandonment of the sucre as the national currency and the formal adoption of the dollar.

**This brief summary of macroeconomic developments in the last three decades before dollarization is useful to identify the key structural patterns that drive Ecuador's macroeconomic performance.** *First*, the dependence on oil is a major theme. The positive aspect of this dependence is that oil booms are a source of short-term economic expansion, potential fiscal savings and foreign exchange earnings. The downside of this dependence is twofold. The most salient effect is to make the economy vulnerable to oil-price volatility. An additional effect is the resultant Dutch disease that causes damage to the competitiveness of the non-oil tradable sectors. *A second major theme* is that the oil-driven boom of the seventies was unwisely managed and this had long-run repercussions that are still felt today. Instead of saving the transitory excess revenues, they were used to finance consumption, the reduction of non-oil taxation and the expansion of the public administration and state enterprises. The collateral of oil was used to contract a huge amount of debt, which today has turned into an inherited burden that is handicapping the conduct of economic policy. *A third theme* is that, with financial liberalization in the early nineties and with the advent of greater degree of capital mobility in the world economy, the nineties brought on new sources of vulnerability for the Ecuadoran economy. In particular, private capital flows came to be capable of driving investment and growth, as in 1993-1994, but also of sinking the economy into crisis and disarray, as in 1998-1999. *A fourth theme* concerns the exposure to natural disasters as an additional factor of vulnerability and a threat to economic growth and macroeconomic stability. In addition, all these patterns have developed in the context of a rentist, conflict-prone and fragmented political economy, adverse to macroeconomic adjustment and monetary and fiscal discipline, whose characteristics will be presently discussed (see paragraph 1.21 below).

## B. The Role of Fiscal Policy in a Dollarization Framework

**Dollarization created a new framework for both private sector economic activity and public sector policymaking.** There is a whole body of literature on the economic costs and benefits of dollarization, which has produced a partial consensus as to the virtues and limitations of this exchange-rate regime, but important differences of opinion remain, and some of the issues

## BOX 1.1: THE COSTS AND BENEFITS OF DOLLARIZATION

A definite *advantage* of dollarization is that it eliminates the risk of a nominal devaluation of the country's exchange rate. In other words, the risk of a currency crisis disappears. This is tantamount to saying that one important component of the country risk premium is eliminated, with the consequence that interest rates on foreign borrowing will be lower. However, while the interest premium attributable to devaluation risk will disappear, sovereign risk will not and, therefore, total country risk and hence interest rate risk premia will, in all likelihood, continue to be different from zero. The absence of currency risk does not insulate a country from swings in market sentiment toward its economic policy and/or prospects. Moreover, foreign lenders will normally perceive that there is a risk that the particular country may default on its obligations. The elimination of currency risk makes it possible for both the government and the private sector to borrow at lower cost with positive effects on the private agents' balance sheets and the governments' fiscal accounts.

Dollarization also rules out one kind of sudden stop in capital flows, namely, that particular type that is motivated by fear of devaluation of the national currency. However, dollarization cannot eliminate the risk of all external crises, as investors may flee because of fears stemming from lack of sustainability of the fiscal position, or about the soundness of the financial system. The elimination of currency risk also removes an important source of vulnerability in the financial systems of emerging market countries. This can contribute to building a stronger financial system, one more capable of actively participating in international financial markets. Financial integration is then facilitated by dollarization. By the same token, there is a cost to this improved integration: if the authorities believed that some insulation of the domestic financial system is needed for the purposes of, say, improving its stability, through, for instance, the imposition of capital controls, they would find that insulating measures are difficult to accomplish, because it would always be possible for the private agents to convert their assets to dollar cash.

Another advantage of dollarization is that the likelihood is high that the inflation regime that would set in will be characterized by lower inflation rates than under alternative exchange rate schemes. The reason is simple. Under dollarization there is no domestic monetary authority that could expand the quantity of money, and thus the greatest potential inflationary factor is eliminated. As a matter of fact, this is a promise on which Ecuador's dollarization is finally delivering, as the rate of inflation dropped from 91.0 percent in 2000 to 6.1 percent in 2003.

Dollarization also makes commercial integration with the rest of the world easier because it eliminates the transaction costs associated with currency exchange. In particular, in the case of Ecuador, dollarization is an obvious advantage for pursuing commercial integration through a trade agreement (bilateral or otherwise) with the United States.

Finally, dollarization has a well-known disciplining effect on fiscal policy in that, in the new system the Central Bank cannot monetize fiscal deficits. However, this does not prevent fiscal indiscipline. This is because it does not prevent excessive borrowing to finance large fiscal deficits. Thus, dollarization increases the incentive to borrow vis-à-vis what would be the fiscal authority's behavior in the alternative scenario of an emerging market country that maintains its own currency. In the same vein, Chang (2000) also argues that, under exchange rate arrangements other than dollarization, changes in exchange rates or interest rates make the costs of a lack of fiscal discipline immediately visible. Dollarization takes those incentives away by allowing the costs of present fiscal profligacy to be shifted to the future (in the form of, say, higher future taxes).

Among the *disadvantages* of dollarization, the most cited are: (a) the sacrifice of an independent monetary policy; (b) the loss of the lender of last resort; (c) the sacrifice of the inflation tax; and (d) the loss of seigniorage. Advocates and opponents of dollarization have debated at length on these issues. A fundamental concern is that the adjustment mechanism to a shock under dollarization has a particularly worrisome feature: After a negative external shock (say, a sudden stop in capital flows), a real exchange rate depreciation is necessary for the economy to return to an equilibrium situation. In a dollarized economy this can only be attained through price deflation. However, if domestic prices and wages are sufficiently inflexible in a downward direction, a prolonged period of deflation may be necessary to carry out the required adjustment. Adding to this, there is

*(continued)*

---

**BOX 1.1: THE COSTS AND BENEFITS OF DOLLARIZATION (CONTINUED)**

the connected issue of the possibility of debt deflation: An unanticipated collapse in prices may lead to bankruptcies, even if the borrowing firms are efficient. Thus, if bankruptcy is costly, debt deflation carries a deadweight loss. Calvo (1999) asserts that debt deflation is perhaps the most serious threat for a dollarized economy. Another related vexing question is that dollarization does not isolate the non-tradable sectors from changes in the real exchange rate. Although the dynamics is quite different from the case of non-dollarized economies (where the nominal exchange rate shoots up), there will be a relative-price pressure on non-tradables, once domestic prices start their adjustment process after a negative shock.

---

raised in the debate warrant further research. Box 1.1 summarizes them.[7] Unlike most discussions of the issue, the box examines the particular adjustment mechanism of a dollarized economy in the presence of negative external shocks.

**There should be no doubt that having given up monetary and exchange rate policies, fiscal policy is the most important tool available for macroeconomic management,** and that a strong fiscal stance is therefore a key prerequisite for the sustainability of dollarization, and the best shield against negative shocks. On the other hand, a policy agenda must address key policy challenges of a dollarized economy such as (i) the risk that adjustment to external shocks should take the form of prolonged deflation and (ii) the lack of a lender of last resort for the financial system. On these issues, two general recommendations follow:

- There is a high probability that adjustment to external shocks will take the form of a prolonged deflation. To prevent this, it is necessary to introduce structural reforms. Reforms should aim at introducing flexibility in goods and factors markets, but especially in the labor market. This will require a social consensus on how to change prices and wages in periods of recession.
- The lack of a lender of last resort requires strengthening the management of liquidity in the financial system. Powell's (2003) proposals are a good starting point. This author suggests that there are definite advantages to centralizing the liquidity that the Ecuadorian financial system has available. He also proposes that the rules and operations of the existing liquidity support mechanisms, including the Liquidity Fund, be improved and that a new contingent liquidity facility be negotiated with a foreign institution.

## C. Structural Constraints on Fiscal Policy

**Ecuador entered the 21st century suffering the deleterious effects of three decades of predominantly wrong fiscal policies.** Throughout 1970–99, there was a sizeable decline in the public sector's net worth, indicating that oil revenues have been largely consumed rather than invested.[8] Estimates of the decline in real net worth calculated in two separate studies[9] range between 32 percent and 48 percent. Figure 1.1 shows the estimated decline trajectories found in the two studies. This erosion of net worth is equivalent to having Ecuador financing its excess consumption through the depletion of a single resource. Moreover, the problem is not only that oil wealth was not invested. It was even worse than that: oil wealth was also used as collateral for a large debt buildup. External indebtedness was the road to financing a long succession of fiscal deficits since 1975. Thus external debt doubled between 1970 and 1975, then increased ninefold from 1975 through 1980.

---

7. This discussion draws heavily upon Calvo (1999); IMF (2000); Berg and Borenzstein (2001); and Antinolfi and Keister (2001).

8. The discussion of public sector net worth draws on Traa (2003), and World Bank (2004).

9. The studies are Traa (2003), and Fierro-Renoy and Naranjo (2003).

10. Data on the growth of external debt in the 1980s can be found in World Bank (1991).

The public external debt kept steadily rising throughout the 1980s[10] and early 1990s and reached an unprecedented level of 87.3 percent of GDP in 1995. During 1996–98, the external-debt-to-GDP ratio dropped to an average level of 66.9 percent, as a result of the 1994 debt-and-debt-service-reduction deal with commercial bank creditors, but, with the advent of the 1999 crisis and the precipitous fall in output that year, the external debt ratio climbed to an all-time high of 98.3 percent, the heaviest burden by far among Latin America's 10 largest economies at that time (Beckerman 2002). During 1970–2000, the budget received an estimated cumulative nominal US$23 billion in direct oil revenues. Nonetheless, the public debt never stopped increasing (Traa 2003).

**The available estimates indicate that there was a pause in the declining trend of public sector net worth during 2000–02 (Traa 2003; UNICEF 2003).** However, with the rate of oil extraction bound to increase with the new heavy crude oil (OCP) pipeline, public sector net worth may resume its declining trend. The decline may even proceed at a faster pace than before, leading eventually to public sector insolvency, unless disciplined fiscal performance prevented this from happening. The fact is that, with the new pipeline, the remaining oil reserves may last less than 30 years.

**Three other structural factors should be added to have a complete picture of Ecuador's current fiscal fragility.** They are: *first*, the high revenue volatility caused by external shocks; *second*, the pro-cyclical character, extreme rigidity, low quality, and limited transparency of spending; and, *third*, the serious liquidity problems of the public sector that prevent it from keeping current in the payment of the public debt.

**The relevant exogenous shocks are well known.** First, the Ecuadorian economy is exposed to the volatility of oil export revenues. Second, it is also exposed to other sources of economic external shocks, prominent among them being those associated with private capital flows. Third, various forces of nature have been another standing source of contingency for Ecuador's economy. As pointed out by Beckerman (2002), the country is prone to earthquakes, volcanic eruptions, landslides, *El Niño* phenomenon, and extended periods of either drought or excessive rain.[11]

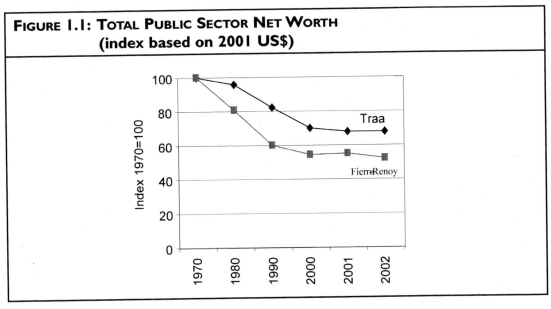

**FIGURE I.1: TOTAL PUBLIC SECTOR NET WORTH (index based on 2001 US$)**

Source: World Bank (2004a).

---

11. Beckerman (2002) points out that while many countries face standing risks from natural phenomena, if one were to list the world's economies according to the frequency and variety of their natural disasters, "Ecuador would surely rank relatively high" (p. 25).

**The ways in which the different exogenous shocks tighten (or ease) the constraints on fiscal policy are also well known.** The volatility of oil prices in the international market translates into volatility of oil fiscal revenue in Ecuador. External financial shocks, through their effects on aggregate demand, aggregate income, and the health of the financial system, have a bearing on fiscal performance. For instance, capital inflows stimulate aggregate demand and output, and may thereby result in increased non-oil tax revenue. Capital outflows, by contrast, may throw the economy into recession and thus lead to falling non-oil tax revenues. Furthermore, they can—and this effect may be even worse—augment the government's contingent liabilities associated with the fiscal costs of financial crises. Just to mention another example, international interest rate shocks can increase the cost of the external debt service, as was the case in the early 1980s. Last, random natural disasters have the double effect of lowering tax receipts (via their effect on output) and prompting increased spending (to cope with the emergency).

**Ecuador's fiscal fragility to shocks does not lie in the external shocks themselves, but in the political economy regime that prevents the country from adopting proper adjustment measures to offset them.** Box 1.2 highlights the conflictive character of this political economy, the towering difficulties faced by the national actors to reach consensus, the acute competition for oil rents, the role of the state in a rent-seeking society, and the ensuing weak governance.

**There exists an internal relationship between the prevailing political-economy regime and some deeply engrained practices and institutions that frame the conduct of fiscal policy.** Throughout the last three decades, the internal connection between the political-economy regime and fiscal policy has been visible in four systemic features of fiscal policy and public finance, namely:

- The size of Government and its role as a producer and provider of non-public goods and services, frequently at subsidized prices.
- The existence of a set of tax expenditures, whose function is to channel (potential) government revenue to the private sector. The main mechanisms for this channeling of rents have been the reduction of the tax burden on non-oil economic activities and the enactment and maintenance of consumption subsidies.
- The fact that policymakers' incentives tend to be biased toward a short-term horizon. In particular, savings-oriented behavior is frequently shunted aside and incentives are biased toward increased expenditure. This is the obvious way of accommodating interest-group pressures, maintaining political clienteles, and "greasing" patronage networks. The lack of a long-term horizon makes public policy in general, and fiscal policy in particular, very sensitive to the varying political shocks occurring in the public sphere. This explains why it is so difficult for Ecuadorian governments to persevere in efforts at fiscal adjustment, as expenditure-reduction measures prompt social and political pressures that may even take the form of rioting and general strikes.
- The deeply flawed institution of earmarking. Lacking a consensus on a set of rules for budget allocation, a number of particular constituencies have attempted to "lock in" their entitlement to public resources. There are more than 50 legal provisions mandating that preestablished percentages of particular taxes, or of oil income, must be given to particular levels of government, agencies, public institutions, or programs. As the 1993 Ecuador Public Expenditure Review pointed out, earmarking of large shares of government revenue has been a trademark of the country's fiscal policy since the 1970s (World Bank 1993). The rationale for this approach was that it would safeguard allocations to particular programs, shielding them from discretionary policy measures. But the abusive expansion of this practice only helped establish entitlement claims that eventually hindered government efforts to adjust to the changing macroeconomic and fiscal realities (ibid.). This is so because earmarking ends up making budgetary allocations arbitrary and automatic, and deters the required review and reassessment of priorities when situations

## BOX 1.2: THE ECUADORIAN POLITICAL ECONOMY

The political economy regime was shaped in the early 1970s under the powerful formative influences stemming from the oil boom. It was born as a response to the key questions of what to do with, and how to distribute, the (then) newly found oil rents.

**The social makeup.** The main social actors in the post-oil-discovery political economy have been (a) the elite class, the backbone of which is a small number of powerful economic groups, some of them family dominated, which own fairly diversified business conglomerates operating in both the financial and non-financial sectors of the economy (de la Torre and others 2001); (b) the powerful military that, as an institution, has participation in oil revenues and is the owner of a number of state enterprises; (c) the unions, particularly the public sector unions, which have traditionally been able to mobilize their membership to exert pressure on governments and politicians; (d) the middle class of professionals, small entrepreneurs, shopkeepers, and bureaucrats; and (e) the indigenous movement that has emerged as a social and political force in the 1990s. The poor have mostly been integrated into the political system as passive recipients of services (and, sometimes, of goods as well) provided through clientelistic networks and a patronage system.

**The conflictive nature of social relationships.** The political system has been appropriately characterized by Eifert and others (2002) as a factional democracy. In the view of those authors, oil-exporting factional democracies have several features that distinguish them from mature democracies. First, income distribution is unequal and social consensus is elusive. Second, politically powerful interests attached directly to state spending, such as bureaucratic and political elites, public sector unions, and the military, tend to capture the State. The driving incentive is the competition for oil rents. Each social group wants to maximize its share of those rents. The diverse, predatory interest groups can be stronger and more continuous than political parties and governments, and try to lock in their claims on the oil rents through devices such as the earmarking of government revenues.

The conflicts around the distribution of oil rents got interwoven with the previously existing regional, ethnic, and social cleavages in Ecuadorian society. Prominent among the preexisting conflicts is the traditional deep-seated division between the dominant classes of the trade-oriented Costa and the agrarian-oriented Sierra (Gelb and Marshall-Silva 1988). It is well known that the socioeconomic differences and rivalries between the dominant two regions go a long way in explaining Ecuador's history of bitter infighting and political instability. Not surprisingly, as the oil boom of the 1970s got under way, the interregional rivalry quickly became woven together, in complex ways, with the disputes around the use of the oil rents, and must be seen, therefore, as an integral element of the prevailing political economy regime. The other major cleavage that plays a role in the Ecuadorian political economy stems from the social exclusion to which the indigenous and Afro-Ecuadorian populations have been subjected (World Bank 2004b). This social exclusion—a lingering legacy of the colonial period—has been a secular feature of Ecuadorian society and shows up in the considerable gaps in income and social indicators between the indigenous and Afro populations, on one hand, and the *mestizo* and white populations, on the other.

**The economic role of the State.** During the oil boom of the 1970s, the decision was made to assign property rights on petroleum resources to the Ecuadoran state. By virtue of this decision the State became both the administrator of the oil rents and the crucial arena where the struggles for oil-rent distribution are waged and the institutional and policy decisions on this crucial matter are made. In consonance with this new role, the government became a producer of goods and services that were sold at subsidized levels, a rescuer of private firms in distress, a subsdizer of credit to the private sector, an employer of last (and sometimes of first) resort, and a builder of infrastructure. (World Bank 1993).

**This political economy breeds weak governance and weak institutions.** Ecuador governments are unstable*; the relationship between the Executive and Congress is very conflictive (Jones 1995; Mainwaring and Shugart 1997; Mejía-Acosta 1999); the political party system is highly fragmented (Coppedge 1998); there is a chronic electoral divorce between parties and voters (Conaghan 1994, 1995); a large number of players are able to wield veto power over governmental decisions (Pachano and others 2004); and "last-ditch" veto play-

*(continued)*

---

**BOX 1.2: THE ECUADORIAN POLITICAL ECONOMY (CONTINUED)**

ers (in the form of, say, popular protest or judicial decisions) have the potential to block the implementation of policies (Pachano and others 2004). Furthermore, political party fragmentation has brought about a crisis of representation. A number of social groups do not feel they are adequately represented by the existing political parties. As a result, social and economic demands are channeled intensively via the social organizations (Jácome 2004) instead of through the political parties, as is the case in mature democracies.

This political economy cannot but breed *weak institutions*. While the country's presidency has considerable legislative powers, including the possibility of introducing fast-track legislation in economic matters (with bills defined as urgent by the President becoming law if Congress fails to act within 30 days) and significant veto powers,[12] presidents have seen these advantages offset by the fact that, as a result of political party fragmentation, they have enjoyed little support in the legislature. On average, since 1979, the president's party has controlled only 26 percent of the seats in Congress and, in that period, no president has ever commanded a single-party majority.

The *efficacy of public administration* is severely damaged in such a context. In addition to the endemic shortcomings of the civil service, the central-government ministries are further weakened by the short tenure of the ministers, a common occurrence in governments whose political base of support is often quite narrow, and are hence vulnerable to external pressures on the ministers to resign, a situation compounded by the use of congressional censure as a political weapon on the part of opposition parties in the legislature. The turnover of key officials has been quite high. Between 1979 and 1998, the average Minister of Finance lasted 336 days in office. On the other hand, in the same period, 22 percent of all cabinet members were subjected to a confidence vote in Congress, and 10 percent were actually censured (Pachano and others 2004). Things have not improved after dollarization though. Between February 2000 and March 2003, the country had six Finance Ministers who stayed in office for an average of just seven months. High cabinet and key-agency instability has a deleterious impact on the Executive's policymaking ability.

As for the Ecuadorian Congress, besides being known for the weakness of the alliances and coalitions, it often lacks the technical skills and staff support needed to deal responsibly with the technical issues involved in legislating on economic and social matters.

* For instance, five presidents governed Ecuador during 1995–98 (Jácome 2004).

---

change or when a budget crisis arises. Earmarking is carefully assessed throughout this report.

A good example of the internal relationship between the political economy and fiscal policy is how oil booms have made possible for Ecuadorian governments to reduce non-oil taxes, mainly through tax exemptions. As oil revenue increased from 3.9 percent of GDP in 1973 to 9.3 percent of GDP in 1982, non-oil tax revenue dropped from 17.0 percent of GDP to 10.5 percent (World Bank 1984). The decline proceeded during the decade of the 1980s, and by 1988 non-oil tax revenue had reached a low value of 9.0 percent of GDP (World Bank 1991). The creation of the Internal Revenue Service in 1997 has brought about a notable recovery of non-oil tax revenue. However, advances made in the non-oil-tax arena are incomplete and fragile. A number of tax exemptions still exist. There is resistance by some interest groups in the political economy to the idea of increased non-oil taxation. The confrontation between reformers and interest groups resisting tax reforms is permanent in Congress. The corporate sector continues to press for tax concessions (IMF 2003b).

---

12. A partial presidential veto can be overridden by Congress only with a two-thirds majority and within 30 days. If the president appeals to a package veto, Congress is prevented from addressing the bill in question for a year (Pachano and others 2004).

# Chapter 2

# FISCAL TRENDS AND CHALLENGES

E cuador's fiscal position at mid-2004 seemed paradoxical. On one hand, oil prices and oil fiscal revenues were flying high. On the other, the fiscal authorities were advocating (and practicing) austerity as they reiterated their commitment to a primary surplus of 5.0 percent of GDP, and had embarked on negotiations with the International Monetary Fund (IMF) about a possible Arrangement. What lied behind this apparent paradox was, a somewhat improved, but still fragile, fiscal position that resulted from a long accumulation of deep, structural vulnerabilities and weaknesses. This chapter analyzes the fiscal situation in seven sections. Section A deals with the volatility of fiscal variables; section B compares Ecuador's fiscal performance in the pre- and post-dollarization periods; section C explores revenue management; section D analyzes expenditure trends; as a way of paving the road for policy recommendations, section E analyzes the Fiscal Transparency, Stabilization and Responsibility Law; section F tackles fiscal sustainability issues; and section G offers fiscal policy recommendations.

## A. The Volatility of Fiscal Variables
While output has been less volatile under dollarization, most fiscal variables—e.g., petroleum and non-petroleum revenue and current and capital expenditure—have been more volatile (Table 2.1). The standard deviation of real GDP growth has declined from 3.98 during 1994–99 to 1.16 during 2000–03. Petroleum revenues have been more volatile than current expenditures. The volatility of expenditure variables has also increased, especially wages and interest payments and, to a lesser extent, capital expenditures.

## B. Fiscal Performance Before and After Dollarization
More disciplined policies in the post-dollarization period have brought a definite improvement in fiscal performance, but the fiscal situation continues to be fragile and requires further consolidation. Both the primary balance and the overall balance clearly improved during 2000–03 compared to 1995–99 (Figure 2.1). The overall balance jumped from an average *deficit* of 3.2 percent of GDP in the pre-dollarization period to an average *surplus* of 1.0 percent of GDP in the post-dollarization period, a turnaround of 4.2 percentage points of GDP. The increase in the primary balance was about equivalent: from an average of 1.4 percent of GDP during 1995–99 to an average of 5.5 percent of GDP during 2000–03.

## TABLE 2.1: VOLATILITY OF NFPS VARIABLES, 1993–2003

| | Standard Deviations | |
| --- | --- | --- |
| | 1993–99 | 2000–03 |
| **Total Revenue** | 1.94 | 1.16 |
| Petroleum | 1.32 | 1.56 |
| Non-Petroleum | 0.63 | 1.74 |
| o/w VAT | 0.26 | 0.61 |
| **Total Expenditures** | 1.38 | 0.87 |
| Current Expenditures | 1.10 | 1.34 |
| Interest | 1.19 | 1.58 |
| Salaries | 0.43 | 1.68 |
| Goods and Services | 0.41 | 0.56 |
| Capital Expenditures | 0.60 | 0.81 |
| Fixed capital formation | 0.44 | 0.38 |
| Central Government | 0.67 | 0.28 |
| Municipal governments | 0.25 | 0.17 |
| **Overall Balance** | 1.99 | 0.63 |
| **Primary Balance** | 1.54 | 1.71 |
| **GDP** | 3.98 | 1.16 |

*Source:* MEF.

Never-the-less, an important caveat is in order. The fiscal improvement reflects in part higher oil revenues, rather than an increased effort at expenditure reduction. Non-oil revenue increased from an average of 20.6 percent of GDP during 1995–99 to an average of 25.2 percent during 2000–03. During the same period, average total non-financial public sector (NFPS) expenditures increased by 0.8 percent of GDP, partly offsetting revenue gains (Table A1).

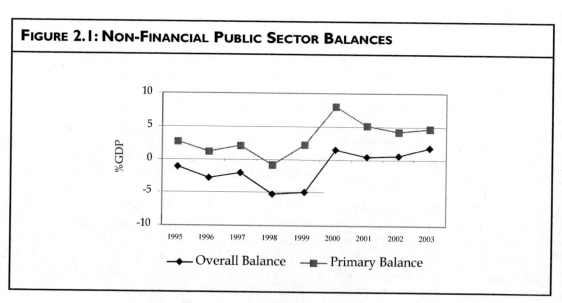

## FIGURE 2.1: NON-FINANCIAL PUBLIC SECTOR BALANCES

*Source:* BCE.

**Estimates of the structural fiscal balance confirm the improvement in the fiscal stance during 2000–03.**[1,2] Table 2.2 shows how the nominal primary balance, the structural primary balance, the fiscal stance, and the fiscal impulse evolved during 1990–2003 (a detailed analysis is in Annex A). The average fiscal stance during 2000–03 is a surplus of 0.8 percent of GDP, in contrast to the average fiscal stance during 1990–99, which was a deficit of 0.2 percent of GDP. The estimates of the fiscal impulse also show an improved fiscal performance: In 2000 there was a strong contractionary fiscal impulse of 3.1 percent of GDP, followed, however, by an expansionary impulse of 1.5 percent of GDP in 2001. In 2002 and 2003, fiscal impulses were again positive (contractionary).

**Several elements reinforce prospects for continued fiscal adjustment and reform but political-economy and institutional factors are still major obstacles to fiscal stability.** Three elements point towards a structurally strengthened fiscal situation in the medium-to-long term. First and foremost, the new institutional framework provided by dollarization creates a structural bias toward fiscal discipline because it prevents monetization of fiscal deficits.[3] Second, both passage of the Organic Law on Fiscal Transparency, Stabilization and Responsibility (FTSRL) and the establishment of the Fund for Stabilization, Investment, and Public Debt Reduction

**TABLE 2.2: ECUADOR: ACTUAL AND STRUCTURAL FISCAL BALANCE, FISCAL STANCE, AND FISCAL IMPULSE, 1990–2003**

(percentages of GDP)

|  | NFPS Primary Surplus | | Fiscal Stance | Fiscal Impulse |
|  | Actual | Structural | | |
|---|---|---|---|---|
| 1990 | 6.8 | 5.8 | + 1.0 | |
| 1991 | 5.2 | 5.6 | − 0.4 | − 1.4 |
| 1992 | 3.5 | 3.5 | 0.0 | + 0.4 |
| 1993 | 4.1 | 5.0 | − 0.9 | − 0.9 |
| 1994 | 4.1 | 4.5 | − 0.4 | + 0.5 |
| 1995 | 2.9 | 3.1 | − 0.2 | + 0.2 |
| 1996 | 1.3 | 0.7 | + 0.5 | + 0.7 |
| 1997 | 2.1 | 1.7 | + 0.4 | − 0.1 |
| 1998 | − 0.6 | − 0.2 | − 0.3 | − 0.7 |
| 1999 | 3.2 | 4.8 | − 1.6 | − 1.3 |
| 2000 | 8.1 | 6.6 | + 1.5 | + 3.1 |
| 2001 | 5.1 | 5.1 | 0.0 | − 1.5 |
| 2002 | 4.2 | 3.7 | + 0.5 | + 0.5 |
| 2003 | 4.7 | 3.4 | + 1.3 | + 0.8 |

*Source:* Annex A.

---

1. This paragraph is based on Artana and Moskovits (2004).

2. The structural balance is a measure of the fiscal balance that is independent of the particular position of the economy in the business cycle at a given point in time. On the basis of the structural balance, the fiscal stance at any given year is defined as the difference between the actual and structural budget balances. When the structural balance approach is chosen, another key concept to bear in mind is the fiscal impulse, defined as the change in the fiscal stance from one year to the next. If the stance remains unchanged, the government is said to have kept fiscal policy neutral (the fiscal impulse is zero). A positive fiscal stance means that the authorities are imparting a contractionary impulse on aggregate demand. A negative fiscal stance is tantamount to the authorities imparting an expansionary impulse on aggregate demand.

3. However, to the extent that it eliminates the foreign exchange risk of external debt, it also, unfortunately, creates incentives toward that particular form of fiscal indiscipline the content of which is excessive indebtedness of the public sector (see Melo 2003).

(FEIREP) considerably strengthened the institutional framework for fiscal discipline. Third, a structural change towards a permanent increase in non-oil tax revenue is in the making, as will be presently shown. These advances are the clear expression of the existence of pro-reform forces in the political economy engaged in a major, medium-to-long-term attempt both at redressing the cumulative effects from past, chronic lack of discipline and at laying the ground for the fiscal institutions and policies that dollarization demands if it is to be sustainable The depth of the 1998–1999 crisis opened a window of opportunity for reform. The arrival of a new Administration in 2003 has, until now, given an upper hand to the advocates of reform. However, medium-term structural adjustment continues to be resisted by an array of forces that, at best are suspicious of fiscal discipline, and, at worst, are adamantly opposed to it. This is why progress made so far is fragile and the timing of reform vulnerable to the contingency of uncertain political alliances.

## C. The Challenges of Revenue Management

**Non-oil tax revenue has recently improved.**[4] One major feature of the Ecuadorian oil-driven political economy over the last three decades has been the reduced burden of taxation on non-oil economic activities. The sizeable increases in public-sector oil revenues in the seventies made it possible for the government to reduce non-oil taxes, mainly through tax rebates and tax exemptions. As shown in Figure 2.2,[5] non-oil tax revenues declined between 1974 and 1984, partially recovered between 1986 and 1989 (due, among other things to president Borja's fiscal reform)

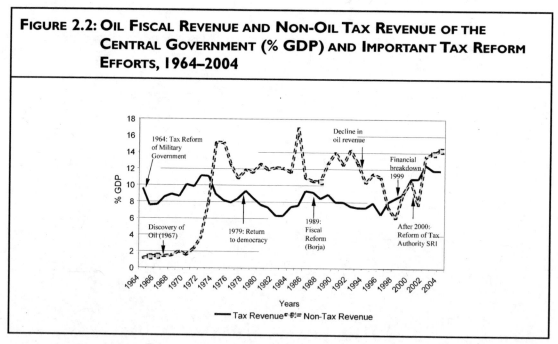

**FIGURE 2.2: OIL FISCAL REVENUE AND NON-OIL TAX REVENUE OF THE CENTRAL GOVERNMENT (% GDP) AND IMPORTANT TAX REFORM EFFORTS, 1964–2004**

*Source:* World Bank staff calculations, based on data from Central Bank of Ecuador (2003). 2004 values are estimates.

---

4. These sections draw heavily from Schenone, Osvaldo (2003), *Tax Policy and Administration,* in Vicente Fretes-Cibils, Marcelo M. Giugale, and José-Roberto López-Cálix, (eds.), *Ecuador: An Economic and Social Agenda in the New Millennium,* World Bank, Washington, D.C., pp. 43–63.

5. In Figure 2.2 "Tax Revenue" stands for non-oil tax revenues and "Non-Tax Revenue" stands for oil fiscal revenues.

**TABLE 2.3: TOTAL REVENUE OF THE NON-FINANCIAL PUBLIC SECTOR (NFPS) AND CENTRAL GOVERNMENT (IN % GDP), 1995–2003**

| | | Central Government Revenue | | | | | | | |
| | | | | | Tax Revenue | | | | |
| | | | | | | | Within SRI | | |
| Year | NFPS | Total | Oil revenue | Outside SRI | Total | Income Tax | VAT | Special Consumption Tax (ICE) | Other Taxes |
|---|---|---|---|---|---|---|---|---|---|
| 1995 | 22.8 | 15.5 | 5.9 | 1.8 | 7.1 | 1.7 | 3.1 | 0.4 | 0.1 |
| 1996 | 21.9 | 15.1 | 7.0 | 1.3 | 6.6 | 1.6 | 3.0 | 0.5 | 0.3 |
| 1997 | 19.9 | 14.6 | 5.1 | 2.0 | 8.0 | 1.7 | 3.3 | 0.6 | 0.4 |
| 1998 | 17.3 | 13.9 | 3.8 | 2.7 | 8.6 | 1.5 | 3.6 | 0.5 | 0.2 |
| 1999 | 21.1 | 16.1 | 6.0 | 2.0 | 8.9 | 0.7 | 3.3 | 0.4 | 2.5 |
| 2000 | 25.9 | 20.4 | 8.8 | 1.4 | 10.2 | 1.8 | 5.2 | 0.5 | 1.2 |
| 2001 | 23.5 | 18.3 | 6.1 | 1.7 | 11.3 | 2.2 | 6.4 | 0.7 | 0.3 |
| 2002 | 25.8 | 18.8 | 5.6 | 1.7 | 11.3 | 2.2 | 6.3 | 0.9 | 0.2 |
| 2003 | 25.7 | 17.8 | 5.8 | 1.4 | 10.4 | 2.2 | 5.9 | 0.7 | 0.2 |

*Source:* SRI (2004).

and declined again between 1990 and 1996. The creation of the Internal Revenue Service (SRI in its Spanish acronym) as an independent entity and its strengthening in the late nineties brought about a significant recovery in non-oil tax revenue. SRI-collected tax revenue increased from 8.0 percent of GDP in 1997 to 11.3 percent in 2002 (see Table 2.3). Following dollarization, policymakers found a real incentive to make tax collection efficient. The SRI was given the managerial autonomy to simplify procedures, impose and enforce sanctions, and work with taxpayers. As a result, the government has improved its fiscal position. The SRI is also supporting modernization of Customs administration, less with the objective of raising revenue, than of facilitating international trade and competitiveness.

**Ecuador does not have a problem of low fiscal revenues but there are obstacles to higher revenues.** The government should deal with three main shortcomings of the tax system, which are constraining the possibility of increasing revenue. These shortcomings are: (a) the proliferation of taxes, with the resulting fragmentation of the tax system; (b) the number and scope of tax exemptions, which narrow the tax base; and (c) the pervasiveness of earmarking.

## A Fragmented Tax Structure

**A central shortcoming of Ecuador's tax structure lies in its fragmentation.** Currently, there are more than 80 taxes (Table 2.4), but, from the standpoint of their revenue-collection potential, most are irrelevant. Five taxes—namely, the value-added tax (VAT), the personal income tax (ISR), the Special Consumption Tax (ICE), customs tariffs, and the vehicle tax—generate more than 75 percent of tax revenues. The Central Government would not lose much revenue by eliminating insignificant taxes. Proliferation of taxes remains a major obstacle for collection and administration. For both the taxpayers and the tax authority it implies unnecessarily high administrative costs. It discourages payment by taxpayers and undermines supervision by the tax authority.

**The SRI has introduced a number of significant improvements to tax administration.** A centralized tax payers registry (*Registro Único de Contribuyentes*, RUC) has been created, with 1.1 million registrants (80 percent individuals and 20 percent legal entities). This allows SRI to impose sanctions on delinquent or tardy taxpayers who, in the past, were able simply to move from one regional office to another to avoid punishment. Under the revamped *Registro* they can

**TABLE 2.4: THE STRUCTURE OF THE TAX SYSTEM**

| Type of Tax | Number of Taxes | Central Gov. | Beneficiaries Munici-palities | Provincial Councils | Other |
|---|---|---|---|---|---|
| Income and Capital Earnings Tax | 5 | 3 | 1 | 1 | |
| Payroll Tax | 1 | | 1 | | |
| Property and Net Worth Tax | 26 | 1 | 11 | 2 | 12 |
| Real Estate Transfer Tax | 24 | | 8 | 2 | 14 |
| Financial Asset Tax | 6 | 1 | | | 5 |
| Sales Tax on Goods and Services | 17 | 7 | 3 | | 7 |
| VAT | 1 | 1 | | | |
| ICE | 7 | 6 | | 1 | |
| Telecommunications | 1 | | 1 | | |
| Electricity | 4 | | 4 | | |
| Public Entertainment | 3 | | 1 | | |
| Betting | 1 | | 2 | | |
| Foreign Trade Tax | 1 | 1 | | | |
| Various Taxes | 4 | 2 | 1 | 1 | |
| Totals | 84 | 15 | 24 | 4 | 41 |

*Note:* The "Other" category is composed of an enormous variety of institutions, including the Guayaquil Beneficence Council, the State University of Guayaquil, the Guayas Transit Commission, the Ecuadorian Social Security Institute, the Osvaldo Loor Foundation, the Potable Water Company, the National Promotion and Development of Sports, the Superintendency of Companies, the Superintendency of Banks, the Ecuadorian Tourism Corporation, and the National Children's Fund.

*Source:* SRI.

no longer do that. The SRI is also using third-party information to increase compliance. Crosschecks during 2001 and 2002 detected approximately 100,000 people not registered in the RUC.[6] As a result of these measures, tax administration indicators show satisfactory levels for 2001–03, as indicated in Table 2.5.

**TABLE 2.5: SELECTED TAX ADMINISTRATION INDICATORS, 2001–03**

| | 2001 | 2002 | 2003 |
|---|---|---|---|
| Debt collected versus outstanding debt | 23% | 41% | n.d |
| Forced collections versus collections under management | 1.7% | 2.8% | 5.7% |
| Taxpayers who declare nothing versus taxpayers who declare a gain | 47.2% | 41.4% | 43.5% |
| Taxpayers who declare versus taxpayers who should declare | 43.4% | 33.5% | 53.7% |
| Notifications to actual non-filers versus (special) non-filers | 94% | 89% | n.d. |
| Notified taxpayers with crosschecked differences versus planned notifications | 47% | 91% | n.d. |

*Source:* SRI.

---

6. The fact that companies and public entities are subject to the VAT offers excellent possibilities for crosschecking information, because when these entities request a reimbursement of VAT credits, they automatically reveal their identities to their suppliers. Because of the large volume of purchases made by the State, the volume of resultant crosschecked information is also very large.

*Tax Exemptions and the Erosion of the Tax Base*
**In Ecuador, the tax base is constantly eroded by exemptions.** Efforts of tax administration authorities to reduce them are permanently offset by waves of new exemptions. Authorities reduced exemptions between 1999 and the first half of 2001, in particular with regard to the VAT.[7] Since then, and within less than one year's time, new exemptions were created or attempted, related not only to the VAT, but also to the personal income tax. Exemptions imply a significant revenue loss for the Central Government and reduce the fiscal space. Calculations of tax exemptions of the internal VAT (that is, excluding the VAT on imports) indicate that in 2001 the tax cost was approximately US$237 million, or 1.1 percent of GDP (Chapter 4).

*Earmarking: The Undermining of Budget Flexibility*
**Historically, earmarking has been a feature of Ecuador's tax system.** Earmarking can be appropriate under certain circumstances. It can establish stable financing for favored programs or services. It may also heighten taxpayer compliance by linking taxes to benefits. Back in the seventies, when this practice was adopted, its rationale was that it would safeguard allocations to particular programs, shielding them from arbitrary, discretionary changes. But the expansion of this practice helped establish entitlement claims that eventually came to hinder the government's efforts to adjust to changing macroeconomic and fiscal realities. When earmarking becomes a widespread phenomenon, it limits the flexibility of government to formulate and execute the budget in response to shifting public priorities. It undermines the possibility of channeling funds into areas where their productivity is higher, promotes an inefficient, and possibly also inequitable, use of tax revenues and reduces the fiscal space. In Ecuador, it has served as a means of appeasing strong local elites and balancing the political interests of different regions. In 2001, there were 32 earmarkings from tax revenues and 25 earmarkings from oil income, the latter being 100 percent earmarked. The FTSRL abolishes earmarking (Article 22), but it remains a standard practice in the country's fiscal system.

**Earmarking undermines the efficiency and flexibility of budget management.** In 2004, earmarked resources represented 4 percent of GDP, of which 2.4 corresponded to pre-budget earmarked tax revenues and 1.4 percent to off-budget earmarked oil resources (Table 4.5). This represents an increase over earmarked revenues of 3 percent of GDP in 2001, of which about 0.7 percent of GDP corresponded to the VAT and 0.8 percent of GDP corresponded to the income tax.

## D. Expenditure Trends
**This section analyzes trends in public expenditures.** First, it looks at the overall and primary expenditure of the non-financial public sector and the Central Government. Second, expenditures are broken down by their economic and sectoral classification focusing particularly on wages and public investment. Detailed data can be found in the Statistical Annex (A1–10).

**An expansionary trend in primary expenditures contrasts with the constant behavior of total expenditure.** Between 1997 and 2002, total and primary expenditures trended upward for both the NFPS and the Central Government (Figures 2.3 and 2.4), though they dipped in 2003.[8] Primary expenditure rose by about 4 percent of GDP during 1997–2003. However, while there has been an upward trend in primary expenditure, total expenditure has remained constant

---

7. The ISR exemption was eliminated for the financial sector on the income from securities and shares issued by the government, for cooperatives and provident societies (except for the ones established by farmers or officially recognized indigenous people), and for promoting development (directed primarily at tourism and industrial endeavors). In addition, the list of items subject to the VAT was replaced with a tax list of VAT-exempt services (fundamentally, housing rentals, and financial services)—which, therefore, leaves all other services subject to the VAT.

8. The Central Government accounts for about three-quarters of the NFPS, which explains why the two series track each other fairly closely.

## FIGURE 2.3: TOTAL AND PRIMARY EXPENDITURES

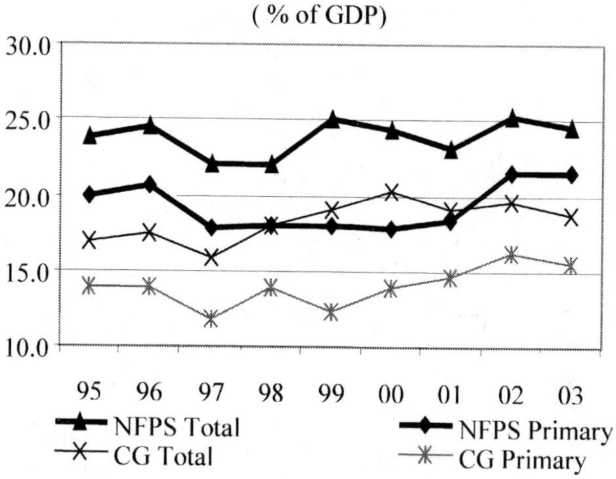

( % of GDP)

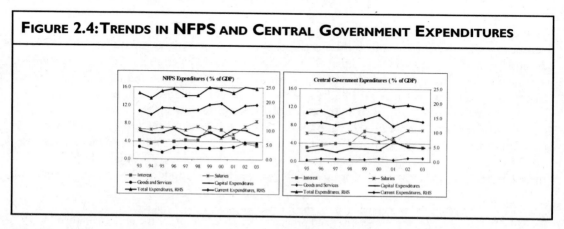

Source: BCE.

around a close 24–25 percent of GDP range, a fact mainly explained by the drop in interest payments as a share of GDP. What is of concern is that the expansionary trend in primary expenditures is more pronounced since dollarization than before.

**The upward momentum on primary expenditures is mainly propelled by current spending and especially the wage and salary component.** While NFPS current expenditures increased from an average of 17.7 percent before dollarization to an average of 18.4 percent since, average capital expenditures increased by just 0.1 percent of GDP The expansionary bias in current spending is partly due to budgetary inertia resulting from public sector wage indexation and to earmarking.[9] Inertia is also reflected in the low volatility of total expenditure (see Table 2.1), which contrasts with the much higher volatility of revenue variables (on this, see also

## FIGURE 2.4: TRENDS IN NFPS AND CENTRAL GOVERNMENT EXPENDITURES

Source: Statistical Annex.

9. Since earmarking implies the ex ante pre-allocation of projected tax revenues in the *proforma* budgets, this implies that any increase in earmarked revenue automatically translates into increased spending.

López-Cálix 2003). Political-economy factors play a major role in explaining both that inertia and the overall trend towards expansion of primary spending. The civil service and state-enterprise unions, the pensioners, the teachers and the indigenous movements have all continuously pressed for increased spending (IMF 2003b). For their part, past governments have often raised public sector wages and/or expand public employment as a way of strengthen their political base and maintain the loyalty of political clienteles.

**The functional composition of Central Government expenditure is relatively constant, but skewed towards defense and public order** (Figure 2.5). Figure 2.5 indicates that average defense and public order spending accounts for about 22 percent of the budget, which is roughly equivalent to the share of health and education expenditures. In a sample of 12 countries (the United States and eleven Latin American countries) Ecuador ranks as the country with the lowest ratios of spending on education and health with respect to GDP, about 3 percent and 1.5 percent of GDP, respectively. Furthermore, education has a relatively large share of spending only because of its large wage bill (Shepherd 2004).

**The rates of growth of some components of current expenditure have been high in recent years, and are unlikely to be sustainable in the medium term.** In real terms, the goods-and-services component grew 12.5 percent in 2001 and 39.0 percent in 2002. The wage and salaries component grew 21.7 percent in 2001, 35.4 percent in 2002, and 19.5 percent in 2003. The most unionized segments have the greatest ability to win concessions, as attested by the fact that real wages in the education sector grew an annual average 18 percent during 2000–02, and the share of wages within education expenditure jumped from 67 percent during 1995–99 to 80 percent during 2000–02. This has had a major impact on both intra-sector and inter-sector budget allocation (see on this Chapter 4).

**Rigidity makes the Central Government's budget a blunt policy instrument because it limits the ability to reduce or reallocate expenditures.** Political-economy constraints shape Ecuadorian public finances and make the budget highly inflexible. There are some expenditure categories in connection with which, once a given level of spending has been reached, it is extremely difficult to cut back to lower levels. This is the case of the wage bill in a highly unionized public sector. It is also the case with most of the earmarked revenues, as its beneficiaries, both social and regional, vehemently defend their share in the public resources. The high degree of budget rigidity is harmful for the design and fulfillment of any comprehensive poverty reduc-

---

**FIGURE 2.5: PUBLIC EXPENDITURE BY SELECTED FUNCTIONS (PERCENT OF TOTAL EXPENDITURE)**

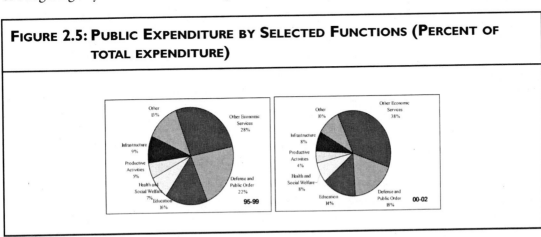

*Note:* In connection with the data on functional composition of expenditure a caveat is in order: these data are inaccurate as they only take into account spending by the institutional sector responsible of the particular function and exclude spending by other institutional sectors in that particular function. For instance, the expenditure in education does not take into account possible education spending by the Defense sector.

*Source:* Statistical Annex Table A6.

tion plan with strategic priorities. Detailed estimates of inertial and rigid spending are developed in Chapter 3. Calculations show that (a) as an average during 2001–04, the rigid components of the Central Government budget added up to 81 percent of total expenditures (including debt amortization); and (b) rigidity rose from 77.6 percent in 2001 to an estimated 82.7 percent in 2004. In addition, (c) the non-rigid components of expenditure include some categories that could appropriately be characterized as inertial expenditures; and these components accounted for 11.9 percent of expenditures in 2001–04. Given these rigidities, the flexible components (namely, a part of investment spending, the whole of the expenditures on goods and services, and certain non-wage, non-interest, and non-transfer components of current expenditures) amounted, on average, to only 7.1 percent of expenditures. Moreover, as the rigid components increased, the flexible components shrank from 13.6 percent of total expenditure in 2001 to 4.0 percent in 2004 (Table 3.5). The budget should be the main instrument to achieve the government's objectives, but these rigidities leave the Ecuadorian government with little scope to act. But above and beyond these considerations the fact stands that flexibility is crucially needed in a small open economy vulnerable to external shocks. Moreover, it should go without saying that the call for greater flexibility must not be seen as equivalent to the return to the old practices of discretionary, unaccountable spending that pre-dated the heavy reliance on earmarking. The flexibility required for macroeconomic purposes is premised on a transparent, accountable management of public finances.

**Wages and salaries account for the largest and fastest growing share of current expenditures, and this trend is unsustainable.** In 2003, 45 percent of current expenditures went to wages and salaries, up from 25 percent in 2000. While the 50 percent salary increase for public employees in 2002 redressed the severe pre-dollarization decline in real wages (about 70 percent), its impact as a permanent expenditure is troublesome, and its expansionary trend is not sustainable. Among middle-income countries, average General Government employment is 4.3 percent of the population.[10] In Ecuador, the equivalent figure is 3.1 percent. When contrasting public employment levels in Ecuador with other countries in Latin America the comparisons are less favorable (see the Statistical Appendix). Nonetheless, by these rough indicators, Ecuador's government is not grossly overstaffed. Public employment has been growing, however. From 2002 to 2004, Central Government employment increased by 7.3 percent (see the Statistical Appendix). Much of the increase occurred during the last year, most notably for police (8 percent) and armed forces personnel (18 percent). Naturally, these employment increases place additional fiscal strain on government. The projected wage bill for 2004 is nearly 27 percent higher in nominal terms than in 2002. Of course, part of this increase is the result of the aforementioned employment increases. However, employees' wages and salaries have grown even faster than employment. Monetary allowances, rather than base pay, account for most of the increase. In 2003, prior to salary unification, base pay averaged only 20 percent of public employees' total remuneration.[11] From 2000 to 2001, while overall employment levels were largely unchanged, the wage bill growth of individual ministries ranged from 21 percent to 114 percent.[12] Increases in pay have slowed since then, but have continued their upward trend. Average nominal remuneration for central government employees is projected to be 18 percent higher in 2004 than in 2002. Other sources of wage-bill expansion and other shortcomings of the current public-employment institutional framework include:

■ The proliferation of salary components, which undermines effective wage policy and administration. On top of base monthly salary, a public employee is paid up to 22 addi-

10. See the World Bank dataset on public employment and wages. These data are for various years from 1996-2000 (http://www1.worldbank.org/publicsector/civilservice/cross.htm).

11. Calculated from salary composition data gathered by SIGEF.

12. Based upon detailed budget figures for the following ministries: *Presidencia y Secretaria General de la Administración, Vicepresidencia de la República, Agricultura y Ganaderia, Bienestar Social, MEF*, and Tourism.

tional components. The net result is salaries that are four to six times bigger than the base salary, making it difficult for the government to control pay policies.

■ The lack of reliable data on public employment. There is no government office collecting the information to provide a comprehensive picture of public employment. There is not even the capacity to ensure that employees who have been released from public service (and duly indemnified) do not return to public employment.

■ Differences in salary levels are frequently inequitable,[13] hiring is not subject to rules but is frequently left to discretion of the hiring officials, and there are cases in which professionals working in similar types of jobs receive widely divergent remuneration.

**The Central Government accounts for about 81 percent of the NFPS wage bill and, within this, a few sectors are dominant.** In 2002, the education sector accounted for 43 percent of the wage bill, a significant increase from the 32 percent in 1995–99. This has been offset by decreases in the shares allocated to defense (21 percent), public order (12 percent), and health and social welfare (11 percent) (Figure 2.6) (Shepherd 2004a).

**The performance of the last two administrations in dealing with the wage bill has differed in some respects.** The Noboa administration approved the 2002 salary raise, which boosted the wage bill by 1.7 percent of GDP. The Gutiérrez administration has taken some measures to contain the growth of the wage bill and, more generally, current expenditures. A 2003 executive decree contained the "Norms on Patriotic Incentives to Savings in the Public Sector." The decree froze wages for regular civil servants, suspended overtime allowances, reduced the President's salary by 20 percent and the salary of political appointees by 10 percent, reduced the number of new positions, and restrained spending on goods and services. The decree was successful in freezing the share of the wage bill in a subset of the Central Government. The decree does not affect, however, some key sectors of the Central Government (see the discussion in Box 2.1). It does not apply either to employees in public enterprises, sectional and provincial govern-

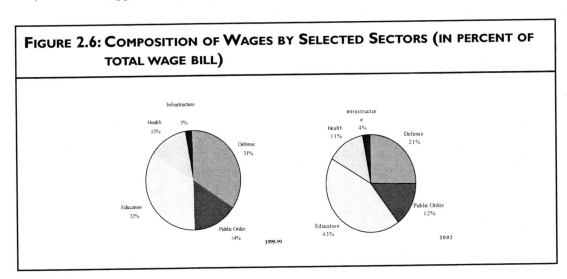

**FIGURE 2.6: COMPOSITION OF WAGES BY SELECTED SECTORS (IN PERCENT OF TOTAL WAGE BILL)**

*Source:* MEF.

---

13. According to Shepherd (2004), who quotes the Ecuadorian *Observatorio de Política Fiscal*, there are substantial differences between the current salaries for employees in the same grade according to whether they work in institutions of the Central Government or in certain decentralized agencies. Whereas the average monthly salaries for employees in the 5th and 11th grades are US$385 and US$959, respectively, for employees at the ministries, employees in the same grades in the Port Authority of Guayaquil earn basic monthly salaries of US$1,300 and US$4,320, respectively.

---

**BOX 2.1: THE CIVIL SERVICE AND THE WAGE UNIFICATION LAW: A STEP IN THE RIGHT DIRECTION**

The *Ley Orgánica de Servicio Civil y Carrera Administrativa y de Unificación y Homologación de las Remuneraciones del Sector Público* was approved on September 28, 2003, and amended on January 28, 2004. It is essential legislation for the government to control public employment and wage expenditures. Though the changes in the law are significant, its coverage is incomplete.

The first key accomplishment of the law is the elimination of a myriad of monetary allowances, except for *décimo tercer sueldo, décimo cuarto sueldo,* and *viáticos, subsistencias, dietas, horas suplementarias extraordinarias, encargos,* and *subrogaciones.* The proliferation of allowances had undermined the coherence of government pay scales and made it difficult to calculate, let alone control, annual increases in the wage bill. The number of permissible allowances has been reduced to a minimum *for those covered by the law.* However, the law exempts teachers, military, police, and civil servants of subnational governments from the salary unification. These groups are 55 percent of all public sector employees.

Total Public Employees (less workers in state enterprises): 360,000
       o/w Armed Forces: 56,000
       o/w Subnational Governments: 34,000
Total Civilian Central Government: 270,000
       o/w Teachers: 113,000
       o/w Police: 26,000
       o/w Judiciary and Legislature: 5,200
  TOTAL COVERED BY THE LAW: about 45 percent of public employees.

To oversee the number of public employees, their classification, and remuneration, the law established a *Secretaría Nacional Técnica de Desarrollo de Recursos Humanos y Remuneraciones del Sector Público* (SENRES). This *Secretaría* was granted broader powers than its predecessor (OSCIDI). Because the law left doubts about the duplicating role of CONAREM, the amendments eliminated it so SENRES will approve the new Unified Monthly Pay Scale. Salary unification will strengthen the government's capacity to monitor and control the wage bill.

The amendments to the law corrected changes that the Legislature introduced in the original bill submitted by the Executive. Congress had frozen employees' social security contributions at the amount paid in September 2003. Therefore, the real value of contributions to IESS would have *declined* over time. In addition, the Legislature raised payments for dismissed workers (raising the cap from US$10,000 to US$30,000), and allowed many public employees who received indemnity payments between 1993 and 1998 to demand a *reliquidación* so that their payment would equal that permitted by law in January 1998. The fiscal impact of this measure was sizable. Amendments to the law not only eliminated such deficiencies, but extended until January 2005 the time for starting to apply the "uniform" salary scale, and increased the transition time for full application to five years, instead of three. In addition, it set a 20 percent gradual increase in the base pay subject to an additional contribution to IESS, to be applied from 2006–10. Since public salaries have been frozen in 2004 and 2005, contribution to the IESS remains the same. Finally, the amended law set the annual ceiling for dismissed workers at 1 percent of the economically active population.

ments, social security institutions, and other autonomous agencies, because all these entities have their own laws and statutes on matters of employment and labor relations.

**A new Civil Service Law was passed in 2003.** The Civil Service and Public Administration Career and Public Sector Remuneration Unification Law represents a significant step towards regaining control over the wage bill. Among other provisions, it reduces salary categories (from 21 grades structure to 14 grades), eliminates or rationalizes monetary allowances, makes wage policy more transparent, and facilitates single registration of public employees (Box 2.1). The drawback is the fact that the law covers only about 45 percent of public servants. As a complementary action, the government has completed reviews of the ministerial staffs and these reviews have identified redundant personnel in a number of ministries. The five largest ministries personnel-wise (agriculture, the central administrative core of the Ministry of Education, social protection, health, and public works) initially remained under the 21-grade scale. However, their staffing reviews were completed in December 2003, so they could move to the 14-grade pay scale in 2004. In addition, the Central Bank has established a consolidated, electronic database for registering the payments and benefits of all public employees. This system will be instrumental in identifying ghost employees.

**Spending on goods and services is decentralized and volatile, leading to limited accountability and poor medium-term management of resources.** The discretion available to fiscal authorities with respect to goods-and-services expenditures is limited by the fact that 65 percent is spent by the local governments, municipal- and province-level government-owned enterprises, and the autonomous institutions, which, together, make up the rest of the General Government. The central budget authorities are not able to track these expenditures, nor control them in the context of fiscal adjustment. A consequence is that in recent years, budgeted operation and maintenance expenditures have been utterly insufficient: while the Ministry of Public Works has estimated US$1.5 billion will be needed over the next five years for the operation and maintenance of roads, the 2004 budget allocated only US$52 million for that purpose. This is very deleterious and costly for the government's net worth, because reconstruction is more expensive than maintenance, and higher levels of future investment will be required simply to maintain the current level of public sector capital stock.

**Deep structural problems make the pension system a major social and fiscal issue.** In 2000-2003, transfers accounted, on average, for 5.6 percent of Central government expenditures. The main types of transfer payments are the social security transfers and the *Bono Solidario*[14] transfers[15]. The discussion here will center on the pension system and will emphasize its fiscal implications.

Ecuador's pension system[16] has serious problems regarding: (i) its low coverage as provider of adequate retirement income for the elderly; (ii) its institutional arrangements, which limit efficiency and transparency; (iii) its redistributive effects, which are not consistent with equitable social development; and (iv) its medium- and long-term sustainability and the burden it implies for the fiscal accounts.

As to the *coverage* issue, only one in seven individuals receives benefits from the system. This low access results from the combination of three factors: the high prevalence of informality at younger ages, which implies that workers end up reaching retirement age without having made enough contributions to qualify for benefits; the contributive character of the system, which is designed to protect only those in the formal sector; and the low percentage of contributors: Ecuador is the LAC country with the second-lowest percentage of contributors to formal pension schemes. When it comes to the *institutional* issues, the main shortcomings are: Ecuador still is one of the few countries in the region where the health service and the pensions fund have not been separated;[17] the absence of a government agency in charge of policy definition and planning in the area of social security, which means that the Ecuadorian Social Security Institute (IESS)

---

14. *Bono Solidario* transfers consist of continuous cash stipends given to unemployed mothers and disabled and elderly people living mostly in poor areas. Recently it was rechristened *Bono de Desarrollo Humano*.

15. Other transfers include those destined to the Defense Board, the Armed Forces Social Security Institute, and the Police Social Security Institute.

16. The discussion on the pensions system draws heavily upon Rofman (2004).

17. However, the 2001 Social Security Law was a significant step ahead as it separated the accounting systems for the four insurance schemes the IESS manages, namely, the pensions, labor accidents, health, and Social Security for Peasants components.

has no counterpart in the Central Government regarding policy decisions; and the lack of transparency, as the IESS does not publish any periodical report providing information on the evolving status of the programs it manages or their expected evolution in the medium and long term. The issue of the *re-distributive* implications of the current social security scheme revolves around the 40-percent mandatory contribution that the Government must pay every year to the IESS (on which, more below). The fact of the matter is that the contribution in question represents a subsidy from the society as a whole to the relatively small, predominantly middle-income segment that receives pension benefits.

From the *public-finance* standpoint, the pension system poses the following problems:

- By law the Central Government is responsible for 40 percent of pension payments, and must transfer those resources to the Ecuadorian Social Security Institute (IESS).[18]
- The 40-percent payment was maintained by the new Social Security Law, with the added problem that it also applies to increases in pension benefits, which are unilaterally determined by the IESS, in what is tantamount to a flawed, moral-hazard-ridden scheme of incentives. The 40-percent transfer creates in fact the wrong incentive as it reduces the cost of raising pensions to social security agencies, inducing them to grant higher pensions than would otherwise be the case.
- The government has accumulated a stock of arrears in its obligations to the IESS on account of the contributions it has to pay as an employer. The 1998 Constitution requires that the government and the IESS reach an agreement on the value of the total debt owed by the government to the IESS, and that it be completely paid by 2009. The IESS estimates this debt is US$2.3 billion, but MEF estimates it is US$500 million.
- High dependency ratios raise concerns about the social security system's actuarial position[19]. Although a young population currently helps the system as a whole to maintain a sound cash flow position, the system shows a large actuarial deficit (more than 30 percent of 2002 GDP) if the government subsidies are excluded from the calculations. Without these subsidies, the IESS would exhaust its reserves in 2038.
- However, the pace at which pensions have been increased in the last several years raises concern that the pension expenditure dynamics may be turning explosive. In 2002 pensions were raised by 30 percent in January, then by 60 percent in July 2002, followed by another 60 percent in October. In 2003, pensions were raised by 27 percent in January, followed by another 27 percent in July. Further increases have been approved in 2004.[20] Expenditure on pensions as a share of GDP increased almost six-fold as it jumped from 0.3 percent in 2000 to a projected 1.8 percent in 2004.

**Taking into account the large weight of public enterprises, capital expenditures ought to be higher.** With respect to total NFPS expenditure, capital expenditures were, on average, 24.7 percent during 1995–99 and 24.3 percent during 2000–03. When compared with the Latin

18. The Central Government became legally required to cover 40 percent of the cost of pensions following the emergence of an actuarial deficit in the public pension fund in 1941. During 1959–64, the Central Government also became obligated to pay military and police pensions, as well as special additional pension schemes for other groups (see World Bank 1991).

19. Bear in mind that this statement refers to the complete social security system, including the IESS as well as the Police and the Armed Forces social security agencies.

20. In June 2004, Congress approved an increase of the minimum pension to US$135.62, a measure that would have an estimated fiscal impact according to MEF of US$210 million. A pension increase of 15 percent was also approved, and its fiscal impact estimated at US$65 million. Similarly, resources from the Reserve Fund could be devolved to pensioners (amount equivalent to US$230 million). Finally, a proposal for retiring pension deposits every three years has been advanced.

American average (14.3 percent), those ratios seem high. But the Ecuadorian public-enterprise sector is large and includes key capital-intensive sectors like oil, telecommunications, and electricity and, from that standpoint, a more relevant benchmark for comparison would be the level of public investment in economies with a strong public-enterprise sector. Such comparisons would show that public investment in Ecuador is pretty much on the low side.[21]

**The role of local governments in implementing public investment has increased significantly, certainly exceeding their capacity, and with little accountability.** As a result of the Distribution Law of 2002, which increased from 10 percent to 15 percent the share of Central Government current revenue transferred to the local governments, local governments have become important executers for public investment. In 2003, local governments accounted for 29 percent of public fixed investment, up from an average of 18 percent during 1995–99 (Figure 2.7). Public investment by the municipal governments increased from an average of 1.0 percent of GDP during 1995–99 to 1.7 percent during 2000–03.

**Resources transferred to the local governments for investment expenditures are sizable and represent about half of total Central Government investment.** In 2003, for instance, out of US$1.3 billion in Central Government capital expenditures, US$642 million (that is, 48.7 percent) consisted of transfers to the local governments. There is some evidence, however, that some transfers are spent on current expenditure items, including wages and goods and services. A number of local governments have limited management capabilities, making it questionable whether they can successfully execute investment projects (Banco Central del Ecuador 2003).

**Public enterprises play a major, albeit declining, role in public investment.** The share of public enterprises within total public investment dropped by almost half (from 33 percent to 18 percent) between the pre-dollarization period and 2003. This is the result of a downward trend in fixed-capital-formation on the part of the non-financial public enterprises. By 2003 investment spending by these firms accounted for 0.8 percent of GDP compared to an average of 1.8 percent during 1995–99 (Shepherd 2004). Public enterprises are handicapped by pricing policies setting tariffs below the true economic costs, and by uneven managerial quality.

**The residual character of capital expenditures leads to their volatility.** NFPS capital expenditure has decreased from an average 5.8 percent of GDP during 1995–99 to 5.4 percent of GDP in 2003 (Table A1), while current expenditures went in the opposite direction. The dif-

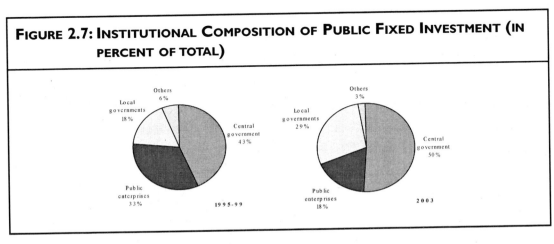

**FIGURE 2.7: INSTITUTIONAL COMPOSITION OF PUBLIC FIXED INVESTMENT (IN PERCENT OF TOTAL)**

*Source: MEF.*

---

21. Venezuela, which has a similarly large public-enterprise sector, boasts a public-investment-to-GDP ratio of about 8 percent, whereas Ecuador's is just about 3.5 percent.

ferences between the behavior of current expenditures and capital expenditures do not bode well for the future of public investment in Ecuador, unless serious institutional changes are implemented that would protect capital expenditures from the effects of fiscal volatility. Due to the inflexibility of the budget, investment spending is the adjustment variable *par excellence* when expenditure needs to be cut. Public investment thus bears the brunt of fiscal adjustment, giving it considerable variability vis-à-vis current expenditures. This pattern also reflects institutional weaknesses like the absence of savings in the good years to finance expenditure in the bad years, and insufficient medium-to-long-term planning capabilities in the public sector.

## E. The Fiscal Transparency, Stabilization and Responsibility Law

**Ecuador's adoption of fiscal rules and stabilization funds is a major step ahead towards an institutional framework favorable to fiscal discipline.** The most important steps Ecuador has taken to offset the vulnerabilities stemming from its volatile revenue base and rigid spending structure are: (i) the fiscal rules contained in the Fiscal Transparency, Stabilization and Responsibility Law and (ii) the setting up of two stabilization funds, namely, the Oil Stabilization Fund (FEP in its Spanish acronym) and the Fund for Stabilization, Social and Productive Investment, and Reduction of Public Debt (FEIREP). Details on these funds are provided in Box 2.2.

### Stabilization Funds

**The main objective of a fiscal stabilization fund in an oil-exporting country is to reduce the impact of volatility of oil prices on government expenditures.** The FEP was created in 1999. It is designed to offset fluctuations in world oil prices by saving when prices are high and enabling the government to draw on the fund when prices are low. Historically, however, FEP funds were earmarked, and little remained as a contingency fund. For its part, FEIREP was created in 2002, with two main sources of funds: (i) some revenues from FEP and (ii) the additional revenues from the opening of a new oil pipeline. FEIREP has three objectives: (a) to repurchase public debt, (b) to function as a macroeconomic stabilization fund, and (c) to contribute to social expenditures.

**An analysis of FEIREP mechanisms finds weaknesses that should be addressed.** The rules for resource accumulation in the fund may force the government to save too much at cer-

---

## BOX 2.2: ECUADOR'S OIL FUNDS

**The Oil Stabilization Fund (FEP).** Article 58a of the Public Finance Reform Act created the FEP, principally using oil revenues that were not foreseen or that were higher than initially budgeted. The FEP is now allocated as follows: 45 percent to the FEIREP; 35 percent for the construction of the Amazon Highway; 10 percent for comprehensive development projects in selected provinces; and 10 percent for the National Police for a period of 5 years, of which half must be spent in the Amazon region.

**The Fund for Stabilization, Social and Productive Investment, and Reduction of Public Debt (FEIREP).** In June 2002, Article 13 of the Organic Law on Fiscal Accountability, Stabilization, and Transparency created the FEIREP.

- Funding sources of the FEIREP are: transportation revenue from state-owned oil rated lower than 23° on the API scale (that is, heavy crude oil) goes to the fund; budget surpluses of the Central Government; and 45 percent of FEP resources.
- FEIREP funds are allocated as follows: 70 percent for the repurchase of public debt and the service of the debt with the Social Security Institute of Ecuador (IESS); 10 percent for health and education expenditures; and 20 percent are destined to a stabilization account of up to 2.5 percent of GDP, to be used to respond to legally declared emergencies and to compensate for the decline in revenue when oil prices are low.

tain times and not enough at others. The formulae also entail a conservative estimate for how long oil reserves will last, forcing the government into a more restrictive fiscal policy than necessary at times, thus increasing the temptation to skirt the rules, as happened in May 2004.

**The goal of accumulating up to 2.5 percent of GDP to fund FEIREP's stabilization component provides insufficient insurance for countercyclical fiscal policy.** This stabilization component aims to provide resources when the price of oil is low or when the country suffers from a natural catastrophe or any other national emergency. Both events reduce fiscal revenues and the latter also raises the demand for public outlays. The amount estimated necessary to provide full insurance for an eventual period of low oil prices, based on average oil revenues for 2000–03, would be 6.9 percent of GDP, compared to 3.9 percent in 1998 (Artana and Moskovits 2004). This is two times higher than the funds available in the FEIREP stabilization component. In addition, the fund is assumed to provide insurance against losses from natural catastrophes. In the last big natural disaster, the El Niño of 1998, the government made an emergency budget allocation of 1.4 percent of GDP, but this was insufficient: the total cost (both public and private) of the damage was estimated at US$2 billion dollars (almost 10 percent of GDP). Although, a priori, the probability distribution of natural catastrophes and low international oil prices are independent, the 1998 period is an example of bad luck when both negative external shocks were present at the same time. Though there is no economic imperative to provide full insurance, authorities should be aware that with FEIREP, they have only partial coverage in a worst-case scenario.

**FEIREP does not accumulate resources in an efficient manner to protect the budget.** A well-designed stabilization fund would have funds entering when the actual oil price is higher than the target price, but Ecuador's funds have a more complicated formula. The FEIREP receives money from two sources: 45 percent of the FEP resources (which capture oil windfalls above a certain price), and fiscal revenues from increases in heavy oil transported through both pipelines beyond a set production level. Now, even if the actual price is lower than the target price set for FEP, FEIREP would still be earning resources from the second source. This would not be the case in an "Ideal" Fund. Adding this result to the previous one shows that the FEIREP may save more than optimally desired when oil prices are lower than the reference price, and less when there is a boom in prices (Figure 2.8).

## FIGURE 2.8: "OPTIMAL" AND ACTUAL STABILIZATION ACCUMULATION SCENARIOS

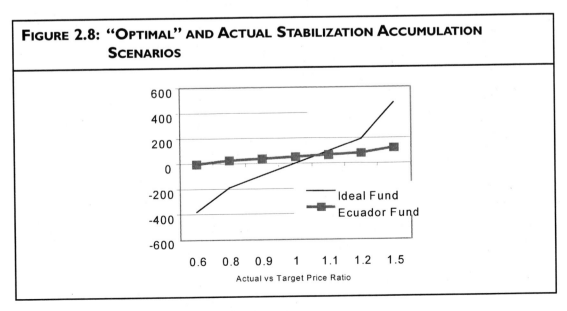

*Source:* World Bank staff calculations.

**Debt repurchasing should be implemented to conserve the country's oil wealth.**
Because a reduction in government debt is similar to the creation of a government asset, using oil resources to repurchase debt can be seen as a way of replacing a dwindling asset. Ideally, the amount of the non-oil deficit should equal the return on the size of the oil wealth. Assuming a 3.5 percent discount rate and a conservative oil outlook, the net present value of Ecuador's oil wealth is US$18.9 billion.[22] Therefore, if Ecuador were able to have a non-oil deficit of US$600 million a year and to save the difference in assets, yielding a 3.5 percent annual return in real terms by the time that crude oil reserves are completely depleted (by 2020), it would have assets equivalent to 35 percent of GDP. Ecuador's rules do not follow this "optimal" path. Table 2.6 compares how much FEIREP would accumulate for debt reduction with the amount that would be saved (or would be available for buybacks of public debt) if Ecuador had an "optimal" rule that would maintain a constant oil wealth. Estimates show that Ecuador saves "too little," or in other words, the country is consuming part of the oil wealth in the current generation (and implicitly transferring to the future more debt or lower assets than under the optimal rule).

### Fine-Tuning Fiscal Rules

**To stabilize the fiscal accounts, the FTSRL introduced quantitative rules for fiscal performance:** (a) primary Central Government expenditures should not increase more than 3.5 percent per year in real terms, or the real growth rate, whichever is lower—this growth rate for expenditures is reduced to 2.5 percent for the operating expenses of the Financial Public Sector; (b) the non-oil deficit of the Central Government should be reduced by 0.2 percent of GDP per year—for this purpose the non-oil deficit is calculated by subtracting oil revenues derived from exports (which is about two-thirds of what the government includes as petroleum revenues) from total revenues; (c) public debt should be reduced by 16 percentage points of GDP during the period January 2003–December 2006 and debt reduction must proceed until a debt-ratio of 40 percent of GDP is reached; thereafter, this 40-percent ratio will remain as the ceiling for public debt; and (d) there are also constraints on sub-national debt: any provincial or municipal government's debt cannot be higher than its annual revenues, and the debt service cannot be higher than 40 percent of the given sub-national government's annual revenue. In addition, Central Government guarantees on private debt are forbidden, and the Executive can only guarantee state debt issued for investment projects.

**The government has largely met its targets.** Although the FTSRL became mandatory in 2003, data for 2002 are also shown to provide some perspective (Table 2.7). In 2004 the rule governing planned real primary spending and the non-oil deficit were met. The scheduled reduction of public debt-to-GDP ratio was also on track in 2003. The executed real primary expenditure, instead of increasing, fell by almost 1 percent of GDP in 2003. Only the non-oil deficit reduction was not achieved in 2003, but after two consecutive years of reduction. This is discussed below as a rather restrictive target.

**The 3.5 percent target for growth in real primary expenditures could be ineffective.** Rules that constrain the growth in public expenditures are easier to control and more understandable by the public than rules that restrict the overall balance or the debt level. However, the design of this rule raises two concerns.

- ◾ **The 3.5 percent target growth is calculated on the budgeted (*proforma*) public expenditures of the previous year, and not on the executed expenditures.**
  Alternatively, it could be the extrapolated state of the expenditures. In the case of the 2004 budget, the rule might become very lenient, since projected real growth in primary spending could end up being about 14 percent in 2004.

---

22. Technical details on this calculation are available from Artana and Moskovits (See Annex A).

## TABLE 2.6: OPTIMAL FUND VERSUS FEIREP FLOWS FOR DEBT REDUCTION (MILNS US$)

| | 2004 | 2005 | 2006 | 2007 | 2008 | 2009 | 2010 | 2011 | 2012 | 2013 | 2014 | 2015 | 2016 | 2017 | 2018 | 2019 | 2020 |
|---|---|---|---|---|---|---|---|---|---|---|---|---|---|---|---|---|---|
| Ecuador Rule (70% of FEIREP) | 191 | 249 | 290 | 331 | 373 | 414 | 420 | 427 | 433 | 440 | 447 | 454 | 460 | 467 | 474 | 481 | 489 |
| "Ideal" Debt Reduction | 329 | 411 | 506 | 591 | 676 | 761 | 796 | 828 | 861 | 895 | 930 | 966 | 1004 | 1043 | 1083 | 1124 | 1167 |

Note: Prices are forecasted as equal to the long-term trend.

Source: World Bank staff estimates.

## TABLE 2.7: EVALUATION OF COMPLIANCE WITH THE FISCAL RULES

| | Application | Measure-ment Unit | Legal Clause | 2002 Executed | 2003 Executed | 2004 Planned (Proforma) |
|---|---|---|---|---|---|---|
| Primary expenditure | central government budget | real growth | 3.5% | 15.1% | −0.9% | 3.4% |
| Non-oil deficit | central government | annual change (% of GDP) | −0.2% | −0.3% | 0.0% | −.02% |
| Public debt/GDP | total public debt | reduction each 4 years[2] | 16.0% 3.8% annually | −12.0% | −5.0% | |

Notes: [1] reported figures are for the central government.   [2] up to 40 percent of GDP.
Source: World Bank staff estimates.

■ **Continuous budget amendments affect compliance of the 3.5 percent rule.** The latter should be applied to the *proforma* budget approved by Congress.

**The condition to reduce the non-oil deficit by on average 0.2 percent of GDP per year is too restrictive on public finances.** Starting from a non-oil deficit of 2.4 percent of GDP in 2003, a 0.2 percent annual reduction would bring the non-oil balance to zero in 12 years, at which point the country would, in theory, no longer depend on oil revenues. Even the most pessimistic estimate assumes that oil reserves will last more than 17 years; therefore, the annual rate of non-oil deficit reduction could reasonably be set at 0.15 percent of GDP per year.

**This condition could be, moreover, unnecessary.** To maintain oil wealth for future generations, it may be sufficient that the reduced non-oil deficit become equal to the future real interest yield on returns from real oil wealth preserved in FEIREP. Should public debt become no longer a significant problem, a well-designed oil fund would generate savings through a well-diversified portfolio that would finance a non-oil deficit equal to the real return on this asset. This would make part of the oil wealth available for future generations.

**To allow flexibility in responding to shocks, Ecuador should reduce its public debt below 40 percent of GDP.** Ecuador's public debt, at 53 percent of GDP, is below the ceiling of 60 percent by the European countries under the Maastricht Treaty. However, for developing countries a sensible ceiling would be about half of what is appropriate for European countries,[23] when due account is taken of the narrowness of domestic capital markets, the higher interest rates, and the lower public revenue in relation to GDP in Latin America.[24] This reinforces the need to increase public savings and lessen the vulnerability associated with a fragile fiscal position. Several factors, including low liquidity, low credibility in the legal framework, and the need to "buy" some confidence after episodes of default on the sovereign debt, suggest that for highly-indebted, oil-rich, emerging countries a lower ratio would be desirable. Thus, it may be better to begin by reducing a government liability, and bring it to a low ratio to GDP to prepare for contingencies, and once an appropriate lower ceiling is attained, to start saving into a government asset. Therefore, while the 40 percent cap on public debt to GDP is acceptable, it would be

---

23. For more details see Artana, López Murphy, and Navajas (2003); or Reinhart, Rogoff, and Savastano (2003).

24. The 60-percent-of-GDP ceiling for European countries, expressed as a fraction of government revenues, turns out to be 150 percent. This is similar to a widely used ratio for private companies, which is the debt-to-sales ratio. Considering that Ecuador Public Sector Revenues are about 25 percent of GDP, a debt ceiling of 150 percent of revenues would yield a "reasonable" debt-to-GDP ratio of 38 percent. The 30 percent "rule-of-thumb" ratio takes into account a higher liquidity risk.

advisable to reduce it in the medium term. Alternatively, a contingent clause could be introduced to further reduce debt ratios in years when the oil price is not excessively low, and there are no natural disasters.

**The FTSRL introduces positive reforms to reduce contingent liabilities.** The Central Government cannot guarantee private debt, and guarantees to provincial and sectional governments' debt are limited to investment projects. Although money is fungible and therefore the loan can end up financing current expenditures, this "golden rule" is a reasonable objective. Together with quantitative restrictions on states' debt, it puts limits on how much debt subnational governments may contract. By doing so it reduces the size of a contingent increase in Central Government debt because of the bailouts of subnational governments that are so frequent in the region.

## F. Issues in Debt Sustainability

**A major weakness of Ecuador's fiscal situation is the high level of public debt, the inherited result of decades of undisciplined fiscal management.** The country experienced a full-fledged debt crisis in 1999 and defaulted on its debt obligations. After a turbulent period of involuntary debt restructuring, including a 40-percent "haircut" in the restructuring agreement, and thanks also to the ongoing economic recovery, Ecuador was able to reduce its public external debt from 102.0 percent in 2002 to 37.2 percent of GDP as of the first half of 2004. Despite this decline, both the debt level and the debt service are still excessive and the risk of default is not negligible. In addition, the Treasury has repeatedly faced liquidity problems in serving its debt, which has frequently forced the country to run sizeable levels of arrears with its creditors. Despite progress in reducing arrears[25], liquidity shortfalls are still a problem as of the writing of this report.

**A Debt Sustainability Analysis (DSA) indicates that primary surpluses between 4.5 and 5.0 percent of GDP are required gradually to reduce the debt-to-GDP ratio to 40 percent, the benchmark defined in the FTSRL.**[26] Most DSA exercises aim at calculating the primary surpluses needed to stabilize the ratio of debt to GDP, that is to say, the fiscal effort needed to avoid an explosive future evolution of the debt ratios. The exercise carried out in this report takes as a parametric point of departure the policy and legal decision to reduce the debt level to 40 percent of GDP, an objective enshrined in the FTSRL, and determines what are the primary balances required to reach this benchmark by 2006. The base case scenario is premised on the assumption that the economic program will be successful in sustaining dollarization (Box 2.3). Focusing on the medium-term, no oil windfall is assumed under the base case scenario. Hence, it is a conservative one (a high case scenario based on higher oil prices is presented in Box 2.3). It assumes that the country would have steady growth and low inflation, favored by slow expansionary spending, an increase in non-oil tax revenues, and sizable primary surpluses. Stability will induce a reduction in interest rates to foster private—foreign and domestic—investment and exports as the main sources of growth. Restructuring of the banking system will continue. Funds from the FEIREP will be used to repurchase debt as mandated by the fiscal rule. All inherited public debt arrears are cleared in 2004, and any default over the next three years is ruled out. Partial grant financing of the priority social expenditure will be given to the GOE to bring adequate protection to the poorest, while minimizing the potentially negative short-term impact of adjustment measures, thus preserving minimum social and political consensus over the difficult measures to be adopted. Under the base case, obtaining primary sur-

---

25. According to Minister of Finance Yépez, President Gutiérrez's government was able to reduce arrears from $780 million in January 2003 to nearly $280 million in early June 2004 (see Reuters, 2004).

26. The baseline DSA is taken from World Bank 2004a.

---

## BOX 2.3 THE DEBT SCENARIOS

**Base Case:** During 2004–06, key assumptions are: growth averaging 4.0 percent, with single-digit inflation rates, converging to international levels (2 percent) by end-period; decline in oil prices in 2005-06, with falling prices partly offset by new oil exports.

- A WTI oil price assumption of $32 per barrel is used for 2004, and $20 per barrel for 2005–06.
- Steady private investment in the oil sector occurs. Oil production would increase by about 40 percent, or 64 million barrels (an increase from 400,000 bpd to 570,000 bpd), during 2003–06. PetroEcuador's production is expected to remain relatively flat, increasing only 9.5 percent during this period, whereas private companies should see their production levels increased 81 percent.
- The increase in oil production will support growth rates of 4.0 percent in the forecast period.
- As a result, the NFPS primary surplus should average 4.5-5 percent of GDP (for an NFPS overall surplus of 2.2 percent of GDP) arising from temporarily increased oil and non-oil tax revenues, austerity measures and declining public spending in real terms.
- Compliance with all fiscal rules contained in the Fiscal Transparency, Stabilization and Responsibility Law is also assumed.

**High Case:** This scenario assumes a higher growth rate of 6 percent in 2004, led by higher oil prices, with similar inflation rates as in the Base Case. The results of the high case show:

- A WTI oil price assumption of $40 per barrel for 2004 and $30 per barrel in 2005 and $26 in 2006.
- Higher primary surpluses are generated, averaging 5.1%, reducing the fiscal financing needs.
- Higher oil revenues also lead to a greater accrual of FEIREP resources and higher levels of debt repurchasing.
- Public debt to GDP ratios will achieve the 40 percent target a year earlier in 2005.

---

pluses between 4.5-5 percent of GDP would allow the government to cover their amortization payments with little additional financing and continue the gradual decline of the public debt-to-GDP ratio to the sustainable ratio of 40 percent of GDP in 2006, (Figure 2.9). The active repayment of expensive domestic and external (global) debt with the primary surpluses is a major factor explaining this result.

**Additional debt sustainability exercises are carried out taking into account shocks to the financing of the current account.** Like all emerging markets, Ecuador faces high volatility of capital inflows. Sudden outflows of capital can be interpreted as a shock to credit or a shock to the capital account and could lead to solvency problems if vulnerabilities are not addressed in advance. A fall in the financing of the current account deficit implies that the country must fol-

## FIGURE 2.9: BASE AND HIGH CASE FOR DEBT SUSTAINABILITY

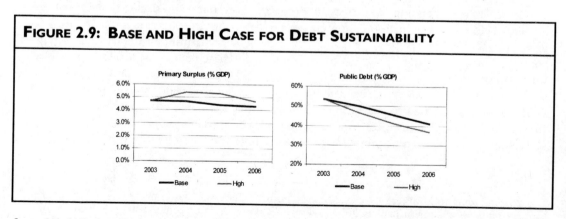

*Source:* World Bank staff calculations.

low a forced adjustment in its absorption of tradable goods. As Izquierdo and Panizza (2003) argue: "To the extent that consumption of non-tradable goods is a complement in consumption of tradable goods, a fall in the latter will imply a fall in the former, leading to a decrease in non-tradable prices. Since, for a small open economy, tradable prices are taken as a given, this implies that the real exchange rate will have to adjust. Adjustment in the real exchange rate will generate valuation effects on the debt-to-GDP ratio, which, in turn, affect fiscal sustainability."

**Ecuador is exposed to direct shocks to the current account that could work just like a sudden stop.** Ecuador's economy is highly vulnerable to a fall in oil prices (or a fall in remittances). This is because the government does not have access to international credit markets and therefore has no tool to smooth out oil price shocks.

**The usefulness of fiscal sustainability exercises lies in their helping policy makers to assess the likely impacts of shocks.** Two exercises aimed at assessing the impact of potential shocks on the economy are presented in what follows. Their theoretical rationale and methodology are developed in Volume II (see Chapter 1). Additional discussion on the theoretical model underlying these exercises is found in Diaz, Izquierdo, and Panizza (2004). All exercises are carried out with reference to the state of the Ecuadorian economy in late 2003, that is, before the recent sharp increase in oil prices, and supplement the conventional fiscal sustainability analysis aimed at identifying the primary surplus needed to achieve a constant debt-to-GDP ratio under given interest-rate and GDP-growth assumptions. The *first exercise* identifies the primary surplus needed for fiscal sustainability, taking into account the change in relative prices required to adjust to the shock and its impact on the debt level. In this exercise two cases are analyzed, a 50 percent drop in the price of oil and a sudden drop in capital inflows. The latter includes an assessment of the additional impact of an increase in contingent liabilities that may surface as a consequence of a depreciation of the real exchange rate needed to adjust to a drop in capital inflows. The *second exercise* gives an indication of how close or far the economy is from being in a crisis situation given its current debt level and the volatility of government revenue.

*Exercise No. 1. Fiscal Sustainability under a Sudden Drop in the Price of Oil, Surge in Interest Rate, or Capital Ouflows*
**A sudden drop in the external resources needed to sustain the level of aggregate demand of the economy (at a given income) has proven very costly in terms of output in developing countries (Calvo and Reinhart 2001).** Ecuador is no exception. Its crisis of the late 1990s was partly the consequence of a sudden stop in capital inflows that led to fiscal solvency and sustainability problems (Izquierdo 2002). A fall in the financing of the current account deficit implies that the country must follow a forced adjustment in its absorption of tradable goods. This implies an adjustment in the real exchange rate that may be accompanied by a materialization of contingent liabilities that would deteriorate fiscal sustainability.

**Impact of an oil shock and an interest rate increase.** A 50 percent drop in the price of oil from US$24 to US$12 per barrel would lead to a drop in net export proceeds equivalent to 13.3 percent of 2003 imports (a proxy for absorption of tradable goods). For this, a 33.3 percent depreciation of the real exchange rate would be required, because the drop in imports would be accompanied by a similar percentage fall in complementary non-tradable goods. This means that tradable goods would become more expensive relative to nontradable goods (e.g, a real exchange rate depreciation). This will not change the value of Ecuador's dollar debt in terms of tradable goods, but it will lower the value of output—that has a large nontradable component—in terms of tradable goods, thus leading to an increase in the debt-to-GDP ratio. At dollar interest rates of 11 percent, Ecuador would require a primary surplus of around 4.4 percent of GDP to sustain 2003 levels of debt. At this interest rate, a drop of 50 percent in the price of oil would require a primary balance of 5.2 percent of GDP, that is, almost 1 additional point of GDP. But, if the shock is accompanied by an increase in 200 basis points in interest rates and a fall of 1 percentage point in GDP growth, the required primary surplus would rise to 7 percent of GDP. Debt sustainability results prove very sensitive to interest rate changes.

**Impact of a sudden stop in capital inflows.** Under the same assumptions, closing Ecuador's 2003 current account deficit would require a primary fiscal surplus of 4.9 percent of GDP. Adding an increase in interest rates of 200 basis points, and a fall in GDP growth of 1 percent would require 2.2 points of GDP in adjustment, bringing the total needed primary surplus to 6.7 percent. If resulting contingent liabilities from the dollarized banking system surface,[27] the public debt would increase by 2.5 points and the economy will require an additional adjustment in the primary surplus of about 0.3 points of GDP, bringing the total to 7 percent of GDP. As a result, when occurring jointly, each of these different elements, that is, contingent liabilities, interest rate increase, and GDP growth deceleration, they would add combined pressure to the less stringent adjustment required if each of those factors were to operate individually and in isolation.

*Exercise No. 2.  Fiscal Sustainability under Tax Revenue Volatility*

**This exercise accounts for tax revenue volatility in a context of expenditure inflexibility and constraints to access international credit markets.** The implicit assumption in this exercise is that the government cannot accumulate more debt than the level it could service if it were to enter a fiscal crisis (defined as the case in which the primary balance remains forever at its lowest possible value[28]). Thus, even under the assumption that the government would always be willing to pay its debt, there would still be a limit above which no additional lending would take place, because the government may not have sufficient resources to pay back under a sustained crisis scenario. While in the standard approach to fiscal sustainability the primary balance (to GDP) that stabilizes the current debt-to-GDP ratio is assumed to be its steady state level, in this exercise only a threshold level of debt to GDP is defined, but this level is neither the equilibrium that will necessarily be observed nor the optimal level of debt. With this information, the government should strengthen fundamentals so that the probability of hitting the upper bound of government debt remains low. Lower values of government revenues per GDP (which would result from taking into account revenue volatility) would require that sustainable debt levels be adjusted downwards, especially if the government cannot commit to large expenditure cuts while facing a shock. Taking into account these considerations, this exercise shows that, with 50-percent probability, it would take six years for Ecuador to reach the debt threshold, and with 35-percent probability it would take three years. This information should help the authorities to correct fiscal imbalances well before hitting debt thresholds.

**Both exercises show additional reasons why Ecuador needs to prepare for potential oil, interest-rate, or capital-outflow shocks by strengthening its fiscal accounts to achieve fiscal primary surpluses at least between 4.4 and 5.2 percent of GDP.** Were authorities willing to protect the economy from the additional potential impact of resultant output slowdown, interest-spread increases, and contingent liabilities, the required primary fiscal surplus should be around 7.0 percent of GDP. As these exercises imply, negative shocks could quickly add substantial pressure to debt sustainability in the future.

## G. Policy Recommendations

**In adopting dollarization, Ecuador chose a very demanding institutional framework for the conduct of economic policy.** The country faces significant challenges stemming from dependence on volatile oil revenues, unpredictable capital flows, and the devastating effects of nature-induced supply shocks. These disturbances are bound to operate regardless of the monetary regime, and would seriously test the most skillful and inspired team of policymakers. But in

---

27. Assumes that 20 percent of loans from the non-tradable sector go bankrupt (see Izquierdo 2004).

28. This lowest possible value is dictated by the lowest possible realization of public revenues and the maximum adjustment in expenditure that would be feasible for the government.

the context of dollarization, the tests are even more stringent. While, from the standpoint of stabilization objectives, dollarization gives policymakers a head start by the sheer impossibility of a currency crisis and hyperinflation it entails, demand management is restricted to fiscal policy, and the buffer of the nominal exchange rate is no longer available. Moreover, the economy's adjustment mechanism after a negative shock is likely to be through recession and deflation, thereby magnifying the challenges. In addition, for all its advantages for financial stability, dollarization in the context of an open capital account needs to be supported by a robust, well-regulated financial system where information-asymmetry problems can be kept under control. Finally, there is the challenge posed by the need to enhance competitiveness in the tradable sectors, where real exchange rate depreciations are costly and painful when, as in the Ecuadorian case, wages and prices are inflexible in the downward direction. To address these challenges, the next recommendations focus on a proposal for a fiscal agenda that could help strengthen the dollarization framework.

**The fiscal agenda, however, face formidable political-economy and institutional obstacles in Ecuador.** As it was pointed out in the first chapter, the ultimate root of Ecuador's fiscal stance lies in the political-economy regime that took shape in the wake of the oil discoveries of the late sixties and is still prevailing. This is the political-economy regime that begets—and keeps reproducing—the incentives that bias fiscal policy towards inertial expenditure expansion and against flexibility of resource allocation. The current oil price boom intensifies the resistance to fiscal adjustment as it creates a public opinion atmosphere where, in the eyes of some social groups, fiscal discipline seems both unjustified and unnecessary. However, in the last several years, large segments of public opinion have come to support the reform camp as the citizenry increasingly understands the inextricable connection between the need for fiscal adjustment and the creation of the fiscal space needed for a poverty reduction strategy.

**Thus, the medium-term objective of fiscal policy is to strengthen and preserve the sustainability of the fiscal accounts.** This could be achieved with the support of an implicit or explicit Fiscal Pact, whose main general goals would be to: (a) deal with the public sector's insolvency risk; (b) carry out a comprehensive tax reform; (c) eliminate the inertial bias toward payroll expansion and investment cutback in the management of public finances; (d) reform the civil service and pensions system; (e) use the oil wealth for debt reduction; (f) while duly complying with the fiscal rule requirements in the short tem (and thereby building credibility), amend in a few years the FTSRL to make it a sharper, more coherent, and more powerful instrument for fiscal consolidation; and (g) address the issue of the Treasury's short-term liquidity problems.

▨ **To lower insolvency risk, the authorities should obtain the large primary surpluses required to reduce the debt to a sustainable level.** Under a base case scenario, the PER's debt sustainability analysis indicates the annual NFPS primary surplus needed to meet interest payments and to reduce the debt ratio to at least 40 percent of GDP during 2004–07. The only way to achieve primary surpluses of this magnitude is to generate new revenues while controlling expenditures. Whereas the 40 percent ratio is the one contemplated by the FTSRL, an additional 5 percent would be desirable to allow for contingencies and shocks.

▨ **The government should persevere in the pursuit of a comprehensive tax reform.** Following a return of oil prices to their historic average level, the objective of tax reform should be to raise the non-oil tax revenues by at least 2.5 percent of GDP. This is equivalent to the amount that must be accumulated in the FEIREP to comply with the FTSRL's rules. Tax reform should be directed toward: (a) eliminating or rationalizing all non-constitutionally mandated earmarked expenditures; (b) eliminating or rationalizing exemptions to VAT, income-tax, and customs duties, with the exception of the VAT exemptions for unprocessed basic foods; (c) simplifying the tax structure, and eliminating taxes that generate minimal revenue; (d) completing Customs reform; and (e) strengthening tax administration. Political-economy obstacles to tax reform are substantial as it affects powerful vested interests. This explains why multiple proposals for new tax legislation have been repeatedly rejected by Congress. However, this only means that the reform camp will have to persevere in the task of creating the political conditions that favor reaching a Fiscal Pact.

- **Eliminate the inertial bias toward payroll expansion and investment cutback.** This can be done through: (a) containing the growth of the wage bill (more details on this below); (b) a review of programs in every spending ministry to find those that can be eliminated because they either do not adequately represent current social priorities or are duplicative or wasteful; (c) better targeting of social programs and elimination of those that cannot be directed sufficiently toward the poor; and (d) using FEIREP funds to repurchase the most expensive debt first (particularly in Global Bonds) to reduce interest payments).

- **Complete civil service reform.** Three measures that the government could consider are: (a) extending the wage unification law to employee categories that were not covered by the FTSRL; (b) a program of public employment retirement, complemented, when necessary, by hiring bans, elimination of vacant positions, and early retirement programs; and (c) permanent review of staffing needs.

- **The pensions system must be reformed so as to render it more equitable; improve its institutional design, make it more efficient and transparent; reduce its current fiscal cost; and preempt future Central Government liabilities.**[29] The Government should develop and implement several policies aiming to solve or reduce the problems of low coverage, inadequate institutional arrangements, costly and inequitable subsidies, and long term sustainability risks. This report suggests: (1) adopting an inclusive approach in the design of the system, providing income security to groups with little or no coverage but great needs, in a fiscally sustainable manner; (2) changing the sector's institutional scheme, by completing the administrative separation of the social security component and the health component and by creating an instance within the central administration in charge of designing and implementing social security policies; (3) reviewing the autonomous status of IESS to avoid political interference in its daily operations; (4) increasing transparency, by adopting a permanent program to prepare, disseminate and evaluate information on the status of IESS and its different programs; (5) eliminating the government contribution to IESS benefits, adjusting the parameters of the system to achieve actuarial sustainability in the medium and long term; and (6) reviewing the system's legal framework to create a simpler, more transparent model. A structural reform (including the creation of individual accounts and private management) may be an option, but only if it can be implemented with a reasonable social and political consensus and in a fiscally sustainable way.

- **Using the oil wealth for debt reduction is an optimal strategy.** Given the large country risk premium on public debt, the best alternative is to use oil revenues to reduce public debt well below 40 percent of GDP in a gradual manner until 2006, and once this ceiling is attained, start accumulating into financial assets that will allow the country to have a reasonable non-oil deficit, even after oil reserves are depleted. This strategy has several advantages. First, it will reduce interest payments for the government. A quantitative exercise shown in the Statistical Appendix demonstrates that, under suitable assumptions as to amount of additional debt repurchases, annual interest payment reductions can be as high as 0.2 percent of GDP in 2005 and 2006 (for details, see Table A76). Secondly, *ceteris paribus*, the fiscal deficit will be lower. Thirdly, real interest rates for the private sector will

---

29. Policy recommendations on how to deal with the social security system's health component are presented in Chapter 4 of Volume II.

also be lower. And this through two channels: (i) government borrowing in domestic capital markets will decrease and (ii) the interest rate for the sovereign, which tends to be a minimum floor for borrowing costs for the private sector, will go down.

- **Buying back the external debt would improve government credibility and strengthen the economy's growth prospects.** This is the debt strategy that will moderate the change in relative prices that is created by the oil windfall and help strengthen the markets' perception that Ecuador's debt sustainability is improving. However, it must be borne in mind that a policy of repurchasing external debt may be politically costly as it is rejected by some segments of public opinion. Indeed, the legal guarantee involved in Global Bonds may raise the debt's repurchasing price in the secondary market, thus reducing initially anticipated savings. Moreover, using available FEIREP resources to buy back domestic debt could add pressure to aggregate demand, unless the holders of domestic debt take their payments out of the country. This is surely not the case with the pension system debt, and is probably not the case with other debt held by residents, either. So, to prevent demand pressure, it must be borne in mind that debt buyback is no substitute for expenditure discipline. If the government cannot cutback inefficient expenditure, the rollover of domestic debt might just be higher domestic debt in net terms. Hence more fiscal vulnerability and lower reduction of the overall debt ratio than projected. Even repurchasing external debt might not prevent this outcome. Hence, assuming expenditure cuts take place, it would then be advisable to keep assessing the advantages and disadvantages of repurchasing domestic or external debt with FEIREP resources. The repurchasing debt policy should weigh the benefits of reducing the country risk and gaining access to financial markets with the increased cost of the renegotiated repurchased price of bonds. In general, expensive debt, such as the Global Bonds, should be exchanged for less expensive one in a transparent process.

- **In the short term, strictly complying with FEIREP rules to prevent diversion of its debt buyback funds would strengthen its credibility.** The pressure to dip into these resources is high, and windfall oil revenues have always been used to finance poorly selected public investments. High oil prices such as currently prevail, make changing FEIREP rules more tempting.

- **FEIREP should start developing its debt repurchases to gain early credibility, but in the future it should clearly separate the stabilization function from the savings and debt-reduction functions.** This will require allocating a higher amount of FEP revenues to the stabilization fund, to deal properly with the volatility in the international price of crude oil. Now, by contrast, the rules force the government to save too much when prices are depressed and too little when prices are high. With regard to the second function, a more precise definition is needed on how much to save for debt reduction and how much for accumulation in financial assets. The current rules force the government to save only about half of what is desirable. All production of crude oil should be involved in this Savings Fund instead of targeting only the increases in production of heavy oil, and how much to save should depend on an estimate of the country's oil wealth and a target for a sustainable non-oil deficit. If the design of the oil fund is improved, the mandatory reduction of the non-oil deficit at an annual rate of 0.2 percent of GDP might be too restrictive in the future.

- **FEIREP resources should be partly invested in highly liquid assets abroad.** Because FEIREP funds will be used when crude oil prices are low, at which time Ecuadorian assets are more likely to be illiquid and depressed in price, it is prudent to invest these funds in liquid financial assets independent of Ecuador's risk. A portion of the stabilization fund should be invested in the same way as the Central Bank's foreign reserves—abroad and in relatively safe assets. However, the downside is the low rate of return on highly liquid assets. Because the size of shocks varies, it is more likely that partial amounts of the fund would be used than all the funds at any given moment. Then, to increase returns, a part of the funds should be invested in a diversified portfolio of longer-term assets with a higher return, but exposed to short-term fluctuations in price. Moreover, a well-designed stabilization fund will also try to offset the macroeconomic consequences of oil price variations (the Dutch disease), by investing abroad.

■ **With respect to other reforms of the FTSRL, it is recommended that discretion be reduced in some additional areas.** One such area is the definition of the reference price for crude oil that is included in the budget. The reference price should be best estimated on the basis of a technical criterion that could be included in the FTSRL. Another improvement would be to apply the criterion of the 3.5 percent growth rate for primary expenditures with reference to the executed budget of the previous year, and not to the approved budget.

■ **The Treasury's short-term liquidity difficulties badly affect the authorities' credibility and the country's reputation.** In early 2004, the public sector has total net financial requirements of US$1.8 billion. Once the identified sources and amounts of financing are taken into account, a financial gap of US$548 still remained. A similar gap is projected for 2005. Given the composition of the public debt, closing the liquidity gap in 2005 is critically dependent on the design of programs of substantial structural reform as a basis for agreements between the government, the IMF, and other multilaterals. Structural reform, supported by sound macrofiscal management will enable the country to obtain cheaper, rapidly disbursing and freely disposable funds from the multilateral agencies. This is also the road to enhanced credibility of the debt reduction plan.

# Chapter 3

# PRO-POOR EXPENDITURES
# AND THE FISCAL SPACE

In May 2004 President Gutiérrez signed a decree committing his Government to developing a **Poverty Reduction Strategy (PRS)**. Finding resources for implement the strategy is a a significant challenge. The task seems enormous, given the structural and fiscal constraints highlighted in other chapters. On one hand, fiscal performance remains mixed. Chapter 2 depicts a fragile consolidation of fiscal accounts during the 2000s. NFPS fiscal revenues have increased in part due to tax receipts, albeit these declined in 2003. Total NFPS expenditure has remained constant, but expenditure composition has worsened in favor of current spending, especially the payroll, and against investment spending. Debt ratios have decreased, but these are still high and their further reduction requires sustained efforts in building sizable primary surpluses in the next several years. On the other hand, expenditure flexibility has worsened with rigid expenditure—wages, earmarkings, and interest payments—accounting for an increasingly large portion of budget revenues and leaving almost no funding for development activities. In this context, serious questions remain about the level and efficiency of public (mainly social) expenditure and the ability to finance an effective poverty reduction strategy. This chapter examines those issues.

**Authorities recognize that the present fiscal stance is inconsistent within the framework of a poverty reduction strategy.** Their goal is to take advantage of the process leading to the PRS to improve the amount and quality of public expenditures: level, composition, and execution capacity while augmenting budgetary flexibility, and diversifying the sources of financing. To do this, they intend to (a) increase the level of education and health spending, to at least a combined 5 percent of GDP; (b) correct the composition of public expenditure between capital and current outlays from a 20:80 ratio to a 25:75 ratio; (c) de-concentrate public investment beyond the three provinces where it is currently concentrated; (d) reduce budget rigidity; and (e) modify the de facto separation of financing of current spending by non-oil tax revenue, and investment by oil revenue (Salazar 2004). Those goals identify important aspects of public expenditure size and "quality" and move in the right direction, but officials will need to further detail their implementation. The answers to four more fundamental questions would be helpful: (a) Is the social spending level enough to support poverty reduction? (b) Are the efficiency and effectiveness (targeting) indicators—two other key aspects of expenditure quality—of resources assigned to the PRS satisfactory? (c) Given needed fiscal retrenchment in the next two to three years, how can the country gain additional fiscal space and improve efficiency and targeting of public expenditures to finance a PRS? and (d) How can the government link expenditure to desired intermediate outcomes and final outputs, especially those related to the Millennium Development Goals (MDGs)? This chapter answers all four questions, and provides policy alternatives. However, it highlights complex trade-offs which require strong political will and the creation of a national consensus.

## A. Is Social Expenditure Enough for Poverty Reduction?

**Budgets for the social sectors are low by regional standards and declining** (Table 3.1). Following dollarization, social sectors expenditures peaked up to 5.1 percent of GDP in 2002, thus reversing a long term decline and almost reaching their level of the early 1980s. However, the levels of education and health expenditures remains low—about half the combined LAC average of 7.5 percent of GDP—and are declining since 2002.[1] There are two main reasons for the increasing trend in social outlays in the post-dollarization context: On the one hand, the need to increase wages and salaries in the social ministries (see Chapter 2); on the other hand, the importance to strengthen the safety net under social welfare programs like the *Bono*. As a percentage of GDP, social welfare programs increased from 0.3 percent of GDP in 1995 to a peak 1.3 percent of GDP in 2002. These programs were especially critical to protect vulnerable groups in a dollarized economy vulnerable to shocks (see Chapter 4 for a detailed review of the performance of the most important programs). Payroll increases have been achieved at certain costs: in education, a significant deterioration of school infrastructure; and in health, severe problems in drug supplies (see below).

**There has been a dramatic decline in real public spending on education and health over the last two decades.** Despite the recovery in recent years, by 2003 the real level of education spending per beneficiary was 40 percent below that of 1980.[2] Because much of education spending is on teacher salaries (about 80 percent of the total in 2000), and recent budget increases have been mainly driven by salary adjustments, by applying the wage deflator, there is no actual recovery in real education spending. This is consistent with the hypothesis that most, if not all, budget increases after 2000 went into raising teachers' nominal salaries. Indeed (a) the shares by educational level have remained fairly constant, such that this factor does not seem to explain the trends in education; (b) private school enrolment has increased somewhat, but not substantially, implying that this is not a relevant reason either; (c) student- teacher ratios have fallen, while enrolment has increased such that declining trends in spending cannot be attributed to a lack of supply of teachers, in primary education the student ratio fell from 30 to 23 students per teacher, and in secondary education it fell from 13 to 11; and (d) rising cost-sharing to cover school maintenance and other operational costs of schools suggests that this is the area where public spending has been faltering. This is, however, difficult to corroborate because of data problems. For its part, public health spending per capita remains among the lowest in Latin America (only Haiti spends less), and recent budget increases have also mainly gone into salary increases for health workers as well. Two additional common factors in both sectors—as well as in the basic infrastructure sector—are the persistent poor targeting of resources and inequalities in access to service delivery. These findings point to the need to assess the pro-poor focus and efficiency of the social and basic infrastructure programs.

---

1. In 2001, according to World Development Indicators, LAC averages for education and health (no pensions included) were 4.1 and 3.4 percent of GDP respectively. An important caveat for Ecuador ratios as suggested by Ecuadorian officials, is that they do not fully comply with the functional budgetary standard classification, but are just proxies.

2. The measurement of the recovery in real education spending from 2000 onward is sensitive to the choice of deflator, not so much for the years prior to that. Here, education spending is deflated using, alternatively, a weighted price for public consumption and investment (weighted for their respective importance in education spending), and a nominal wage index for public employees (Vos and Ponce 2004).

**TABLE 3.1: ECUADOR: SOCIAL EXPENDITURE[1] OF CENTRAL GOVERNMENT AS A PERCENTAGE OF GDP[2]**

|  | 1973 | 1975 | 1980 | 1985 | 1990 | 1995 | 2000 | 2001 | 2002 | 2003 | 2004[3] |
|---|---|---|---|---|---|---|---|---|---|---|---|
| Total Social Expenditure | 3.5 | 3.3 | 5.3 | 4.7 | 4.4 | 3.6 | 4.0 | 4.3 | 5.1 | 5.0 | 4.9 |
| Education | 2.9 | 2.5 | 4.3 | 3.5 | 2.8 | 2.4 | 1.9 | 2.2 | 2.7 | 2.6 | 2.6 |
| Health | 0.5 | 0.7 | 0.9 | 1.1 | 1.3 | 0.9 | 0.8 | 0.8 | 1.3 | 1.3 | 1.2 |
| Social Welfare | 0.1 | 0.1 | 0.1 | 0.1 | 0.3 | 0.3 | 1.3 | 1.3 | 1.1 | 1.1 | 1.1 |
| Cash transfer programs |  |  |  |  |  |  | 0.8 | 0.7 | 0.5 | 0.6 | 0.6 |
| Other | 0.1 | 0.1 | 0.1 | 0.1 | 0.3 | 0.3 | 0.5 | 0.6 | 0.5 | 0.5 | 0.5 |
| Memo: Education & Health | 3.4 | 3.2 | 5.2 | 4.6 | 4.1 | 3.3 | 2.7 | 3.0 | 4.0 | 3.9 | 3.8 |

Notes:
[1] Social expenditures refer to the Central Government budget only. Social expenditures include education, health, social welfare, and labor, and cash transfer programs. Cash transfer programs refer to the Bono Solidario for 1999–2002, and include Beca Escolar and Bono de Desarrollo Humano thereafter.
[2] The social expenditure share of GDP is calculated on the basis of constant price series in dollars of 2000. The share at current prices is slightly higher on average (0.3 percentage points for the 1990s, and 0.1 percent for the whole series), but the trends are the same. The difference between the constant and current price shares is explained by the difference in deflators for government spending and GDP, the former being—on average—slightly higher.
[3] Numbers for 2004 refer to the provisional budget for social expenditure data and Central Bank projection of GDP growth.

Sources: Central Bank and MEF data. Series from Vos and others (2003), updated and adjusted by Vos and Ponce (2004).

## B.  Is Social and Basic Infrastructure Expenditure Pro-Poor?

*Main Social Programs*

**About half of total social spending is not pro-poor.** Incidence analysis allows examining to what extent expenditure is pro-poor (that is, a negative differential between the share of spending received by the richest and poorest quintiles, thus favoring the consumption levels of the poor relatively more than those of the rich, and hence reduces consumption inequality), mixed or non-pro-poor.[3] In 2003, and in absolute terms, the poorest quintile received 12 percent of social expenditure, compared to 27 percent to the richest quintile (Vos and others 2003). Table 3.2 combines findings from Vos (2003) with the actual amount of subsidies in 2003, which gives a broadly disaggregated picture of pro-poor and non-pro-poor social expenditure. In Ecuador:

- **About 45 percent of total social expenditure can be considered non pro-poor**, since a significant amount of spending benefits households in the top of income distribution.
- **Primary education and, to a mixed extent, secondary education, are pro-poor**, and combined they account for about two-thirds of education spending.
- **The Health Ministry's spending (MSP) can be considered pro-poor**, but combined with the *Seguro Social Campesino* financed by the Social Security Institute, account for barely one-third of the health sector.
- **Tertiary education (universities) and IESS spending are most relevant among non-pro-poor spending**, and represent about one-fifth and one-third of education and health sector resources.
- **All social welfare—targeted—programs (school breakfast, infant care, and the cash transfer *Bono Solidario* [recently converted to BDH]) are pro-poor**, but together represent only about 10 percent of social expenditure. Notice that these programs still have, however, significant improvements to do both in terms of targeting and nutritional impact.
- **The subsidy to the cooking gas is definitely not pro-poor**, and represents a meaningful 10 percent of all social expenditure (equivalent to resources allocated to all focalized social welfare programs).

**Incidence analysis allows ranking social expenditure and energy subsidies from less to more pro-poor.** Taking the difference between the richest and poorest quintiles, it appears that the school breakfast, primary school spending, and the *Bono* cash transfer, in that order, are the most pro-poor programs (Figure 3.1).[4] At the bottom of the classification, university education, IESS health care and the cooking gas appear to be the most non-pro-poor outlays. Before its disappearance in 2003, the gasoline subsidy, in particular, did not have any impact on the two poorest quintiles, and 85 percent of this subsidy was concentrated on the richest quintile. If public expenditure needs to be reoriented toward financing of a PRS, these findings point to key areas of reform.

---

3. A mixed ranking represents a close to nil differential, and a non-pro-poor a positive differential (see Figure 3.1 for a graphic representation). Notice that incidence analysis also allows examining progressivity or regressivity of social spending. Progressivity is defined as the degree to which spending improves the consumption levels of the poor with the rich under a non-proportional distribution. Conversely, a social program can be non pro-poor if proportionally higher resources are allocated to the richest quintiles. For concrete examples on Ecuador, see World Bank (2004b).

4. Two important caveats to these findings are that (a) even though the School Breakfast and the *Bono* appear as more pro-poor, that does not mean that they do *not* require important re-targeting efforts (both programs are rather fine-tuning their database of beneficiaries); and (b) the *Seguro Social Campesino* do not depend on the Central Government, but on IESS, which makes more difficult to channel increased resources to it directly.

## TABLE 3.2: PRO-POOR AND NON PRO-POOR SOCIAL EXPENDITURES, 2003

| Type of Expense | Type of Program | Fiscal cost US$M, 2003 | Direct Distributive Effect (in US$M, 2003) | | | Direct Distributive Effect (with respect to the equity line) | | |
|---|---|---|---|---|---|---|---|---|
| | | | Pro-Poor | Non Pro-Poor | Mixed | Pro-Poor | Non Pro-Poor | Mixed |
| **UNIVERSAL** | | 1,706.6 | | | | | | |
| Education | | 1,123.8 | | | | | | |
| Primary | Universal | 453.4 | 453.4 | | | X | | |
| Secondary | Universal | 304.0 | | | 304.0 | | | X |
| University (public)[1] | Universal | 366.4 | | 366.4 | | | X | |
| Health | | 582.8 | | | | | | |
| Per service provider | | 387.5 | | | | | | |
| IESS | Affiliates | 191.4 | | 191.4 | | | X | |
| SSC[2] | Universal | 35.9 | 35.9 | | | X | | |
| MSP | Universal | 160.2 | | | 160.2 | | | X |
| Per care service | | 195.3 | | | | | | |
| Hospitals | Universal | 114.4 | | 114.4 | | | X | |
| Centros de salud[3] | Universal | 80.9 | | 80.9 | | | X | |
| **FOCALIZED** | | 254.6 | | | | | | |
| School breakfast | Focalized | 17.0 | 17.0 | | | X | | |
| Infant care | Focalized | 77.7 | 77.7 | | | X | | |
| Bono Solidario[4] | Focalized | 159.9 | 159.9 | | | X | | |
| **SUBSIDIES** | | 221.0 | | | | | | |
| Cooking gas | Universal | 221.0 | | 221.0 | | | X | |
| **TOTAL** | | 2,182.2 | 743.9 | 974.1 | 464.2 | | | |

Notes: 1. Refers to earmarked transfers to universities.
2. This program is not financed by the Central Government, but by the Social Security Institute, and by employee and employer payroll contributions.
3. Includes sub-centros de salud y puestos de salud.
4. Excludes the Beca Escolar.
Source: Vos and others (2003), MEF, and Bank staff's estimates.

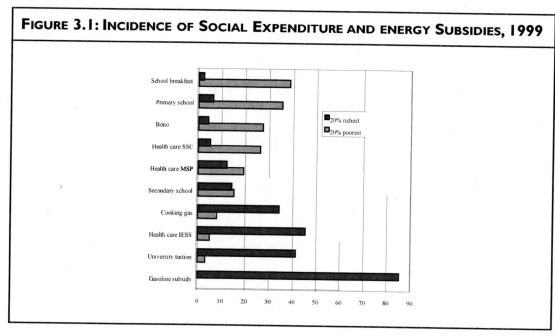

**FIGURE 3.1: INCIDENCE OF SOCIAL EXPENDITURE AND ENERGY SUBSIDIES, 1999**

*Source:* Vos, Ponce, Cuesta, and Borobrich (2003).

The pro-poor share of total social expenditure is even lower. Social expenditure is defined in a wider sense, since it includes off-budget financed programs—like IESS health care payments or the *Seguro Social Campesino* outlays, and excludes self-financed ones—like IESS pensions.[5] Combining the distribution per quintile of household income found by Vos and others (2003) for 1999 with the actual amount of social expenditure and subsidies in 2003 allows disaggregating cumulated outlays by quintile. Table 3.3 extracts these conclusions:

■ Social subsidies are progressive. They represent a higher share of poor income households, inasmuch as they represent two-thirds of their household budget (67.2 percent).

■ The cooking gas (41 percent) and university tuition (24 percent) subsidies, and IESS health care (16 percent) together represent 80 percent of total subsidies to the richest households quintile. Notice that IESS health care payments are off-budget and financed through an earmarked payroll tax, not through the Central Government budget.

■ In aggregate terms, the poorest quintile receives 17.4 percent of total outlays, compared to 21.4 percent for the richest quintile.

■ The most pro-poor program, school breakfast, receives an annual amount (US$17 million) that represents less than 1 percent of total social expenditure, and is 20 times less than the most regressive subsidy, the one devoted to the university tuition. Notice that the gasoline subsidy was rightly eliminated in 2003 with the increase in gasoline prices early adopted by the Gutierrez's administration. Notice that despite this finding, the school breakfast—served by PAE—still has important shortcomings regarding its targeting and nutritional impact, and is under review (see Annex C).

■ The pro-poor SSC health care receives 5 times less resources (US$35.9 million) than the non-pro-poor IESS health care spending.

---

5. Table 3.3 does not include all social outlays. Important missing ones are IESS, ISSFA and ISSPOL pensions, which are all very sizable and regressive (e.g. IESS spends about US$500 million in pensions per year).

# TABLE 3.3: SOCIAL EXPENDITURE AND ENERGY SUBSIDIES, BY INCOME QUINTILE, FROM LESS PRO-POOR TO MORE PRO-POOR, 1999 AND 2003

|  | Less Pro-Poor Outlays | | | | | | | More pro-poor outlays | | | | |
| --- | --- | --- | --- | --- | --- | --- | --- | --- | --- | --- | --- | --- |
|  | Gasoline Subsidy | University Tuition | Health Care IESS | Cooking Gas | Secondary School | Health Care MSP | Health Care SSC | Bono | Primary school | School breakfast | Total | Percent of total |
| **Social Subsidies as Percent of Household Budget, 1999** | | | | | | | | | | | | |
| 20% poorest | 0.0 | 2.0 | 2.1 | 12.0 | 8.0 | 6.7 | 0.7 | 14.8 | 17.2 | 3.7 | 67.2 | |
| Second quintile | 0.0 | 4.9 | 1.7 | 12.5 | 6.9 | 4.2 | 0.4 | 8.5 | 6.7 | 0.9 | 46.7 | |
| Third quintile | 0.1 | 4.5 | 3.7 | 11.6 | 5.3 | 2.8 | 0.2 | 5.1 | 3.4 | 0.4 | 37.1 | |
| Fourth quintile | 0.2 | 5.2 | 2.5 | 9.5 | 3.0 | 2.0 | 0.2 | 2.1 | 1.5 | 0.7 | 26.9 | |
| 20% richest | 0.6 | 3.4 | 2.3 | 5.8 | 0.9 | 0.5 | 0.0 | 0.3 | 0.4 | 0.0 | 14.2 | |
| **Composition of Social Subsidies in Percent of Total, 1999** | | | | | | | | | | | | |
| 20% poorest | 0.0 | 3.0 | 3.1 | 17.9 | 11.9 | 10.0 | 1.0 | 22.0 | 25.6 | 5.5 | 100.0 | |
| Second quintile | 0.0 | 10.5 | 3.6 | 26.8 | 14.8 | 9.0 | 0.9 | 18.2 | 14.3 | 1.9 | 100.0 | |
| Third quintile | 0.3 | 12.1 | 10.0 | 31.3 | 14.3 | 7.5 | 0.5 | 13.7 | 9.2 | 1.1 | 100.0 | |
| Fourth quintile | 0.7 | 19.3 | 9.3 | 35.3 | 11.2 | 7.4 | 0.7 | 7.8 | 5.6 | 2.6 | 100.0 | |
| 20% richest | 4.2 | 23.9 | 16.2 | 40.8 | 6.3 | 3.5 | 0.0 | 2.1 | 2.8 | 0.0 | 100.0 | |
| **Incidence of Social Subsidies in Percent, 1999** | | | | | | | | | | | | |
| 20% poorest | 0.0 | 3.0 | 5.0 | 8.0 | 15.0 | 19.0 | 26.0 | 27.0 | 35.0 | 38.0 | | |
| Second quintile | 1.0 | 12.0 | 7.0 | 14.0 | 23.0 | 23.0 | 35.0 | 28.0 | 26.0 | 15.0 | | |
| Third quintile | 4.0 | 16.0 | 21.0 | 20.0 | 26.0 | 22.0 | 13.0 | 25.0 | 20.0 | 12.0 | | |
| Fourth quintile | 10.0 | 28.0 | 22.0 | 24.0 | 22.0 | 24.0 | 21.0 | 16.0 | 13.0 | 33.0 | | |
| 20% richest | 85.0 | 41.0 | 45.0 | 34.0 | 14.0 | 12.0 | 5.0 | 4.0 | 6.0 | 2.0 | | |
| Total | 100.0 | 100.0 | 100.0 | 100.0 | 100.0 | 100.0 | 100.0 | 100.0 | 100.0 | 100.0 | | |
| **Incidence of Social Subsidies in Millions of US Dollars, 2003** | | | | | | | | | | | | |
| 20% poorest | 11.0 | 9.6 | | 17.7 | 45.6 | 30.4 | 9.3 | 43.2 | 158.7 | 6.5 | 332.0 | 17.4 |
| Second quintile | 44.0 | 13.4 | | 30.9 | 69.9 | 36.8 | 12.6 | 44.8 | 117.9 | 2.6 | 372.9 | 19.5 |
| Third quintile | 58.6 | 40.2 | | 44.2 | 79.0 | 35.2 | 4.7 | 40.0 | 90.7 | 2.0 | 394.6 | 20.7 |
| Fourth quintile | 102.6 | 42.1 | | 53.0 | 66.9 | 38.4 | 7.5 | 25.6 | 58.9 | 5.6 | 400.6 | 21.0 |
| 20% richest | 150.2 | 86.1 | | 75.1 | 42.6 | 19.2 | 1.8 | 6.4 | 27.2 | 0.3 | 408.9 | 21.4 |
| Total | 366.4 | 191.4 | | 221.0 | 304.0 | 160.2 | 35.9 | 159.9 | 453.4 | 17.0 | 1909.2 | 100.0 |

Note: Data exclude free meals and Armed Forces health program subsidies.

Sources: Vos and others (2003); Ministry of Finance; and STFS.

▧ The *Bono* receives a little less resources than IESS (US$160 million compared to US$191 million), but the number of beneficiaries is four times larger than the number of retirees in the pension system (Rofman 2004).

**Incidence analysis has several caveats but they do not affect the main conclusions presented.** First, not all social programs are designed exclusively for poor households. Second, even if a program is targeted to the poor, its level of progressiveness depends on how effective the targeting mechanism is. As a result, the higher the leakages in public spending, the larger the losses in progressiveness. Third, the cost of providing a service may vary across groups or areas, and often service delivery to poor areas, especially rural areas, is more expensive. Fourth, even pro-poor programs, like the *Bono*, have difficulty maintaining adequate pro-poor targeting, but the welfare index—known as SELBEN (the *Sistema de Identificación y Selección de Beneficiarios de Programas Sociales*)—which ranks Ecuadorian households according to demographic and structural characteristics—remains a solid targeting instrument for social programs located in the first and second quintiles (World Bank 2004b).[6]

**Ecuador has had a mixed performance in *education* indicators.**[7] Despite the significant amount of non-pro-poor expenditure in tertiary levels, Ecuador has good coverage of primary education. Poor quality and low transition ratios to secondary education remain the major issues in the sector. Inequality in access to education has also increased between urban and rural populations, and between the rich and the poor. Only the gender gap in education appears to be by-and-large closed. Positive educational outcomes show the advantage of making education expenditures more efficient.

**Educational outcomes.** Indicators continued to improve during the 1990s and into the new millennium:

▧ **There has been continuous growth in the average level of schooling since the 1970s:** in 2001, the average adult had completed 7.3 years of schooling, up from 6.7 years in 1990. This level is above the Latin American mean, and is about the same as that of East Asia's population.

▧ **By 2001, the gender gap had practically been closed:** 7.5 years for males compared to 7.1 years for females. Thus, educational levels of the female population have risen much faster than that of males, such that, in terms of net enrollment rates, girls already outperform boys at all educational levels.

▧ **Net enrollment** in primary education increased from 88.9 to 90.1 percent between 1990 and 2001, approximating the MDG of primary education for all.

**Important concerns, however, remain in the education sector.** *First*, the transition rates from primary to secondary education and from secondary to tertiary did not improve in the 1990s. *Second*, important disparities remain, affecting rural, indigenous, and black populations. The average level of schooling of the rural population is less than half the one of the urban population, and the gap is even larger for the indigenous and black populations. This is also the case for illiteracy rates. *Third*, the overall quality of education is poor, with math and language test scores worsening between 1996 and 2000 and starting from an extremely low baseline (Ecuador scores lowest for the Latin America region). Fourth, internal efficiency indicators, measured by desertion and repetition rates, have also worsened, with the number of years pupils need to com-

---

6. In 2003, the estimated targeting errors of the BDH are as follows: (a) using income poverty, the exclusion error is 23.4 percent and the inclusion errors 9.7 percent; and (b) using SELBEN, these percentages are respectively 22.2 and 7.3 percent (Table A54).

7. This section draws from Vos and Ponce (2004).

plete primary education increasing from 6.7 years to 6.9 years between 1995 and 2001, a decline concentrated in urban schools; and higher dropout by girls in secondary rural schools and by boys in urban schools, seemingly for economic reasons. Retention rates and education quality also appear affected by the high rate (15 to 18 percent) of teacher absenteeism and frequent teacher strikes in Ecuador (Box 3.1).[8] *Fourth*, budget allocations to primary education schools are not approved according to standards in terms of coverage, vulnerability and poverty ratios, students/teacher ratios by school, and type of school establishment.

Ecuador has also improved *health* conditions and this is another reason why an increased social budget would help improve living conditions. Since 1970, infant mortality rates have been cut by 70 percent to 34 per 1,000 live births. Health provisioning has shifted toward greater emphasis on primary health care in public provisioning, and inpatient hospital care by private health providers. Health policy reforms have included increases in user fees for public services, decentralization of public services, special programs providing free health care for the poor (including the free maternity program), and introduction of demand subsidies for health through the conditional cash transfer program *Bono de Desarrollo Humano*. However, reforms as implemented so far have yet to address some fundamental problems in health service delivery, including access to services, the quality of services, and inequalities across social groups and geographic areas. Important inequalities remain, showing much higher mortality rates and limited access to health care for the indigenous population, the poor, and those living in rural areas. Inequalities in access to health facilities have also increased, partly because of expensive user fees and partly because health inputs (particularly drug supplies) have fallen well behind requirements. Reforms were implemented under tight budget constraints, because the health budget (in real per capita terms) declined for most of the 1990s. However, continued expansion of the immunization program and the introduction of the Free Maternity Program have compensated for this effect, at least for young children and pregnant women. This could explain the continued decline in infant mortality during the 1990s.

**Health outcomes.** Health indicators have also improved during the 1990s and into the new millennium:

- Life expectancy at birth increased from 48 years to 72 years between 1950 and 2000. This upward trend was sustained during the 1990s, adding another 5 years to life expectancy.
- Parallel declining trends are found in child and infant mortality rates. The overall mortality rate dropped from 13.8 per 100,000 inhabitants in 1960 to 4.5 per 100,000 inhabitants in 2001. This rate did not change much during the 1990s. In contrast, since 1970, the infant mortality rate has fallen by 70 percent in Ecuador, which is as impressive as the achievements in the rest of the Americas, where the rate has fallen on average at a similar rate.[9] The infant mortality rate has followed an almost linear trend since 1950, reaching 33 per 1,000 live births during 1995–2000, down from 140 during 1950–55. Child mortality rates follow similar trends because they mainly reflect infant mortality since most child deaths are concentrated in the first year of life (WHO 2003).
- The drop in infant mortality coincides with a long-term decline in fertility rates. Fertility dropped from almost 7 per woman in the 1950s and 1960s to 2.8 during 2000–05. During the 1990s, fertility dropped faster in rural than in urban areas, but the rate is still 1.5 times higher for rural women. Fertility and infant mortality may be mutually dependent, because higher fertility raises the risk of early childbirth, whereas infant deaths may induce higher fertility due to a replacement effect.

---

8. When compared to other countries, though, the Ecuadorian absence rate is in the low range (Rogers and others 2004).

9. Only achievements in Chile, Costa Rica, and Cuba have been more impressive, with reductions of over 80 percent.

---

## BOX 3.1: ECUADOR: TEACHER ABSENCE IN PRIMARY SCHOOLS

As part of the PER work, and in collaboration with a multicountry study initiated by the World Bank as a background paper for the World Development Report 2004, a pioneer national teacher tracking survey was carried out in Ecuador. (See Rogers et al. 2004 in Volume II.) It aimed to determine teacher absence rates and their main correlates in Ecuador. During 2002–03, survey teams interviewed a random sample of 720 teachers in 102 primary schools in 51 randomly selected *parroquías* were surveyed. Each school was visited twice, in December 2002 and again in January–February 2003, to allow two observations of teacher attendance.

Of the 670 fulltime teachers who would normally have been teaching at the time of the survey visit, 86.5 percent. On average, teachers were found in the classroom (or accompanying the enumerator) 79 percent of the time, although in a fifth of those occasions the teacher was not teaching at that moment. The overall teacher absence rate, measured as the fraction of teachers who could not be found anywhere in the school, was about 14 percent, with a relatively small number of teachers apparently accounting for a larger share of the absence than in other countries. About half of the overall absences were not accounted for by the school directors.

| Percentage of time the teacher was found ... | December 2002 | January–February 2003 | Total (both rounds) |
|---|---|---|---|
| In the classroom teaching | 59.5 | 64.8 | 62.1 |
| In the classroom not teaching | 16.0 | 14.9 | 15.5 |
| Out of class on scheduled break | 0.0 | 0.0 | 0.0 |
| Out of class but in school premises | 6.0 | 5.1 | 5.6 |
| Doing administrative work | 2.2 | 1.6 | 1.9 |
| **Cannot find/absent** | **14.6** | **12.5** | **13.5** |
| Accompanying surveyor | 1.8 | 1.1 | 1.1 |

*Source: Rogers et al. (2004).*

The study also analyzed the correlates of (and hence possible reasons for) absence, with some notable results. Overall, Bangladesh, India, Indonesia, Papua New Guinea, Uganda, and Zambia all recorded higher teacher absence rates than Ecuador, and only Peru's absence rate was lower (Chaudhury et al 2004). Surprisingly, in Ecuador absence is not more likely in remote, rural areas—as is often found in other countries—but rather in urban areas. In fact, teachers in urban schools (outside Quito) are absent at twice the rate of teachers in the most remote rural schools, perhaps because of greater employment opportunities and distractions in the urban areas. Also, one-teacher schools (escuelas unidocentes) are not associated with higher teacher absenteeism, although multi-teacher polidocente schools apparently are; thus as a general matter, the effects of having to teach various grades at the same time are ambiguous. In general, a better community (lower poverty rate) and institutional environment are associated with reduced teacher absence, whereas individual characteristics of teachers (age, tenure, education, union membership) do not seem to make much of a difference. Some factors that might be expected to raise performance through formal monitoring and enforcement of attendance—notably, proximity to a Ministry of Education office, and the past use of discipline by the school director—are indeed associated with lower absence. On the other hand, active parent committees, per se, do not appear to reduce teacher absence. Finally, and perhaps more significant, contract teachers (especially those not hired at the school level) have a higher probability of absence than regular teachers, despite the greater leverage that schools and communities might be thought to have over contract teachers. Hence, special contracts may not be the right "quick fix" for the problem.

In the analysis of access to education, no doubt absenteeism will affect the quality of education, but the survey is less clear to what extent it will influence school enrolment. As indicated, rural school enrolment rates are much lower than enrolment rates in urban areas, and are thus seemingly unrelated to teacher absence. Also, teacher quality does appear to have a positive influence on school enrolment, but does not affect absence.

**Important concerns remain.** *First,* the decline in fertility and the increase in life expectancy are changing Ecuador's demographic profile. *Second,* the epidemiological profile (causes of mortality) is moving away from traditional child diseases (malnutrition, respiratory and infectious diseases) toward diseases associated with higher levels of economic well-being and urban lifestyle (cardiovascular and cancer health risks). *Third,* preventable diseases remain the main causes of child (1 to 5) and infant (0 to 1) mortality. *Fourth,* the prevalence of AIDS has increased, with 10 times more cases reported in 2002 than in 1990. *Fifth,* malaria trends remain closely associated with the occurrence of the El Niño effect.

## Subsidies in Basic Infrastructure Services

**The water and sanitation, electricity, and telecommunications sectors face similar problems.** These are poor coverage (especially in rural areas), low efficiency and quality of services, irregular allocation of resources for new investment, and—with the exception of the electricity sector—incomplete regulatory and institutional frameworks. In general, the Government should encourage greater local, national, and international private sector participation, consolidating institutional and legal agreements, and—especially in the water supply/sanitation sector—transferring resources from the center to improve services and coverage. In addition, the individual sectors face some specific problems (Giugale, Fretes-Cibils, and López-Cálix 2003):

- The **water and sanitation** sector is characterized by poor cost recovery through rates, and high dependence on transfers from the Central Government to cover deficits. There is no integrated national system for managing water resources. Since all water and sanitation services are decentralized, providers depend on municipal governments, and the Central Government has limited its role to improving the quality and efficiency of services, and guaranteeing coverage to urban and rural populations not yet served.
- The **electricity** sector problems include heavy power losses and operational inefficiencies in companies, an incomplete sector reform process, institutional vulnerability, the questionable sustainability of the Electric Wholesale Market (MEM), the need for rate adjustments to ensure the sector's financial sustainability, incomplete implementation of the sectoral environmental policy, and the lack of a rural energy strategy.
- The **telecommunications** sector faces challenges including artificially low and unsustainable rates for fixed and residential telephone service; limited competition in the cellular market, resulting in user costs that are among the highest in the region; very limited Internet access; and an outdated institutional and legal framework not suitable to attract greater participation from the private sector in the capital of ANDINATEL and PACIFICTEL.

**From the point of view of public expenditure, subsidies to basic infrastructure have little impact on the poor.** Subsidies to electricity, water and sanitation, and telephone service represented about US$341 million in 2003, equivalent to 1.3 percent of GDP. They divert funds from other priorities without effectively reaching the poor. They can hardly be justified on economic grounds.

- There are high losses in the power sector and a large portion is due to theft and inappropriate billing—these can be considered implicit subsidies (Lecaros 2004).
- The water sector has had massive shortfalls of resources for non-wage and maintenance expenditures. Subsidies to the sector, both from the Central Government and municipalities, have more than halved from US$146 million in 2001 to US$67 million in 2003. The Ministry of Urban Development and Housing's (MIDUVI's) transfers for municipality investments have been drastically reduced to less than one-tenth their amount in 2002—from US$52 million to US$5 million in 2002. Seventy percent of sector resources are concentrated in Quito and Guayaquil (Sotomayor 2004).

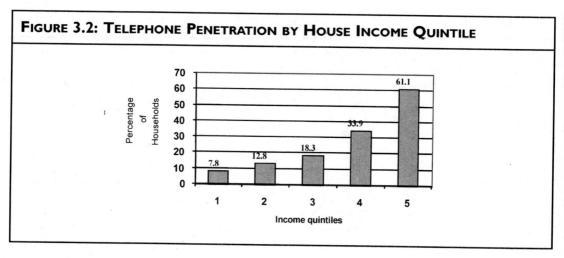

**FIGURE 3.2: TELEPHONE PENETRATION BY HOUSE INCOME QUINTILE**

*Source:* ECV, 1998–99.

▪ The telecom sector has poorly targeted subsidies in a context of low operational surpluses for the telephone companies. First, by the nature of the service, poor and rural users are less likely to have a fixed-line telephone connection: in 1999, telephone penetration was almost 10 times lower in the poorest quintile (Figure 3.2), and only one out of twenty rural households had telephone service in 1999. Second, targeted subsidies require substantial financial capacity, but the financial burden of the current subsidy scheme is very high. Third, many users that can afford to pay unsubsidized tariffs are being benefited because they reside in eligible areas. Thus, subsidies benefit all residential consumers, regardless of their income level, which has no rationale whatsoever (Gómez and Vidal 2004).

**The next important question is, to what extent do the poor benefit from the subsidies?** Without reliable data, and with the decentralized system of water, which makes it virtually impossible to estimate the water subsidies, a feasible approximation can be based on household income distribution from the 1990s (Table 3.4).

**TABLE 3.4: BASIC SERVICES SUBSIDIES BY EXPENDITURE QUINTILE, 2003**

| Subsidy | Consumption Expenditure Quintile | | | | | Overall | Source |
|---|---|---|---|---|---|---|---|
| | 1st | 2nd | 3rd | 4th | 5th | | |
| | (In millions of US dollars) | | | | | | |
| Electricity[1] | 12.8 | 18.2 | 24.9 | 35.6 | 60.5 | 152.1 | Central Bank |
| Water | 5.3 | 8.1 | 10.2 | 15.9 | 28.0 | 67.5 | WB staff estimate[2] |
| Telephone | 6.1 | 10.9 | 15.7 | 30.3 | 58.1 | 121.0 | Gómez and Vidal (2004) |
| TOTAL | 24.2 | 37.2 | 50.8 | 81.8 | 146.6 | 340.6 | |
| | (% distribution) | | | | | | |
| Electricity | 8.4 | 12.0 | 16.4 | 23.4 | 39.8 | 100.0 | LSMS (1994) |
| Water | 7.9 | 12.0 | 15.2 | 23.6 | 41.3 | 100.0 | LSMS (1994) |
| Telephone | 5.0 | 9.0 | 13.0 | 25.0 | 48.0 | 100.0 | ECV (1998–99) |
| TOTAL | 7.3 | 11.2 | 15.0 | 23.9 | 42.6 | 100.0 | |

*Notes:*
[1] Data obtained by MEF and CONELEC for electricity (*deficit tarifario*).
[2] Excludes subsidies from municipalities.

---

**BOX 3.2: HOUSEHOLD EXPENDITURES ON WATER: THE CASE OF MACHALA, EL ORO**

Machala is a city with 90 percent water coverage. Those not covered are the poorest segments of the population. It is possible to estimate the surprising differences in price and consumption for the poor, and the impact in terms of his or her monthly expenditures on water and sanitation as a percentage of family income. The table below shows that an average family served by a water connection consumes three times more than an average family without a water connection. Those households without a connection spend about 9 percent of their monthly income for a service of lower quality, while those with access to the network spend less than 1 percent of their monthly income on water.

Machala: Monthly Expenditure on Water of Households
With and Without a Connection to the Water Network

| Concept | User | |
|---|---|---|
| | With Water Connection | Served by Tankers |
| Estimated average monthly consumption of a poor family (in m$^3$) | 15 | 4 to 5[a] |
| Estimated average monthly payment (in US$) | 1.20[b] | 29.00 |
| Monthly expenditure in water as a percentage of monthly family income | 0.4 | 9.0 |

Notes:
  a. Estimated by Yepes and Gomez based on average consumption of approximately 30 liters per person per day.
  b. Tariff depends on house characteristics. The indicated value is based on the lowest tariff.
Source: Yepes, Gomez, and Carvajal (2002); and Sotomayor (2004).

---

- Overall, subsidies to basic services are not pro-poor: 7.2 percent accrue to the poorest households located in the lowest income quintile, while 43 percent accrue to the richest households. This means that the poorest households are receiving about one sixth as much subsidy as the richest households.
- Comparing these subsidies to those of the social sectors, their non-pro-poor level is similar to the most unequally distributed one: those devoted to university tuition.
- Among the three main public services, subsidies to telephone rates are the most regressive. About half of them benefit households in the richest income quintile. Again, in nominal terms, this means that the poorest households are receiving only about one-tenth as much subsidy than the richest households.
- Electricity and water have similarly regressive distributions: the two richest quintiles "capture" about two-thirds of subsidies to both sectors.

**Inequality is higher when one considers that water and sanitation services are highly subsidized for those households that have a connection (the more affluent segments), while they are not subsidized for those with no connection.** As a consequence, service to the poorest segments of the population end up being of higher cost and/or lower quality (Box 3.2).

## C. How Much Fiscal Space is Available for a Poverty Reduction Strategy?

**Ecuador's fiscal space is declining.** "Fiscal space" is the sum of resources available to finance the current—both non-wage and non-pension—primary expenditure required by individual programs and investment projects associated with the PRS.[10] Between 2001 and 2003, and as a percentage of GDP, public investment declined from 6.6 percent to 5.4 percent of GDP. This cut was almost equivalent to the one-third of the increase in the public payroll in the same period from 5.5 to 8.5 percent of GDP, which shows the fiscal space lost by accommodating wage increases. An important finding is that interest payments on public debt opened new fiscal space, as they declined by almost 2 percent of GDP in the same period. These "savings" were mostly used to finance Central Government (CG) transfers to the Ecuadorian Social Security Institute (IESS).[11]

**Identification of financing mechanisms is a major issue in the design of a PRS.** In heavily indebted poor countries (HIPCs), for example, PRS financing has been provided by the debt relief obtained from debt reduction. In some middle-income (non-poor) countries developing a PRS, the little progress of their strategy has been associated with poor targeting and insufficient internal resources to meet its goals. Failure was due not to donor delays in financing, but to confusing priorities between the PRS and other "national" agendas, and low local implementation capacity. Hence, creating fiscal space, externally or domestically financed, is not enough to finance a PRS. Consensus about and clarity of agreed PRS objectives, and the effectiveness and efficiency in the use of dedicated resources, are also extremely important.

**At present, Ecuador has a small fiscal space to finance a PRS.** For a country that has a budget envelope of 24 percent of GDP—in the top Latin America and the Caribbean (LAC) range—and public spending that can reach 30 percent when off-budget activities are included, finding an extremely small fiscal space may sound odd or suggest severe inefficiencies. Indeed, between 2001 and 2004, CG public investment declined from 4.2 percent to 2.2 percent of GDP, a cut of 2 percentage points in four years. As a result, the amount of resources that, in strict terms, could be reallocated to a PRS under the 2004 budget framework is around 0.5 percent of GDP (US$145 million), that is, the flexible part of the budget devoted to investment (Table 4.1). This amount is not adequate for an effective strategy and the government needs to find additional resources. Hence, implementing a PRS requires Ecuador to solve the paradox of having a relatively big budget coupled with a small fiscal space.

### Reversing Current Expenditure

**Budget inertia has raised rigid expenditure to unsustainable levels.** Within the 2004 Central Government budget—the *Presupuesto General del Estado* (PGE)—rigidity in the use of funds (besides earmarking) is also substantial, and an already-tight fiscal situation is becoming an unsustainable trend (Table 3.5). **In the budget, about 83 percent is rigid, composed of 32 percent for wages and salaries, 30 percent for debt service, and 21 percent for transfers** (mainly to sectional governments, but also to the IESS) and the BDH. The "rigid share" of the budget is driven by payroll, the share of which has increased by about 50 percent since 2001, and now represents almost one-third of total CG expenditure. CG transfers, especially to IESS, also show a similar increase in their "rigid share" during this period. Both trends have offset the savings obtained from debt service reduction in the last four years.

---

10. This is an intermediate definition of fiscal space between two extremes. A stricter definition would restrict it to investment spending, but this would exclude goods and services required to implement it, e.g. on basic infrastructure maintenance (roads). Alternatively, an extended definition would include wage and benefits, especially outlays associated to human capital formation (like teachers' salaries and pensions). However, this would associate pension increases to pro-poor spending (which is not the case, even when restricted to the social sectors).

11. Transfers to municipalities from the Central Government, which could partly be considered as fiscal space—for most transfers should be invested—also declined in the same period.

## TABLE 3.5: RIGIDITY OF THE CENTRAL GOVERNMENT BUDGET, 2001–04

| | Percent of Budget | | | | Percent of GDP | | | |
|---|---|---|---|---|---|---|---|---|
| | 2001 | 2002 | 2003(p) | 2004(e) | 2001 | 2002 | 2003(p) | 2004(e) |
| **Rigid Component** | **77.6** | **81.8** | **81.9** | **82.7** | **19.0** | **21.1** | **18.4** | **18.3** |
| Debt Service | 39.9 | 30.9 | 31.9 | 30.2 | 9.8 | 8.0 | 7.2 | 6.7 |
|   Amortization | 21.7 | 17.8 | 18.2 | 16.2 | 5.3 | 4.6 | 4.1 | 3.6 |
|   Interest | 18.2 | 13.1 | 13.7 | 14.0 | 4.5 | 3.4 | 3.1 | 3.1 |
| Wages and Salaries | 21.1 | 26.7 | 30.9 | 31.6 | 5.2 | 6.9 | 6.9 | 7.0 |
| Transfers[1] | 13.8 | 22.1 | 16.3 | 17.8 | 3.4 | 5.7 | 3.7 | 3.9 |
|   o/w Municipalities | 10.9 | 9.9 | 10.6 | 10.4 | 2.7 | 2.5 | 2.4 | 2.3 |
|   o/w Social Security | 0.7 | 2.5 | 2.8 | 3.6 | 0.2 | 0.6 | 0.6 | 0.8 |
| Bono Solidario | 2.9 | 2.2 | 2.8 | 3.1 | 0.7 | 0.6 | 0.6 | 0.7 |
| **Non-Rigid Component** | **22.4** | **18.2** | **18.1** | **17.3** | **5.5** | **4.7** | **4.1** | **3.8** |
| *Inertial Expenditures* | 8.7 | 12.2 | 13.2 | 13.3 | 2.1 | 3.1 | 3.0 | 2.9 |
|   Services | 2.3 | 4.9 | 5.2 | 5.8 | 0.6 | 1.3 | 1.2 | 1.3 |
|   Investment | 6.5 | 7.3 | 8.0 | 7.5 | 1.6 | 1.9 | 1.8 | 1.7 |
|     External credit (*predestinado*) | 4.7 | 4.4 | 4.3 | 3.8 | 1.2 | 1.1 | 1.0 | 0.8 |
|     Domestic credit (*Banco Estado*) | 1.2 | 1.3 | 1.0 | 0.7 | 0.3 | 0.3 | 0.2 | 0.2 |
|     Autogestion | 0.5 | 1.1 | 1.1 | 1.8 | 0.1 | 0.3 | 0.2 | 0.4 |
|     Grants/Counterpart | na | 0.4 | 1.6 | 1.2 | na | 0.1 | 0.4 | 0.3 |
| *Flexible Expenditures* | 13.6 | 6.0 | 4.9 | 4.0 | 3.3 | 1.6 | 1.1 | 0.9 |
|   Goods | 0.1 | 0.2 | 0.2 | 0.2 | 0.0 | 0.0 | 0.0 | 0.1 |
|   Other Current Spending | 3.0 | 3.4 | 1.5 | 1.4 | 0.7 | 0.9 | 0.3 | 0.3 |
|   Investment[2] | 10.5 | 2.4 | 3.2 | 2.4 | 2.6 | 0.6 | 0.7 | 0.5 |
| **Total Expenditures + Amortizations** | **100.0** | **100.0** | **100.0** | **100.0** | **24.5** | **25.8** | **22.4** | **22.2** |

*Notes:* p = Preliminary; e = Estimate.
[1] In 2002, there was a US$467 million transfer to water, sewer, and electric companies.
[2] In 2004, allocated to other (*arrastre*) projects and other commitments with external projects.
*Sources:* BCE, IMF, and WB.

Reversing the rigid share of the budget for current expenditure should bring the structural investment rate to 5.7 percent of GDP. In the last five years, the difference between the actual and structural primary surpluses has been an annual average of 0.3 percent of GDP (Annex A). In the same period, the average investment rate has been 5.9 percent of GDP. Subtracting the latter from the former gives a structural investment ratio of 5.6 percent of GDP. This coefficient would also be consistent with an estimated structural fiscal surplus of 4.8 percent of GDP. As a result, and taking into account that the investment ratio is projected at 5.4 percent of GDP in 2004, structural reform efforts concentrated on the CG budget—aimed at reducing the wage payroll and/or the burden from pensions—should target potential savings of about 0.2 percent of GDP, in order to bring the investment ratio back to its structural level. The austerity decree of 2003 and the recent passage of the new civil service law are encouraging steps in the right direction (Chapter 2) that should prove Ecuador being able to curb payroll expenses this time, despite unsuccessful attempts in the past.

Barely 2 percent of the total budget is actually non-rigid and flexible (Table 3.5 and Figure 3.3). In the non-rigid component, equivalent to 17.3 percent of the budget, three aggravating factors are that: (a) an additional 13 percent of the budget is inertial due to investment precommitments (counterpart funds and others) and temporary salaries being paid through the "serv-

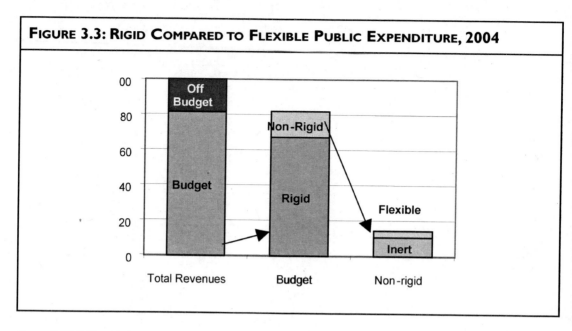

FIGURE 3.3: RIGID COMPARED TO FLEXIBLE PUBLIC EXPENDITURE, 2004

*Source:* BCE, IMF, and WB.

ices" component[12]; (b) the flexible share has rapidly decreased to minimum levels (4 percent of the budget) in the last four years; and (c) the flexible investment share is about half of such amount (2.4 percent of the budget). This residual investment is equivalent to about US$145 million (0.5 percent of GDP). **Should this pattern continue, the flexible part of the budget devoted to public expenditures would disappear in 2007.** Potential fiscal space in inertial investment is capped at 1.7 percent of GDP in 2004, but its materialization depends on the authorities' ability to shift resources to a pro-poor PRS.

### Making an Optimal Selection of Public Investment

**Institutional constraints that affect public investment planning further restrain the small fiscal space remaining.** Under the new administration, the Executive has made noteworthy improvements in public investment planning: projects are now validated at the Ministry of Economy and Finance (MEF), a public investment central database (*Banco de Proyectos*) has been created, and limited monitoring of selected projects has been introduced. However, despite these improvements, authorities recognize that there are still misallocations of the fiscal space. During interviews, authorities conjectured that about half (1.1 percent of GDP) of the non-rigid investment budget goes to non-priority projects, and that at least one-fifth of it (0.2 percent of GDP) could be reoriented. In addition:

- MEF lacks tools to plan and monitor effectively all public investment and to overcome several institutional shortcomings (WB/IADB 2004).
- There is no national system of public investment. There are, instead, two public entities with duplicative and uncoordinated roles at the planning stage: ODEPLAN in the Office of Planning in the Presidency, and the Secretariat of Public Investment at MEF.

---

12. If we assume that all investment financed by external credit and grants (including counterpart funds) is inertial, but addressing PRS needs, their combined amount still remains small: 1.1 percent of GDP in 2004.

■ No coordination mechanisms exist between ODEPLAN and the Secretariat of Public Investment and INECI, at the Ministry of Foreign Affairs, which prevents effective coordination with external grants.

■ No information system, or physical and financial indicators, are available for past or current monitoring of public investment projects, and the time series are not consolidated.

■ There is no unified or consistent methodology for formulating public investment projects.

■ Congress approves the investment envelope by sectors and expenditure item, but does not assign the allocations project per project, which limits transparency and social accountability about approved projects.

■ Projects executed by public enterprises and autonomous institutions are not included in the investment envelope of the annual budget. These are simply off budget.

## Assessing Defense Spending

**Another potential source of intra-budget fiscal space may be defense spending.** It is necessary to examine Ecuador's own military expenditures and see how these fit within budget priorities, but this analysis is not developed here. Indeed, whether a defense budget is high or low can only be determined relative to the perceived threats to national security and the government's goals and intentions, which is not the purpose of this report. However, some international comparisons are relevant. Can Ecuador afford to continue increasing military expenditures, especially now, during a time of severe fiscal adjustment, or do they contain a potential source of fiscal space in the near term? This is what a thorough analysis could further develop.

**The number of members of the Ecuadorian armed forces is increasing.** According to 2003 budget numbers, Ecuador has roughly 57,000 armed forces personnel. This is equivalent to 0.5 percent of the population in 2000. This percentage is high compared to the LAC regional average of 0.3 percent, albeit average when compared to the 0.5 percent found in middle-income countries. However, from 2003 to 2004, the number of army members registered in the budget increased by 18 percent, or 10,000 new *effectifs* (Table 3.6). Police members also increased by about 3,600 during the same period. This represents a costly payroll increase for a country making important efforts to streamline its wage payroll. Collier and Hoeffler (2002) show that foreign aid helps countries to raise their military spending outside their income level. In Ecuador's case, foreign assistance to combat drug traffickers from neighboring countries and to facilitate coca eradication efforts may have temporarily increased personnel numbers and military expenditures. The problem is that aid is temporary, but current expenditure created associated to it tends to persist over time.

**TABLE 3.6: ECUADOR: PERSONNEL INVOLVED IN DEFENSE AND SECURITY (2002–04)**

|  | 2002 | 2003 | 2004 |
|---|---|---|---|
| National Police | 26,008 | 33,303 | 36,907 |
| Armed Forces | 56,193 | 56,193 | 66,193 |

Source: Central Government Budget, 2004; MEF.

**The defense budget is also high by international standards.** When comparing Ecuador to LAC and developed economies, in GDP terms, the country's military expenditures (above 3 percent) were almost double the LAC mean (1.6 percent), and higher than the developed economies mean (2.4 percent). The same result is found when military expenditures are assessed as a share of total government expenditure. Again, Ecuador significantly outspends its LAC neighbors and developed economies. Only Chile, in LAC, devotes a higher share of its budget to defense (Figure 3.4).

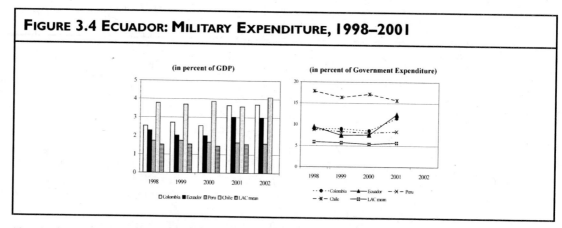

### FIGURE 3.4 ECUADOR: MILITARY EXPENDITURE, 1998–2001

*Note:* LAC mean not available for 2002 as a percent of GDP.
*Source:* International Institute for Strategic Studies (IISS) Yearbook 1997–2003.

**Bringing Ecuador's defense budget back to its historic level of spending would generate a potential fiscal space of about 1 percent of GDP, but this should be preceded by a thorough assessment.** The rising level of military expenditure in a given country appears "strongly influenced by the levels chosen by its neighboring governments" (Collier and Hoeffler 2002). Ecuador confirms that pattern, closely following Colombia's recently increased defense spending. Colombia, Ecuador's northern neighbor, has faced internal conflict for over 50 years, but since 2000, it has deepened its campaign against drug traffickers and guerillas with foreign assistance. Ecuador has followed such a trend, raising its defense budget from an average ratio of close to 2 percent of GDP by the end-1990s to 3 percent in the early 2000s. Among its immediate neighbors, however, Peru shows a very contrasting picture. To finance its pro-poor agenda, President Toledo deliberately shifted its budgetary priorities away from defense spending, by reducing it by more than half a percentage point of GDP between 2000 and 2003 (World Bank and Interamerican Development Bank, 2003). Thus, Peru made a conscious decision to shift spending from defense to the social sectors and, not less important, to make military expenses fully transparent and information about them available to the public through its financial management system on the Internet. Peru's reform of military spending demands Ecuador's close attention.

## D. How Much Off-Budget Fiscal Space Can Be Found for a Poverty Reduction Strategy?

### Reducing Off-Budget Activities

**Off-budget activities, especially budget earmarking are, in general, bad for budget flexibility.** Although some tax or expenditure earmarking can benefit specific goals, provided they are adequately targeted and monitored, in general they have caused several shortcomings in Ecuador's budgetary policy (Reis 2003):

■ Fiscal policy becomes constrained, because the government's ability to shift resources or modify the budget is significantly reduced.
■ In a process of a budget adjustment mandated by a fiscal rule, such as the one for Ecuador, rigid earmarking provoke the compression of public investment, the flexible variable in the budget.
■ Perverse incentives develop, as the pressure for cutting expenditure brings additional requests for additional earmarking.
■ Prospects for a countercyclical fiscal policy become dim, because inertial cyclical spending leaves little room (and resources) for countering a recession.

**There is also potential fiscal space arising from the elimination of off-budget activities** (Table 4.5). There are two main types: pre-budget taxes, off-budget oil revenues, and off-budget subsidies also financed from oil revenues.

▨ *Most pre-budget earmarking of taxes* is constitutionally man-dated and mainly affect allocations to provincial and sectional governments, and universities. There is very little that can be done about them, short of amending the Constitution. In 2004, they account for about 2.4 percent of GDP (8.2 percent of the total budget) (Figure 3.5).

▨ *Off-budget earmarked oil revenues* amount to 1.6 percent of GDP (5.5 percent of the budget) in 2004. These include resources to the Fund for Stabilization, Investment, and Public Debt Reduction (FEIREP) (1 percent of GDP), which is well targeted, has a well-defined purpose, and is adequately monitored. Discounting FEIREP, their elimination would open a potential fiscal space of 0.6 percent of GDP. Regressive subsidies financed by PetroEcuador, e.g. (gas, diesel, and electricity) are an expenditure "quasi-earmarking." In 2004, these subsidies represent 1.3 percent of GDP and could generate some fiscal space by reform, but this would depend on the proposals adopted (see Table 4.5).

*Reducing Tax Expenditure*

**The fiscal space is also constrained by tax exemptions (also known as tax expenditures).** Exemptions narrow the tax base, make tax administration more complex, and deviate resources needed to finance priority public expenditure. Authorities reduced the value-added tax (VAT) exemptions between 1999 and the first half of 2001,[13] but since then new exemptions were created or proposed on the VAT and the personal income tax (Schenone 2003).

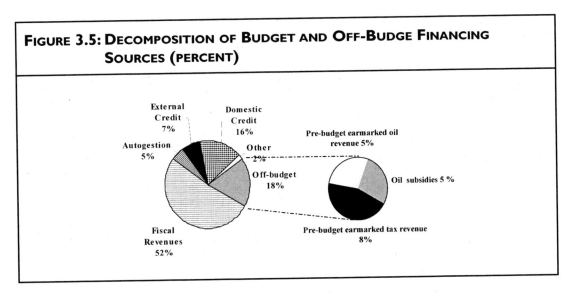

**FIGURE 3.5: DECOMPOSITION OF BUDGET AND OFF-BUDGE FINANCING SOURCES (PERCENT)**

*Source:* Budget Office, MEF, and Table A25.

---

13. The personal income tax (ISR) exemption was eliminated for the financial sector on the income from securities and shares issued by the government, for cooperatives, and provident societies (except for the ones established by farmers or officially recognized indigenous people), and for promoting development (directed primarily at tourism and industrial endeavors). In addition, the list of items subject to the VAT was replaced with a tax list of VAT-exempt services (fundamentally, housing rentals and financial services)—which, therefore, leaves all other services subject to the VAT.

TABLE 3.7: ESTIMATED TAX EXPENDITURE OF THE INTERNAL VAT
EXEMPTIONS, 2001
(millions of U.S. dollars)

| Sector | Total Income | Export of Goods and Services | Taxable Income Before Exempt | Income Actually Taxed | Exempted Estimated Income | Tax Credit on Purchases | Fiscal Cost |
|---|---|---|---|---|---|---|---|
| Agriculture | 1,339 | 363 | 976 | 86.6 | 889.4 | 533.6 | 42.7 |
| Commerce | 7,162 | 507 | 6,655 | 5,148.6 | 1,506.4 | 903.8 | 72.3 |
| Construction | 523 | 1 | 522 | 467.8 | 54.2 | 32.5 | 2.6 |
| Energy and gas | 572 | 0 | 572 | 89.9 | 482.1 | 289.3 | 23.1 |
| Energy & mining | 571 | 431 | 140 | 65.3 | 74.7 | 44.8 | 3.6 |
| Finance and insur. | 1,499 | 63 | 1,436 | 1,190.0 | 246.0 | 147.6 | 11.8 |
| Industry | 5,468 | 899 | 4,569 | 3,469.9 | 1,099.1 | 659.5 | 52.8 |
| Others | 25 | 1 | 24 | 13.0 | 11.0 | 6.7 | 0.5 |
| Comm. services | 3,089 | 909 | 2,180 | 1,982.4 | 197.6 | 118.6 | 9.5 |
| Transp. & comm. | 1,405 | 30 | 1,375 | 998.7 | 376.3 | 225.8 | 18.1 |
| **Total** | **21,654** | **3,204** | **18,450** | **13,512.4** | **4,936.6** | **2,962.2** | **237.0** |

Source: Schenone (2003) based on MEF data.

**Tax exemptions increase income inequity.** They are often regressive and benefit the poor least. In 1999, out of every 100 sucres the IRS could not collect because of the exemptions on education, books, health, transportation, water, and electricity (in other words, except basic food items, house rental, and financial services), 43 sucres benefited the richest 25 percent of the population and only 14 sucres benefited the poorest 25 percent (Kopits and others 1999). Except for VAT exemptions—which could most likely be eliminated without changing incidence significantly—tax expenditures re-enforce Ecuador's income inequality. Two factors favor such distortions: the proliferation of taxes, and the concentration of high-income taxpayers in a small but well organized group that is able to shift the tax burden to a large number of "small" taxpayers. In Ecuador, about 3,000 large companies generate 80 percent of revenue collected by the *Servicio de Rentas Internas* (SRI).

**Tax expenditures entail a significant revenue loss of about 3.8 percent of GDP for the Central Government.** Although there are no reliable estimates of overall tax expenditure in Ecuador, broad calculations of tax expenditure on the internal VAT (that is, excluding the VAT on imports) indicate that in 2001, its cost was approximately US$237 million, or 1.1 percent of GDP (Table 3.7).[14] Approximately half of this was related to the retail and manufacturing sectors. Then, tax exemptions on customs tariffs and the VAT on imports amounted to 1.4 percent of GDP. Finally, according to SRI data, tax expenditure on the income tax is estimated to have a fiscal impact of 1.3 percent of GDP (1 percent for firms and 0.3 percent of GDP for individuals). Hence, a 25 percent reduction of VAT and SRI tax exemptions, such as authorities indicated in their initial multiyear reform program (World Bank 2003b), would bring fiscal space for about 0.9 to 1.0 percent of GDP.

14. Based on a sample of 3,055 large taxpayers. An alternative estimate, using national accounts data, gives a combined result of VAT tax exemptions and evasions of 1.9 percent of GDP (SALTO/AID 2003). This result is not inconsistent with the figures presented above.

*Making Transparent and Integrating Off-Budget Public Investment*
**There are other potential sources of fiscal space in the budget.** Other off-budget or quasi-fiscal activities are those developed by (a) public enterprises grouped under the Solidarity Fund; (b) regional development agencies (*Organismos Regionales de Desarrollo*, ORDs); and (c) provincial and sectional governments.[15]

■ The Solidarity Fund (*Fondo de Solidaridad*) is an autonomous body, created in 1995, to address human development through education, health and public services. It is the sole holder of the 5 power generation companies, 1 power transmission company, 19 power distribution companies, and 3 telephone companies (ANDINATEL, PACIFICTEL, and TELECSA). Its pricing policy and financial balances and activities are subject to strong political interference, which leads to complex and non-transparent cross-subsidies, and important quasi-fiscal activities. Their audited financial balances are unknown, and this prevents making any estimates about the potential fiscal space that could be created through reform of their pricing policies. Worst of all, the Solidarity Fund might be a source of contingent liabilities. Indeed, the IMF estimated that the stock of debt of the power distribution companies was US$571 million up to December 2002 (IMF 2003). The *minimum* fiscal space that could be generated is 0.1 percent of GDP.

■ Regional development agencies (ORDs) depend on the Executive, but receive off-budget earmarked revenues and manage their budget independently. Some of their projects are known by the Investment Office at MEF, but there is no accountability and transparency about their pro-poor impact. In 2003, RDBs managed a budget of US$246.8 million (equivalent to 0.9 percent of GDP) (Table A26). Making these investments fully transparent and/or evaluating their use prior to integrating them into the budget are reasonable options to consider while looking for additional fiscal space.

■ Provincial and sectional governments are autonomous, but receive earmarked transfers and also have their own sources of revenue. There is no estimate of their contingent liabilities. A significant step, however, has been the database of municipal finance that MEF has recently developed. The system will be fully running in November, cover subnational fiscal accounts, and be opened to the public. Subnational transfers represented 2.4 percent of GDP in 2003 and, in theory, 70 percent should have been devoted to investments. In practice, MEF authorities believe that the actual investment share of transfers is around 50 percent, and that the ensuing investment by subnational ("sectional") governments is mostly disconnected from the priorities of the Central Government's expenditure agenda.[16] Had municipalities agreed devoting at least one-third of their receipts to the priorities of a PRS agenda would generate about 0.4 percent of GDP of additional fiscal space.

## E.  Toward a Results-Oriented Budget: Attaining the Millennium Development Goals

**Ecuador has to accelerate progress to meet the Millennium Development Goals (MDGs).** MDGs are integral to the Government's social strategy and goals (Table 3.8). Progress toward meeting them is mixed. According to official statistics, the government has already achieved the gender ratio gap and, provided progress in primary education is sustained, it is in line to achieve universal enrollment in primary education. Similarly, on health indicators, the target for reducing

---

15. Other public entities, like the Central Bank, the Deposit Guarantee Agency, or the group of 22 enterprises associated to the army that are registered as *Sociedades Anónimas*, also develop quasi-fiscal activities, which are not always duly registered and transparent.

16. According to Pablo Lucio Paredes, a well-known Ecuadorian economist, "sectional" governments devote less than 10 percent of their total transfers to education and health needs.

## TABLE 3.8: PROGRESS BY ECUADOR IN MEETING THE MILLENNIUM DEVELOPMENT GOALS

| Millennium Development Goals Target | Ecuador's Performance |
| --- | --- |
| 1. Reduce by half the share of population earning less than US$1 a day (extreme poor), from 17.7 percent in 1998 to 8.9 percent in 2015, and reduce by half the share of children under age 5 with prevalent malnutrition, from 38 percent in 1990 to 19 percent in 2015. | There are no reports on the share of population earning less than US$1 a day and on prevalent child malnutrition in recent years. The World Bank projects a reduction in the share of the population living below the extreme poverty line from 28 percent in 1990 to 22 percent in 2007 (World Bank 2004a). However, more recent estimates found that the share of the population living below the national poverty line increased during 1990–2001. There are no more recent data available (World Bank 2004b). |
| 2. Enroll all children in primary school by 2015 and increase the share of male and female pupils starting grade 1 and reaching grade 5 from, respectively, 40 percent and 41 percent in 1990/91 to full completion in 2015. | Net primary enrolment was 90 percent in 2003. The share of male and female pupils starting grade 1 and reaching grade 5 increased to, respectively, 77 percent and 79 percent in 2001/02. |
| 3. Make progress toward gender equality and empowering women by increasing the female-to-male enrolment ratio in primary and secondary school of 97 percent in 1990/91. By 2015, gender disparities at all levels of education should be eliminated. | *The female/male net primary enrolment has been met.* The ratio of female-to-male enrolments in primary and secondary school increased to 100 percent in 2001/02. |
| 4. Reduce infant (aged 0 to 1) mortality rate by two-thirds, from 61.3 per 1,000 live births in 1990 to 20.4 in 2015, and child mortality (aged 1 to 5) rate by two-thirds, from 57 per 1,000 live births in 1990 to 19 in 2015. Increase immunization against measles and DPT in children aged 12 to 23 months from, respectively, 46 percent and 51 percent of children aged 12 to 23 months in 1990 to full coverage. | Infant mortality rate per 1,000 live births declined to 25 in 2002, and the child mortality rate per 1,000 live births declined to 29 in 2002. Alternative figures released by the Government of Ecuador show infant and child mortality rates of, respectively, 11.5 and 34 in 2003. Immunization against measles and DPT increased in 2002 to, respectively, 80 percent and 89 percent of children aged 12 to 23 months. |
| 5. Reduce maternal mortality rate per 100,000 live births by three-quarters, from 150 in 1990 to 50 in 2015, and increase the rate of births attended by skilled health staff, from 66 percent in 1990 to 100 percent. | Data on maternal mortality are not very reliable and what can be safely said is that this rate has fallen considerably over recent decades. For instance, according to INEC, this rate dropped from 203 per 100,000 live births in 1971 to 46 in 2002, but according to ENDEMAIN, maternal mortality had an average of 302 per 100,000 live births in 1981–87 and 159 in 1988–94. Births attended by skilled health staff increased to an average 69 percent during 1995–2000. |
| 6. Halt and reverse the spread of HIV/AIDS. Eliminate incidence of malaria, tuberculosis, and measles from, respectively, 15 cases, 160 cases, and 15 cases in 1990 to zero by 2015. | Prevalence of HIV increased from 0.8 to 6.0 per 100,000 between 1990 and 2002. In 2003 the number of reported cases were respectively 797 (HIV: 497, AIDS: 300). Incidence of tuberculosis per 100,000 inhabitants was 52 in 2002. In 2002, there were 149 cases of measles, down from 779 in 2000. In 2002, there were 87,547 reported cases of malaria (that is 692 per 100,000 inhabitants, down from 775 per 100,000 inhabitants in 2000. |

*Sources: World Development Indicators (2003); PAHO (1994, 2002); MOH.*

by two-thirds mortality for girls aged 1 to 5 has already been achieved, and a simple linear extrapolation suggests that the goal for infant mortality (aged 0 to 1) could be reached by 2010 for boys and 2008 for girls (Vos 2004).

**Despite progress, unfavorable poverty trends and budget constraints raise questions about whether the goals will be reached.** Social expenditure is declining, and its level is low. Unless dedicated efforts are made, special population groups—like indigenous, Afro, and rural

---

**BOX 3.3: MAIN CONCLUSIONS OF THE WORLD BANK ECUADOR POVERTY ASSESSMENT**

- **Poverty is increasing in Ecuador.** Over the decade 1990–2001, the national poverty rate deteriorated from 40 to 45 percent, and the number of poor increased from 3.5 million to 5.2 million. According to the most recent survey and census, headcount poverty rates in urban areas, both in the Sierra and the Costa, experienced a sharp increase of 100 percent and 80 percent, respectively, whereas rates in rural areas appeared stable over the decade.
- **In contrast to 1990, in 2001 the poor population appeared concentrated in urban areas**—the Sierra (20 percent) and the Coast (26 percent). As a result, the absolute number of poor people increased by 500 percent in the urban Sierra and by 300 percent in the urban Coast. Most surprisingly, growth in the number of poor in urban areas far surpasses that of the total population in those areas, and this poses formidable challenges both in terms of employment and in provision of basic social services
- **Patterns of domestic migration suggest that over 30 percent of the population live in a place different from where they were born.** About one-third of all internal migration occurs within provinces, and two-thirds occurs across provinces. Most migratory movements (60 percent) are urban-to-urban, rather than rural-to-urban, and Quito and Guayaquil alone are the destination of 20 percent of all internal migrants, with 13 percent and 16 percent, respectively.
- **Poverty increased significantly in 44 out of 220 cantons over the decade.** The largest increases (15 to 25 percentage points) occurred in cantons located in the provinces of Azuay, Bolivar, Cotopaxi, Guayas, Manabí, and Pichincha.
- **Individuals heading poor households are more likely to be self-employed and less likely to be public salaried workers than heads of non-poor households.** In particular, 40 percent of poor heads of households are self-employed, compared to 30 percent of non-poor ones. Similarly, only 4.5 percent of poor heads of households are public sector servants.

---

poor—could be left further behind. Indeed, the most recent data showed that the national poverty rate increased from 40 to 45 percent during 1990–2001 (Box 3.3), especially in the urban areas.

**The implications for achieving the MDGs are consistent with the general principles that should guide expenditure in the social sectors and the budget as a whole.** The standard justification for public spending depends on how well the expenditure line item compares with other sectors and programs on the following three grounds: efficiency, ability to implement, and equity. While equity issues have already been addressed, this section examines efficiency and ability to implement. To do so, an input–output model is used in a two-step method innovated by Vos and Ponce (2004). The model allows estimating financing requirements for meeting three MDGs—primary and secondary enrolment and infant mortality—and comparing them to financing requirements for other selected goals estimated under alternative approaches (UNDP/UNICEF 2003). Only models for primary enrolment and infant mortality are explained below. For a full explanation of the model applied to secondary enrolment, see Vos and Ponce (2004).

**An innovative input-output method is introduced to estimate the financial inputs required to achieve specific MDGs.** It aims to (i) define a production function for specific outputs, (ii) isolate the main determinants of such output; (iii) estimate cost per unit of producing such output, and, based on estimated elasticities and unit costs ensuing from above, (iv) calculate the financing needs of reaching a key MDG. This is similar to the World Bank model known as *SimSip* (see World Bank, 2004b), but its main difference is that its estimated coefficients are Ecuador-based, while those assumed in *SimSip* result from LAC averages.

**Meeting universal primary education.** Estimation proceeds in two steps. First a model of the determinants of schooling is estimated. Second, unit costs are assessed. This allows the identification of the various determinants of schooling, and their unit cost, making it possible to establish input–output relationships between policy interventions and expected educational outcomes measured by net enrolment rates.

**First step.** The schooling model establishes the relative importance of each possible determinant of enrolment in primary education. It finds an elasticity expressing the impact of a 1 percent change of a given determinant on school enrolment. Then, these determinants are linked to unit costs to obtain a basis for making budget projections for alternative resource allocations. Complete details about elasticity results of the determinants of net enrolment and coefficients of cost-effectiveness in primary education are found in Table A42.

**Second step.** Three *static* cost-effectiveness simulations are performed for the main determinants chosen, that is, inputs change to approach a given target (say, 100 percent net enrolment in primary education) using model elasticities and unit costs to estimate the costs of three selected interventions: (a) an increase in the shares of trained teachers to 100 percent, (b) an expanded *Beca Escolar* (now tranformed into BDH), and (c) a combination of the two previous policies and an increase of rural school infrastructure.[17] However, there are two basic assumptions: (a) the pupil–teacher ratio is kept fixed during the simulation period; (b) the baseline (no policy change) scenario keeps all inputs constant (although the number of teachers may rise as a result of the fixed pupil–teacher ratio assumption), except unit costs which adjust for projected inflation only. As a result, the primary education budget remains at 1.3 percent of GDP, and the budget for secondary education remains at 1.2 percent of GDP, while net enrolment rates do not improve from their 2003 levels in the baseline scenario.

Following are results from the three budget scenarios (Table 3.9):

▨ The *share of trained teachers increases to 100 percent* (up from 90 percent in 2003) and the *share of teachers with central appointments decreases* to 84 percent (down from 94 percent) by 2007. This scenario works to get all urban non-poor children in school by 2007, and induces the urban poor to a net enrolment rate of 97 percent (up from 89 percent in 2003). This policy should also help increase enrolment among the rural poor, but without additional investment in rural school infrastructure the effect will be more than offset by the ensuing increase in the number of pupils per classroom. The budget implications of this policy are minimal. All other things being equal, it would require an increase of about 7 percent in the (nominal) education budget by 2007, or about US$30 million per year compared to a baseline of no policy change (0.1 percent of GDP).[18]

▨ *The Beca Escolar (Bono) program is expanded to cover all urban poor.* School subsidies (or reduced schooling costs) appear to significantly influence enrolment for this population group only. This involves additional budgetary costs, not just from the increase in coverage of the cash transfer program, but also due to rising teacher costs as enrolment increases and the pupil–teacher ratio is kept fixed. Having all urban poor in school by 2007 would involve a slightly smaller additional budget effort of 6 percent over the baseline projection by 2007, or about US$28 million (0.1 percent of GDP) per year.

▨ *Combining the two policies and allowing for an increase in rural school infrastructure* by a sufficient amount such that the rise in the number of pupils per classroom does not have a

---

17. Interaction effects are included. For instance, an expansion in the conditional cash transfer program would lead to higher school enrolment, but also to a higher number of students per classroom, which has a negative effect on enrolment for some groups of the school-age population unless more is invested in classrooms.

18. This policy can be as effective, and even cost saving, if the assumption of a fixed pupil–teacher ratio of 23 is dropped and the ratio is allowed to increase to 25, implying a 3 percent reduction in the number of teachers (or about 3,700 teachers).

negative effect on enrolment of the rural poor. This combination of policies leads to universal access to education for the urban population, but leaves the rural population without any visible benefit. The cost would be only marginally higher than for the second budget scenario (reaching 0.2 percent of GDP by 2006), mainly due to the extra investment in schooling infrastructure and the rise in demand for teachers as enrollment increases.[19]

## TABLE 3.9: ESTIMATED FISCAL COST OF ATTAINING KEY MDGS AND SOCIAL TARGETS
### (in percent of GDP)[20]

| Year | Primary Education | Secondary Education | Basic Health | Infant Mortality | Child Nutrition* | Child Care | Total |
|------|-------------------|---------------------|--------------|------------------|------------------|-----------|-------|
| 2004 | 0.1 | 0.2 | 0.3 | 0.02 | 0.1 | 0.1 | 0.82 |
| 2005 | 0.1 | 0.3 | 0.3 | 0.02 | 0.1 | 0.2 | 1.02 |
| 2006 | 0.2 | 0.4 | 0.3 | 0.02 | 0.1 | 0.3 | 1.32 |
| 2007 | 0.2 | 0.6 | 0.5 | 0.02 | 0.1 | 0.5 | 1.92 |

Notes: * Includes only the free school meals (colación escolar and others by the Programa de Alimentación Escolar).
Sources: Vos and others (2004) for primary and secondary education, and infant mortality; and UNDP (2003) for others.

**Meeting the Infant Mortality Target.** The same methodology is applied: an input–output relationship in health is established, that is, between policy interventions and expected health outcomes measured by infant mortality (Vos et al. 2004).

**First step.** The relative importance may be expressed as the elasticity measuring the impact of a 1 percent change of a given determinant on, respectively, the probability of professionally assisted child delivery and child survival. This is linked to unit costs, to make budget projections for alternative resource allocations. Elasticity results of the determinants of infant mortality and cost-effectiveness coefficients for infant mortality are found in Table A54a.

**Second step.** Three static simulations are considered: First, modifying the impact on access to health services. This specification is for the probability of professionally assisted childbirth and prenatal controls. The key policy variables are access to health insurance and availability of health services and medical personnel. In addition, we assume that expansion of the free maternity program will increase professionally assisted childbirth commensurately.[21] Second, results of policy simulations on the demand for maternal care (at child delivery and prenatal controls) are subsequently used in the health "production function" for child survival. A survival model further suggests that breastfeeding has a strong positive effect on avoiding early child death. According to the model findings, this leaves the coverage of the immunization program as the policy variable

---

19. This policy package could be financed by allowing for a gradual increase in the pupil–teacher ratio to 27.5 by 2007, but requiring a reduction of 9 percent in the number of teachers (that is, affecting about 11,000 teachers).

20. Estimates for secondary education follow the same two-step procedure indicated above for primary education. For a complete description of the exercise, see Vos and Ponce (2004). The input variables that require financing in this case are the number of teachers with a university degree (for urban enrolment), the coverage of students with Beca Escolar (Bono) in secondary education (the one with expected major impact on rural poor students) and, to a minor extent, some increase in infrastructure (especially urban).

21. Household determinants include the educational level of the mother and per capita household consumption. The averages of these two variables are assumed to change at fixed rates of 1.5 percent per year, thus imposing a trend in rising access to health services due to improving socioeconomic conditions. We assume further that use of prenatal controls has similar determinants and impact as the probability of medically assisted child delivery.

with the most important expected effect on reduction of infant mortality. Ethnicity and female education variables are considered the relevant household variables in determining infant mortality. Third, unit cost estimates are added for relevant public health input variables, such as salaries of health workers, construction and maintenance of hospitals and health centers, and of the special programs, specifically the Immunization and Free Maternity Programs. Key assumptions are that the nominal health budget (for all items) is adjusted for a given inflation rate (3 percent per year) to account for changes in input costs, and nominal salaries of health workers are adjusted this way, and thus real wages for doctors and nurses are kept constant.

Results from the three budget scenarios target an overall reduction of infant mortality from 34 to 19 per 1,000 live births between 2004 and 2015. For the poor, the reduction should be from 42 to 22 per 1,000 live births, and for the indigenous population reduction should be from 66 to 33. Baseline simulation projects improvements in education and per capita consumption forward to 2015 under the assumptions indicated above, but assumes that health programs show no further expansion from their coverage reached in 2003. The baseline then projects that without health input improvements, infant mortality would reach only 30.5 per 1,000 live births by 2015.

- *Neither reaching full coverage of the Immunization Program* nor the expansion of the Free Maternity Program targeted at the poor by themselves is sufficient to reach the MDG targets for infant mortality. The expansion of the Immunization Program would reduce infant mortality to 20.1 per 1,000 live births by 2015. Because this program is universal and initial coverage does not differ much across population groups, this policy would reduce infant mortality for all, but would not narrow differences between poor and non-poor or indigenous and non-indigenous.
- *A targeted expansion of the Free Maternity Program* would narrow such gaps. Generating unrestricted access to medically assisted child delivery and maternal care for the poor and indigenous population would reduce the overall infant mortality rate to 28 per 1,000 live births. The higher probability of early child deaths among the poor compared to the non-poor would fall from 45 percent around 2000 to 21 percent in 2015, and the gap between the indigenous and non-indigenous population would be almost halved from 118 percent to 67 percent.
- The *additional budgetary cost of the expansion of these programs* as simulated would be about the same for each: between US$3 million and US$4 million per year (or 0.01 percent of GDP). Combining the two would sum to an annual cost of US$7.2 million over the baseline budget (or 0.02 percent of GDP). The combination of these two policies would be sufficient to reach the MDG targets for the poor and indigenous population groups, but would still fall slightly short for the non-poor (Table 3.9).

## F. Policy Recommendations

**In the context of fiscal adjustment, an efficient and effective allocation of increased resources could make substantial inroads into poverty.** Finding additional fiscal space is not the only concern for Ecuadorian authorities. Current spending on the education and health sectors in Ecuador have already led to positive educational and health outcomes and there is room for significant improvements in equity. The value of targeted spending in selected programs of the education, health and social welfare sectors is underscored by the opportunities foregone when budgetary resources are used for less-priority and non-pro-poor items. Thus, ensuing policy recommendations open additional room for redirecting social spending and subsidies to basic infrastructure. However, the emphasis on targeting and a more equitable distribution of resources should not preclude addressing the institutional aspects of poor performance. This is why the next chapter deals with institutional shortcomings in social programs, very relevant in a context of resource constraints. In the meantime, here is a set of proposed actions.

## FIGURE 3.6: CHILE FONDO CONCURSABLE

- Started in 2000 (combined with policy rule)
- Eliminates traditional incrementalist practices
- New and reformulated projects must apply every year
- Old projects compete with new projects
- Current spending associated to projects is also considered

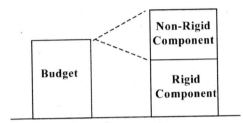

*Source:*

**To Shift Public Expenditure Toward a Pro-Poor Focus**
**Developing a poverty reduction strategy is something that just cannot be done with a non-pro-poor budget.** Therefore, reviewing the non-rigid part of the budget to increase its pro-poor focus is also critical for a PRS. This implies:

■ **Making sure that the additional fiscal space created is allocated entirely to pro-poor spending,** especially in the education, health, and social protection sectors.

■ **Revising the current allocations of social expenditure and projects.** The development of a Competition-Based Fund (*Fondo Concursable*) could be tantamount to a cooperative "game" among uncooperative "players" in a cash-rationed budget. Indeed, there are not many choices for Ecuador except to optimize the use of existing resources. In that context, a modified version of the *Fondo Concursable* could deal, with at least, the non-rigid share of the budget whose size is about 1 percent of GDP (Figure 3.6 and Box 3.4).[22] In this case, the Ecuadorian *Fondo* would deal with assigning residual monies according to some pre-established priorities within line ministries throughout in-year modifications, as opposed to the goal of the Chilean Fund of getting national priorities reflected in the annual and multi-annual allocation of resources. Other modifications could include: (a) the definition of a streamlined project approval procedure for projects below a ceiling amount, in accordance with the small amount of resources involved; (b) the upgrade of procedures in the present *Banco de Proyectos,* so as to significantly reduce the average 6-months delay actually taken in assessing a project, (c) simplified criteria for selecting projects; and (d) simplified forms for project formulation. It should be noticed that such proposed Fund would not contribute to solve the issue of priority setting, but at least allow MEF to maintain budgetary and technical control over the use of resources, which is desirable to maintain fiscal discipline and prevent policy discretion in the assignment of resources.[23]

---

22. Some LAC countries, like Guatemala, also integrate investment by subnational governments into the *Listado Nacional de Proyectos* that accompany the budget *proforma,* but Ecuador is barely starting to simply register such projects.

23. Some caution should accompany this recommendation, since the Chilean Fund works because it has a technically competent budget office, within a Cabinet-level Expenditure Review Committee that initially prepares a medium-term financial programming (although not a detailed multi-year budget). Ecuador does not have a similar body.

---

### BOX 3.4: THE CHILEAN COMPETITION-BASED (CONCURSABLE) FUND FOR PUBLIC PROGRAMS

**Goals and Requirements.** The Fund's goals are to provide better information on the budget-making process and improve the allocation of public resources to new, restructured, or substantially enlarged programs, thereby reducing the inertial nature of the budget. Since 2001, the budget has been prepared using a procedure that differs in significant ways from the system applied in previous years. This procedure has two main steps:

1. Ministries develop their budget proposal based on information from a budgetary framework linked to their inertial spending (determined by laws, medium- and long-term commitments, and so forth). This enables them to assign all residual resources to a Central Fund for government priorities (*Fondo Concursable*). This Fund examines all new, restructured, or substantially enlarged projects.
2. The initiatives submitted to the Fund must be presented in a standard format. This includes background to allow study on the need for and relevance of the initiative. Most of the headings included in this form correspond to those used in the standard methodology of evaluation of government programs. This methodology is the basis for the analysis and selection of initiatives for financing.

**Focus and Methodology.** The public institution prepares a Program (Project) Presentation file in a required format of the draft budget. The main features of this format are: justification, target population and beneficiaries, budgetary cost and budget request, goal and purpose, description of components, monitoring indicators, and means of verification.

**Institutional Framework and Actors Involved.** Projects are presented as part of the overall framework of annual budget preparation. The Finance Ministry, originally through its Budgets Office, is the responsible authority for assessing them. Projects to be financed by the Fund are selected in meetings with the President of the Republic at which the overall budget for public spending is presented. The selected ones become part of the draft annual Budget, which must be debated and approved by the National Congress, which scrutinizes it. Beginning with the 2002 budget, the initiatives are presented to the Ministry of Planning (MIDEPLAN) for review and assessment of the basic prerequisites, thus becoming jointly involved with the Budget Office in the decision-making process of the draft budget at the Ministry of Finance.

**Monitoring.** The selected projects included in the budget are monitored annually, based on previously established performance indicators and a well-established project evaluation methodology.

---

- **Making optimal use of the available targeting instruments, like SELBEN, to unify targeting criteria and consolidate programs.** The GOE has reconsidered retargeting the gas subsidy using SELBEN. This is a pro-poor proposal that would significantly improve upon the current status quo, since most spending would be directed to households at the bottom of the income distribution, that is, poorest households. This measure is considered to be welfare enhancing over the alternative of complete elimination of the cooking gas subsidy, which is not recommended (World Bank 2004b). The World Bank (1996) estimated that without proper compensation, the pure elimination of the subsidy would lead to a welfare loss (reduction in consumption) of more than 5.3 percent for the very poor. A detailed analysis of the alternatives for retargeting the cokking gas subsidy is included in Annex E.
- **Implementing a new Household and Living Conditions Survey is essential.** The last one was performed in 1999, before dollarization. This would allow an updated poverty map (crossed with the census) and benefit incidence analysis of public subsidies. It would also help analyze most recent poverty trends.

### To Re-Target Public Subsidies

**None of the three subsidies to basic infrastructure services caters to the poor, and they are highly distortive from an efficiency perspective.** The implicit subsidy for telephone service is the most unequally distributed, followed by the largest subsidy, for water. While tackling the telecom and electricity subsidy is a priority for the Central Government, dealing with the water subsidy requires collaboration from subnational governments.

- **Electricity** would be, in theory, the easier sector to tackle. Restructuring the tariff system to reduce the total subsidy to consumers below a maximum amount of electricity consumption should not have a major impact on the electricity companies, or on non-poor consumers. An alternative to further lower the 15 percent actual subsidy to residential consumers below 300 Kilowatt-hours would be to modify the ceiling itself to target the truly poorest households.
- **The telecom sector** should start by reducing the tariffs for public telephones, which are 10 times higher than tariffs for residential users; and by eliminating cross-subsidies through completion of the tariff rebalancing between domestic and international rates approved by CONATEL in 2003.
- **The water sector** is the more complex to handle, due to its decentralized management. Cross-subsidies should be linked to operational performance, and the amount of subsidy allocated per connection should be defined considering the size and income level of the population, to avoid existing disparities in transfers that actually benefit the largest and richer water companies.

**While the bias in social expenditure is much less pronounced for pro-poor expenditure than in subsidies for basic services, it is nevertheless not desirable.**

- Reduction in overall university tuition subsidies could finance access for poorer groups, for instance, to secondary education.
- Retargeting of the subsidy of the cooking gas makes sense in the context of an increase to a well-targeted and fully financed *Bono de Desarrollo Humano*, or a revamped *SELBEN*. In the past, the BDH was in fact introduced to compensate the poor for the elimination of the subsidy on gas. Therefore, retargeting is an appropriate policy substitute to the cooking gas subsidy, since welfare losses would be compensated through an increased BDH and its revised database of beneficiaries or revamped SELBEN, and fiscal savings would be generated from lower administrative costs and reduced leakages.
- Pro-poor programs, like primary education and school breakfast, should be a priority, but these efforts should be accompanied by rapid completion of the on-going re-targeting process in the school breakfast. Once this is achieved, increasing its very small budget is also justified.
- As raising the budget of the *Seguro Social Campesino* faces legal and institutional constraints inside IESS, other low-budget pro-poor programs providing similar services, like the *Ley de Maternidad Gratuita* should see an increased budget allocation.
- All pro-poor programs would highly benefit from a results-oriented, performance-based budgeting. This would imply defining standard monitoring indicators and evaluation mechanisms, and promoting civil society participation through social accountability mechanisms.

**Ecuador has multiple medium-term sources of a potential fiscal space for pro-poor spending adding up close to 6 percent of GDP.** Most possible sources of fiscal space for Ecuador are identified in Table 3.10. Identified sources tax policy and tax administration changes (other than removal of selected tax exemptions, i.e. not tax reform is considered. This provides authorities with several options to consider, both intra- and off-budget. Intra-budget sources represent about one-third and off-budget two-thirds. Due to the lack of information, contingent liabilities are not included, but the table does include most off-budget and some quasi-fiscal

## TABLE 3.10: POTENTIAL SOURCES OF FISCAL SPACE AND ESTIMATED ANNUAL IMPACT

| Measures | Percent of GDP |
| --- | --- |
| *Intra-budget* | |
| Curb capital spending ratio toward the "structural" level (paragraph 3.23) | 0.2 |
| Interest savings from debt repurchase (Table A76) | 0.2 |
| Reduce defense spending to end-1990s level (paragraph 3.29) | 1.0 |
| Make optimal use of public investment (paragraph 3.25) | 0.2 |
| *Off-Budget* | |
| Reduce selected off-budget earmarking of oil revenues (paragraph 3.31) | 0.6 |
| Incorporate oil-subsidies to budget (gas, diesel, and electricity) (paragraph 3.31) | 2.3 |
| Eliminate 25 percent of overall tax exemptions (paragraph 3.34) | 1.0 |
| VAT | 0.7 |
| Internal | 0.3 |
| External | 0.4 |
| Income | 0.3 |
| Firms | 0.2 |
| Individuals | 0.1 |
| Rationalize spending of ORDs (paragraph 3.35) | NA |
| Integrate 10% of subnational spending with national priorities (paragraph 3.35) | 0.4 |
| Allocate resources from Solidarity Fund to the PRS (paragraph 3.35) | 0.1 |
| **TOTAL** | **6.0** |

*Source:* World Bank staff calculations.

activities. It is important to remember that the materialization of these sources is constrained by the annual quantitative ceilings set by the fiscal rule on primary spending, non-oil deficit, and public debt reduction. In other words, whatever solutions are adopted, they will have to be accommodated within the annual fiscal ceiling mandated by the rule.

### Trade-Offs between In- and Off-Budget Fiscal Space

In the process of assessing alternatives, it is important to consider several rules of thumb:

- **Curbing the increase in wage payroll—in GDP terms—is absolutely essential to prevent full elimination of the very small fiscal space remaining in the budget.** There is simply no choice. This could also imply considering expanding the coverage of the civil service law to the rest of uncovered public servants. Ditto for the growth in transfers to IESS.
- **Off-budget activities, by definition, should gradually go into the budget.** Perhaps easier to handle are those that depend on the Executive alone. A natural candidate is oil-financed (and non-pro-poor) subsidies (cooking gas, diesel, and fuel oil). It is important to realize that their introduction to the budget does not mean their full elimination, but rather their reorientation, and increased monitoring and transparency.
- **The level of tax and expenditure earmarkings should not only go into the budget, but be reduced in real terms.** Their elimination has been attempted several times in the past decades with little success. It has also been suggested to start by eliminating those that are non-constitutional. In reality, there might be two feasible alternatives: (a) freeze the level of the earmarking in real terms, which preserves its existence, but prepares beneficiaries for its gradual phase out; or (b) adopt a temporary reduction of a group of them, which allows obtaining fiscal space faster. Reis (2003) suggests that a 20 percent across-

the-board suspension of all earmarkings, (including transfers to subnational governments), would generate annual savings of about US$400 million. Resources from such a temporary suspension could go to a trust fund (*fideicomiso*), following the best-practice experience of Brazil, and be closely scrutinized in their use by social accounting mechanisms.[24]

■ **Defense expenditure may be evaluated, so as to identify possible sources of fiscal savings.**

### To Reach Selected MDGs

**Selected MDGs are within reach by Ecuador provided social expenditure is well targeted, effective, and financed by low-cost programs explicitly linked to specific outcomes.** In the past decade, net primary education enrolment and infant mortality rates have come down steadily, despite low education and health expenditures, apparently poorly functioning education systems, a significant amount of non-pro-poor spending in both sectors, and a high incidence of malnutrition. Continued overall improvements in education, urbanization, fertility rates, and sanitary conditions explain these paradoxical trends. However, no linear extrapolation guarantees that these trends will continue to improve. Using an input–output model, however, that identifies the main factors (inputs) that determine achieving key goals, there is a way to target cost-effective interventions that may guarantee reaching at least three key MDGs: universal primary and secondary enrolment, and infant mortality. These four cost-effective factors are teacher training and the expansion of the Bono de Desarrolo Humano for primary and secondary education, and expansion of the coverage of the Immunization and Free Maternity Program for infant mortality. Notice, however, that significant institutional shortcomings can impede progress: high rotation of personnel, deviation of resources toward non-priority items, corruption and lack of transparency, and political clientelism in the allocation of spending remain. Some of these shortcomings have been identified in Chapter 4. Linking budget support to performance requires:

■ **Providing the additional budget needs, which are reasonably small, but focused on specific key programs.** Financing the four cost-effective factors amounts to a combined additional budget representing about 0.3-0.4 percent of GDP per year for 2004–05, and 0.6-0.8 percent of GDP per year for 2006–07 (Table 3.9). Taking advantage of complementary estimates done by UNDP/UNICEF (2003) and using a very different methodology, it is also possible to approach the low cost of meeting a wider number of MDGs, also including those of child malnutrition, basic health, and child care. Their inclusion would raise total additional budget needs to about 0.8 percent of GDP in 2004, 1 percent of GDP in 2005, and almost 1.9 percent of GDP in 2007.

■ **Defining a set of performance indicators that would allow monitoring progress.** Performance indicators ought to be an integral part of the PRS and result from a consensus-building exercise. In the case of the main two goals examined, most frequently used indicators are: planned and actual expenditures in the associated programs, enrolment rates for boys and girls, number of teachers trained, cost of primary education, differences in unit costs, and immunization rates. Obviously, high data quality, participation by civil society, and transparency and accountability of executing agencies favor a good tracking of progress. An interesting conclusion of this approach is that not all sector budgets need to be linked to performance indicators, but only those that are critical for achieving the goals of the PRS (including the MDGs).[25]

---

24. This mechanism has been extended three times and will last 14 years in Brazil, until 2007. However, the initial earmarkings considered eligible for the Fund have been reduced by the exclusion of those for subnational governments following the first extension.

25. In the European Union, perhaps the most advanced region in developing results-oriented budgeting, so far only 30 percent of the European Commission's budget is linked to performance indicators (World Bank 2004c).

# Chapter 4

# PERFORMANCE OF PUBLIC EXPENDITURE MANAGEMENT

**T**his chapter examines public expenditure management (PEM) in Ecuador, introducing an innovative methodology for reviewing budgeting by social programs and subnational governments. It assesses the country's capacity to maintain discipline in overall fiscal balances, allocate resources to policy priorities, and channel resources to expenditure programs efficiently, effectively, and with transparency. Thus, this assessment completes the standard three-level PEM analysis (Table 4.1). As discussed in Chapter 2, Ecuador has made progress in regaining aggregate fiscal discipline in the early 2000s and in reverting unsustainable fiscal trends. As shown in Chapter 3, it has also reached positive outcomes in the social sectors, despite declining outlays, a sizable share of non pro-poor social spending and a very small and reducing fiscal space. In this Chapter, it is showed that such progress is fragile, but for an additional reason: the multiple and severe institutional shortcomings surrounding the budget process. Under any scenario, no effective poverty reduction is possible without institutional and structural reforms in the budget system. Hence, there are legitimate questions as to whether current PEM practices support fiscal discipline or makes it difficult to sustain, facilitates an optimal pro-poor allocation of resources or distributes them with little prioritization, and implements an efficient mix of resources in the social sectors or wastes them.

**Poor performance of social expenditure in Ecuador is closely linked to PEM shortcomings.** Recent reviews of international experience with poverty reduction strategies have concluded that in many countries, the practice of PEM is an obstacle to the achievement of poverty reduction objectives (Judge and Klugman 2003). Ecuador is no exception. Failures in the budget process and institutional bottlenecks systematically lead to underexecution of social programs. These shortcomings result in underbudgeting or in long interruptions and delays in the channeling of budgeted resources. Perhaps the most important failures are unrealistic budget planning, deviations between budgets approved and executed—with a bias in favor of defense and security forces and against spending in the social sectors—a lack of effective interventions resulting from budget fragmentation through a myriad of overlapping social programs, the presence of significant off-budget funds, and delays in the actual transfer of resources, arising from cash rationing and poor execution capacity at the level of line agencies. This chapter explores all those issues in detail.

**Developing an effective poverty reduction strategy for Ecuador requires, as a precondition, an overall reform of the budget process and, more broadly, of all levels of PEM.**

| TABLE 4.1: BASIC ELEMENTS OF PUBLIC EXPENDITURE MANAGEMENT: THE "THREE-LEVEL ANALYSIS" | |
| --- | --- |
| **Aggregated Fiscal Discipline** | Budget totals should be the result of explicit, enforced decisions, not merely accommodate inertial trends and spending demands. Aggregate ceilings on totals should be set before individual budget decisions are made, and these should be sustainable over the medium term. |
| **Allocation to Strategic Priorities** | Budget allocations should be based on government priorities and on effectiveness of public programs. The budget system should shift resources from lesser to higher priorities and from less to more effective programs. |
| **Operational Efficiency** | Line agencies should produce goods and services at a cost that achieves ongoing efficiency gains and is competitive with market prices. |

*Source:* Schick (1998).

A sound PEM is the key policy instrument that articulates the country's fiscal ceilings and rules with, on one hand, priorities reflected in the budget and, on the other hand, improvements in public sector performance and service delivery. Hence, PEM reform requires an enhanced performance of the budgeting system, rapid upgrading of its budget and financial management procedures, a complete overhaul of budgeting procedures by social agencies in charge of priority social programs and of provincial and sectional governments receiving transfers, transparent information access at all levels of government to allow results-oriented budgeting in the future, and, only when previous reforms have gained ground, a medium-term expenditure framework that would allow aligning expenditure inputs with expected social outcomes.

## A. The PEM Process and its Recent Performance

**The PEM process in Ecuador takes place in a framework where the role of the Central Government is being diminished.** In 2003, the Central Government directly accounted for about 60 percent of total spending, down from 64 percent in 1998 (Figure 4.1 and Table 4.2). Fiscal decentralization has meant that the relative share of the rest of the public sector (mainly the Social Security Institute of Ecuador (IESS), and municipal and provincial governments) has increased by 7 percent during this period. Public enterprises, on the other hand, have also had a declining trend: overall, their share has declined by 3 percent since 1998.

**Since 2003, Ecuador has taken significant steps to improve its overall PEM.** The passage of the Fiscal Law (FTSRL), in 2002, has provided a significant impetus to this effect.

## FIGURE 4.1: CHANGES IN SHARE OF NFPS EXPENDITURES, BY GOVERNMENT TIER

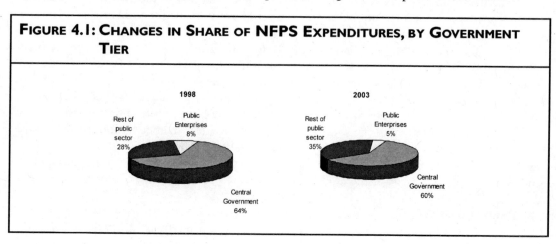

*Source:* BCE.

**TABLE 4.2: ALLOCATION OF PUBLIC SPENDING BY TIERS**

|  | 2001 | | 2002 | | 2003 | |
|---|---|---|---|---|---|---|
|  | US$ Mln | Percent | US$ Mln | Percent | US$ Mln | Percent |
| **Non-Financial Public Sector** | 4,853 | 100.0 | 6,117 | 100.0 | 6,585 | 100.0 |
| Central Government (less transfers) | 3,206 | 66.1 | 3,773 | 61.7 | 3,952 | 60.0 |
| Rest of Public Sector | 1,281 | 26.4 | 1,992 | 32.6 | 2,289 | 34.8 |
| o/w Subnational Government | 706 | 14.5 | 982 | 16.1 | 1,102 | 16.7 |
| o/w IESS | 252 | 5.2 | 546 | 8.9 | 656 | 10.0 |
| o/w Universities and Technical Schools | 171 | 3.5 | 222 | 3.6 | 305 | 4.6 |
| Public Enterprises* | 252 | 5.2 | 356 | 5.8 | 295 | 4.5 |
| o/w PetroEcuador | 164 | 3.4 | 282 | 4.6 | 210 | 3.2 |

Note: * Only includes nonoperating and capital expenditures.

Source: BCE, MEF, and IMF.

Efforts include setting quantitative rules for budget formulation,[1] initiating the groundwork for multiyear budgeting, and requiring subnational entities to submit monthly revenue and expenditure reports. Besides the Law, in recent years Ecuador has also been prudent in its budget formulation: despite high oil prices, it has adhered to using a conservative oil price estimate of US$18 per barrel, though average oil prices were above US$24 per barrel in the last two years. Excess oil revenues are feeding the Fund for Stabilization, Investment, and Public Debt Reduction (FEIREP). In addition, it has also reinitiated the expansion of coverage of its integrated financial management system (SIGEF), with the goal of covering 90 percent of the Central Government by end-2004; built a single database for Central Government-financed public investment; developed an interbank payment system (IPS) at the Central Bank that records salary payments to public employees; started to develop a central registry database for all government employees at SIGEF; and developed CONTRATANET, an electronic public procurement system, on a pilot basis and initially as an informational system.

**Despite these improvements, a standard overall assessment of the Ecuadorian PEM reveals significant shortcomings in all areas.** Since the late 1990s, the International Monetary Fund (IMF) and the World Bank have jointly developed a survey tool called the Country Assessment and Action Plan (AAP) questionnaire to evaluate budgetary management practices worldwide (World Bank 2003c). This survey involves a series of 16 indicators covering the various stages of budget management, including 7 on formulation, 4 on execution, 2 on reporting, 2 on auditing, and 1 on public procurement. The survey was originally designed to help heavily indebted poor countries (HIPC) identify key budget management areas for improved execution and tracking of increased poverty reducing expenditures. Indeed, this assessment was a precondition for preparing HIPCs for the upcoming debt relief, which would increase funding to be made available for poverty reduction. Likewise, Ecuador is also experiencing an increase in revenues associated with the new oil pipeline. Although 70 percent of these revenues are devoted to debt reduction, 20 percent are assigned to countercyclical policy and 10 percent to social invest-

---

1. In this respect, three important measures were taken. First, a limit is set on the real growth of the non-financial portion of the budget at the lower of either the previous year's growth rate or a growth cap of 3.5 percent on real noninterest expenditure. Second, the debt-to-GDP ratio is to be brought down to below 40 percent of GDP, and henceforth capped at that amount, which means that fiscal surpluses are needed, as well as savings from FEIREP mostly devoted to repurchase public debt, which also prevents diversion from its resources to current expenditure. Third, the non-oil deficit is to decrease by 0.2 percent of GDP per year.

ment, especially in education and health. Besides setting a baseline, applying this survey to Ecuador highlights areas for improving budget management.

**The survey results show that Ecuador barely meets 1 of the 16 global benchmarks (Table 4.3).** According to IMF/WB standards, if less than half (7 or fewer) of the benchmarks are met, the country's PEM system requires substantial upgrading. Ecuador's performance is dismal across the different budget stages. *On the formulation side*, an outdated classification system and significant amounts of extrabudgetary resources limits the government's ability to plan, control, and direct expenditures. In addition, coverage of general government activities is insufficient, and there is a lack of a medium-term expenditure framework. An important caveat for the only satisfactory item—the overall ratio between the executed and approved budget—is that the execution performance by sector widely varies from 0.31 in housing, and 0.35 in social welfare to 1.45 in energy and 2.05 in administration, which reduces the budget reliability as a guide to resource allocation. *On the execution side*, the key reason for Ecuador's low scoring is the persistence of significant domestic arrears and cash-rationing mechanisms arising from the lack of timely and centralized information managed by Treasury. This cash rationing does not really reflect the Government's true cash situation: While Treasury knows how much budgetary resources are transferred from the *Cuenta Unica* to private accounts from public institutions, these funds are either kept in deposit at some 2,400 accounts at the Central Bank, or in the private bank accounts, because they are not necessarily immediately disbursed by these institutions. Hence, whereas Treasury is short of funds and must raise money, in reality there are undisbursed funds lying in the institutional accounts. *On the reporting side*, the lack of prompt and virtual consolidation of the budget executed (the so-called *devengado*) by SIGEF, and shortfalls in auditing, mainly explain low scores. Despite recent efforts to expand its coverage, SIGEF's decentralized system is based on separate software databases, which produces a virtual disconnect among themselves, and problems in collecting reliable data from one institutional database to SIGEF central, a shortcoming that is expected to be corrected by year's end. No legal requirement to audit the fiscal accounts exists, and there is high-level political interference at the General Comptroller's Office (CGE) by political parties, which prevents substantive cases from being presented or sanctions being applied.

**In the same vein, Ecuador PEM global ranking is low compared to those of HIPCs.** Ecuador fares worst on about half of all indicators, thus placing it in the group of less-advanced countries (Table 4.4). Alternatively, when compared to Peru, a strong Latin America and the Caribbean (LAC) performer in PEM, Ecuador fares worse in all but three indicators. This is in part due to Peru's usage of a well-functioning integrated financial management system supported by a sound regulatory framework. The gap has widened since the survey was taken, because Peru has made strides in participatory multiyear budgeting and PETS piloting.

## B. Budget Management Review in the Central Government

Whereas the previous section provides valuable insights and benchmarking, this section highlights budget formulation and execution features that are relevant to understand key shortcomings in line agencies and subnational governments. More comprehensive and detailed analysis of budget management has been developed in parallel with the IMF Report of Observance of Standards and Codes (ROSC) (IMF 2003), and the WB/IADB Country Financial and Accountability Assessment (CFAA) (WB/IADB 2004). Annex B also presents an overview of the budget cycle in Ecuador.

### Budget Formulation

**There are several technical and institutional weaknesses that inhibit Ecuador from having an effective budget formulation.** The main ones include (a) extensive off-budget activities, especially through earmarking of revenues and expenditures (see Chapter 3), which constraints the scope of the budget as a policy instrument; (b) incrementalism, whereby allocations are

## TABLE 4.3: REVIEW OF ECUADOR'S PUBLIC EXPENDITURE MANAGEMENT AND BENCHMARKS

| International Benchmark (in parentheses) | Ecuador Rating | Rationale for Ecuador's Rating |
|---|---|---|
| **Formulation** | | |
| 1. **(A)** Fiscal reporting matches the IMF definition of general government sector with coverage (by value) of at least 95 percent, whether it is funded through the budget or not. | B | Coverage of the general government budget is 78 percent of the NFPS (and 90 percent of non-financial public enterprises). Consolidated reporting of the general government is weak and untimely, especially ex post. Ex ante reporting of activities by subnational government data is available, but ex post reporting is available only since 2004, and does not include quasi-fiscal activities. |
| 2. **(A)** Government activities are funded through extrabudgetary resources, but these funds represent less than 3 percent of total spending. | C | There is no comprehensive and reliable information estimating extrabudgetary resources, but they are significant (above 10 percent). Earmarked revenues not included in the budget represent 23 percent of total budget (corrected by off-budget financing) in 2004 alone. The budgets from the social security agencies for the army and the police, public enterprises, and autonomous institutions are not reported and, since only recently, their financial accounts are expected to be known. |
| 3. **(B)** The level and composition of the budget outturn is quite close to the original budget appropriations (deviations between 5 and 15 percent) for at least two years. | **B** | **During 1995–03, deviations represented an average 6 percent of under-budgeting. Although there was no dominant pattern of under- or overexecution in those years, systematic underexecution of public investment appears (and overexecution of wages—see Table A57).** |
| 4. **(A)** Budget reports, full ex ante and timely ex post—include data on external financing—external loans or grants. | B | Ex post reports on budget execution are neither timely nor complete. Grants, especially in-kind, are partly incorporated into the budget, and with delays. |
| 5. **(B)** Classification of budget expenditure is done on an administrative, economic, and detailed functional and programmatic basis. | C | Budget classification does not conform to international standards (ROSC 2003). There are no programmatic classifications. Ecuador's economic and functional classifications do not fully conform to the accepted international standards. |
| 6. **(A)** Identification of poverty reducing expenditure is clear, through a virtual or an actual poverty fund. | C | Poverty reducing spending is not tagged. The lack of a virtual poverty fund, or the establishment of a special tracking mechanism for pro-poor expenditures adds to the lack of a programmatic classification as a major obstacle to identify pro-poor spending. |
| 7. **(A)** Multiyear sectoral expenditure projections exist, and are integrated into the budget formulation cycle as indicative ceilings. | C | The FTRSL approved a multiyear program, but its proposed implementation is delayed to 2005. The lack of functional and program classification could prevent the adoption of detailed inter- and intrasectoral benchmarks. |
| **Execution** | | |
| 8. **(A)** No stock of payment arrears (or very few), with little accumulation of arrears over the previous year. | C | The level of arrears has declined, but still is about 5 percent. It manages a cash-rationing system, with priority social spending protected up to a certain extent. |
| 9. **(A)** Internal control system is effective. | C | Internal financial audits are weak in their breadth, depth, and frequency. |
| 10. **(B)** Public expenditure tracking surveys (PETS) of funds are piloted to supplement weak internal control as a second best. | C | No PETS have been piloted or implemented. CGE does financial but not performance audits, sometimes verifies whether resources reach the final users or service providers, and does not publish its audit findings and recommendations. |

*(continued)*

### TABLE 4.3: REVIEW OF ECUADOR'S PUBLIC EXPENDITURE MANAGEMENT AND BENCHMARKS (CONTINUED)

| International Benchmark (in parentheses) | Ecuador Rating | Rationale for Ecuador's Rating |
|---|---|---|
| **Formulation** | | |
| 11. **(A)** Satisfactory reconciliation of fiscal and banking accounts is undertaken monthly. | B | The *Cuenta Unica* is reconciled daily and through electronic means, but institutional accounts can take longer than one month. Statistical discrepancies in monthly reporting are still significant. |
| **Reporting** | | |
| 12. **(B)** Internal budget execution reports are received between two and four weeks of the end of the relevant period. | C | Delays in receiving institutional reports of budget execution from spending units may last much longer than a month. Delays are particularly significant in decentralized execution units. |
| 13. **(A)** Good-quality classification of poverty reducing spending is reflected in regular in-year budget reports. | C | Because there is no virtual fund or an alternative permanent tracking mechanism of poverty reducing expenditure, reporting is made on an ad hoc basis, and its quality is poor, in terms of both a functional or programmatic classification basis. |
| 14. **(A)** Routine transactions are entered into the main accounting system within two months after the end of the fiscal year. | B | Transactions are entered within a six-month period. Full extension of SIGEF is reducing these delays. |
| 15. **(B)** An audited record of the financial outturn should be presented to the legislature between 6 and 12 months of the end of the fiscal year. | C | Audits are made ad hoc, and there is no legal requirement to audit overall fiscal accounts, which significantly reduces accountability for financial results. |
| **Procurement** | | |
| 16. **(A)** The public procurement system promotes efficiency and effectiveness in the use of public resources, through clear rules that promote competition, transparency, and value for money. | C | The procurement system has unclear rules and weak enforcement. There have been numerous cases of suspected corruption in public procurement contracts. An interinstitutional commission is preparing a new legal framework. CONTRATANET has been used as an informational tool, but not yet as a transactional tool. |
| **Benchmarks met** | I | |

*Notes:* Bold = Benchmark met. A = Good, B = Fair, and C = Poor.
*Source:* ROSC and CFAA, and WB/IADB staff survey.

decided mostly as semiautomatic adjustments to the previous year's allocation and turn budgeting into a very rigid exercise; (c) bad incentives to overestimate revenues in the initial budget, so as to "armor" it before facing Congress's proposed reallocations that often are far from best budgetary practices; (d) absence of a results-oriented budget, shown in the lack of physical and financial indicators and, more generally; (e) absence of a multiyear budgeting framework (MYBF).

**A central problem in budget formulation is the sizable extent of off-budget resources, mainly earmarked revenues.** When off-budget resources are significant like in Ecuador, they make the size and financial situation of the government opaque, complicate Treasury management, and reduce budget transparency (Table 4.5). Budget fragmentation also weakens the government's capacity to prioritize policies and expenditures.

■ From a total of US$3.9 billion projected to be collected in taxes in 2004, about US$705 million, or 18 percent) are "preassigned" to different entities including local governments, the (*Fondo de Desarrollo Seccional*) (FODESEC), universities, the *Fondo*

## TABLE 4.4: RANKING OF ECUADOR'S PEM IN RELATION TO PERU, BOLIVIA, AND HIPC INDICATORS

| Indicator | Ecuador 2004 | Peru 2001 | Bolivia 2001 | HIPCs Average 2000/01 | Detailed HIPCs Distribution (24 countries, 2000/01) A | B | C |
|---|---|---|---|---|---|---|---|
| **Formulation** | | | | | | | |
| 1. Good coverage of general government | B | A | B | B | 8% | 67% | 25% |
| 2. Full reporting of extrabudgetary sources | C | B | A | A | 54% | 38% | 8% |
| 3. Reliable budget as programming tool | B | A | C | B | 0% | 67% | 33% |
| 4. Registered data on external financing | B | B | A | B | 42% | 54% | 4% |
| 5. Sound classification of transactions | C | B | C | B | 17% | 38% | 46% |
| 6. Tagging of poverty reducing spending | C | B | B | A | 46% | 38% | 17% |
| 7. Integration multiyear & annual budget | C | C | C | B | 17% | 46% | 38% |
| **Execution** | | | | | | | |
| 8. Timely reporting of payment arrears | B | A | B | A | 46% | 33% | 21% |
| 9. Good quality of internal control system | C | B | C | B | 13% | 71% | 17% |
| 10. Regular spending tracking surveys done | C | C | C | C | 8% | 46% | 46% |
| 11. Proper reconciliation of accounts | B | A | B | B | 38% | 38% | 25% |
| **Reporting** | | | | | | | |
| 12. Timely budget reporting | C | B | C | B | 8% | 71% | 21% |
| 13. Regular reporting of pro-poor spending | C | A | C | B | 23% | 54% | 23% |
| 14. Timely accounts recording and closure | B | A | A | B | 25% | 42% | 33% |
| 15. Timely audited accounts | C | A | C | C | 0% | 17% | 83% |
| **Procurement** | | | | | | | |
| 16. Efficient and effective procurement | C | na | na | na | na | na | na |

Note: A = Good, B = Fair, and C = Poor.

Source: World Bank/IADB (2003a); and response to WB/IMF survey.

*Salvamento Cultural*, the *Comisión de Transito de Guayas*, the *Centro de Rehabilitación de Manabi*, water companies, the *Corporación Aduanera Ecuatoriana* (CAE), and the *Servicio de Rentas Internas* (SRI).

▪ Off-budget resources from oil revenues are also sizable. From a total of US$2.1 billion projected to be collected in oil revenues, about US$855.5 million (or 40 percent) are "preassigned" to different entities—FEIREP, sectional governments, the army, and others.

▪ As part of oil revenues, PetroEcuador's off-budget resources are remarkable as well. While about 57 percent of Petroecuador's net oil surplus (revenues–expenditures) of US$2.7 billion is assigned to budgetary operations, the remaining 43 percent (US$1.2 billion) is assigned to off-budget activities, including about one-third (US$387 million) going to subsidies (cooking gas, power companies, and diesel), and the remainder to FEIREP and other earmarkings to institutions and regions.

▪ An overall total of about one-fifth of the total public resources (including off-budget activities) beyond the government's control—and earmarked (*preasignado*) resources— represents a major limitation on the government's ability to shift budgetary resources to pro-poor policy priorities, especially if Ecuador is committing to a poverty reduction strategy.[2]

### TABLE 4.5: SOURCES OF GOVERNMENT FINANCING, 2004
#### (in US Mlns, Percent of Total, Percent of GDP)

|  | 2004 Proforma | Percent Financing | Percent of GDP |
|---|---|---|---|
| Budgetary Sources | 7022.6 | 81.8 | 24.2 |
| Fiscal revenues | 4501.3 | 52.4 | 15.5 |
| Tax | 3243.6 | 37.8 | 11.2 |
| Petrol | 1257.7 | 14.7 | 4.3 |
| Autogestion* | 391.3 | 4.6 | 1.4 |
| External credit | 584.0 | 6.8 | 2.0 |
| Domestic credit | 1401.5 | 16.3 | 4.8 |
| Other | 144.4 | 1.7 | 0.5 |
| Local counterpart | 99.6 | 1.2 | 0.3 |
| Nonreimbursable (grants and technical assistance) | 44.8 | 0.5 | 0.2 |
| Off-Budget Sources | 1560.9 | 18.2 | 5.4 |
| Pre-budget earmarked non-oil tax revenues | 705.4 | 8.2 | 2.4 |
| Off-budget oil revenues | 855.5 | 10.0 | 3.0 |
| Pre-budget earmarked | 468.5 | 5.5 | 1.6 |
| o/w FEIREP | 292.1 | 3.4 | 1.0 |
| Subsidies (gas, diesel, electricity) | 387.0 | 4.5 | 1.3 |
| Total | 8583.5 | 100.0 | 29.6 |
| Total tax revenues | 3949.0 | 46.0 | 13.6 |
| Total oil surplus revenues | 2113.3 | 24.6 | 7.3 |

*Note:* *Self-generated revenues from fees, and other sources.
*Source:* Budget Office, MEF and Table A25.

---

2. An aggravating factor is that for earmarked taxes, increasing revenue collections automatically triggers additional spending resources to the earmarked entity, thereby diminishing added revenue to the Central Government from improved tax collection.

## TABLE 4.6: BUDGETARY ASSUMPTIONS AND ACTUAL VALUES

|  | 2002 | | 2003 | | 2004 |
|---|---|---|---|---|---|
|  | Assumption | Actual | Assumption | Actual | Assumption |
| GDP (US$ mln) | 19702 | 24311 | 27092 | 26913 | 29707 |
| GDP growth | 5.0% | 3.3% | 3.5–4% | 2.6% | 5–5.5% |
| Inflation year end | 8–10% | 9.4% | 6–8% | 6.1% | 4–5% |
| Current revenues (US$ mln) | 4239 | 4572 | 4503 | 4771 | 4429 |
| Crude oil price | 20.0 | 21.8 | 18.0 | 25.7 | 18.0 |
| Petroleum production (Mln barrels) | 157 | 143 | 152 | 152 | 192 |

*Source:* MEF, BCE, and IMF.

**Budget incrementalism has raised inertial expenditure to unsustainable levels.** Within the Central Government's budget—the *Presupuesto General del Estado* (PGE)—rigidity in the use of funds (besides earmarking) is also substantial, making an already tight fiscal situation run an unsustainable trend that is exhausting an already small fiscal space. Overall, in the total budget, about 83 percent is rigid, comprised of 32 percent for wages, 30 percent for debt service, and 18 percent for transfers (mainly for municipalities), and 3 percent for the *Bono de Desarrollo Humano* (see Chapter 3).

**Some overestimated budget assumptions prevail, although deviations have been declining.** These overestimations appear as contingencies to offset Congress's proposed modifications in the budget approval process. Congress has no capacity to modify the ceiling on total expenditure set by the *proforma* proposed by the Executive. However, it can modify its sector allocations arbitrarily, often with few technical criteria. To offset this, the Executive is tempted to overestimate its budgetary assumptions (Table 4.6), although deviations have been declining. This has not prevented Congress from approving a few budgetary malpractices. For instance, in the debate on the approval of the 2004 *proforma*, Congress arbitrarily reduced the amount of interest payments to make room for additional increases in other categories of current spending. This decision placed Ecuador in potential debt default, a very dangerous move for a country slowly rebuilding credibility with domestic economic agents, and its reputation in international markets. This move forced the Executive to readjust current spending in other areas, but ex post, only after Congress approved it.

### Execution

**The practice of using Emergency Decrees to modify the approved budget has also steadily increased.** Between 1998 and 2003, their annual number rose from 3 to 9 (Figure 4.2). Emergency Decrees have two important implications: (a) they overcome cumbersome procurement procedures, while opening room for eventual corruption in direct contract allocations; and (b) they modify budget priorities while shifting resources from the original budget, further reducing the already small fiscal space for social investment. Certainly, among the recent list of emergency decrees, in most cases there is a reasonable justification linked to a natural disaster, but this is not always the case: in recent years, a few budget modifications not linked to natural disasters have also occurred.[3] In the absence of a contingency budget reserve, as is typical in other LAC countries, these emergency situations should rather be considered as eligible for the use of FEIREP resources, as is now mandated by the FTRSL.

---

3. For example, in 2002, an emergency decree was issued during a period of public unrest that led to road closures and work stoppages in the construction of the new oil pipeline.

**FIGURE 4.2: EMERGENCY DECREES**

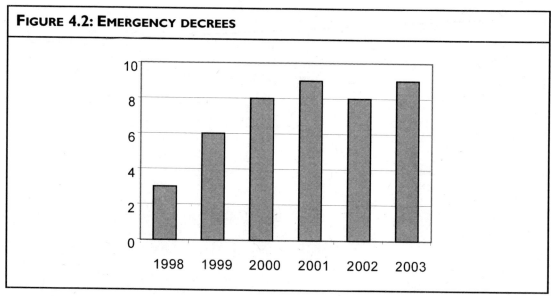

Source: MEF.

**Absence of a Results-Oriented Budget Framework.** The budget has an extremely simple format, and does not contain any fiscal ratio (IMF/ROSC 2003), or any physical or financial indicator. Lack of a medium-term expenditure framework that ties expenditure priorities to government policies also prevents the government from allocating resources in line with its long-term goals. This makes virtually impossible to shift resources between and within sectors in accordance with medium term goals, and plan capital investments that require multiyear commitments. Thus, decisions on budget trade-offs are not based on systematic analysis grounded in clearly articulated policy, and expenditures tend to be biased towards short duration projects or towards current spending.

**Whereas the reliability of the overall budget has improved in recent years, its decomposition shows big winners and losers.** In examining Ecuador's actual versus budgeted expenditures over the past seven years, several noteworthy features emerge (Table 4.7). First, the reliability of the budget has generally increased after dollarization, particularly in 2002, when actual expenditures accounted for 98 percent of budgeted expenditures. An average underspending of 6 percent during 2000–03 means a marked improvement compared to overspending of 12 percent of the budget during 1995–99. Second, although overspending dominates underspending over the whole period—5 out of 9 years—there is no persistent trend. Third, there is a considerable variance in the under/overspending by individual sectors, the overall trend showing fewer sectors with a greater than 15 percent deviation in 2003 compared to 1995 (10 compared to 16). Fourth, very disturbing, however, is the constant underspending in the social sectors—particularly in social welfare, which during 1995–2002, on average spent only half its budget. Other continuously underspending sectors include environment, labor, and tourism. Fifth, on the flip side, sectors with a general history of heavy overspending—some with an average of over 200 percent during 1995–2003—include administration, finance, energy, other general services and, particularly, defense.

**There is heterogeneity among sectors as to the relationship between their weight in the overall allocation of budget resources and the degree to which they exhibit over- or under-spending (Table 4.8).** For example, whereas executed spending in "Other General Services" averaged 300 percent higher than budgeted during 1995–2003, it accounted for only 0.2 percent of the executed budget, and therefore was not critical to the overall budget allocations. By

## TABLE 4.7: LEVEL OF BUDGET EXECUTION OF SECTOR EXPENDITURES, CENTRAL GOVERNMENT, 1995–2003[1]

| Sector | 1995 | 1996 | 1997 | 1998 | 1999 | 2000 | 2001 | 2002 | 2003 | 1995–2003 | 1995–99 | 2000–03 |
|---|---|---|---|---|---|---|---|---|---|---|---|---|
| Legislative | 1.69 | 1.11 | 0.98 | 0.89 | 1.43 | 0.95 | 0.92 | 1.06 | 0.98 | 1.11 | 1.22 | 0.98 |
| Judiciary | 1.37 | 1.23 | 1.08 | 1.09 | 1.02 | 0.66 | 1.28 | 1.12 | 0.88 | 1.08 | 1.16 | 0.99 |
| Administration | 3.47 | 4.34 | 2.25 | 1.47 | 0.53 | 1.92 | 1.31 | 2.05 | 1.57 | 2.10 | 2.41 | 1.71 |
| Planning | 0.59 | 0.56 | 0.60 | 0.86 | — | — | 1.50 | 0.77 | — | 0.65 | 0.65 | — |
| Environment | — | — | — | — | 0.31 | 0.24 | 1.50 | 0.77 | 0.45 | 0.65 | 0.31 | 0.74 |
| Interior | 1.81 | 1.63 | 1.48 | 1.02 | 0.96 | 0.85 | 0.90 | 0.99 | 0.86 | 1.17 | 1.38 | 0.90 |
| Defense | 1.37 | 1.14 | 1.29 | 1.24 | 1.00 | 1.06 | 1.11 | 0.90 | 1.19 | 1.15 | 1.21 | 1.07 |
| External Affairs | 1.14 | 1.06 | 1.01 | 1.13 | 2.37 | 1.02 | 0.95 | 0.44 | 0.55 | 1.08 | 1.35 | 0.74 |
| Finance and economic services | 2.08 | 3.04 | 1.50 | 5.81 | 1.20 | 5.06 | 1.23 | 1.14 | 0.79 | 2.43 | 2.73 | 2.06 |
| Social Sectors | 1.01 | 1.09 | 0.93 | 0.87 | 0.84 | 0.60 | 1.02 | 0.91 | 0.86 | 0.90 | 0.95 | 0.85 |
| o/w Education | 1.09 | 1.20 | 0.93 | 1.01 | 1.20 | 0.80 | 1.08 | 1.15 | 0.89 | 1.04 | 1.09 | 0.98 |
| Social Welfare | 0.56 | 0.76 | 0.64 | 0.28 | 0.30 | 0.22 | 0.68 | 0.35 | 0.84 | 0.51 | 0.51 | 0.52 |
| Health | 1.11 | 1.03 | 1.12 | 0.91 | 0.94 | 0.82 | 1.24 | 0.83 | 0.83 | 0.98 | 1.02 | 0.93 |
| Labor | 0.61 | 0.29 | 0.71 | 0.93 | 0.82 | 0.52 | 0.88 | 1.11 | 0.88 | 0.75 | 0.67 | 0.85 |
| Agriculture, Fishing & Livestock | 0.72 | 0.97 | 0.76 | 0.47 | 1.03 | 0.31 | 1.52 | 0.63 | 0.92 | 0.82 | 0.79 | 0.85 |
| Energy | 1.54 | 0.47 | 6.82 | 15.64 | 2.47 | 0.92 | 2.20 | 1.45 | 1.08 | 3.62 | 5.39 | 1.41 |
| Industry | 0.76 | 1.00 | 1.11 | 0.98 | 0.91 | 0.45 | 1.32 | 1.10 | 1.41 | 1.01 | 0.95 | 1.07 |
| Tourism | 0.48 | 0.31 | 1.11 | 0.75 | 0.11 | 0.16 | 0.70 | 0.91 | 0.62 | 0.57 | 0.55 | 0.60 |
| Transport & Communications | 0.68 | 1.04 | 1.41 | 0.83 | 1.39 | 0.52 | 0.61 | 0.60 | 1.21 | 0.92 | 1.07 | 0.73 |
| Housing & Urban Development | 1.11 | 0.51 | 0.47 | 1.23 | 0.21 | 0.95 | 2.61 | 0.31 | 0.93 | 0.93 | 0.71 | 1.20 |
| Other General Services[2] | 8.21 | 5.06 | 6.45 | 15.64 | 1.04 | 1.38 | 1.33 | 1.03 | 0.96 | 2.95 | 4.36 | 1.18 |
| Public Debt | 1.82 | 1.55 | 1.13 | 1.05 | 1.85 | 0.65 | 1.16 | 1.17 | 0.90 | 1.25 | 1.48 | 0.97 |
| Others[3] | 0.91 | 0.75 | 0.92 | 1.27 | 0.82 | 0.59 | — | — | 0.94 | 0.88 | 0.94 | 0.76 |
| **TOTAL** | **1.34** | **0.74** | **1.10** | **1.09** | **1.34** | **0.76** | **1.11** | **0.98** | **0.92** | **1.04** | **1.12** | **0.94** |

*Notes:*
[1] Ratio of executed "devengado"/initially approved (planned) budget per year. Shaded areas reflect over- or under-spending above 15 percent.
[2] Includes the Electoral Tribunal and the Constitutional Court.
[3] Includes transfers to subnational governments.

*Source:* Ministry of Finance.

## TABLE 4.8: CHANGES IN THE BUDGET SHARE BETWEEN EXECUTED AND APPROVED

| | 1995 | 1996 | 1997 | 1998 | 1999 | 2000 | 2001 | 2002 | Average 95–02 |
|---|---|---|---|---|---|---|---|---|---|
| Legislative | 0.1 | 0.4 | -0.1 | -0.2 | 0.0 | 0.1 | -0.1 | 0.0 | 0.0 |
| Judiciary | 0.0 | 0.9 | 0.0 | 0.0 | -0.3 | -0.1 | 0.1 | 0.2 | 0.1 |
| Administration | 1.4 | 3.4 | 0.8 | 0.2 | -0.5 | 0.5 | 0.1 | 0.3 | 0.8 |
| Planning | -0.2 | -0.1 | -0.2 | -0.1 | ... | ... | ... | ... | -0.1 |
| Environment | 0.0 | 0.0 | 0.0 | 0.0 | -0.2 | -0.1 | 0.1 | -0.1 | 0.0 |
| **Interior** | **1.8** | **6.8** | **1.7** | **-0.4** | **-1.4** | **0.4** | **-0.9** | **0.1** | **1.0** |
| **Defense** | **0.2** | **5.7** | **1.5** | **1.4** | **-2.4** | **2.3** | **0.0** | **-0.8** | **1.0** |
| External Affairs | -0.1 | 0.4 | -0.1 | 0.0 | 0.5 | 0.3 | -0.1 | -1.2 | 0.0 |
| **Finance** | **0.6** | **2.5** | **0.3** | **3.9** | **-1.0** | **12.2** | **0.4** | **0.5** | **2.4** |
| Education | -3.1 | 8.9 | -2.1 | -1.1 | -1.0 | 0.4 | -0.3 | 1.9 | 0.5 |
| **Social Welfare** | **-2.2** | **0.1** | **-1.0** | **-2.7** | **-5.8** | **-4.0** | **-1.5** | **-2.5** | **-2.4** |
| Labor | -0.2 | -0.6 | -0.1 | 0.0 | -0.1 | 0.0 | 0.0 | 0.0 | -0.1 |
| Health | -1.0 | 2.1 | 0.1 | -0.8 | -1.1 | 0.2 | 0.4 | -0.8 | -0.1 |
| **Agriculture** | **-3.2** | **1.8** | **-1.7** | **-2.5** | **-1.5** | **-1.7** | **1.2** | **-1.3** | **-1.1** |
| Power and Natural Resources | 0.0 | -0.5 | 1.3 | 3.7 | 0.4 | 0.0 | 0.1 | 0.1 | 0.7 |
| Industry | -0.1 | 0.1 | 0.0 | 0.0 | -0.1 | -0.1 | 0.0 | 0.0 | 0.0 |
| Tourism | -0.1 | -0.1 | 0.0 | 0.0 | -0.1 | 0.0 | -0.1 | 0.0 | 0.0 |
| **Transport and Communications** | **-4.0** | **2.4** | **0.9** | **-1.0** | **0.1** | **-1.3** | **-2.9** | **-2.5** | **-1.1** |
| Housing and Urban Development | -0.3 | -0.6 | -1.4 | 0.1 | -1.3 | 0.1 | 1.4 | -2.2 | -0.5 |
| Others General Services[1] | 0.5 | 0.8 | 0.3 | 0.0 | 0.0 | 0.1 | 0.0 | 0.0 | 0.2 |
| **Public Debt** | **11.0** | **37.3** | **1.3** | **-1.6** | **14.5** | **-7.7** | **2.2** | **8.1** | **8.1** |
| Others[2] | -1.4 | 0.1 | -0.9 | 1.2 | -3.3 | -1.6 | ... | ... | -1.0 |
| Memo: Social Sectors | -6.3 | 11.1 | -3.0 | -4.6 | -7.9 | -3.4 | -1.4 | -1.4 | -2.1 |

*Note:* Shares are estimated as a percentage of the total budget. Changes are the difference between the executed and approved shares per sectors. A negative amount reflects executed share that is lower than the approved share.

*Source:* Ministry of Finance

**FIGURE 4.3: STOCK OF ARREARS (US$ Mn)**

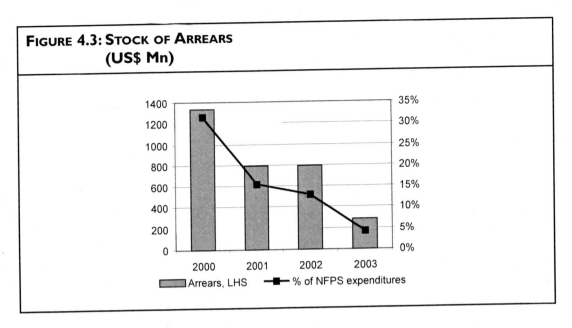

*Source:* MEF.

contrast, overspending greatly impacted the allocation of budget resources in Defense and Interior, which accounted for 2.0 percent of the budget; in Finance, which accounted for 2.4 percent of the budget; and on Public Debt, which accounted for 8.1 percent. The latter case reflects a weak technical capacity to properly budget for what are foreseeable expenditures. Overspending in these sectors was mainly compensated by underexecution in social welfare (2.4 percent of the budget), Transport and Communications (1.1 percent), and Agriculture (1.1 percent), that is, a significant underspending in critical social and infrastructure sectors, which appear more vulnerable to fiscal cuts.

**Budget cuts were made with inadequate information.** A shortcoming of the current SIGEF is the delayed recording of expenditures made by public institutions, making it very difficult for the Ministry of Economy and Finance (MEF) to consolidate executed expenditures with accuracy. In this way, while MEF is aware of the amount it transfers to institutions, reconciling its transferred amounts with actual spending can be delayed by several months, which in turn impacts the decision on how much Treasury should over- or under-assign to the executing line agency.

**Cash rationing is declining, but arrears still represent a recurrent problem in budget management.** Another direct consequence of poor budget execution management has been the occurrence of arrears. In Ecuador, these are particularly problematic, and the large size of arrears carried into the next fiscal calendar year weakens the execution of that year's budget allocation. Figure 4.3 illustrates the stock and size of the arrears relative to expenditures in the last four years. Less than 5 percent is the international benchmark; however, Ecuador substantially exceeded that amount in the previous three years. Problems also arise in defining arrears, which the government classifies as the difference between budgetary transfer requests and actual budgetary transfer payments, though the former may not reflect actual expenditures, thereby leading to a potential overestimation of arrears. Nor does the budgetary accounting system used provide the Central Government with timely information on the size and composition of the arrears. Accumulating arrears impacts the government's credibility and lead to disruptions in the delivery of goods and services.

## C. Budget Management Review in Social Programs and Subnational Governments

This section introduces an innovative approach to review budgeting—especially at the execution stage—in two key segments of Ecuador public sector: social programs and subnational governments. The Central Government has persistently under-executed both social programs and transfers to provincial and municipal governments. For instance, the combined cutbacks on approved expenditures for education, health, and social welfare were 16 percent during 2000–02, from an average of only 5 percent during 1995–1999. This section reviews the main reasons for this deteriorating budget underperformance within social sectors, particularly within those priority social programs (PSPs) considered of utmost importance by the Government of Ecuador (GOE). The next section deals with subnational governments. Following an overview of the institutional arrangements underpinning the provision of social service, the budget process within social programs is reviewed in detail, using a spending tracking methodology focused on time execution delays, rather than on resource flows. Taking into account the multiplicity of social programs, out of a sample of the 45 existing programs, a sample of five PSPs was selected according to size, targeting, and sources of financing. The sample includes: the *Bono de Desarrollo Humano* (BDH), *Plan Ampliado de Inmunizaciones* (PAI), *Ley de Maternidad Gratuita y Atención a la Infancia* (LMG), *Programa de Asistencia y Desarrollo Comunitario* (PRADEC), and *Programa de Alimentación Escolar* (PAE). Results are revealing.

Work on reviewing budgeting procedures in line agencies is in the pioneer stage worldwide. It builds upon seminal work developed in LAC in the nineties, particularly on institutional reviews and staff tracking surveys for Honduras (The World Bank, 1997 and 2001) and, more recently, on public expenditure tracking surveys for Peru (The World Bank and IDB, 2003). The surveys in Honduras were able to identify the main constraints to personnel management and the relationship between trends in budgetary assignments and unobserved in health and education outcomes, especially because either resources never reached the programs in whose names they were consigned or inefficient service delivery arrangements prevailed. Those from Peru were able to identify shortcomings in the transfer of resources, and quantify leakages at each ladder of the chain of the delivery of resources until the final beneficiary. Instead, the Ecuador budgeting review focus on quantifying perceived delays in the transfer of resources and institutional shortcomings at the level of social programs and subnational governments that explain, to a significant extent, observed budget underexecution.

The tracking methodology employed has some limitations and its limited focus has some pros and cons. On the pros, it identifies major bottlenecks in expenditure execution, while showing systemic problems (either at the level of Treasury or the line ministries) that are in need of reform. On the cons, the limited scope—five social programs—does not negate its contribution, but also raises further few questions that would require additional work. For instance: how did the multiplicity of programs come into being and did the donors have to do with it? what are the social ministries' capacities for budget management—especially at the Ministry of Social Welfare that shows a significant under-execution capacity? and do these programs have performance indicators, if any? So, it must be beard in mind that to fully understand some of the key issues that are identified in this review would have required a complementary study at the sectoral level that was beyond the scope of this PER.

### Social Programs

The institutional organization of social programs is very simple, and involves increasing local participation. It consists of (a) the management structure—within the social ministry and/or local agency administering it; (b) the service intermediary, generally the ministerial *Dirección Nacional* or *Provincial*; and (c) the service provider.

**TABLE 4.9: FORMS OF LOCAL PARTICIPATION WITHIN SELECTED PRIORITY SOCIAL PROGRAMS**

| Program | Local Participation |
|---|---|
| Bono de Desarrollo Humano (BDH) | n/a |
| Programa Ampliado de Inmunizaciones (PAI) | 76 comites cantonales promoting vaccination programs, and 176 municipios participating in the provision of services |
| Programa de Maternidad Gratuita (LMG) | 40 out of 220 municipios participating in the provision and supervision of services |
| Programa de Asistencia y Desarrollo Comunitario (PRADEC) | 443 out of 786 juntas parroquiales participating in the provision and supervision of services |
| Programa de AlimentaciXC59,1n Escolar (PAE) | n/a |

Note: n/a = Not available.

Source:

■ The management in each social program consists of a technical administrator, a planning committee (the *Comité de Gestión*), and a supervisory committee (the *Comité de Vigilancia*). The *technical administrator* is the social program's executing entity, and has main responsibility for its direction. The *planning committee* is composed of representatives of the social ministry and local organizations who design the scope of the program and make arrangements about the technical role of all players participating in the program, including setting up activities. The *supervisory committee* is also composed of representatives of the government and local constituencies to ensure that the program is adequately executed and in conformity with the technical and budget planning.

■ The *treasury function* is part of the management structure, and is carried out by the ministry hosting the social program. It executes any financing arrangement agreed between the program and MEF, autonomous agencies, or other entities. In general, budgetary resources of the social program for either the current operational expenses or capital investment are transferred by MEF to the social ministry, which acts through its intermediary agencies to finally reach the service provider. Diverse forms of local participation have recently developed, but these are rather exceptions (Table 4.9).

■ Service providers are institutions that serve local communities. They are either a school or a health unit in a local community, paid either through the intermediary social ministry or directly by MEF. PAI, for instance, has hospitals and other health centers devoted to the vaccination of infants and children to prevent tropical diseases. For its part, PAE has a significant degree of local communities' participation. It delivers food to the education units, and mothers' committees prepare breakfast and lunch for children. Monetary contributions are also frequent. Others, like PRADEC, manage food supplementary activities through *comedores comunitarios*, meeting the needs of children and elderly populations in the poorest areas.

**Priority social programs have grown increasingly fragmented and disorganized.** The number and volume of PSPs has almost tripled to 45 in 2004, from 17 in 2001, and their approved budgetary resources have climbed to US$398 million (1.3 percent of GDP) in 2004, from US$62 million (0.3 percent of GDP) in 2001. In particular, the budget for PSPs in the social welfare and health sectors skyrocketed to 10 times its 2001 level. Their creation reflects the GOE's response to political and social pressures and reverse poor household income losses that resulted from the economic crises and the transition to full dollarization. They address the needs of the poorest and most vulnerable groups, including women, school children, disabled and elderly people, and indigenous groups. However, this effort has not been supported by sound

**TABLE 4.10: BUDGET OF PRIORITY SOCIAL PROGRAMS GROUPED BY SOCIAL SECTOR, 2001 AND 2004**

| Sector | 2001 | | | 2004 | | |
|---|---|---|---|---|---|---|
| | Number of Programs | Budget | | Number of Programs | Budget | |
| | | US$Mn | % | | US$Mn | % |
| Education | 6 | 27.6 | 44.7 | 8 | 49.9 | 12.5 |
| Social welfare | 5 | 23.0 | 37.3 | 14 | 279.5 | 70.3 |
| Health | 2 | 4.4 | 7.2 | 10 | 37.5 | 9.4 |
| Housing and urban development | 4 | 6.7 | 10.8 | 8 | 30.0 | 7.5 |
| Labor | 0 | 0.0 | 0.0 | 5 | 1.0 | 0.2 |
| Total | 17 | 61.7 | 100.0 | 45 | 397.8 | 100.0 |

Source: STFS.

budgetary practices. Consequently, the existence of too many social programs translates into too many overlapping administrations to control, less-efficient service delivery, diversity of financing arrangements, and discretionary government intervention (Table 4.10).[4]

**Overall, budget formulation in the PSPs suffers from the same discretionary and unreported amendments made to budget approval ex post.** The major problems, however, are located at the stage of budget execution, and budget evaluation and control, due to inadequate cash management, budget reporting, and limited technological resources and trained personnel in line agencies.

**Discretionary government intervention reduces the budget initially approved for social programs, especially for those depending on the Ministry of Social Welfare.** Their budgets are formulated in conformity with a preestablished timeline, accounting and classification procedures, and within overall expenditure ceilings. Once approved, there is no transparent timely reporting of changes in the amended budget (*codificado*) throughout the year. Thus, cash constraints originating from reduced tax collection drive MEF to amend its budget without discussing it at a technical or local level with the program managers. It turns out that not only programs, but ministries, frequently do not have the most updated version of their budget. Therefore, changes in the budget are unknown, which prevents decisionmakers and stakeholders from knowing *ex ante* and *ex post* how public funds are actually reassigned in agreement with government priorities. As a result, in 2003, all PSPs had an average 11 percent reduction in their budget, but those grouped under the Ministries of Education or Social Welfare—particularly PAE, BDH, and PRADEC—suffered major cutbacks—close or above 20 percent—of their initial budget (Table 4.11).

**Other relevant problems are found in other aspects of budget execution.** Indeed, bureaucratic hurdles and delays in the transfer of resources contribute to program execution falling behind schedule (Figure 4.4).

---

4. The cluster of programs grouped as "Aid to Rural and Indigenous Households" is the one with the largest number of social programs, totaling twenty-one. This cluster provides 6 different services to mainly rural and indigenous women, including a conditional cash transfer for consumption (BDH), a credit for productive activities (*Credito Productivo Solidario*), eight low-cost housing programs including the *Vivienda Bono Solidario*, four labor development and training programs, and three primary health programs including a mobile station service, all managed through four different ministries. The next-largest cluster is the one for "Child and Infant Support," with ten programs or activities embodying four food security and nutrition programs (PAE, PANN, PRADEC, and Micronutrientes), five shelter and development programs (*Direccion de Proteccion de Menores*, FONDEJU, *Nuestros Niños*, ORI, and *Erradicacion del Trabajo Infantil*), and 1 primary care program (*Cuidado Materno Infantil*), all dispersed in four ministries as well.

## TABLE 4.11: BUDGET APPROVED AND EXECUTED FOR PRIORITY SOCIAL PROGRAMS, 2003

### (in millions of US dollars, except where otherwise noted)

| Sector/Program | Approved | | | Executed | |
| --- | --- | --- | --- | --- | --- |
| | Initial Budget (Pro Forma) | Revised (Codificado) | % Change (over initial) | Devengado | % Change (over initial) |
| **Ministry of Economy and Finance** | | | | | |
| Bono de Desarrollo Humano[1] | 203.1 | 164.6 | −19 | 161.8 | 80 |
| **Ministry of Social Welfare** | | | | | |
| PRADEC | 12.2 | 10.0 | −18 | 7.0 | 57 |
| **Ministry of Health** | | | | | |
| PANN 2000 | 5.7 | 5.7 | −1 | 5.7 | 99 |
| PAI | 10.0 | 9.0 | −10 | 9.1 | 91 |
| Ley de Maternidad Gratuita | 19.9 | 25.5 | 28 | 23.9 | 120 |
| **Ministry of Education** | | | | | |
| PAE | 30.7 | 17.0 | −45 | 14.2 | 46 |
| Investment expenditure[2] | 90.8 | 98.4 | 8 | 26.0 | 29 |
| **Total** | **372.4** | **330.2** | **−11** | **247.7** | **66** |

Notes:
[1] Includes *Beca Escolar*. It will be transferred to MSW in 2005.
[2] Includes *Secretaria Nacional de Deportes*.

*Source:* Shepherd (2004).

**Bureaucratic hurdles include an excessive and duplicative number of required documents.** Three documents are required for budget execution: (a) a monthly *Programación Periódica de Caja* (PPC) form to MEF requesting Treasury to establish a cash commitment up to the amount indicated therein; (b) an electronic entry of progress indicators updating the database system (SIGOB); and (c) a *Liquidación de Gastos* or *Resultados Económicos* spreadsheet of the social programs submitted to the Budget, Public Investment, and Accounting Departments in MEF. There is room for elimination of eventual duplications among these requirements, to counteract the strong complaint that these hurdles are deliberately set to delay transfers of resources.

**Cash rationing induces multiple budgetary malpractices.** These include:

▓ **The lack of knowledge about any technical criteria that the Budget or Treasury Offices apply to approve—partially or in full—or disapprove a PPC.** The rationale for cutting the planned budget follows directives of fiscal discipline, as MEF adjusts expenditures to the amount of actual revenues collected during the year. But apart from such a general directive, there is little knowledge about what specific criteria are actually considered to reallocate resources. The lack of a Cash Committee, made up at least of representatives of Treasury, Budget, Public Credit, and Economic Policy only makes this matter worse.

▓ **The proliferation of informal financing arrangements to avoid major disruptions in program operations.** This includes the use of off-budget funds—through autonomous agencies or donor resources—that often are not registered or are registered late in the initially approved budget. For example, in 2003, the PAI raised about one-third of its additional budget through resources not reported in the pro forma, which were donated by the Government of Luxembourg and multinational private firms (Shepherd 2004).

▓ **An ineffective intermediation of ministries in channelling resources, resulting in delays or leaks.** Once MEF transferred resources to ministries, e.g. MED or MSW, often

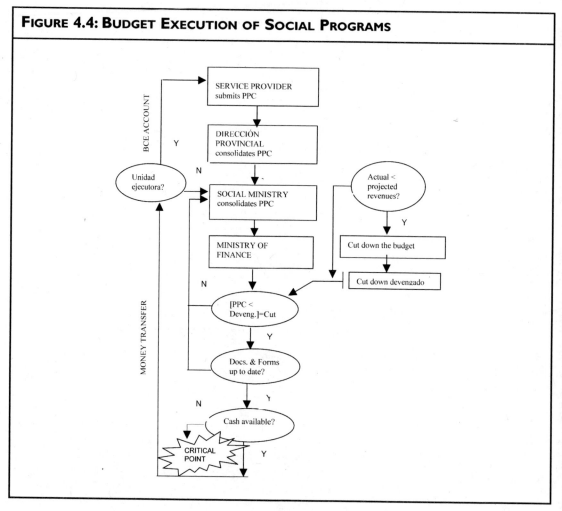

**FIGURE 4.4: BUDGET EXECUTION OF SOCIAL PROGRAMS**

Source: MEF.

these ministries held funds in their accounts before actually delivering them to the decentralized executing units, programs or service providers (Annex C). Not surprisingly, the one PSP—the Free Maternity Program (LMG)—that has an appointed Executing Unit (EUs) was the most successful in terms of budget execution in 2003. This is due to the fact that it is ruled with autonomy, has its own special account and received non budgeted exceptional financing from the Solidarity Fund.

▪ **Missclassification of PSP spending as between current and capital spending is common.** No clear-cut criteria are defined. For instance, the classification of expenditure assigned to the BDH as a current transfer is questionable, because this operation could also be conceived to be a temporary capital investment that produces a return of an increased number of children attending schools, particularly in the poorest areas. Bear in mind, however, that these expenditure classification problems are endemic and appear in most social (and cash transfer) programs worldwide.

**Institutional hurdles and budgetary malpractices are the main reasons for budget underexecution of priority social programs.** Budget protection had a mixed performance in 2003. All PSPs, except the LMG, underexecuted their approved budget, but the level of under-

## TABLE 4.12: BUDGET EXECUTION AND TRANSACTIONAL DELAYS WITHIN PSPs, 2003

|  | BDH | PAI | LMG | PRADEC | PAE | Average |
|---|---|---|---|---|---|---|
| 2003 Initial Budget (in US$ millions) | 203.1 | 10.0 | 19.9 | 12.2 | 30.7 | |
| Revised budget (in percent)[1] | 81% | 90% | 128% | 82% | 55% | 87% |
| Budget execution, *devengado* (in percent)[1] | 80% | 91% | 120% | 57% | 46% | 79% |
| Transaction delay (days in average) | | | | | | |
| Intermediary being reimbursed at least 50%[2] | 78 | 63 | 32 | 43 | 47 | 53 |
| Intermediary being reimbursed in full[2] | 93 | 74 | 65 | 62 | 62 | 71 |
| Service provider being paid in full[3] | 30 | 92 | 73 | 73 | 85 | 71 |
| Program administration services (overhead) paid | ... | ... | 65 | 102 | 135 | 107 |
| Purchasing order processed[4] | ... | 62 | ... | 47 | 112 | 74 |
| Purchases being reimbursed[5] | ... | 134 | ... | 113 | 172 | 140 |

Notes:
[1] In percent of the initial budget approved by Congress.
[2] Funds actually transferred by MEF to the intermediary (PPC *Aprobado y Recibido*), in percent of the initial.
[3] Funds actually transferred to the service provider (PPC *Aprobado y Recibido*).
[4] Includes the time since the order was processed up to Customs clearance that takes 35 days. Purchases ordered twice a year.
[5] Refers to international cooperation agencies contracting with suppliers and then getting reimbursed by Treasury.
*Sources:* Ministry of Finance; and social programs estimates.

execution, however, was significant—below 80 percent—only in three out of six selected programs (Table 4.12).

A simple tracking survey of transactional steps in the channelling of resources managed by the PSPs reveals that delays are significant, and that programs with the worst budget performance are, not surprisingly, those with most significant disbursement delays. This innovative survey, based essentially on interviews and records collection, tracks not only processing delays in payments—especially by MEF—to intermediaries and service providers, but also processing and reimbursement of purchasing orders by social ministries and all five PSPs in 2003 (Table 4.12). Even though this analysis has a limitation, for it is very difficult to discriminate exactly on who is responsible for each type of delay—MEF or the executing ministry/agency—it provides insights and sets a baseline performance benchmark for each procedure analyzed. The main survey results for 2003 are worth highlighting:

- **On average, an intermediary—ministry or agency—got fully reimbursed by MEF after more than two months.** There were cases, such as the BDH, whose reimbursements took more than three months. On the other extreme, the LMG takes only one month.
- **In a similar vein, the payment of overhead fees for program administration—frequently incurred by donors—took on average more than three months.** It could go to four months in the case of the BDH. Moreover, purchase orders took an average of more than two months just to be processed, and more than four months to be fully reimbursed.
- **The more effective PSP was the LMG, in part due to the existence of an Executing Unit, and to support from international cooperation agencies in the latter.** Other programs, like PRADEC, signed a technical cooperation with the UN World Food Program (WFP) that has provided not only advanced financing, but also a transfer of technology and training in an entrepreneurial-like management environment. Similar arrangements with the WFP and UNDP are in place regarding the PAE, and also with

---

**FIGURE 4.5: SEASONAL PATTERNS IN BUDGET FOR SOCIAL PROGRAMS, 2003 (Flows, US$mn)**

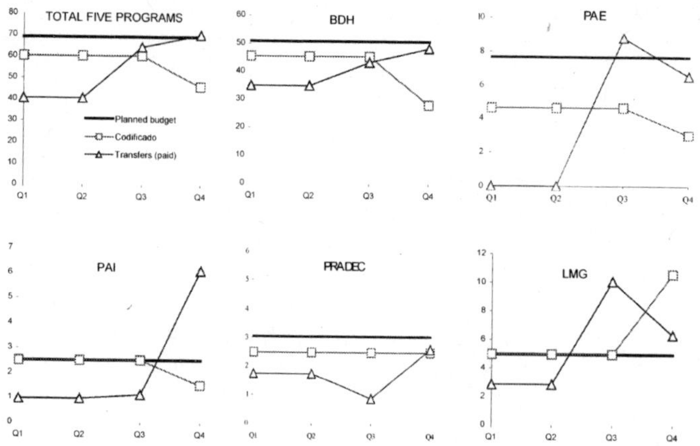

*Source:* Secretaría Técnica del Frente Social.

PAHO in regard to the PAI, but transactional delays remained very high for both paying overhead administrative services and reimbursing purchase orders.

**The same tracking survey found a strong seasonality in budget execution for the five PSPs.** In aggregate terms, data show the following:

■ In 2003, the amount of cutbacks in the approved budget were constant until the third quarter, but deepened in the last quarter. Data for all five programs show that the modified (*codificado*) budget for PSPs was reduced drastically in the last quarter (Figure 4.5).

■ Evidence suggests that MEF held back its transfers to the PSPs in the first half of the year—an average reduction of US$30million (43 percent) per quarter, but then went on to comply with the committed average level of US$70 million. This suggests that cash rationing was the real budget constraint.

■ In individual terms, it is clear that BDH, PAE, and PAI show a common trend in their modified budget, whereas wide diversity is found in actual transfers.

■ Among all five programs, PAE was clearly the program most severely affected because it received no budget resources in the first half of the year. However, it recovered its level of budget execution in the third quarter and peaked in the last quarter, reaching about 100 percent of committed resources for the year.

Finally, it would have been interesting to explore whether these trends—individual or aggregate—reflect a seasonal pattern in tax collection, but no complete data were obtained from Treasury to explore this question.

### Provincial and Municipal Governments

**Perhaps the most outstanding shortcoming of budget formulation by sub-national governments is the unrealistic projection of the level and timeliness of Central Government transfers.** This is largely due to the particularities of the management of inter-governmental transfers in Ecuador. Although the 15-Percent Law is formally a revenue-sharing arrangement, which

**FIGURE 4.6: PLANNED COMPARED TO EXECUTED TRANSFERS OF THE 15-PERCENT LAW, 1997-2003**

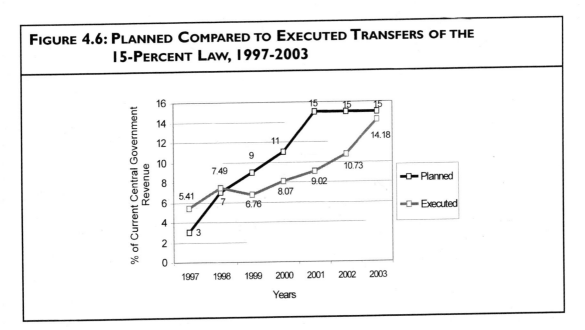

*Source:* Frank (2004).

mandates that resources are transferred to local levels based on revenue availability, actual budgetary practices differ from this norm. In theory, in January of each fiscal year, the MEF commits itself to a certain level of transfers, formalized in *Acuerdos Ministeriales*, which lists both the revenue sources and the amounts to be transferred. Local governments then take these *Acuerdos* as a reference for their own budget formulation. However, in practice, despite a significant improvement in 2003, the amount of total revenue transferred deviated substantially from the amount planned for many years back (Figure 4.6).[5] Under the current system, intrayear budget adjustments are frequent, and local budgeting, especially for subnational governments heavily dependent on transfers, becomes a cash-strapping, year-long, continuous exercise, perversely affecting their budget execution.

**Budget formulation at the local level replicates similar deficiencies at the central level.** Most municipalities and provincial councils do not align their spending priorities with those from the national level, have no strategic plan, and have no incentives for allocative and productive efficiency. Emphasis is placed more on budget recording than on reporting and planning. Most of them consider budget formulation a routine exercise that provides little value added for effective government.

■ **Since 2000, most municipalities and provincial councils formulate their budgets in isolation from national strategic directives**, either because there was no legal requirement to do so[6]; because of lack of knowledge of national objectives; or because of the inability of central institutions to formulate national objectives, communicate them, and build consensus.

---

5. This is a general disadvantage of revenue-sharing arrangements, not attributable to the particular circumstances in Ecuador. It is therefore highly unrealistic to introduce multiyear subnational budgets as mandated by the Fiscal Law (Art. 20). Even the mandatory quarterly budgetary projections are difficult to achieve (Art. 34).

6. The Fiscal Law, adopted in 2002, expressly exempts municipalities and provincial councils from sending their operational plans to the MEF (Art. 2, LRF).

▨ **As far as sub-national governments are concerned, the Fiscal Law (FTSRL) provides a weak framework for fiscal discipline.** For instance, the Law establishes limits for yearly budget growth,[7] but subnational governments are excluded from it. Therefore, the only formal budget constraint on municipalities and provincial councils is the maximum allowed level of indebtedness, which itself is problematic.[8] Because their maximum level of debt is measured against *current* revenue, and this includes intergovernmental grants, its implications are obvious: subnational governments achieve higher debt ceilings if they obtain a higher level of transfers. LAC experience has shown that this rule can result in an unsustainable debt path.[9]

▨ **Budget formulation is not used as a means of raising allocative efficiency and matching public services with the priorities of citizens.** Moreover, participatory budgeting is rarely performed, and only a few public entities, mostly municipalities, engage communities regularly. An outstanding exception is the Cuenca municipality, where the rural *Juntas Parroquiales*—elected nationwide since 1998—are formally involved in the yearly budget exercise. In addition, a minor share of its municipal budget is now directly executed by this social committee.[10]

▨ **Future expenditures are projected based on past levels**, which replicates inefficiencies and rigidities of central management. No incentives are given to local politicians to find creative solutions in terms of costing exercises for improving their budget efficiency.[11]

**Budget execution is affected by arrears in transfers, not only on a yearly, but on a monthly basis.** In contrast to other LAC countries—Bolivia and Colombia, for example—that apply revenue-sharing arrangements, payments to subnational government in Ecuador are not made on a daily basis, but on an irregular basis: each month there can be several payments, only a single payment, or none at all. Consequently, the amount of transfer payments is very volatile. In 2003, for instance, transfers remained relatively low until the middle of the year, but in the second half, MEF scaled up the amounts in order to meet the agreed yearly target (Figure 4.7). Similar seasonal trends can be observed in 2001 and 2002 (Frank 2004). Oil revenue volatility accounts for most of transfer volatility. When oil is excluded from the revenue base that is used to distribute the 15-Percent Law, the volatility of funds appears lower, and the flow of funds much smoother (Frank 2004). The volatility of transfers undermines the ability of municipalities and provincial councils to cover the cost of services that are used regularly. It also impedes efficient delivery of local services in the water, sewerage, and road sectors, and often leads to interruptions in service provision.

**Since 2003, however, MEF has strictly complied in keeping monthly transfers stable, but this has increased rationing in a cash-strapped Treasury.** Transfer volatility does not necessarily affect the monthly amount of total transfers made to subnational governments. However,

---

7. 3.5 percent in real terms (Art. 3).

8. A debt stock relative to current revenue 100 percent; debt service lower than 40 percent of current revenue (Art. 7, LRF).

9. Bolivia is probably the clearest example. After 1999, nine, mostly large municipalities—among them La Paz, Cochabamba, and Santa Cruz—went bankrupt. A rescheduling of debt showed its positive effect in local government returning to solvency a few years later.

10. Other examples of participatory budgeting include the Guamote municipality in Chimborazo province, and the Cotacachi municipality in Imbabura province, both of which have a high share of indigenous population residing in the local jurisdiction.

11. Some advances for costing have been made in the education sector and the Ministry of Education (MEC). With *Cooperación Técnica Alemana* (GTZ) assistance, a costing methodology has been developed where transfers would take into account the number of students attending a particular school.

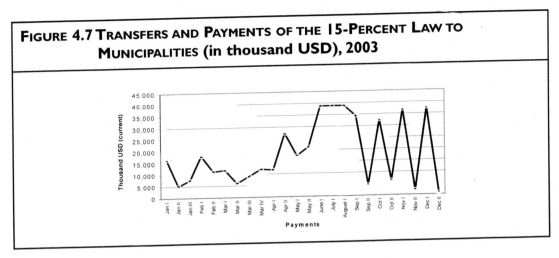

**FIGURE 4.7 TRANSFERS AND PAYMENTS OF THE 15-PERCENT LAW TO MUNICIPALITIES (in thousand USD), 2003**

*Source:* Frank (2004), based on information provided by MEF.

instead of letting transfers fluctuate according to actual revenue obtained each month (or each day), MEF has predetermined (and complied with) its own schedule of transfers, but at the cost of sacrificing other financing priority needs of the Central Government (Figure 4.8)[12]. Therefore, a new subnational spending "cycle" has emerged, featuring "savings" by the National Treasury when actual monthly revenue has exceeded the level of transfers; or "borrowing," when the reverse occurs, that is, when there is a shortfall of revenue. In the former, MEF has used the uncommitted part of funds to finance expenditures in sectors, other than the subnational governments. Unfortunately, these "savings" have become contingent liabilities of the Central Government that are later claimed by mayors and prefects.

**Budget control and monitoring in subnational governments remain weak and cumbersome.** Both municipalities and provincial councils conduct their own internal auditing. In addition, there is external monitoring from the Comptroller General, which has the formal powers to

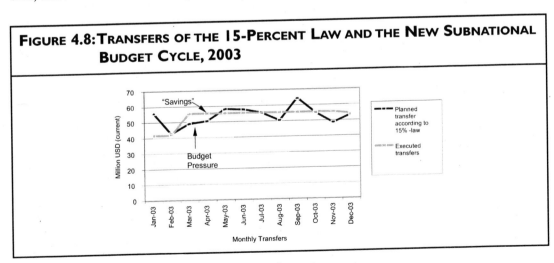

**FIGURE 4.8: TRANSFERS OF THE 15-PERCENT LAW AND THE NEW SUBNATIONAL BUDGET CYCLE, 2003**

*Note:* Monthly transfers that are displayed may consist of several payments.
*Source:* Frank (2004), based on information provided by MEF (2004).

---

12. The fact that the Ministry of Economy and Finance is now, since January 2004, planning the level of transfers based on the quarterly average will not substantially improve this situation.

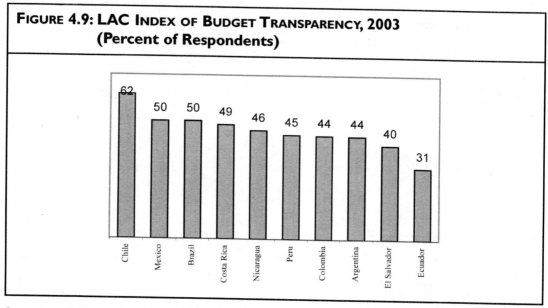

**FIGURE 4.9: LAC INDEX OF BUDGET TRANSPARENCY, 2003 (Percent of Respondents)**

*Source:* Latin American Index of Budgetary Transparency (2003).

initiate administrative sanctions. Annually, roughly 150 municipalities are found in conflict with administrative rules and regulations. The majority of subnational governments are able to justify legal behavior ex post, but a minority of administrations—roughly 20 a year, or 10 percent of the total of 220—is subject to judicial procedures. Much weaker is budgetary oversight and monitoring by citizens and users.

Reporting on local budgets remains poor. Only since 2003, has the Central Government made an effort to improve the information flow among levels of government. Reports on executed municipal and provincial budgets are now required by MEF before the end of March of every year, but a considerable number of local administrations still send incomplete information, or simply disregard this rule entirely. Although there are no official data on compliance, roughly 20 percent of municipalities and provincial councils still do not send their executed budget back to MEF: as of April 2004, about 177 of the 220 municipalities had reported their 2003 executed budget.

## D. Budget Transparency, Accountability, and Participation

Ecuador has the lowest LAC regional ranking in budget transparency. In a 2003 regional survey of budget transparency, Ecuador ranked last among 10 Latin American countries, with only about a third of respondents saying budget policy was transparent in Ecuador (Figure 4.9 and Table 4.13).

- In the survey, positive responses fluctuated between 0 and 36 percent. The variables with the highest percentages of positive responses were: information on macroeconomic criteria (36 percent), time given to the Legislature for analysis of the national budget (42 percent), and quality of information and statistics (24 percent). However, these values were below the average of the selected group of LAC countries.

- Areas with dramatically low positive responses were the evaluation of the internal comptroller (0 percent), budgets developed on a National Development Plan (0 percent), reported budget execution information that allows its monitoring (0 percent), information on public servants' salaries and benefits (0 percent), and timeliness of budget information being made public during the execution and auditing phases (0 percent).

## TABLE 4.13: POSITIVE QUALIFICATIONS PER COUNTRY
(as percentages of positive responses)

| Attribute | Brazil | Colombia | Chile | Ecuador | Peru |
|---|---|---|---|---|---|
| **A. Citizenship Participation in the Budget Process** | 20 | 15 | 14 | 3 | 7 |
| Mechanisms exist that incorporate civil opinion during the approval phase of the budget process. | 11 | 5 | 4 | 3 | 4 |
| **B. Legislative Attributes and its Participation on the Budget Process** | 49 | 40 | 39 | 26 | 35 |
| Time given to the Legislative Branch for analysis and discussion of the federal budget is enough. | 50 | 46 | 63 | 42 | 41 |
| There is an extensive debate in the Legislative Branch over the Executive proposal of the budget. | 31 | 29 | 31 | 22 | 15 |
| **C. Macroeconomic Criteria** | 53 | 43 | 76 | 36 | 58 |
| The Executive Power publishes the macroeconomic assumptions on which the budget proposal is planned. | 67 | 65 | 88 | 54 | 88 |
| Income projections are reliable. | 40 | 21 | 65 | 18 | 27 |
| **D. Budget Allocation** | 39 | 31 | 44 | 14 | 14 |
| Budget allocation is basically inertial, that is, it is based on previous allocations. | 24 | 20 | 16 | 19 | 6 |
| Annual budgets are formulated on the basis of policies established in the National Development Plan. | 54 | 39 | 41 | 0 | 10 |
| **E. Budget Adjustments** | 35 | 37 | 20 | 12 | 30 |
| **F. Budget Supervising** | 37 | 40 | 48 | 4 | 18 |
| The resources exercised by government-owned enterprises are properly supervised. | 37 | 54 | 45 | 3 | 24 |
| The resources exercised by decentralized organizations are properly supervised. | 42 | 50 | 33 | 10 | 24 |
| **G. Institutional Powers of the External Comptroller** | 42 | 40 | 48 | 13 | 12 |
| The external comptroller verifies that the Executive complies with the programmatic and non-financial objectives of the budget. | 33 | 31 | 29 | 2 | 9 |
| The external comptroller has the capacity to efficiently supervise federal spending. | 50 | 55 | 43 | 33 | 22 |
| **H. Evaluation of the Internal Comptroller** | 33 | 4 | 33 | 0 | 6 |
| **I. Accountability** | 33 | 24 | 39 | 10 | 14 |
| The federal Executive Branch periodically publishes information that informs about the progressive accomplishment on its programs goals. | 26 | 13 | 29 | 0 | 10 |
| The reports of the execution of the budget have disaggregated information of all of the decentralized organizations and government-owned enterprise expenditures. | 17 | 14 | 14 | 2 | 7 |

(continued)

## TABLE 4.13: POSITIVE QUALIFICATIONS PER COUNTRY (CONTINUED)
### (as percentages of positive responses)

| Attribute | Brazil | Colombia | Chile | Ecuador | Peru |
|---|---|---|---|---|---|
| **J. Supervision of Federal Officials** | **36** | **36** | **35** | **11** | **18** |
| It is possible to know with certainty the salaries of federal officials. | 42 | 61 | 39 | 13 | 15 |
| Information on federal officials' benefits, such as bonuses, medical insurance, use of autos, is public. | 22 | 38 | 18 | 0 | 9 |
| An official misusing the budget for his or her own benefit or the benefit of others is penalized. | 32 | 34 | 53 | 8 | 19 |
| **K. Information Regarding Federal Debt** | **31** | **32** | **49** | **15** | **30** |
| When federal debt is contracted, its destination is made public. | 25 | 27 | 39 | 8 | 25 |
| **L. Quality of the Information and Statistics** | **42** | **35** | **61** | **24** | **25** |
| **M. Responsibilities from Different Levels of the Government** | **35** | **34** | **49** | **14** | **14** |
| **N. Timeliness of Budget Information** | **33** | **23** | **35** | **10** | **16** |
| Timeliness that budget information is made public during the execution phase. | 26 | 15 | 39 | 0 | 26 |
| Timeliness that budget information is made public during the oversight–supervision/auditing phase. | 24 | 18 | 16 | 0 | 4 |

*Source:* Latin American Index of Budgetary Transparency (2003).

▓ In between these extreme ratings, low ratings were also received on proper verification of non-financial objectives of the budget by the Comptroller (2 percent), proper supervision of resources managed by public enterprises (3 percent), citizen participation in the budget process (3 percent), and budget oversight by civil society (4 percent). This reflects that despite recent efforts developed by the Fiscal Policy Observatory and other civil society organizations, there is still a scarcity of effective institutional mechanisms (and tools) to incorporate social auditing and accountability norms into the budget process.

## E. Are There Sufficient Conditions for a Multiyear Budgeting Framework in Ecuador?

**A well designed Multiyear Budgeting Framework (MYBF) should lie at the core of government efforts to build a poverty reduction strategy and Ecuador's commitment to meeting the Millennium Development Goals.** The MYBF is the core instrument available to articulate the country's poverty reduction strategic spending priorities within the projected and sustainable fiscal resources envelope. It has three objectives: improved macroeconomic performance, especially fiscal discipline; better inter- and intra-sectoral resource allocation; and more efficient use of public resources. Complementary objectives are greater budgetary predictability for line ministries, increased political accountability for public expenditure outcomes through more legitimate decision making processes, and greater credibility of budgetary decision making by enforcing political constraints conveyed ex ante. Finally, budget flexibility can also be enhanced by continuously reviewing budget priorities and managing the budget in the context of hard budget constraints.

**The MYBF provides the framework that allows expenditures to be driven by policy priorities and disciplined by budget realities.** It combines a top-down fiscal resources envelope with a bottom-up estimation of the current and multiyear costs of existing national policies and, ultimately, the matching of those costs with available resources in the context of a multiyear budget process. The "top-down" resource envelope—often known as the "ceiling" expenditure—is determined by a macroeconomic model that projects fiscal ceilings and estimates target revenues and expenditure for the next years. As such, it also requires a pre-definition of the priorities of the national agenda. The "bottom-up" approach—often called the "floor" minimum spending—summarizes the sectors' review of their main program and project priorities, with an eye to optimizing the minimum allocations. Whereas the top-down approach is often determined by the central fiscal authorities, some fully developed MYBFs—like those of Brazil or Uganda—have developed the bottom-up approach in a participatory way with subnational governments and civil society. Once the country becomes ready for a MYBF satisfying a series of pre-conditions (see below), it will essentially have to cover six stages (Box 4.1). A variant of this approach could consider starting a pilot MYBF focused in the social sectors. If such pilot process becomes successful, it would give credibility to medium-term programming.

**Ecuador is not ready for a MYBF.** International experience collected in the implementation of poverty reduction strategies (PRSs) has, however, concluded that malpractice in public expenditure management is an obstacle to achieving the full benefits of an MYBF. In addition, the fiscal space is extremely reduced for a multiyear investment plan. Improving budget formulation in a multiyear fashion should not be seen as a panacea to solving the multitude of PEM problems that exist, and it even risks distracting attention away from the need to improve the basic framework. To its credit, Ecuador budget practices have several positive aspects: (a) macro-fiscal projections were realistic and within an reasonable range until 2003; (b) deviations between budget formulation and budget execution were not significant until 2002[13]; (c) budget ceilings

---

13. The lack of closure of the 2003 budget accounts has prevented authorities from updating budget execution at the sectoral level for 2003.

---

### BOX 4.1: THE SIX STAGES OF A COMPREHENSIVE MULTIYEAR BUDGETING FRAMEWORK

1. Development of a Macroeconomic Fiscal Framework: A macroeconomic model that incorporates projections of revenue and expenditures in the medium term (multiyear).
2. Development of Sector Programs: Agreement on sector objectives, outputs, and activities review, development of programs and subprograms, and preliminary cost estimation.
3. Development of Sector Expenditure Frameworks (SEFs): Analysis of intra- and inter-sector trade-offs.
4. Definition of Sector Resource Allocations: Setting current and medium-term budget ceilings.
5. Preparation of Sector Budgets: Medium-term sector programs based on the matching of sector priorities with budget ceilings.
6. Final Political Approval: Presentation of budget estimates to cabinet and Parliament for approval.

*Source:* World Bank (1998).

---

are introduced in line agencies to ensure their plan is consistent with overall macro aggregates; and (d) financial information is slowly becoming more disaggregated, timely, reliable, and transparent. However, key issues that Ecuador needs to resolve in order to have a complete MYBF are:

- Negotiations between line agencies and MEF typically do not involve technical discussions on trade-offs, but are focused on the extent of inertial allocations.
- Line ministries rarely consult with spending units to get informed costing exercises of selected goals, so there is no alignment of expenditures (inputs) with strategic outcomes.
- Few agencies collect data systematically on activities or program results, so there is little scope to link budget allocations with agency performance.
- While in a well designed MYBF, capital and current spending budgets should be integrated, in Ecuador they are currently determined by separate entities, and these should be integrated in an MYBF.
- Municipal budgets have no clear connection with defined national priorities and lack adequate budget formulation, reporting, and control.

**The MYBF should be seen as a complement to—not a substitute for—basic budgetary reform.** A piecemeal approach is likely to fail, since improvements in one area will not translate into gains through the budget cycle. By preceding the formulation of annual budgets, the MYBF may have at least a partial, but significant, impact especially at the budget formulation stage. Henceforth, the approach to the introduction of an MYBF should necessarily be gradual. It can start by defining ceilings on the major aggregate fiscal variables and on key sectoral spending. Then, a multiyear sector budget could be piloted in those ministries where predictability of funding and transparent outturns would warrant good monitoring. Those building blocks should be in place before moving forward to more advanced stages of an MYBF in the foreseeable future.

### F. Policy Recommendations

**The performance of PEM needs to improve in all levels.** Priorities might be to first consolidate annual budget procedures that support aggregate monitoring of fiscal discipline, while simultaneously introducing measures to improve the strategic allocation and operational effectiveness not only at the central level, but at the level of subnational governments. In the short term, developing austere and realistic budgets (Chapter 2) and sound budget management of a still cash-rationed economy are priorities for fiscal consolidation. In the medium term, continued

---

**BOX 4.2: MAIN RECOMMENDATIONS OF THE IMF–ROSC**

In December 2003, an IMF Report on the Observance of Standards and Codes (ROSC) evaluated Ecuador's fiscal transparency practices compared to the IMF *Code of Good Practices on Transparency in Monetary and Financial Policies.* The ROSC recommended the following measures:

- **Improve the legal framework for fiscal management:**
  - Approve a new organic budget law regulating the main aspects of budget management.
  - Simplify tax legislation and eliminate unproductive taxes and exemptions.
  - Periodically review private sector regulations and procedures to maintain transparency.
- **Increase the comprehensiveness of the budget:**
  - Apply gross budget accounting (that is, not netting out expenditures from revenues).
  - Bring all fiscal policy activities carried out in entities into the Central Government budget.
  - Report in the budget all quasi-fiscal activities, tax expenditures, and contingent liabilities.
- **Bolster operational control:** SIGEF should be redesigned to collect timely, relevant fiscal information.
- **Increase audit transparency and effectiveness:**
  - Make public the audited government accounts and public enterprise financial statements.
  - Publish and enforce the conclusions and recommendations of audit reports.
  - Increase the number and training of audit personnel.
- **Improve the presentation of the budget:**
  - Present clearly the revenue, expenditure, overall balance, and financing components in the budget, and in reports of budget execution.
  - Present the functional, economic, and program classification of revenues and expenditures.
  - Include in the budget a discussion of the main objectives of the different budget programs.

---

efforts to refine the design of the poverty reduction strategy, and to develop adequate sector strategies will guide intra- and inter-sector allocation and program prioritization (Chapter 3).

**Key recommendations to sound budget management are well summarized by a recent ROSC completed by the IMF** (Box 4.2). Besides those general recommendations, a few essential ones derived from this chapter analysis are to:

- **Create a Cash Committee at MEF,** composed of representatives of the Budget, Treasury, Public Credit, Public Investment, and Economic Policy Offices. Its main function would be to design and implement a cash management policy, based on clear and simple prioritization criteria. In the short term, and while arrears still exist, define temporary rules for applying cash rationing through in-year budget modifications. All resolutions from the Cash Committee should be made public, to allow social accountability.
- **Revert inertial budgeting through structural change.** Curbing the positive growth of the wage bill is critical. There is no substitute for this and it cannot be emphasized enough.
- **Gradually integrate off-budget activities into the Treasury *Cuenta Unica* gradually.** This would bring Treasury control of resources now sleeping in commercial bank accounts. For instance, an obvious candidate is PetroEcuador subsidies.

Regarding *budget management in social programs,* it is clear that that the budgets in many social programs have no relationship to their goals and expected outputs. The fact that many social programs have a lower than 80 percent level of execution is a problem. Critical recommendations are to:

■ **Review budgeting policy in social programs so as to establish a close association between budgets and goals/results.** Setting monitoring—financial and physical—indicators is a first step. These should include coverage, targeting, and cost efficiency indicators.

■ **Review the overall budget protection policy.** Budget protection policy has two sides: on one hand, it increases budget rigidity; on the other hand, in a context of fiscal retrenchments, it guarantees that cash-rationed mechanisms do not affect essential pro-poor expenditure. A first step would be to assess existing protected programs. For example, budgetary protection is actually given to seven priority social programs (PSPs), five of which are examined in this Chapter: LMG, BDH, PRADEC, PAE, PANN, PAI and investment by the ministry of education. Then, some criteria should be defined and applied for reconfirming programs to receive budgetary protection annually, so as to make sure they effectively represent key priorities of the national agenda. International experience indicates that the number of selected programs should be small. Finally, the amount of resources to be protected should be seen as a function of past and present execution capacity, as well as of the outcomes to be produced. In any case, programs should receive the minimum amount of resources needed to achieve their goals.

■ **Consider the possibility of converting the de facto budget protection policy into a "Virtual" Poverty Fund.** This enhanced mechanism would consist of tagging selected budget programs that are poverty-reducing, i.e. the PSPs (the so-called "virtual" fund). Drawing from the experience of Uganda's Poverty Action Fund (Box 4.3), virtual funds rapidly expanded through Highly Indebted Poor Countries (HIPC).[14] In some countries, its setting up has also involved making changes to the existing budget and accounting systems (Zambia); or introducing new reporting templates to track spending lines (Mauritania, Mozambique and Tanzania); or producing additional information on all poverty-reducing spending (Honduras) (The World Bank and IDB 2003). A Virtual Poverty Fund, tailor-made to Ecuadorian budgetary protection policy, would essentially require adding two new features: (i) the development of its institutional framework by creating a coordination body and facilitating open access and reporting; as well as (ii) the definition of monitoring indicators and evaluation mechanisms to be followed in a participatory way with civil society (an Observatory of Social Policy, for instance). Such a proposal would definitely strengthen a medium-term social policy with one of the finest tools for a solid poverty reduction strategy.

■ **Merge or eliminate duplicative social programs.** The current number of 45 social programs is too high and suggests waste of resources (Table A58).[15] Obvious candidates for elimination are those programs that show a significant degree of low budget and/or significant budget underexecution and/or poor targeting. A first step is to assess the performance of existing programs, and also find out whether these are donor-financed, which would improve chances of their coordination. Impact evaluations would help deciding which programs are more effective and deserve to take the lead in a particular area. For instance, the creation of the *Sistema Integrado de Alimentación y Nutrición—SIAN* is a

---

14. In 1996, the IMF and the World Bank launched the HIPC initiative to reduce the debt stock of debt-stressed countries. In 1998, they launched the Enhanced HIPC initiative to provide faster, deeper and broader debt relief, and strengthen the links between debt relief and poverty reduction through a poverty reduction strategy produced by the country. Uganda is committed to channel cash-flow savings on interest payments resulting from the reduction of the stock of debt under HIPC toward selected poverty programs.

15. The generation of fiscal space should *not* be the guiding criteria in merging or phasing-out programs, but the elimination of inefficiencies and prevention of overlapping areas of work. In Ecuador, 3 social programs take about 75 percent of the overall budget. Besides, there are important political economy considerations to consider, especially when programs are administered by different sector ministries, or particular constituencies have been created around programs, e.g. indigenous groups.

---

**BOX 4.3: ECUADOR: INSTITUTIONALIZING A VIRTUAL POVERTY FUND: A LOOK AT BEST-PRACTICE UGANDA**

The virtual Poverty Action Fund (PAF) is focused on implementing the Government of Uganda's highest priorities within the Poverty Eradication Action Plan (PEAP). The PAF is funded by a combination of HIPC debt relief, donors—general or sector-earmarked—support, and Government's own resources. The *operational framework* of the virtual PAF has the following components: (i) budget priorities are defined by a rolling 3-year MTEF; (ii) it is not a separate Fund, but a subset of the overall budget; (iii) the Government commits not to cut its funds; (iv) all expenditures fall under full Congress and auditor general oversight; (v) it is managed by sector and ministerial level Working Groups; and (vi) PAF programs have a structured and participatory institutional framework that ensures that they are properly planned, budgeted and implemented. This includes:

*Eligible Criteria:* A program qualifies if it meets 4 criteria: it is part of the PEAP; it directly reduces poverty (with involvement by the poor); it delivers a service to the poorest 20th of the population; and has a well-developed implementation plan (with costs, outcome, and output targets clearly identified). Programs are reviewed once a year.

*Administration:* 5 percent of PAF resources are set aside for improving program effectiveness and transparency;

*Size:* at least a constant proportion of the original budget;

*Reporting:* An overall quarterly report by central or local governments should be produced by the Ministry of Finance and distributed countrywide. Biannual sector performance evaluations are also required. Audits should cover all Central Government-led and at least 60 percent of district-led programs. Sector expenditure tracking studies are required when there is inadequate audit information. Civil society independently monitors reviews.

*Safeguards:* (i) in case of budgetary shortfalls, under-allocation to PAF should be lower than cuts in non-PAF programs; (ii) in case of under-performance, funds can be reallocated to other PEAP programs or to PAF programs in the following fiscal year.

---

very positive step in the right direction and should be replicated. The on-going retargeting of the BDH, PAE and PRADEC is also a welcome development.

- **Eliminate cash constraints in the first half of the year.** Arrears reappeared in the first quarter of 2004. Preventing them in future years would require proper planning of cash management by the proposed Cash Committee.
- **Rationalize, simplify, and if possible automate, budget procedures and forms for requesting reimbursement of payments.** Bureaucratic controls over individual commitments and payments could be replaced by an advanced quota system covering an overall envelope of resources planned in the monthly PPCs. This process, however, would depend on the extent to which SIGEF records proper and timely information about budget execution. A system of management contracts should be designed combining incentives for timely reporting of financial and physical indicators and sanctions for non-compliers in selected PSPs.
- **Resist the temptation to convert an additional number of PSPs to Executing Units, even though it might produce short-term improvements in budget execution.** Another variant of this approach that should also be prevented is the creation of further "trust funds" as a financing alternative that would allow those programs to have a special regime of operational and procurement procedures.

**Regarding** *budget management in provincial and municipal governments,* **it is essential to revert to a sound process of budget decentralization.** Problems have arisen in LAC from arrangements that involved automatic unconditional transfers from the center through rigid tax-revenue-sharing formulas such as those applied in Ecuador. Critical recommendations are to:

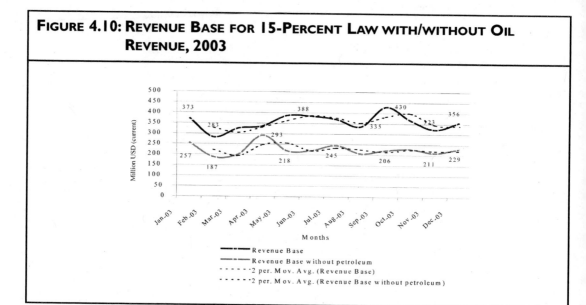

**FIGURE 4.10: REVENUE BASE FOR 15-PERCENT LAW WITH/WITHOUT OIL REVENUE, 2003**

*Note:* Dotted line represents trend line (moving average).
*Source:* Frank (2004) based on information provided by MEF.

■ **Design a strong regulatory and institutional framework that clearly assigns expenditure responsibilities, accompanying the devolution of revenue, and in line with subnational government administrative capacity.** This framework can consider establishing standard incentives for the transfer of resources in exchange for devolved expenditure responsibilities (for example, standardized per student criteria in assignment to education).

■ **Isolate oil revenue from intergovernmental transfers, which would smooth fluctuations in the planned flow of funds toward subnational levels.** When oil is excluded from the revenue base that is used to distribute the 15-Percent Law, the flow of transfers appears smoother on a monthly basis (Figure 4.10). This is necessarily so because oil revenue amounts for roughly one third of the volume of transfers related to the 15-Percent Law.

■ **Adopt daily automatic transfers based on revenue available on daily accrued income as is often an international practice.** This would prevent accumulation of local "savings" in transfers.

■ **Condition actual delivery of transfers on timely and reliable budget reporting by subnational governments as mandated by the Fiscal Law.** This would constitute the minimum conditions that are required to achieve more transparency.

■ **Promote responsible subnational borrowing by establishing further legislation under which the Central Government might intervene in those local governments that violate the fiscal rules, specifying the main elements of subnational fiscal adjustment programs, reprogramming debts, and excluding the possibility of any bailout.**
The budget should be made more accountable, transparent, and participatory.

■ **In 2003, the government prepared a Transparency Plan based on three actions that should be taken:** (a) complete the upgrade of the SIGEF financial management system to consolidate NFPS financial statements and produce monthly, timely, and reliable reports on consolidated executed expenditure to be published on the government's website

(Portal) beginning in 2004; (b) support the e-government system—CONTRATANET—to perform transactional public procurement; and (c) build a national public investment system, starting with a central database and project bank.

- **In the medium term, budgetary transparency should be institutionalized at all levels of government, including subnational governments, while civil society participation should be encouraged.**[16] This may include a national dialogue on the multiyear program, possibly within the context of the ongoing preparation of the poverty reduction strategy. This would facilitate civil society organizations, such as the Fiscal Observatory, playing a better-informed and more effective watchdog and advocacy role in the implementation of key fiscal reforms, like those of Customs and of the civil service.
- **The recent approval of the Law of Access to Public Information represents an important milestone,** but its *Reglamento* (norms) is pending approval. Norms should guarantee gradual access to information on all public budget sectors, including defense, to ensure detailed oversight and monitoring.

**Developing a MYBF requires fulfilling a number of prerequisites and carrying out several preparatory actions.** A credible MYBF requires strong political support from the President and the Cabinet. Politicians must be aware that a MYBF will tie their hands and reduce their discretionary bargaining powers on budget issues. Therefore, developing a consultative process at the outset is both legitimate and desirable, since this would prevent Legislative and public pressure from dissuading the Executive to change its priorities in further years of implementation of the MYBF. Initial measures are to:

- **Define national priorities and a reduced set of key target outcome indicators, as part of the PRS.** Ecuador already has identified a few social indicators, which should serve as a good starting point.
- **Continue improving the realism of growth and revenue budget projections, as well as of sector budget ceilings.**
- **Prepare the first MYBF, including an overall macro framework and propose sector expenditure ceilings.**
- **Consider the implementation of a competition-based Fund for investment.** The Chilean Fund is a positive reference the main feature of which is the simplicity of its focus to allocate the flexible component of budget expenditure (see Chapter 3).
- **Reclassify the budget per programs,** which is an extremely helpful prerequisite to match strategic priorities to the PRS, prepare groundwork for integrated costing (capital and recurrent), and develop monitoring indicators.
- **Select pilot ministries for preparing sector expenditure frameworks** (strategy, objectives, key programs and costs, and performance indicators), **especially focused on the sector priorities of the PRS. In advanced stages of the MYBF, this would lead to defining budgetary *floors* for selected PSPs.**
- **Appoint a highly qualified staff to an interministerial executive body of the MYBF.** It should develop a roadmap encompassing stepped-up phases for the preparation of a MYBF (in some best practice countries—like South Africa—this team has even standardized its procedures in a Manual on Financial Planning and Budgeting).
- **Convey national priorities to municipalities, to induce the alignment of their budgets.** This can be achieved through expenditure ear-marking (provided there is the possibil-

---

16. The Civic Anti-Corruption Commission was established in 1999 to combat corruption in Ecuador. It was established as an independent entity not controlled by the Executive. Its president is elected by civil society organizations every four years under the supervision of the Superior Electoral Tribunal. It is 95 percent financed by public funds, and the remaining 5 percent comes from international donors.

ity of monitoring and sanctioning) or through co-sharing arrangements such as matching grants. These and other incentives must be established in such a way that subnational budgets are aligned to national priorities.

■ **Set a clear schedule between the multiannual and annual budgeting processes during each year's budget formulation process.** Successful MYBF countries conclude a first draft by April each year, just in time to use it as a key input in the guidelines for the preparation of the annual budget to line ministries.

# Annex A

# AN ESTIMATION OF THE POTENTIAL OUTPUT AND THE STRUCTURAL FISCAL BALANCE IN ECUADOR[1]

## Why Estimate a Structural Fiscal Balance?

It has long been recognized that the nominal budget balance is an imperfect indicator of the government's true fiscal stance.[2] The problem is that, in general, the fiscal balance depends not only on authorities' tax and expenditure decisions, but also on the extent to which autonomous spending decisions by the private sector are reflected in the country's output and national income levels, and thereby on tax collection. Thus, if the economy enters a recession, because of, say, a reduction in private investment, tax revenue automatically declines, irrespective of the authorities' fiscal stance, and the fiscal balance worsens. Conversely, if an autonomous increase in private spending leads to an increase in national income, tax revenue increases and the fiscal balance improves. These changes in the fiscal balance take place automatically for a given tax structure. This implies that the nominal fiscal balance is a distorted measure of whether government fiscal policy is expansionary or contractionary. A given fiscal stance is consistent with a worsening or an improvement in the nominal balance, depending on whether private spending decreases or increases.

To address the issue of the need to have a measure of fiscal policy that is independent of the particular position of the economy in the business cycle, the concept of cyclically adjusted or structural budget balance has been developed in the macroeconomics literature.[3] The basic idea is to carry out a simple decomposition of the nominal budget balance (B) into two unobservable components—the structural component (SB) and the cyclical component (CB)—in such a way that the following equation holds for period t:

$$B(t) = SB(t) + CB(t) \qquad (1)$$

---

1. This Annex was prepared by Daniel Artana and Cynthia Moskovits.
2. Most of this section is based on Annex B of the Public Expenditure Review for Peru (World Bank 2003).
3. See, for instance, Hagemann (1999) and Marcel and others (2001).

Under the admittedly inaccurate, simplifying assumption that government spending is not a function of the state of the business cycle, the structural component is defined by[4]:

$$SB(t) = SR(t) - G(t) \tag{2}$$

where $SR(t)$, the structural revenue, is the fiscal revenue that would be collected if actual output in t were the level of output determined by the long-term trend, which will be called trend output. $G(t)$ is total government spending. $SR$ is estimated by means of the following equation:

$$SR(t) = R(t)[TY(t)/Y(t)]^ß \tag{3}$$

where $R(t)$ is the observed value for the government revenue, $TY(t)$ is the economy's trend output, $Y(t)$ the actual level of output, and ß is the income elasticity of total government revenue. Completion of the calculations implied by equations (2) and (3) requires that estimates for both trend output and the income elasticity of revenue be generated.[5]

To estimate the potential output, two alternatives are used: a production function and the estimation method proposed by Hodrick and Prescott (1997). The second alternative is used in most cases because it is easier to calculate. In terms of this method, if the logarithm of $Y(t)$ is denoted $y(t)$, the time series for $y(t)$ can be decomposed in its trend component $ty(t)$ and its cyclical component $cy(t)$:

$$y(t) = ty(t) + cy(t) \; ; \text{ for } t = 1, \ldots, T \tag{4}$$

then the Hodrick–Prescott (HP) trend output, $hpy(t)$, is the series that minimizes the expression:

$$\Sigma \; cy(t)2 + \lambda \; \Sigma \; \{[ty(t) - ty(t\text{-}1)] - [(ty(t\text{-}1) - ty(t\text{-}2)]\}^2 \tag{5}$$

where the sums are carried out from t = 1 to t = T and $\lambda$ is a parameter that determines how smooth the trend line will be. The method's idea is to minimize the sum of two terms where the first term is the sum of squares of the cyclical component and the second term is the sum of squares of the trend component's second differences.

In the case of oil-producing countries, the adjustment to the nominal budget balance should take into account the impact of volatility of the price of crude oil. Therefore, a first adjustment is to recalculate the nominal balance net of the effect of fluctuations in the price of oil (these should better be saved in an oil stabilization fund). A second step is to correct for the cyclical component of tax revenues to get a structural budget balance.

## Estimating the Output Gap and the Public Sector Structural Balance

This section applies GDP at 2000 constant prices during 1960–2003. Data came from the IMF and the Central Bank of Ecuador. As is customary in this exercise, some additional years are added to moderate the instability that the estimate has at the tails of the sample period. For 2004

---

4. In the European Community expenditures are also adjusted by excluding expenses related to the business cycle (for example, payments of unemployment insurance). As in most Latin American countries, private firms compensate fired employees directly through severance payments, and it has been customary to adjust only government revenues for the cyclical component (see Marcel and others 2001). Another issue is the impact of inflation on interest payments. This correction is not necessary when the focus of the analysis is on the primary balance of the public sector. Focusing on the primary balance is a good approximation when nonresidents hold most public debt.

5. Equation (3) considers only the effect on tax revenues of the economic cycle. But in a more sophisticated estimate it would be better to allow for other changes in revenues produced by the cycle (some countries adjust for the changes in the tax base of capital gains or take into account different lags in the perception of taxes (see for example, Donders and Kollau 2002 and Braconier and Forsfält 2004). These topics are not very relevant for Latin American countries because taxation of capital gains is usually low and fiscal lags are relatively short in the most relevant taxes.

## FIGURE A.A.1: ACTUAL AND POTENTIAL REAL GDP

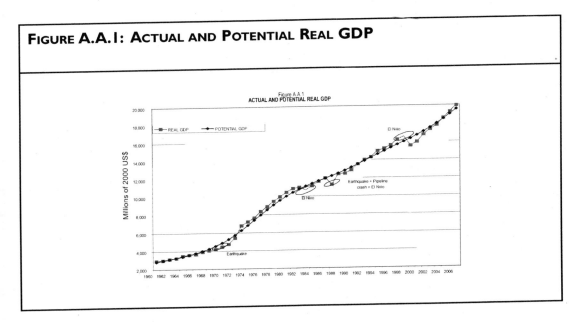

Source: Author's calculations on Banco Central del Ecuador (BCE).

and 2005, most conservative estimates provided by Consensus Forecasts as of April 2004 and from 2006 onward were assumed: a real annual growth rate of 3.5 percent. Several alternatives for adding years (3, 5, or 10) were applied, but they did no major changes. Hence, the series produced forecasts for only three years.

### The Output Gap

To determine the output gap, the potential GDP must first be estimated. Two alternative methods are available: (a) assessing a production function; or (b) filtering actual real GDP (the most common filter is that built by Hodrick and Prescott). Though the first alternative is probably more accurate, it is not available for Ecuador. The results obtained by making use of the second method, with the usual $\lambda = 100$ parameter for annual time series, cover 1960–2006 (Figure A.A.1).

Natural disasters proved to injure the economy during 1970, 1982/83, and 1987, although it cannot be detected from the data in the last El Niño phenomenon that took place during 1997–98. Barely minor differences appear when extending the actual GDP estimates up to 2010, 2015, and 2020, respectively, in order to avoid the "tails problem" of the Hodrick–Prescott filter (Artana 2004).

### The Structural Fiscal Balance

In a second step, the structural fiscal balance is estimated. The information available is on the Non-Financial Public Sector for 1983–2003 of the Central Bank of Ecuador and the World Bank. Expenditures were not adjusted by cyclical components because there are no payments directly related to the cycle (like unemployment insurance). In a preliminary analysis, this assumption appears to be supported by the data, which suggests that expenditures are independent of the business cycle in Ecuador. For simplicity, oil revenues are considered only those originated in exports of crude oil. Although a fraction of the revenues obtained from sales for derivatives could also be included, as collected at the upstream level, its adjustment is small. To remove the impact of the volatility of the crude oil price, oil revenues are recalculated every year according to the average export price for the Ecuador mix during 1991–2003 (equal to US$17.2 per barrel). The adjusted series is named Structural Oil Revenues. To estimate them, equation

(3) has to be estimated with different values for the income elasticity of tax revenues. Results are virtually the same as using an income elasticity of 1.1. Following this, the Structural Primary Balance (surplus in the case of Ecuador) can be obtained (Table A.A.1).[6] Figure A.A.2 compares Actual and Structural Primary surpluses for every year since 1983. The line shows the impact of departures of the crude oil price from its long-term reference.

In most years, the volatility in oil prices and its effect on oil revenues accounts for most of the difference between Actual and Structural Primary Surpluses. This underlines the importance of oil prices in the economy and of improving the design of the Oil Stabilization Fund.[7]

- It is also apparent than in periods of high export prices of crude oil, the government relaxes the collection of non-oil tax revenues (for example, in 1990, 2000 to 2003), and the opposite holds in periods of low prices (1993 to 1995, 1997, and 1998).[8] This is clearly the case with the revenues obtained from sales of derivatives in the domestic market, which are negatively correlated with the price of oil.

- Previously, during the 21-year period for which we had statistics, the cumulated actual primary surplus was slightly higher than the cumulated structural one (1 percent of GDP, for an annual average of less than 0.05 percent of the GDP). If the sample is restricted to the last 10 years, this figure grows to 1.4 percent of GDP (a similar figure is obtained for the last five years), equivalent to an annual average of about 0.3 percent of GDP.

- The Structural Fiscal Balance is in surplus after dollarization. In particular, the level of the Structural Primary Surplus was 3.9 percent of GDP in 2003. Recent excess actual surplus over the Structural Primary Surplus is explained by high oil prices and the need to devote additional fiscal resources to debt reduction.

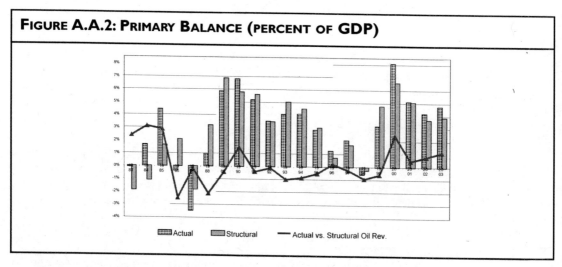

**FIGURE A.A.2: PRIMARY BALANCE (PERCENT OF GDP)**

Source: Author's estimates on BCE, Ministerio de Economía y Finanzas (MEF) and IMF.
Source: Based on Table A.A.1

---

6. A comparison for a longer period of time is available in Figure A.A.2, and data are available from the authors.

7. The Output Gap measured for every year of the period 1991–2003 is relatively small. There is a puzzle in the data, because 1998 appears with a Potential GDP below Actual GDP in spite of the impact of El Niño. This puzzle is also present in the estimates done in IMF (2003 b).

8. This has been done mostly through tax exemptions and incentives, introducing distortions that should be avoided.

## TABLE A.A.1: STRUCTURAL FISCAL BALANCE
(percent of GDP)

| | Primary Expenditure | Non-Oil Revenues | | | Oil Revenues (Exports) | | | Primary Surplus | | |
|---|---|---|---|---|---|---|---|---|---|---|
| | Actual | Actual | Structural | Difference (Act.-Struct.) | Actual | Structural | Difference (Act.-Struct.) | Actual | Structural | Difference (Act.-Struct.) |
| 1990 | 20.0% | 17.2% | 17.6% | -0.4% | 9.6% | 8.1% | 1.5% | 6.8% | 5.8% | 1.0% |
| 1991 | 19.9% | 18.0% | 18.0% | 0.0% | 7.1% | 7.5% | -0.4% | 5.2% | 5.6% | -0.4% |
| 1992 | 21.5% | 17.4% | 17.2% | 0.2% | 7.7% | 7.8% | -0.1% | 3.5% | 3.5% | 0.0% |
| 1993 | 18.8% | 17.6% | 17.5% | 0.1% | 5.2% | 6.3% | -1.0% | 4.1% | 5.0% | -0.9% |
| 1994 | 17.7% | 18.3% | 17.9% | 0.5% | 3.5% | 4.4% | -0.9% | 4.1% | 4.5% | -0.4% |
| 1995 | 19.9% | 19.4% | 19.0% | 0.4% | 3.4% | 3.9% | -0.5% | 2.9% | 3.1% | -0.2% |
| 1996 | 20.6% | 17.5% | 17.1% | 0.3% | 4.4% | 4.2% | 0.2% | 1.3% | 0.7% | 0.5% |
| 1997 | 17.9% | 17.3% | 16.6% | 0.7% | 2.6% | 2.9% | -0.3% | 2.1% | 1.7% | 0.4% |
| 1998 | 17.9% | 16.2% | 15.6% | 0.6% | 1.1% | 2.0% | -0.9% | -0.6% | -0.2% | -0.3% |
| 1999 | 17.9% | 16.6% | 17.6% | -1.0% | 4.5% | 5.1% | -0.6% | 3.2% | 4.8% | -1.6% |
| 2000 | 17.8% | 17.8% | 18.7% | -0.9% | 8.1% | 5.6% | 2.4% | 8.1% | 6.6% | 1.5% |
| 2001 | 18.3% | 18.9% | 19.3% | -0.4% | 4.5% | 4.1% | 0.5% | 5.1% | 5.1% | 0.0% |
| 2002 | 21.6% | 21.8% | 22.1% | -0.3% | 4.0% | 3.2% | 0.8% | 4.2% | 3.7% | 0.5% |
| 2003 | 21.5% | 22.5% | 22.8% | -0.3% | 3.8% | 2.6% | 1.1% | 4.8% | 3.9% | 0.9% |

# Annex B

# SUMMARY OF THE BUDGET PROCESS

## Budget Formulation

The national budget formulation process in Ecuador begins in July, when line ministries and institutions must develop their annual proforma budgets.[1] These are then passed and reviewed by the Budget Office (*Subsecretaria de Presupuesto*) in the Ministry of Economy and Finance (MEF), and incorporated into the pro forma annual budget, which the Development Policy office also reviews. The pro forma annual budget is then sent in September to Congress, which can change allocations, but cannot raise the budget ceiling. Congress has until November 30th to approve the budget, and on December 1st, the new budget (*Presupuesto General del Estado*, PGE) becomes effective.

The national budget does not include provincial and municipals expenditures. Formulation of these budgets is not covered by the PGE, except for the assignment of transfers to the subnational governments.

## Budget Execution

Budget execution is the responsibility of the Treasury and Budget Offices in the MEF. Movement of most of the public funds is done through the Treasury's *Cuenta Unica* (Single Account). Tax and petrol revenues, and external and domestic financing, fund this account and, in turn, the account channels budgetary transfers to the institutions, makes subnational transfers, and pays the debt. This account is reconciled on a daily basis. Figure A.B.1 illustrates the flow of funds in the budget process.

Each public institution has three accounts: two in the private banks and one in the Central Bank. Of the two accounts in the private bank, one is for deposit of *autogestion* (self-generated revenues from fees, and so forth). These deposits remain there for four days before being automatically transferred to the institution's account in the Central Bank. This holding period was introduced as a means to help support private sector banks after the banking crisis in 1999. The second private bank account is a payment account on demand. Checks are written against the institution's private bank, not the one from the Central Bank. Payments withdraw the money transferred to the private bank account from the institution's account in the Central Bank. Thus, in essence the second private bank accounts have zero balance. Although withdrawal of the funds is codified using a two-digit classification, a recurrent problem is the lack of control over whether withdrawals are consistent with their assigned budget classification. The only control is

---

1. This Annex was prepared by Elaine Tinsley.

## FIGURE A.B.1: FLOW OF BUDGETARY FUNDS

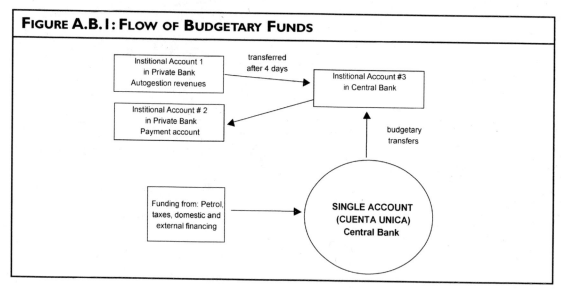

Source: World Bank

that the amount withdrawn cannot exceed the institution's account balance in its Central Bank account.

The institution's account in the Central Bank is funded from *autogestion* revenues and from budgetary transfers from the *Cuenta Unica*. Each institutional budget has a payment plan—the *Programación Periódica de Caja* (PPC)—stating the monthly amount of budgetary transfers to be made to the institution. The PPC is initiated by the Budget Office in MEF. However, this is not necessarily the monthly amount that is transferred from the *Cuenta Unica* to the institution's account. Instead, it provides a "promise of payment" that is merely indicative of the intention to pay, but is not enforceable. The actual amount transferred depends on Treasury cash availability and MEF's decision to transfer.

Decentralization of expenditure management to virtually all public institutions creates severe cash management problems for Treasury. While money is flowing to decentralized spending units that do not report whether they have actually spent the money in deposit in their private bank accounts, Treasury finds itself short of funds. This generates artificial arrears in Treasury's *Cuenta Unica*, even though there is cash sitting in the institutions' private accounts. While Treasury is empowered to and does take back some of the sitting funds, institutions strongly resist this. In 2003, cash management shortfalls forced Treasury to raise short-term money on the markets, and hence increase budget-financing costs. However, with the recent build-up of the old oil stabilization fund (FEP), Treasury now borrows short term against it. Still, in 2004, it has become apparent that this action has not resolved severe cash management problems. If the government had cash management under control, it would allow it to implement the budget more efficiently, minimize the cost of borrowing, and maximize return on government deposits.

Financial management is also weak. Although Ecuador has an integrated financial management system (SIGEF) in place, this system is primarily used for budgetary formulation and accounting, rather than execution. With only 70 percent of Central Government institutions covered by it, SIGEF does not permit timely and complete consolidation of fiscal information yet. As a result, the Government of Ecuador does not have access to complete and accurate budget execution information, which could be used as an indispensable tool for decisionmaking and management control. There are also problems in assessing the impact of expenditures and targeting future expenditures on poverty reduction programs. Expenditure monitoring is partial and done through two mechanisms. First, the Central Bank uses the fiscal database to detect expenditure withdrawals using a two-digit classification from the institution's account in the Central Bank. However, as explained above, there is no way to verify that this institution used resources as approved. Second, SIGEF provides some expenditure reporting that is later used by Treasury to verify payments.

## Budget Control

In the public sector, there are two levels of controls—internal control units and the external *Controlaría General de Estado* (CGE). There are about 300 internal control units employing some 800 auditors. The CGE itself has about 1,740 personnel, of which 55 percent are auditors (957). Internal control units report to and are hired by the CGE, though their wages come from the respective line ministries. The CGE also approves their work program, which is based on a series of ad hoc tasks. Once internal units have issued their reports to the CGE, their task is done, because only the CGE has the authority to further investigate, or issue fines and penalties for infractions. Each institution is to be audited at least once every five years, though the overall fiscal accounts are not audited. According to the CGE, public institutions have the capacity to conduct an annual internal audit of the fiscal accounts; however, because they have not been required, they have not done so.

**Internal auditing.** The internal control environment is weak, due to ineffective accounting and information systems, inadequate control over fixed assets, and inadequate monitoring of controls. Internal audit capacity relies excessively on external auditing. The internal audit function in line ministries is not oriented to providing assurance on the control environment, but rather to performance of ad hoc special reviews. The internal financial audits are weak in their breadth, depth, and frequency, with procedures mainly done manually. Norms governing internal audit have not been adequately promulgated. Internal control units do not do routine analysis, or auditing of accounts; this is mainly the responsibility of the CGE. Instead, internal control units investigate processes, and report on noncompliance of civil and administrative problems to the CGE. It also examines whether the budgets match the development goals. There is no full auditing of the budgets of public institutions, only parts. Reports about internal audits (and external audits) are not published—though names of people committing infractions are published in the papers.

**External auditing.** The CGE covers all public sector entities and private entities that receive public funding. In general, the norms and procedures governing external audit are adequate and in agreement with international standards. CGE's principal activity is to conduct financial audits, although recently it has started a pilot plan to conduct performance audits. It does not audit the public debt. Audit functions are not directed toward efficiency gains, but rather toward ex ante and ex post compliance. The CGE also takes an active role in monitoring public works and preapproval of public contracts. Despite its role of monitoring the use of public resources, the CGE does not publish the conclusions and recommendations of its audits, though it does monitor the fulfillment of the recommendations it makes. Political interference is seen as the main reason why the CGE has not tackled larger cases of corruption. Though it enjoys a reputation for its thoroughness, its work has targeted minor infractions rather than greater allegations. The process of the Comptroller's selection is subject to political interference. The President selects the Controller General from three candidates presented by Congress. This is often problematic in a multiparty Congress having difficulty agreeing on the initial three candidates, who often represent different political parties. As a result, the Controller General's position remained vacant for over a year.

## Budget Reporting

With expenditure management decentralized to the institutions, reporting is another particularly weak area of public expenditure management throughout the whole spending cycle. The MEF receives information from each institution on the execution of the PGE. In some cases, this information is transmitted by internet via SIGEF, and is timely. However, about 40 percent of public institutions do not send their information in a timely manner. This leads to delays in processing by the Budget Office, which in turn authorizes monthly budget transfers to the institutions through Treasury, which materializes the transfers and delivery of funds to the institutions. Because the spending information is not delivered in a timely way, Treasury has a hard time finding the information to make the appropriate decisions on budgetary allocations. Published budget information is also too broad and does not reflect all fiscal activities. Periodic reports mainly contain information about the central administration. The budgetary information is reported on a cash basis, but authorities have indicated their intention to move to an accrual basis. The strong decentralization of the budget does not facilitate the conciliation of data over and under the line.

**Reporting by public enterprises.** The government's Accounting Office receives financial statements from the subnational governments. This includes information on an accrual basis, and on cash transactions. In addition, public enterprises are legally required to publish their financial audits, but this is not being done. Part of the problem is the lack of a legal definition of a public enterprise. For instance, companies of the Solidarity Fund are considered autonomous and subject to the Law of Companies, and therefore are classified as private companies rather than public. Lack of a legal definition of public enterprises also results in overlapping jurisdictions. For example, the electricity companies of the Solidarity Fund, due to their quasi-public/private status, are subject to five different levels of controls: internal audit controls, the Comptroller's Office, the Superintendency of Companies, private external auditors (international), and a so-called *Comisario*, the functions of which are not well known.

# Annex C

# MAJOR BUDGETARY ISSUES IN PRIORITY SOCIAL PROGRAMS

## The Institutional Framework and Budgetary Constraints

Following is a description of the organization of five priority social programs.[1] It helps explain the institutional weaknesses of the budget process detailed in Annex D.

**The *Bono de Desarrollo Humano* (BDH).** The *Bono de Desarrollo Humano* was originally created in late 1997 on a smaller scale, as the *Bono Solidario*. While the program started in 1998 with a budget of US$57 million, its budget was increased from US$151 million in 2002 to US$202 million in 2004. The BDH is now Ecuador's biggest social program. The Central Government has primary responsibility for it, and the number of beneficiaries will rise by 40 percent in 2004, as 12 new provinces gradually become part of the program.

**The BDH has a dual organization: a treasury authority and a technical administrator.** The treasury authority is the Ministry of Finance's responsibility for transferring cash stipends to beneficiaries through the private bank system, BANRED. The technical administrator is the Ministry of Social Welfare (MSW), which has responsibility for technical administration, development, and supervision and control activities.

**This duality of mainstream responsibilities is setting an undesirable, embittering precedent and creating serious cleavages within the BDH institutional structure.** The existing law designated the MSW to be the only entity responsible for the functioning of this and other related subsidy programs. The BDH's *Decreto 486-A*, of June 7, 2000, was issued to regulate the operation of subsidy programs, while replacing other legal provisions that mandated the Ministry of Finance (MEF) to administer subsidies at first, then passed the responsibility on to the President of the Republic's National Modernization Commission (CONAM), and finally to the MSW. The law instituted the creation of the Social Protection Program (PPS), and charged it with the responsibility to, among other things, "administer and transfer focalized subsidies for development of projects of social compensation directed to most vulnerable population groups." In practice, however, it was the MEF that ended up taking over the treasury and financial management functions, and transgressing the legal mandate, while subordinating the technical management functions to the PPS' 39 staff members. At present, MEF transfers the monies to the beneficiaries and has the power to stop their flowing without prior consent or discussion with PPS. The BDH does not have a planning committee that gathers rural women and other key beneficiaries. Rather, that task is performed by PSS in coordination with the Beneficiaries

---

1. This Annex was prepared by Jorge Shepherd.

## FIGURE A.C.1: ORGANIZATION OF BDH OPERATING IN 14 PROVINCES

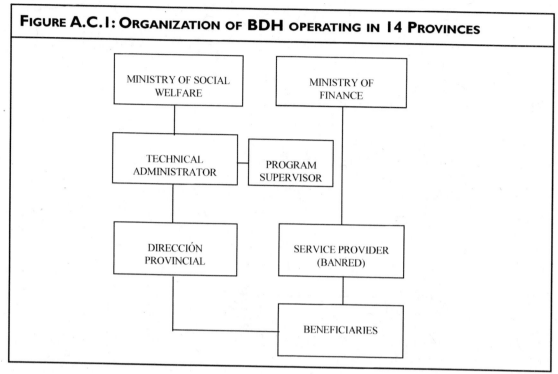

*Source:* Programa de Proteccion Social (PPS)

Selection Service's (SELBEN) specialists in order to verify the actual compared to projected number of beneficiaries.

**A major organizational flaw is that the founding law does not recognize the BDH as an executing unit[2] and, consequently, funding is channeled by MEF either through MSW or directly to the service provider (Banred).** Usually, MSW receives the funds transferred from Treasury for administrative purposes, and then withholds them. There were serious delays in the functioning of the program. These became critical during its implementation in 12 Provinces, when Treasury transferred the planned budgetary resources in the third quarter of 2003, but MSW withheld the funds for 124 days, and then only partially released them. In Figure A.C.1, the current organization shows the dual organization in administering and providing the subsidy through the private banks network.

**The BDH has suffered cutbacks.** Its budget in 2003 was originally approved in the amount of US$203 million, or 0.8 percent of gross domestic product. BDH has reportedly benefited 1,043,826 mothers, as well as 226,848 elderly people, and 8,840 handicapped people living in the first and second quintiles of the population, mainly in rural areas. The goal in 2003 was to help 1,025,882 mothers, 244,234 elderly people, and 9,884 handicapped people. BDH faced major financing problems in the second half of 2003. Its budget was reduced by 20 percent, to $165 million. Cutbacks were attributed to the changes of authorities in MSW. When measured by the approved initial budget, BDH executed 80 percent of the social program in 2003 (Table A.C.1). The program is entirely financed by the Treasury.

---

2. An executing unit is any official entity lawfully endowed with an administrative capacity and autonomy, which reports use of public budget funds directly to the Ministry of Finance. Even though the budget of an executing unit is part of the hosting ministry, the ministry will neither be able to control nor intervene in any way in the funds that were approved by Congress and conveyed with the financing sources at the beginning of the fiscal year.

**TABLE A.C.1: BUDGET EXECUTION AT BDH, BY FINANCING SOURCE**
(in millions of US dollars)

| | Total | Treasury | Fondo de Solidaridad | WFP | Others |
|---|---|---|---|---|---|
| Initial budget | 203.1 | 203.1 | 0.0 | 0.0 | 0.0 |
| Revised budget | 164.6 | 164.6 | 0.0 | 0.0 | 0.0 |
| Executed (*devengado* basis) | 161.8 | 161.8 | 0.0 | 0.0 | 0.0 |
| Executed (cash basis) | 161.8 | 161.8 | 0.0 | 1.0 | 0.0 |

*Source:* STFS.

**There is a major problem with the supervision and administration of the BDH.** Its expenses, as stated earlier, were repaid late by Treasury and then withheld by MSW. That led the technical administrator (PPS) and universities to go unpaid for a longer time, and paralyzed the regular supervision tasks for the Second Phase. Evidence shows that the Treasury took two months to transfer about US$1 million to the program and, after an additional five months, MSW released only one-third of it, in mid-March 2004. Today, it is still uncertain when and how much of the remaining two-thirds will be released by MSW. This jeopardizes the planning of the program.

**The Plan** *Ampliado de Inmunizaciones* **(PAI).** Since 1989, the Pan-American Health Organization (PAHO) has made it possible for the PAI to arrange purchases of vaccines and other inputs through a revolving fund PAHO created to help countries in the region eradicate, in a more efficient manner, polio, measles, tuberculosis, and other major diseases affecting children. PAHO helps facilitate good planning of the program by paying in advance for the purchase of vaccines, and getting reimbursed by the government later. Effective and instrumental as PAHO has been, however, it is clear that the MEF does not reciprocate by reimbursing PAHO in a timely manner for the purchases and distribution expenses. Table 3.12 shows that MEF took more than three months on average to repay PAHO for such purchases.

**PAI is one the finest and most efficient social programs, but is not yet protected by law.** Program operations are regulated by the Immunizations Law at the Ministry of Public Health (MPH), and aim to ensure adequate provision and programming of primary immunizations (immunization campaigns). Institutionally, the program continues to run the risk of government intervention because it is funded entirely by the Treasury. Official funding is enabled by the Constitution, which states that Ecuadorians are entitled to free access to primary vaccination services. Yet, despite this constitutional mandate, PAI was not instituted as an executing unit that could otherwise permit protecting its approved budget from future reductions. For the first time, in 2004, the approved budget was cut—and reduced in half under the commitment of FEIREP to provide the other half of financing. This arrangement has still not been agreed in writing by FEIREP and the Central Government.

**Another example of good formulation, planning, and supervision when local communities are involved.** Formulation and programming of immunization campaigns (nationwide information campaigns on regular or extraordinary vaccination programs supported principally by the government) are prepared in accordance with the basic needs of the population detected in the prevalence and incidence statistics collected through various local surveys. Vaccinations are planned ahead of time and executed by the Ministry's Provincial Branches (*Direcciones Provinciales*) through the District Branches (*Areas de Salud*) to the 1,743 hospitals throughout the country. Hospitals include the Health Centers, Health Sub-Centers, Health Posts and providers belonging to the *Hospital Materno Infantil* network. There are also Immunization Brigades, groups of health staff who provide the service in the Amazon region and other remote areas of the country. MPH created a technical administration office to direct the formulation, planning, and supervision activities in coordination with local health providers and communal organizations. There is active participation by local constituencies in the planning and implementation efforts through the Canton Committees, the Watch Committees, and the Immunization Brigades, which are acknowledged as being key players in the improvement and vigilance of the services provided by PAI. In fact, PAI is acknowledged to be one of the most successful social programs, helping to reduce extreme poverty by eradicating polio 12 years ago and measles 6 years ago.

**There are no major operating problems identified within service intermediaries and providers.** Problems related to unpaid wages in recent months have not led to disruptions in the service. At present, 176 of 220 municipalities participate in the provision of vaccination services, and it is expected that all municipalities will participate in next year's nationwide campaign. There are numerous individual bilateral agencies and non-governmental organizations (NGOs) participating in the verification of the service delivery. Among those are the U.S. Agency for International Development (USAID) and Physicians Without Borders, each working in different regions. In other areas such as technological development and training, there has also been enormous support provided by international cooperation programs and private donors. Among those are the Government of Luxembourg, PAHO, the United Nation's Children's Fund (UNICEF), Petroecuador, and multinational firms such as Glaxo Smith Kline Laboratories.

**The PAI operates well, but is supported with extra-budgetary resources.** The initial budget for PAI approved by Congress for 2003 was US$10.0 million, but it was cut to US$9 million (Table A.C.2). According to PAI, however, the actual budget was US$13 million, the difference funded by extra-budgetary resources other than Treasury. Like most social programs, PAI is funded entirely by the Treasury, which makes its operations vulnerable to changes in projected tax revenues and other urgent cash payments by Treasury. However, to avoid delays in purchases of vaccines, PAI entered into an agreement with PAHO. This international organization set a revolving fund available for all countries in the region to make advance payments to the supplier and thus ensure timely delivery of the vaccines to areas at risk. This has helped significantly in the vaccination planning, and has saved valuable time, considering that it takes 50 to 73 days on average for the purchase order to be processed through the PAHO bureaucracy, and then shipped and cleared in customs.

### TABLE A.C.2: BUDGET EXECUTION AT PAI, BY FINANCING SOURCE
#### (in millions of US dollars)

|  | Total | Treasury | Fondo de Solidaridad | WFP | Others |
|---|---|---|---|---|---|
| Initial budget | 10.0 | 10.0 | 0.0 | 0.0 | 0.0 |
| Revised budget | 9.0 | 9.0 | 0.0 | 0.0 | 0.0 |
| Executed (*devengado* basis) | 9.1 | 9.1 | 0.0 | 0.0 | 0.0 |
| Executed (cash basis) | 9.1 | 9.1 | 0.0 | 0.0 | 0.0 |

Note: * *Devengado* is the executed budget. It is the sum of budget commitments recognized by Treasury and supported by documentation certifying the service delivery.
Source: STFS.

**The major problem with PAI lies in the funding of the operational expenses to the service providers.** In that respect, Treasury has transferred the monies to the program, but often the MPH holds resources for unknown reasons. Interviews suggest that MPH owes about US$2 million of the US$11.1 million, inclusive of overdue payments from the previous year, transferred by the Treasury to the program. Yet, despite this problem, budget execution generally has been high, reaching 91 percent of the approved initial budget and 101 percent of the revised budget.

**Another problem detected with budget execution at PAI is the circumvention of external and other financial and technical assistance off the budgetary process.** In addition to the

## FIGURE A.C.2: ORGANIZATION OF PAI OPERATING NATIONWIDE

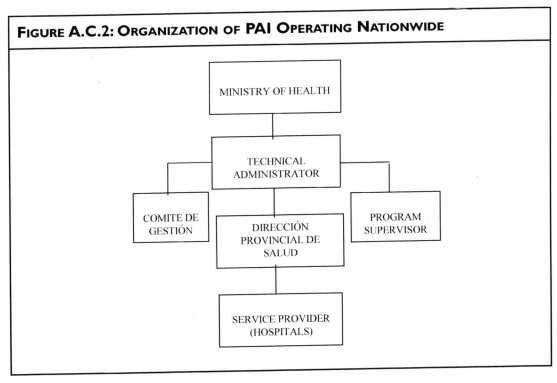

*Source:* Ministry of Health

US$9.1 million that the Treasury transferred through the Ministry of Health, there were extra-budgetary resources in the amount of US$2.9 millions, that is, 32 percent more than was originally allocated to the program's budget. These are funds donated with the official cooperation of Luxembourg (US$2.7 million), consisting of cold storage rooms and other equipment necessary to improve the local cold storage chain to ensure that adequate vaccinations are available, especially in the remotest areas of the country. Other donations included those from PAHO, UNICEF, Petroecuador, and the vaccine supplier Glaxo Smith Kline Laboratories.

**PAI, nevertheless, was successful in reaching almost 90 percent of the target population nationwide during 2003.** A total of 5.1 million vaccines were provided to infants, school-age children, and females aged 10 to 49. The following vaccines were administered: 355,000 doses against Bacillus Calmette-Guérin (BCG); 552,349 triple doses against diphtheria, tetanus, and polio; 657,110 against *pentavalentes* (a vaccine that immunizes against diphtheria, tetanus, pertussis, type-B influenza, and hepatitis B); 1,382,750 doses against polio alone; 90,558 doses against hepatitis B alone; 295,201 doses against measles; 518,332 doses against diphtheria and tetanus for children, and 1,085,912 doses against diphtheria and tetanus for women; and 157,882 doses against yellow fever. The goal for 2003 was to administer 5,264,991 vaccines to beneficiaries. An evaluation of beneficiaries has been successfully conducted by the Watch Committees and NGOs.

**The Free Maternity and Infant Care Program (LMG).** The LMG provides health services to pregnant women and to children under age 5, and preventive health services for women, such as screening for cancer, HIV, and other infectious diseases related to women and infants. This is the only priority social service administered under executing units and is administered in an autonomous manner. That is, it has its own executive organization, and its funding is deposited directly into a special account at the Central Bank of Ecuador, without any interference from the Ministry of Health.

## FIGURE A.C.3: ORGANIZATION OF LMG OPERATING IN 40 MUNICIPIOS

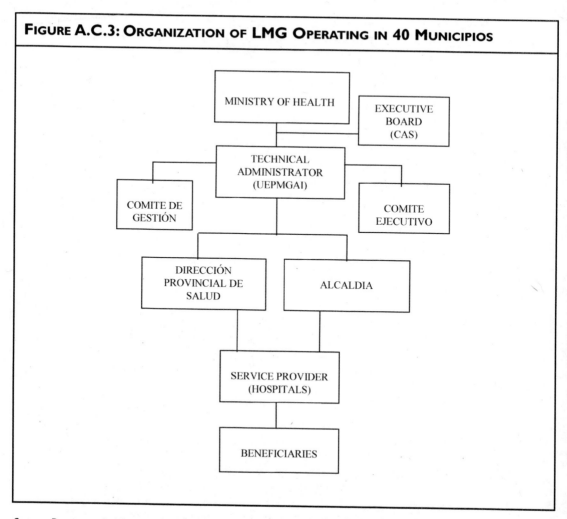

*Source:* Programa de Maternidad Gratuita y Atencion a la Infancia (LMG)

**The program has an organization with ample grassroots participation involving key official institutions and special-interest groups.** There is a top executive board (the Support and Monitoring Committee) chaired by the First Lady, as head of the National Institute for Children and the Family, and includes the MPH, the Executive Director of the National Women's Committee (CONAMU), and the President of the National Association of Municipalities (AME), among others. The Board appoints the Technical Administrator, the Executive Committee, and the Local Management and Monitoring Committees. Technical administration resides in the Executing Unit of the Free Maternity and Infant Care Program (UEPMGAI), which was created in mid-2002 to provide technical, financial, supervisory, and training services to social providers nationwide. The Executive Committee comprises representatives of other local and international agencies. Finally, the Local Management and Monitoring Committee comprises representatives of health intermediaries and providers, women, and indigenous organizations, and local governments. Service providers are all hospitals belonging to the MPH and the LMG system (Figure A.C.3).

**In 2003, LMG reached a women and infant population coverage ratio of 16 percent within 40 of the 220 municipalities participating in a pilot maternal and infant care program.** In contrast with other social programs, LMG is enabled by its charter to get the municipalities and other local organizations involved in the development and provision of the social service. The Solidarity Fund provides most of the funding for the program, but financial arrangements with this agency are subject to annual revision and renewal. According to LMG data, maternal care in rural areas expanded its coverage significantly in 2003: 90 percent of pregnant women received first and subsequent pre-delivery tests, and three of five pregnant women even received dental care services. However, only very low numbers of pregnant women received HIV tests and sexually transmitted disease exams.

**The LMG was created by a law, and is supported by a broad-based structure of powerful women and indigenous organizations, which gives it the capacity not only to protect and execute the budget as initially planned, but also to retrieve large overdue funds not paid in the previous year.** As a result, the program was able to raise 28 percent more of budget resources than initially planned in 2003, as Treasury funding was doubled to US$10.4 million, from US$4.8 million. In 2003, LMG reported a budget execution of 120 percent, when measured by the approved initial budget of US$19.9 million. The program's budget execution declined to 94 percent when measured by the revised increased budget of US$25.5 million (Table A.C.3). This is the only social program the initial budget of which grew, and considerably, whereas the revised budgets (*codificado*) of other programs mostly declined.

### TABLE A.C.3: BUDGET EXECUTION AT LMG, BY FINANCING SOURCE
#### (in millions of US dollars)

|  | Total | Treasury | Fondo de Solidaridad | WFP | Others |
|---|---|---|---|---|---|
| Initial budget | 19.9 | 4.8 | 15.1 | 0.0 | 0.0 |
| Revised budget | 25.5 | 10.4 | 15.1 | 0.0 | 0.0 |
| Executed (*devengado* basis) | 23.9 | 8.9 | 15.0 | 0.0 | 0.0 |
| Executed (cash basis) | 22.1 | 7.1 | 15.0 | 0.0 | 0.0 |

*Source:* STFS.

**LMG is funded mostly by the Solidarity Fund (59 percent) and by earmarked tax revenues (41 percent).** The Solidarity Fund provides a fixed amount every year (US$15.1 million), whereas the earmarked fund represents the 3 percent of the Special Consumption Tax . As mentioned, the program operates as an executing unit within the MPH. This provides the advantage of getting all budgetary resources deposited directly by Treasury and the *Fondo de Solidaridad* into a special account at the Central Bank of Ecuador. In principle, this prohibits the MPH from using these resources for other purposes. Once the funds are deposited in the program's main account they are transferred by the program, according to its own evaluation guidelines and controls, to the service providers' individual bank accounts within the Provinces, but through the program's intermediaries (the Management Committee).

*The Food and Community Development Program* (**PRADEC**). A reformed social program with an entrepreneurial vision, PRADEC provides food security services to children aged 2 to 6, and to handicapped and elderly people. In addition, it provides technical assistance in the development of productive activities that can improve the income and consumption of rural households. PRADEC has undergone a major organizational change, starting to reshape its managerial and monitoring strategies through more vigorous community participation and more efficient use of financial resources. Compared to previous years, supervision and evaluation of the service are now monitored more closely.

**Like the PAI, PRADEC conducts its financial management and food purchases through an arrangement with an international cooperation agency.** In this case, the UN World Food Program (WFP) has valuable expertise in the financial management and provision of PRADEC's food and its connection with multinational food suppliers. The financial manager agrees to execute the funding arrangement with Treasury, and the purchaser agrees to advance

**FIGURE A.C.4: ORGANIZATION OF PRADEC OPERATING IN 443 JUNTAS PARROQUIALES**

Source: Programa de Alimentacion y Desarrollo Comunitario (PRADEC)

the purchases of food, and then get reimbursed by the Government of Ecuador. This facilitates better planning and helps avoid major disruptions in times of liquidity stress at Treasury. Another reason for PRADEC's performance is its revamped internal organization and the active participation of local communities. Service providers are the community cafeterias (*comedores comunitarios*), facilitated by the Ministry of Social Welfare in coordination with the parish committees and local communities. There are practically no intermediaries because food deliveries are made directly by the financial manager through a chain of distributors that is regulated by internal rules, and are executed by the program's technical administrator (Figure A.C.4).

**PRADEC suffered a heavy budget cut in 2003.** Treasury, its sole financial source, reduced its funding due to emerging conflicts over the reporting of expenses. As a result, budget execution was 57 percent when measured by the approved initial budget, and 70 percent when measured by the revised *codificado* budget (Table A.C.4). The program, however, progressed rapidly as the role of the parish committees evolved positively by enhancing the supervision and control functions through a system of inspectors. In spite of the budget reduction, the program was able to meet the service goals within the first and second quintiles of the population, and the food supplies were purchased and delivered in a timely fashion.

**The School Nutrition Program (PAE).** PAE, like PRADEC and PANN are part of the Integrated System of Children Care—known as SIAN). It is the second biggest social program in Ecuador. It provided lunch services in the Sierra Region to nearly 520,00 children aged 5 to 14

(120 days) during 2003. In the Coastal Region, lunch services were provided to 751,710 students and breakfast to 371,821 students, for 40 days each. The goal for 2003 was to provide lunch services to 1,450,000 during a minimum of 160 days. Over the years, PAE has turned out to be the most ambitious of all food programs in Ecuador, aimed at providing both breakfast and lunch supplements to school-age children for a period of 160 days in the Coast and the Sierra. Compared to other countries, this program is much larger, because only breakfast is provided by most countries (such as the Glass of Milk Program in Peru). As a result, the budget increased from US$17.5 million in 2001 to US$30.7 million in 2003. Yet, the budget is not protected against possible reductions by the Central Government, the Solidarity Fund, or other parties.

### TABLE A.C.4: BUDGET EXECUTION AT PRADEC, BY FINANCING SOURCE
#### (in millions of US dollars)

|  | Total | Treasury | Fondo de Solidaridad | WFP | Others |
|---|---|---|---|---|---|
| Initial budget | 12.2 | 12.2 | 0.0 | 0.0 | 0.0 |
| Revised budget | 10.0 | 10.0 | 0.0 | 0.0 | 0.0 |
| Executed (*devengado* basis) | 7.0 | 7.0 | 0.0 | 0.0 | 0.0 |
| Executed (cash basis) | 7.0 | 7.0 | 0.0 | 0.0 | 0.0 |

*Source:* STFS.

**The organizational structure is embedded in a frail Education Ministry.** As ambitious as the coverage of this program is becoming, the fact is that the organization is facing increasing institution building and absorption challenges. The Program's technical administrator is not able to adequately program and evaluate the services because the education sector faces enormous institutional problems, and the PAE services have become politicized at the local level. To prevent budget execution problems, PAE has arranged for the financial management function to be conducted through an independent entity, the United Nations Development Program/World Food Program (UNDP/WFP).

**As the program is not executed through an executing unit , its reliance on transfers from the Solidarity Fund** negatively affects the quality of social expenditure. In 2003, more than half of the funding was not transferred because the second-largest partner of the program, the Solidarity Fund, did not comply with the agreed financing. In fact, PAE had the largest budget cutback in 2003 of all priority social programs.

### TABLE A.C.5: BUDGET EXECUTION AT PAE, BY FINANCING SOURCE
#### (in millions of US dollars)

|  | Total | Treasury | Fondo de Solidaridad | WFP | Others |
|---|---|---|---|---|---|
| Initial budget | 30.7 | 16.0 | 12.0 | 2.7 | 0.0 |
| Revised budget | 17.0 | 16.0 | 0.0 | 1.0 | 0.0 |
| Executed (*devengado* basis) | 14.2 | 13.2 | 0.0 | 1.0 | 0.0 |
| Executed (cash basis) | 15.2 | 14.2 | 0.0 | 1.0 | 0.0 |

*Source:* STFS.

**The lack of a formal institutional agreement that allows steady execution of the budget process and proper financial arrangements, particularly with the Solidarity Fund, is a major problem.** In 2003, Congress approved an initial budget of US$30.7 million, more than half funded by Treasury. Later, however, it was cut by 45 percent because the program's major partner, the Solidarity Fund, did not transfer the US$12 million it contributed in the previous year (Table A.C.5). The Solidarity Fund alleges that the program neither justified nor reported

## FIGURE A.C.5: ORGANIZATION OF PAE OPERATING IN THE COAST AND SIERRA

Source: Programa de Alimentacion Escolar (PAE)

the quarterly expenses, but the program's authorities claimed the contrary. Also, the UN WFP reduced its commitment in the approved budget by one-third, to only US$1 million. This international agency alleges that MEF did not comply with its obligation to reimburse the UN agency for the purchases of food in a timely fashion. Currently, it takes an average of 172 days for Treasury to refund WFP for these purchases, and the first transfer of last year was realized in July 2003.

**PAE also suffers from a severe pro-poor targeting problem.** In 2003, among all programs belonging to SIAN, PAE had the poorest targeting ratio in quintiles 1 and 2. Whereas PANN and PRADEC reached 67 and 100 percent of their intended beneficiaries, PAE barely reached 60 percent. Hence, close to half of their intended beneficiaries were not reached by this program.

**Poor targeting is also compounded by an inadequate selection of its main beneficiaries.** According to studies developed by SIAN, the nutritional impact of PAE on its intended beneficiaries, children from 6 to 15 years, is almost nil, and this explains why SIAN is gradually shifting food-aid resources toward children in the 0-5 years range, where malnutrition rates are highest and needs strongest.

**Other issues are the slow reporting of** *justificaciones*[3] **to MEF, and the bureaucratic delays in payments.** As stated, the financial management of the program is conducted by UNDP and WFP, which also subcontract and purchase the food supplies. These international agencies pay in advance for the food items to the suppliers, and then are reimbursed by the MSW. Given delays in MEF transfers, this method has proven very useful also enabling the program to operate with transparency.

---

3. *Justificaciones* are the documented explanations on the use given to public funds transferred by the Treasury to the social programs that are required to justify the next payment.

# Annex D

# BUDGETARY FRAMEWORK OF DECENTRALIZATION IN ECUADOR

Since 1997 Ecuador has developed into an increasingly decentralized unitary state.[1] After repeated failures in the preceding years, subnational government successfully gained access to additional national tax and oil revenue. The centerpiece of this fiscal bargain is the "15-Percent Law," which transfers a portion of Central Government revenue to municipalities and provincial councils in a revenue-sharing arrangement. As a result of the implementation of this law, the amount of all 17 intergovernmental grants has increased significantly: while in 1996 transfers represented 1.2 percent of gross domestic product (GDP), this share rose to 2.7 percent in 2003,[2] and in terms of current Central Government revenue, the share increased from 8.4 percent in 1996 to 16.5 percent in 2003 (Figure A.D.1). From an international perspective, this represents a fairly advanced degree of fiscal decentralization. Similar degrees of transfers are employed, for instance, in Bolivia and Venezuela.[3] Both in depth and speed, in recent years the decentralization process in Ecuador has advanced significantly—at least on the revenue side.

**Much less pronounced was decentralization on the expenditure side.** With a few exceptions, transfers of responsibilities in the health, education, and roads sectors do not occur on a large scale or in a consistent manner, and only a few municipalities have adopted new responsibilities in those sectors. To break this inertia, during 2001 and 2002 a large-scale bargaining process took place for the transfer of expenditure responsibilities in the environment, agriculture, roads, and tourism sectors. Yet this attempt also ended in deadlock. Although several agreements were signed among Central Government ministries, provincial councils, and municipalities,[4] they were not applied in practice. Expenditures today remain as centralized as

---

1. This Annex was prepared by Jonas Frank.

2. This is still much less than the 6 percent GDP that federal Argentina makes available to its provinces; however, they are responsible for health and education services, and the fiscal problems Argentina faced due to a deficient intergovernmental setup speak for themselves.

3. Both Bolivia and Venezuela also transfer roughly 20 percent of Central Government revenue to subnational governments. This, however, is not a degree of fiscal decentralization comparable to Colombia, which makes roughly 45 percent of Central Government revenue available to departmental and municipal governments. However, Ecuador is far more advanced than many Central American countries, where the share of transfers usually does not exceed 5 percent. During the 1980s and early 1990s, Ecuador transferred roughly 9 percent of current revenue to subnational levels.

4. In total 140 of 220 municipalities, and all 22 provincial councils, formally participated in this bargaining process.

127

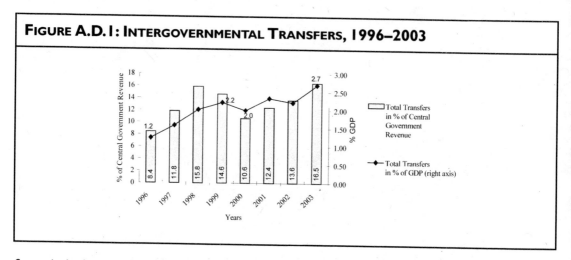

**FIGURE A.D.1: INTERGOVERNMENTAL TRANSFERS, 1996–2003**

*Source:* Author's calculations based on information provided by MEF (2003) and Central Bank (2003).

they were in the 1970s, when the oil boom led to unparalleled public sector growth. So far, decentralization of expenditures has fallen short of expectations.

**This particular type of decentralization came at a cost, however—a cost that is only beginning to emerge and become fully apparent.** The sudden increase in transfers of revenue was not followed by a commensurate transfer of expenditure responsibilities. Municipalities and provincial councils—as well as their associations, AME and the *Consorcio de Consejos Provinciales del Ecuador* (CONCOPE), respectively—have repeatedly and expressly refused to link transferred revenue to the explicit adoption of new expenditure responsibilities, and the center has so far been unable to convince local politicians of the need to overhaul the fiscal framework in order to regain the much-needed budget flexibility—a condition to sustain dollarization.

**This has put additional fiscal stress on the national government.** As shown above, never were transfers higher in terms of GDP, and never was a higher share of Central Government revenue transferred to subnational government than in 2003. In the medium to long term, this implies a severe sustainability problem for the national level: while the real average GDP growth during 1996–2003 was 1.8 percent, and Central Government revenue grew an average 3.4 percent, the increase in transfers during the same period was 14 percent without any further accountability in return. In other words, intergovernmental grants have grown over-proportionately relative to the growth of the economy and the revenue the nation was able to raise. To comply with the amount of intergovernmental grants, the center has sacrificed budget flexibility on one hand, and fiscal responsibility on the other.

**Some of the dilemmas originate in the way transfers are administered.** A particular feature is earmarking of revenue. This type of management comes in two forms: (a) for transfers in general revenue-sharing arrangements, which are applied, among others, for the 15-Percent Law,[5] and (b) for transfers that tap resources before entering the national budget ("off-budget assignments"). While the first form of earmarking provides subnational government with a transparent form of financing, the second form is worrisome since it establishes discretionary property over some sources of revenue. Thus, subnational governments receive earmarked revenue from, among other sources, the income tax, oil revenue, the vehicle tax, surpluses of public enterprises,

---

5. The establishment of the *Fondo de Desarrollo Seccional* (FODESEC) in 1990 represents the first regular revenue-sharing arrangement in Ecuador, and hence a break from the past and the practice of transferring extrabudgetary funds.

## FIGURE A.D.2: SOURCES OF REVENUE FOR TRANSFERS TO SUBNATIONAL GOVERNMENTS (IN PERCENT), 1991–2002

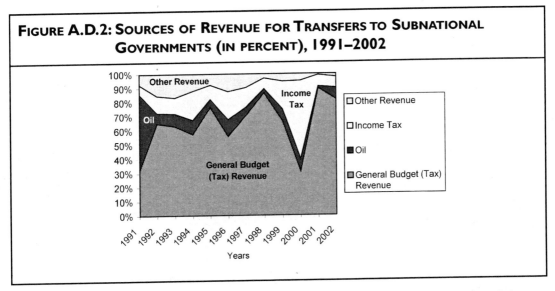

*Note:* "Other Revenue" includes transfers from Central Government agencies (*Contraloria*, among others) that are transferred separately and directly from different agencies. The beneficiaries of earmarked funds obtain a share of the vehicle tax, a share of the surplus of public enterprises, a share of import taxes, and a share of taxes of domestic credit operations. General Budget (Tax) Revenue includes a share of oil pertaining to the 15-Percent Law (1997 onward).
*Source:* Author's calculation based on Development State Bank (BEDE) (*Sistema de Información Municipal* [2001]) and (unpublished) information provided by the Ministry of Economy and Finance (the yearly *Acuerdos*, which define the sources and amounts for transfers to subnational governments).

import taxes, and a tax on domestic credit operations.[6] Off-budget earmarking is a threat to budget flexibility and undermines transparency.

**Although negative from an overall perspective, earmarking is appealing for subnational governments.** Not only does it protect financing in an environment of competing claims on scarce resources, but, more important, earmarking acts like a countercyclical revenue policy tool for municipalities and provincial councils. Recipients of earmarked funds usually receive funds in a timely, stable, predictable way. In contrast, recipients of allocated non-earmarked resources from the national budget suffer in particular during times of economic crisis. This is evidenced by the crisis years 1999 and 2000, when transfers from earmarked resources remained stable, and hence their share in the amount of total transfers increased significantly (Figure A.D.2). In a volatile economic environment, as often prevails in Ecuador, earmarking fulfills an important stabilizing function for subnational governments—despite its negative impact on national public finances.

**Consequently, earmarking has historically been high during economic crises.** This has led to an inefficiently high level of earmarking. The rationale behind this is that social groups in Ecuador were trapped into a social dilemma: all of them could have been better off if they reneged unilaterally on earmarking. But a unilateral restraint would have benefited all others, a perverse incentive mechanism that prevented them from achieving collectively superior outcomes. Local politicians and the different provinces were trapped into this very dilemma.

**While the recent trend in fiscal decentralization came at a cost for the Central Government, the level of executed spending and service delivery efficiency at the local levels has been undermined from at least four perspectives.** First, the intergovernmental transfer system establishes a fragmented and contradictory incentive framework that sends confusing sig-

---

6. This is channeled through the FODESEC Fund.

| Table A.D.1: Current and Capital Spending of Municipalities and Provincial Councils (in thousand USD), 2003 | |
|---|---|
| **Total Expenditure** | **1,102** |
| Current Expenditure | 621 |
| Wages and salaries | 169 |
| Purchases of goods and services | 352 |
| Interest payments | 3 |
| External | 3 |
| Current transfers | 97 |
| To IESS | 10 |
| To other public sector | 27 |
| To private sector | 60 |
| Capital Expenditure | 480 |
| Fixed capital expenditure | 480 |
| Other | 0 |

Source: MEF.

nals to subnational governments. Transfers are based on 17 different grants. Each of these grants establishes different criteria for resource distribution (see Table A.3 in the Annex), thereby creating a complex web of rules and regulations for the use of funds. Although there is no earmarking for specific expenditures—for instance health and education—there are multiple rules limiting their use for current and investment spending. The 15-Percent Law, for instance, mandates that at least 90 percent of these resources must be used for investment purposes, and 10 percent for current spending. However, in practice, current expenditures take a much higher share of municipal and provincial government budgets: in 2003 some 56.4 percent of expenditures were destined to wages and salaries, and goods and services. Only 43.6 percent were used for proper investment purposes (Table A.D.1). Yet monitoring of and sanctions[7] on the use of resources remain cumbersome, and are not applied regularly.[8]

**Municipalities and provincial councils have taken advantage of an underregulated subnational sector.** In an environment where the national level has failed to signal spending priorities to local government, they have quite naturally developed their own expenditure patterns and priorities. The lion's share of subnational expenditures is destined to providing two services: urban streets and roads (32.9 percent) as well as a number of non-specified public works (Table A.D.2). The importance of these two sectors is contrasting with expenditures that are funded only by a minor share of municipal budgets. Ecuador must decide whether these local spending purposes are justified when looking at the high level of transfers—particularly low are investments in the education (3.6 percent) and health (0.5 percent) sectors, yet it is these services that traditionally require a high share of Central Government grants. This is particularly so because of the positive externalities associated with these services. In other words, transfers compensate subnational government for producing benefits that spill over into other local jurisdictions. A high level of transfers would precisely constitute an appropriate incentive framework not only to deal with positive externalities, but also to give the Central Government the leverage to redirect

---

7. Each year roughly 150 of 220 municipalities are notified or alerted by the Comptroller's Office for inappropriate budget management practices. Most of them are able to justify budget management ex post, but a small number of municipalities are subject to judicial processes.

8. However, monitoring of classifications for current and capital investment is always difficult to establish. In addition, the *Ley Orgánica de Administración Financiera y Control* (LOAFYC) states that municipalities can by request to the Ministry of Economy and Finance amend their budget classifications so that current spending is classified as investment expenditures, by, for instance, listing "*recursos humanos para inversion.*"

## TABLE A.D.2: PRIORITIES OF SUBNATIONAL INVESTMENT SPENDING, 2002

| Service and Sector | Amount of Investment in US$ million | In Percent of Total Investment |
|---|---|---|
| Urban Planning and Cadastre | 0.3 | 0.1 |
| Bus terminal | 0.4 | 0.1 |
| Slaughterhouses | 0.5 | 0.1 |
| Cemetery | 0.8 | 0.2 |
| Solid waste | 1.7 | 0.3 |
| Health | 3.1 | 0.5 |
| Markets | 5.6 | 1.0 |
| Community Works | 10.0 | 1.7 |
| Recreation | 16.6 | 2.9 |
| Education | 20.6 | 3.6 |
| Water | 29.8 | 5.2 |
| Sewage | 35.7 | 6.2 |
| Streets and roads | 189.9 | 32.9 |
| Other public works | 261.9 | 45.4 |
|  | 577.0 | 100.0 |

Source: Author's calculations based on information provided by MEF (2004).

subnational expenditures into sectors it feels provide most value added to communities and socioeconomic development. Transfers in the form of earmarking, matching grants, and other means, are specific models of fiscal management that could be used to achieve this goal. None of these, however, has been applied in Ecuador in a consistent manner.

Second, transfers have weakened accountability relationships with local citizens and users of services. Because of the high level of transfers, mayors and prefects do not necessarily need to tax their citizens, and hence become accountable to the center. Local own revenue did not grow proportionate to the level of transfers. In fact, between 1997 and 2002, the share of own revenue available to local government declined (Figure A.D.3). This caused an increase in vertical fiscal imbalances, and a higher share of subnational expenditures is now financed by the center through transfers. Yet given the high proportion of transfers in local portfolios, mayors and prefects "do not feel the pain of the marginal tax dollar" they spend. This, in turn, does not create incentives for efficient, cost-effective, and fiscally sustainable service delivery.

Third, the particular purpose of intergovernmental transfers remains vague. The criteria that are used for compensation do not clearly focus on either fiscal *capacity* or expenditure *needs*. By putting weight on Unsatisfied Basic Needs (NBI) and population, transfers explicitly compensate for neither low fiscal capacity nor expenditure needs. The current transfer system is a hybrid between these two options. This is not to say that transfers do not compensate for either low fiscal capacity or spending needs at all, but a clearer focus could establish a more coherent incentive framework for subnational governments.

Fourth, the transfer system rewards the inefficient distribution of responsibilities that exists across levels of government. No clear delineation of responsibilities has emerged among munici palities, provincial councils, and the Central Government, and the large number of implementing agencies that exist. The dual political structure on each subnational level, whereby elected and delegated authority coexist, is a major obstacle to accountability.[9] A series of autonomous agen-

---

9. Dual authorities exist on each subnational level: on the provincial level (appointed Governor and elected Prefect), on the cantonal level (appointed teniente político and elected mayor), and on the parish level (appointed Jefe Político and elected Presidente de la Junta Parroquial Rural). The Constitutional Reform of 1998 eliminates both the Teniente Político and the Jefe Político, but they still exist in practice.

**FIGURE A.D.3: OWN REVENUE AND EXPENDITURES PER LEVEL OF GOVERNMENT (IN PERCENT) AND VERTICAL FISCAL IMBALANCES, 1997 AND 2002**

Note: Incomplete reporting on subnational governments for 2002 (mostly on own revenue); in particular larger provincial councils have not reported their own revenue, including Guayas and Manabí.
Sources: Author's calculation, based on information provided by MEF (2004) and Central Bank (2002).

cies exist in parallel to sector ministries and subnational governments. Regional development authorities,[10] with budgets that often exceed those of municipalities and provincial councils, execute many responsibilities that could be decentralized. This includes responsibility over rural roads, secondary roads, school buildings, hospitals, rural development programs, water and irrigation systems, and electrification programs, among others.[11] Whereas municipalities are responsible for many urban services—streets, water and sewerage, electricity, markets—no clear delineation regarding provincial councils has emerged. This is compounded by the fact that the jurisdiction of provincial councils is ambiguous with regard to urban and rural areas. Though it is constitutionally mandated that provincial councils are responsible for rural areas, they often provide services in urban areas. If involved in urban areas at all, the involvement is based on informal arrangements and personal understandings with municipal authorities. The transfer system, however, rewards this inefficient institutional setup because it allows subnational government to pay for duplications and overlaps in responsibilities.

---

10. The more important regional development authorities include Centro de Reconversión Económica del Azuay (CREA), Centro de Desarrollo de la Cuenca del Guayas (CEDEGE), Centro de Reconversión del Manabí (CRM), and Unidad de Desarrollo del Norte (UDENOR).

11. No data are available with regard to sectoral allocation of investments carried out by regional development authorities.

## TABLE A.D.3: CAPITAL SPENDING OF MUNICIPALITIES AND PROVINCIAL COUNCILS IN THE HEALTH AND EDUCATION SECTORS, 2002

| Regions | Health | | Education | | Total Investment | |
|---|---|---|---|---|---|---|
| | In US$ million | In Percent | In US$ million | In Percent | In US$ million | In Percent |
| Costa | 1.4 | 45.3 | 4.3 | 21.1 | 300.2 | 43.3 |
| Oriente | 0.6 | 19.6 | 5.8 | 28.4 | 87.9 | 12.7 |
| Sierra | 1.1 | 35.1 | 10.3 | 50.5 | 305.4 | 44.0 |
| Total | 3.1 | 100.0 | 20.4 | 100.0 | 693.5 | 100.0 |

*Note:* Costa includes the Galápagos Islands.
*Source:* Author's calculation, based on MEF (2004).

**While the fiscal decentralization framework is questionable from many perspectives, ironically it may constitute a favorable framework for *some* services, particularly in the social sectors.** Public services in health and education typically require a high level of transfers to compensate for positive externalities that are associated with service delivery, and that spill over into other local jurisdictions. Grants made available by the Central Government usually provide incentives for municipalities and provincial councils to spend in those sectors, even though the benefits—in terms of higher educational attainments (education) or disease control (public health)—do not accrue only to the population residing in those areas. Yet the misfortune herein is that the involvement of municipalities and provincial councils in these sectors is, as yet, minimal: both subnational governments spend only 0.5 percent of their investment budget on health, and 3.6 percent on education. In other words, less than 5 percent of subnational investment expenditures are destined to the social sectors (Table A.D.3). The challenge remains for local politicians to venture into these new, largely unexplored areas of service delivery.

**This picture is corroborated by taking a closer look at the education and health sectors separately.** In the education sector, municipal involvement is stronger in the pre-primary and primary levels compared to the secondary level. However, it remains very limited overall. In the education sector—at the pre-primary, primary, and secondary levels—only a minor share of teachers (0.4 percent of the total number of teachers), schools (0.4 percent of the total number of schools), and students (0.5 percent of the total number of students) are administered by municipalities (Table A.D.4). Both the Central Government and a large number of semi-autonomous or private entities deliver most of the country's educational services. To date, Ecuador's education system has either not taken advantage of municipalities, or has selected other service delivery models that emphasize deconcentration and school autonomy as a form of strengthening service providers directly.[12]

**This situation is similar in the health sector.** Less than 1 percent of total public health spending is executed by municipalities. Given their population size, the Quito and Guayaquil municipalities are outliers in terms the budget destined to the health sector. Their involvement far exceeds those of any other municipal government. Expenditures remain heavily centralized in the Ministry of Public Health, or are administered by a wide range of other autonomous or semi-autonomous institutions (Table A.D.5). As yet, however, and with few exceptions, no consistent involvement of subnational governments in the health sector has developed.

**Aligning increased transfers with expenditure responsibilities remains the most important challenge on the road to decentralized government, in particular in the social sectors.**

---

12. This includes models, such as *Redes Amigas*, supported by the international donor community (Inter-American Development Bank, among others; and previously, the World Bank).

## TABLE A.D.4: ADMINISTRATION OF SCHOOLS, TEACHERS, AND STUDENTS IN THE EDUCATION SECTOR, SCHOOL YEAR 2000–01

| Education Level | Administration | Schools | | Teachers | | Students | |
|---|---|---|---|---|---|---|---|
| | | Number | Percent | Number | Percent | Number | Percent |
| Pre-primary schooling | Central Government | 2,694 | 52.8 | 5,020 | 36.5 | 109,685 | 55.0 |
| | Municipal Government | 17 | 0.3 | 58 | 0.4 | 915 | 0.5 |
| | Other (private or semi-autonomous schools) | 2,388 | 46.8 | 8,677 | 63.2 | 88,988 | 44.6 |
| | Total | 5,099 | 100.0 | 13,755 | 100.0 | 199,588 | 100.0 |
| Primary schooling | Central Government | 14,004 | 77.7 | 55,472 | 65.5 | 1,436,124 | 73.5 |
| | Municipal Government | 74 | 0.4 | 455 | 0.5 | 10,063 | 0.5 |
| | Other (private or semi-autonomous schools) | 3,936 | 21.9 | 28,831 | 34.0 | 508,873 | 26.0 |
| | Total | 18,014 | 100.0 | 84,758 | 100.0 | 1,955,060 | 100.0 |
| Secondary schooling | Central Government | 1,938 | 55.8 | 51,988 | 64.1 | 662,666 | 69.2 |
| | Municipal Government | 7 | 0.2 | 178 | 0.2 | 3,134 | 0.3 |
| | Other (private or semi-autonomous schools) | 1,529 | 44.0 | 28,905 | 35.7 | 292,261 | 30.5 |
| | Total | 3,474 | 100.0 | 81,071 | 100.0 | 958,061 | 100.0 |
| All education levels | Central Government | 18,636 | 70.1 | 112,480 | 62.6 | 2,208,475 | 71.0 |
| | Municipal Government | 98 | 0.4 | 691 | 0.4 | 14,112 | 0.5 |
| | Other (private or semi-autonomous schools) | 7,853 | 29.5 | 66,413 | 37.0 | 890,122 | 28.6 |
| | Total | 26,587 | 100.0 | 179,584 | 100.0 | 3,112,709 | 100.0 |

Note: "Other" school types include *escuelas fiscomisionales* and clerical schools. Central Government schools include *escuelas fiscales*. Secondary education equivalent to *nivel medio* (*ciclo básico, post ciclo básico, bachillerato en ciencias, bachillerato técnico, postbachillerato*).

Source: Author's calculation based on information provided by the *Sistema Nacional de Estadísticas Educativas del Ecuador* (SINEC).

## TABLE A.D.5: PUBLIC SPENDING IN THE HEALTH SECTOR (IN THOUSAND USD), 1997

| | Total Spending | Percent of Total Spending |
|---|---|---|
| Ministry of Health | 176.3 | 47.3 |
| Quito Municipality | 0.6 | 0.2 |
| Guayaquil Municipality | 1.1 | 0.3 |
| Other Municipalities | 0.3 | 0.1 |
| Other Institutions* | 194.5 | 52.1 |
| Total | 372.8 | 100.0 |

Note: * "Other institutions" include the Servicio de Erradicación de Malaria (SNEM), Instituto Nacional de Higiene (INH), Centro Estatal de Medicamentos e Insumos Médicos (CEMEIM), Patronato San José, universities, military, police, Seguro Social Campesino, Social Security Institute (IESS), and Military Social Security Institute (ISSFA). No updated and more recent information exists.

Source: Author's calculations based on *Cuentas Nacionales de Salud* (1997:17).

A future decentralization process in the social sectors would have a considerable impact on both national and subnational budgets. Municipalities and provincial councils and their associations have repeatedly refused to adopt new expenditure responsibilities commensurate with the new funds that are made available. Therefore, they mistakenly claim that any new responsibilities would need to be financed with additional transfers. This, under the present framework, would further deteriorate vertical fiscal imbalances and dependency rates of subnational levels of government. It would also most likely imply that the share of local current spending would increase, to come up with the needed wages for teachers, nurses, and doctors. In the education sector, in particular, improved service delivery may require emphasis on current as opposed to investment expenditures. Consequently, possibilities for fiscal adjustment on subnational levels may even further deteriorate as spending becomes more rigid. A deepening of decentralization—for example, in the social sectors—within the current institutional setup is therefore possible only if subnational governments first make optimal use of increased current transfers to finance new expenditure responsibilities. Only when they become supported by results-oriented and well-monitored mechanisms, and when fiscal space allows them to free additional resources, should Ecuadorian municipalities and provincial councils be exposed to an additional transfer push within sustainable levels.

# Annex E

# ALTERNATIVES FOR COOKING-GAS SUBSIDY REFORM[1]

## Introduction

The objective of this Annex is to promote the discussion of the cooking-gas subsidy reform in Ecuador. It is divided in two parts. The first part presents a series of results on alternative reform scenarios, which stems from the World Bank's Ecuador Poverty Assessment. The second part evaluates the various mechanisms that could be used to implement reform.

## Diagnosis, Targeting Options and Impact

The gas subsidy, in its current format, is universal (every household in the country has a right to this subsidy). Consequently, and given the fact that gas consumption is higher in richer households than in poorer ones, the subsidy follows a regressive distribution (richer households benefit relatively more from the subsidy than poor households (Table A.E.1).

Indeed, most of the subsidy is distributed to white and Mestizo households, while only a small portion reaches indigenous and Afro-Ecuadorian homes, since the latter are mostly poor and exhibit a low consumption of gas. This does not mean, however, that the subsidy is not an important portion of these households' consumption, which explains the strong resistance to the reform or elimination of the subsidy within the indigenous movement, for example (Table A.E.2).

The subsidy is not only targeted inadequately, but it is also expensive. It cost the government of Ecuador approximately 0.9 percent of the GNP per year. All of the above points to a need to reform. Improving its targeting is an option, so as to provide more benefits for the poor, or considering its complete elimination is another option.

A series of simulations were conducted with the purpose of evaluating the impact of various reform alternatives and/or eliminating the cooking gas subsidy. Following is a description of the methodology used and a summary of findings.

Simulations are based on data obtained from the *Encuesta de Condiciones de Vida 1999* (LSMS Survey 1999), which assumes a subsidy equal to US$3.4/liter (the difference between market price—US$5/liter—and the price consumers paid—US$1.6/liter—at the time these calculations were made). Although these amounts might have changed over the past months, ren-

---

1. This Annex was prepared by Carolina Sánchez-Páramo.

**TABLE A.E.1: Subsidy Distribution by Consumption Deciles**

| Consumption Deciles | Percentage of Total Consumption | Percentage of Total Spending in Subsidy |
|---|---|---|
| 1 (poorer) | 2 | 3 |
| 2 | 3 | 5 |
| 3 | 4 | 7 |
| 4 | 5 | 8 |
| 5 | 6 | 9 |
| 6 | 7 | 10 |
| 7 | 9 | 12 |
| 8 | 1 1 | 1 3 |
| 9 | 1 6 | 1 6 |
| 10 (richer) | 37 | 17 |

*Source:* Vos et alia (2003).

**TABLE A.E.2: Distribution of the Cooking-Gas Subsidy by Ethnic Group**

| Ethnic Group | Number of people | Percentage of Total | Percentage of Total Using Gas |
|---|---|---|---|
| Indigenous | 824,189 | 6.8 | 42.9 |
| Afro-Ecuadorian | 267,196 | 2.2 | 89.5 |
| Other | 1,257,466 | 10.45 | 92.9 |

*Source:* Authors' calculations using the Population Census 2001.

dering the estimated fiscal savings a mere approximation, the exercise continues to be informative with regard to the impact caused by the various policy options being considered.

- ▇ Scenario 1: Current Situation
- ▇ Scenario 2: Complete elimination of subsidy along with an equal drop in the price of total consumption in the household
- ▇ Scenario 3: Complete elimination of subsidy along with a distribution of generated fiscal savings to poor households, in the form of transfers
- ▇ Scenario 4: Complete elimination of subsidy along with a distribution of generated fiscal savings to poor households in SelBen's quintiles 1 and 2
- ▇ Scenario 5: Retargeting subsidy to households in the System of Selection of Beneficiaries' (SelBen's) quintiles 1 and 2

The economic impact is measured based on two variables: fiscal savings generated by the reform, and the effect of the latter on the monetary poverty rate and gap.[2]

Under these assumptions, Scenarios 2 and 5 generate the largest fiscal savings (100 and 76.3 percent, respectively), and Scenario 3 reaches the lowest poverty rate, followed by the status quo (Table A.E.3).

---

2. To carry on estimations, and with the purpose of simplifying some of the calculations needed for the simulations, it is assumed that: (i) there are no changes in household consumption patterns in response to changes in (the amounts of) subsidy (partial balance analysis); and (ii) the poverty line remains constant for all scenarios. The poverty line used is US$1.3 per person per day.

## TABLE A.E.3: EFFECT OF VARIOUS REFORM SCENARIOS FOR THE COOKING-GAS SUBSIDY

| | Fiscal Savings (percent of subsidy) | Poverty Rate | Poverty Gap |
|---|---|---|---|
| Scenario 1 | 0.0 | 49.7 | 19.3 |
| Scenario 2 | 100.0 | 51.0 | 20.3 |
| Scenario 3 | 0.0 | 47.0 | 17.4 |
| Scenario 4 | 0.0 | 50.3 | 18.5 |
| Scenario 5 | 76.3 | 51.0 | 19.7 |

Source: Authors' calculations using the LSMS Survey "Encuesta de Condiciones de Vida 1999" and the Population Census 2001.

While fiscal savings results are the obvious consequence of the described mechanisms, the impact of the different monetary poverty rate scenarios requires a more elaborate explanation.

First, it is important to note that, although there is a correlation between monetary poverty and poverty measured according to the SelBen Index (quintiles 1 and 2), both rates are not the same, since they assess different dimensions of wellbeing. Monetary poverty reflects the lack in a household's income level and/or consumption, while SelBen's poverty measures structural scarcity (e.g., access to sanitation, electricity, and other services).

Second, as a result, and given the fact that the analysis measures the impact of reforms on monetary poverty (and not on poverty measured by SelBen), the scenarios considering redistribution or retargeting mechanisms based on monetary poverty (Scenario 3) will have a greater effect on said poverty than those using the SelBen (Scenarios 4 and 5).

This does not mean that the SelBen is an inadequate tool for targeting. On the contrary, using this index provides two important advantages:

- Transparency: The use of the SelBen index as a targeting instrument has contributed to its positioning as the main tool to select beneficiaries in government social programs—thus increasing transparency in the distribution of resources allocated to social assistance
- Cyclical Variation and Leakage: Given its nature, the SelBen Index is less susceptible to cyclical changes in the economy than monetary poverty. This helps minimize any leakage created by cyclical changes in income and consumption. In addition, SelBen is a less costly tool, as it does not require constant updates.

Given these arguments in favor of using the SelBen, it would be advisable to consider scenarios 4 and 5 as top choices. And, between those two, scenario 5 should have preference given its capacity to generate larger fiscal savings. Figure A.E.1 shows the effect of applying scenario 5 to benefit distribution. It is clear that this distribution would be significantly more progressive and pro-poor than the current one.

### Possible Implications of Offsetting the Retargetting of the Cooking-Gas with a BDH Increase

The Government of Ecuador has considered several alternatives for the cooking-gas subsidy reform, along with a possible increase in the Human Development Bonus (BDH: *Bono de Desarrollo Humano*) in an amount still to be determined. This section offers some comments about this option, comparing it to the scenarios considered above, and analyzing possible pros and cons with respect to its implementation.

Eliminating the subsidy with a simultaneous increase of the BDH could be considered a variation of scenario 4 (eliminating subsidy along with a distribution of generated fiscal savings to poor households in SelBen's quintiles 1 and 2), depending on the amount of fiscal savings devoted to the BDH increase.

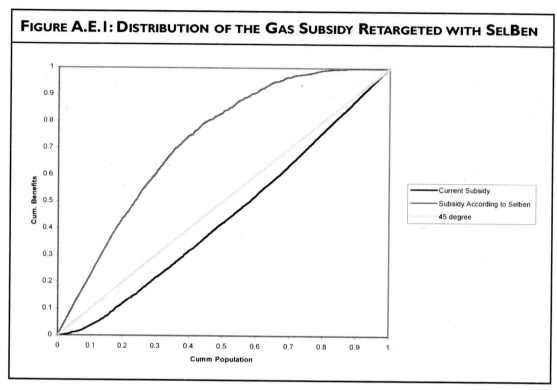

**FIGURE A.E.1: DISTRIBUTION OF THE GAS SUBSIDY RETARGETED WITH SELBEN**

*Source:* Author's calculations using ECV 1999.

Using the BDH as a means for compensation provides some advantages. The main ones are the simplicity of logistics in this mechanism, which would enable applying (new) transfers almost immediately. The the fact that these are fixed transfers and not a single subsidy facilitates the task of estimating future costs for this measure.

However, it also presents some drawbacks. The first one has to do with coverage of the target population by the compensatory measure. According to the BDH's establishment decree, the program's target population are all households in SelBen's quintiles 1 and 2—approximately 1,200,000 households. In practice, out of 1,050,000 beneficiary households currently in the program, 850,000 belong to quintiles 1 and 2, and the rest are households in quintile 3—primarily seniors and/or physically challenged individuals. This suggests that: (i) not all households in quintiles 1 and 2 are receiving the BDH, and (ii) not all BDH beneficiary households belong to quintiles 1 and 2. Thus, an increase in the BDH as a compensatory measure for the elimination of the gas subsidy will not benefit all households considered as poor by the SelBen. Only those which are currently part of the program and comply with the required co-responsibility conditions will benefit.

The second drawback to consider is the loss of flexibility in identifying and determining the target population. The link between subsidy reform and changes in the BDH imply that the compensatory measure will only benefit quintiles 1 and 2 of the SelBen. It is possible, however, for there to be a desire to extend coverage to other groups (i.e., SelBen's quintile 3) in order to minimize a negative reaction from the population as a response to the elimination of the subsidy. This flexibility is lost when implementing the change through the BDH, unless an increase in coverage of this program is considered for the same group—a measure which, at present time, does not appear to be advisable, given its elevated fiscal cost, among others.

Lastly, it is essential to note that there have been other attempts in the past to eliminate the gas subsidy through the creation of compensatory programs (in this case, the Solidarity Bonus). These attempts failed and gave place to a situation where the subsidy did not disappear and new liabilities emerged in the form of transfers. The political economy to eliminate the subsidy is complex and deserves additional actions. Even if the BDH amount is increased, strong political opposition must not be discarded.

## Conclusion

There seem to be two viable action plans: the first one would consider eliminating the subsidy along with a simultaneous increase of the BDH, and the second one would consider retargeting the subsidy independently. Although implementation of both instances must be accompanied by a very good communications campaign, the steps to follow will depend on the action plan selected.

The first option will require:

- A decision on the amount of increase in the BDH and cost of this measure, considering the number of program beneficiaries—both current and potential;
- A strong communications campaign;
- Good planning and funding to implement a device to respond to an increase in BDH participation, which will be likely to occur once the measure is announced.

The second option will require:

- A decision about the beneficiary population (preferably using the SelBen Index);
- A strong communications campaign;
- Development of a new targeted subsidy payment device. For such purpose, it will be necessary to: (i) provide recipients with an identification (ID, card or something similar), (ii) enable a payment method (direct deposit, ATM withdrawals with a card, reimbursable coupons). The political viability of the device should be determined on a smaller scale (pilot program) before implementing it at a national level.

# STATISTICAL APPENDIX

## TABLE A1: NON-FINANCIAL PUBLIC SECTOR
(Nominal, GDP)

| | 1993 | 1994 | 1995 | 1996 | 1997 | 1998 | 1999 | 2000 | 2001 | 2002 | 2003 | Average 1995–99 | Average 2000–03 |
|---|---|---|---|---|---|---|---|---|---|---|---|---|---|
| **Millions of US$** | | | | | | | | | | | | | |
| **Total Revenues** | 3440.5 | 4051.7 | 4599 | 4656 | 4714 | 4027 | 3515 | 4126 | 4933 | 6271 | 6908 | | |
| Petroleum | 1194.5 | 1194.4 | 1329 | 1575 | 1270 | 913 | 1049 | 1460 | 1352 | 1390 | 1664 | | |
| Non Petroleum | 1877 | 2328.2 | 2717 | 2607 | 3134 | 3096 | 2334 | 2516 | 3475 | 4695 | 5090 | | |
| o/w VAT | 449.1 | 562.1 | 621 | 633 | 779 | 831 | 591 | 893 | 1457 | 1667 | 1737 | | |
| Operating surplus on the non-financial public enterprises | 369 | 529.1 | 553 | 475 | 310 | 18 | 132 | 150 | 106 | 187 | 155 | | |
| **Total Expenditures 1/** | 3455 | 3952 | 4804 | 5221 | 5220 | 5145 | 4165 | 3889 | 4853 | 6117 | 6585 | | |
| Current Expenditures | 2516.7 | 2874.8 | 3616 | 3773 | 3970 | 3990 | 3165 | 3095 | 3457 | 4536 | 5124 | | |
| Interest | 630 | 665.8 | 786 | 831 | 995 | 987 | 1183 | 1052 | 996 | 869 | 820 | | |
| External | 555.8 | 589.1 | 669 | 659 | 751 | 749 | 837 | 853 | 779 | 665 | 634 | | |
| Domestic | 74.2 | 76.7 | 117 | 173 | 243 | 238 | 346 | 199 | 217 | 205 | 186 | | |
| Salaries | 1011.9 | 1227.9 | 1426 | 1482 | 1542 | 1691 | 991 | 761 | 1163 | 1761 | 2288 | | |
| Goods and Services | 409.3 | 370.1 | 305 | 533 | 600 | 569 | 397 | 410 | 579 | 901 | 948 | | |
| Others | 465.6 | 610.9 | 1099 | 927 | 833 | 744 | 594 | 871 | 719 | 1005 | 1069 | | |
| Capital Expenditures | 938.3 | 1077.2 | 1188 | 1449 | 1250 | 1155 | 1000 | 795 | 1396 | 1582 | 1460 | | |
| Fixed capital formation | 876 | 981.1 | 998 | 1265 | 1246 | 1143 | 982 | 782 | 1161 | 1417 | 1431 | | |
| Central government | 119.7 | 365.7 | 381 | 498 | 478 | 602 | 485 | 425 | 645 | 611 | 660 | | |
| Non-financial public enterprises | 414 | 440.1 | 389 | 544 | 486 | 199 | 245 | 83 | 143 | 236 | 254 | | |
| Municipal governments | 108.7 | 122.4 | 159 | 154 | 190 | 260 | 224 | 246 | 329 | 459 | 480 | | |
| Others | 233.6 | 52.9 | 69 | 69 | 91 | 82 | 27 | 29 | 44 | 111 | 38 | | |
| Other capital | 62.3 | 96.2 | 190 | 184 | 4 | 12 | 18 | 12 | 236 | 165 | 29 | | |
| **Balance** | –14.5 | 99.7 | –205 | –566 | –506 | –1118 | –650 | 237 | 80 | 154 | 323 | | |
| Discrepancy 2/ | | | 45 | 30 | 0 | 84 | 168 | 10 | 5 | 0 | 130 | | |
| **Overall Balance** | –89.2 | –34 | –250 | –595 | –506 | –1202 | –818 | 227 | 75 | 154 | 453 | | |
| Primary Balance | 541 | 632 | 536 | 236 | 489 | –215 | 366 | 1280 | 1071 | 1023 | 1273 | | |
| **In percent of GDP** | | | | | | | | | | | | | |

## TABLE A1: NON-FINANCIAL PUBLIC SECTOR (CONTINUED)
### (Nominal, GDP)

| | 1993 | 1994 | 1995 | 1996 | 1997 | 1998 | 1999 | 2000 | 2001 | 2002 | 2003 | Average 1995–99 | Average 2000–03 |
|---|---|---|---|---|---|---|---|---|---|---|---|---|---|
| **Total Revenues** | 22.9 | 21.8 | 22.8 | 21.9 | 19.9 | 17.3 | 21.1 | 25.9 | 23.5 | 25.8 | 25.7 | 20.6 | 25.2 |
| Petroleum | 7.9 | 6.4 | 6.6 | 7.4 | 5.4 | 3.9 | 6.3 | 9.2 | 6.4 | 5.7 | 6.2 | 5.9 | 6.9 |
| Non Petroleum | 12.5 | 12.5 | 13.5 | 12.3 | 13.3 | 13.3 | 14.0 | 15.8 | 16.5 | 19.3 | 18.9 | 13.3 | 17.6 |
| o/w VAT | 3.0 | 3.0 | 3.1 | 3.0 | 3.3 | 3.6 | 3.5 | 5.6 | 6.9 | 6.9 | 6.5 | 3.3 | 6.5 |
| Operating surplus on the non-financial public enterprises | 2.5 | 2.8 | 2.7 | 2.2 | 1.3 | 0.1 | 0.8 | 0.9 | 0.5 | 0.8 | 0.6 | 1.4 | 0.7 |
| **Total Expenditures 1/** | 22.9 | 21.3 | 23.8 | 24.6 | 22.1 | 22.1 | 25.0 | 24.4 | 23.1 | 25.2 | 24.5 | 23.5 | 24.3 |
| Current Expenditures | 16.7 | 15.5 | 17.9 | 17.7 | 16.8 | 17.2 | 19.0 | 19.4 | 16.4 | 18.7 | 19.0 | 17.7 | 18.4 |
| Interest | 4.2 | 3.6 | 3.9 | 3.9 | 4.2 | 4.2 | 7.1 | 6.6 | 4.7 | 3.6 | 3.0 | 4.7 | 4.5 |
| External | 3.7 | 3.2 | 3.3 | 3.1 | 3.2 | 3.2 | 5.0 | 5.4 | 3.7 | 2.7 | 2.4 | 3.6 | 3.5 |
| Domestic | 0.5 | 0.4 | 0.6 | 0.8 | 1.0 | 1.0 | 2.1 | 1.2 | 1.0 | 0.8 | 0.7 | 1.1 | 1.0 |
| Salaries | 6.7 | 6.6 | 7.1 | 7.0 | 6.5 | 7.3 | 5.9 | 4.8 | 5.5 | 7.2 | 8.5 | 6.8 | 6.5 |
| Goods and Services | 2.7 | 2.0 | 1.5 | 2.5 | 2.5 | 2.4 | 2.4 | 2.6 | 2.8 | 3.7 | 3.5 | 2.3 | 3.1 |
| Others | 3.1 | 3.3 | 5.4 | 4.4 | 3.5 | 3.2 | 3.6 | 5.5 | 3.4 | 4.1 | 4.0 | 4.0 | 4.2 |
| Capital Expenditures | 6.2 | 5.8 | 5.9 | 6.8 | 5.3 | 5.0 | 6.0 | 5.0 | 6.6 | 6.5 | 5.4 | 5.8 | 5.9 |
| Fixed capital formation | 5.8 | 5.3 | 4.9 | 5.9 | 5.3 | 4.9 | 5.9 | 4.9 | 5.5 | 5.8 | 5.3 | 5.4 | 5.4 |
| Central government | 0.8 | 2.0 | 1.9 | 2.3 | 2.0 | 2.6 | 2.9 | 2.7 | 3.1 | 2.5 | 2.5 | 2.4 | 2.7 |
| Non-financial public enterprises | 2.7 | 2.4 | 1.9 | 2.6 | 2.1 | 0.9 | 1.5 | 0.5 | 0.7 | 1.0 | 0.9 | 1.8 | 0.8 |
| Municipal governments | 0.7 | 0.7 | 0.8 | 0.7 | 0.8 | 1.1 | 1.3 | 1.5 | 1.6 | 1.9 | 1.8 | 1.0 | 1.7 |
| Others | 1.6 | 0.3 | 0.3 | 0.3 | 0.4 | 0.4 | 0.2 | 0.2 | 0.2 | 0.5 | 0.1 | 0.3 | 0.2 |
| Other capital | 0.4 | 0.5 | 0.9 | 0.9 | 0.0 | 0.1 | 0.1 | 0.1 | 1.1 | 0.7 | 0.1 | 0.4 | 0.5 |
| **Balance** | -0.1 | 0.5 | -1.0 | -2.7 | -2.1 | -4.8 | -3.9 | 1.5 | 0.4 | 0.6 | 1.2 | -2.9 | 0.9 |
| Discrepancy 2/ | 0.0 | 0.0 | 0.2 | 0.1 | 0.0 | 0.4 | 1.0 | 0.1 | 0.0 | 0.0 | 0.5 | 0.3 | 0.1 |
| **Overall Balance** | -0.6 | -0.2 | -1.2 | -2.8 | -2.1 | -5.2 | -4.9 | 1.4 | 0.4 | 0.6 | 1.7 | -3.2 | 1.0 |
| **Primary Balance** | 3.6 | 3.4 | 2.7 | 1.1 | 2.1 | -0.9 | 2.2 | 8.0 | 5.1 | 4.2 | 4.7 | 1.4 | 5.5 |
| Note: Nominal GDP US$Mln | 15057 | 18573 | 20196 | 21268 | 23636 | 23255 | 16674 | 15934 | 21024 | 24311 | 26913 | | |

Source: BCE, IMF for 2003

1/ Expenditures on accrued basis.
2/ Includes reduction of personnel and costs of strengthening the private financial system.

## TABLE A2: NON-FINANCIAL PUBLIC SECTOR
(Real, Growth)

| | 1993 | 1994 | 1995 | 1996 | 1997 | 1998 | 1999 | 2000 | 2001 | 2002 | 2003 | Average 1995–99 | Average 2000–03 |
|---|---|---|---|---|---|---|---|---|---|---|---|---|---|
| **Millions of 2000 US$** | | | | | | | | | | | | | |
| Total Revenues | 3261 | 3260 | 3462 | 3408 | 3230 | 2864 | 3267 | 4126 | 3930 | 4465 | 4525 | 3246 | 4261 |
| Petroleum | 1132 | 961 | 1000 | 1153 | 870 | 649 | 975 | 1460 | 1077 | 989 | 1090 | 929 | 1154 |
| Non Petroleum | 1779 | 1873 | 2045 | 1908 | 2148 | 2202 | 2170 | 2516 | 2768 | 3342 | 3334 | 2095 | 2990 |
| o/w VAT | 426 | 452 | 467 | 463 | 534 | 591 | 549 | 893 | 1161 | 1187 | 1138 | 521 | 1095 |
| Operating surplus on the non-financial public enterprises | 350 | 426 | 416 | 347 | 212 | 13 | 123 | 150 | 84 | 133 | 101 | 222 | 117 |
| **Total Expenditures 1/** | 3275 | 3179 | 3616 | 3822 | 3577 | 3660 | 3872 | 3889 | 3866 | 4355 | 4313 | 3709 | 4106 |
| Current Expenditures | 2385 | 2313 | 2722 | 2762 | 2721 | 2838 | 2942 | 3095 | 2754 | 3229 | 3357 | 2797 | 3108 |
| Interest | 597 | 536 | 591 | 609 | 682 | 702 | 1100 | 1052 | 794 | 619 | 537 | 737 | 750 |
| External | 527 | 474 | 504 | 482 | 515 | 533 | 778 | 853 | 621 | 473 | 415 | 562 | 591 |
| Domestic | 70 | 62 | 88 | 126 | 167 | 169 | 322 | 199 | 173 | 146 | 122 | 174 | 160 |
| Salaries | 959 | 988 | 1073 | 1085 | 1057 | 1202 | 921 | 761 | 926 | 1254 | 1499 | 1068 | 1110 |
| Goods and Services | 388 | 298 | 230 | 390 | 411 | 405 | 369 | 410 | 461 | 641 | 621 | 361 | 533 |
| Others | 441 | 491 | 828 | 678 | 571 | 529 | 552 | 871 | 573 | 715 | 700 | 632 | 715 |
| Capital Expenditures | 889 | 867 | 894 | 1060 | 857 | 821 | 929 | 795 | 1112 | 1126 | 957 | 912 | 997 |
| Fixed capital formation | 830 | 789 | 751 | 926 | 854 | 813 | 913 | 782 | 925 | 1009 | 937 | 851 | 913 |
| Central government | 113 | 294 | 287 | 365 | 328 | 428 | 451 | 425 | 514 | 435 | 432 | 372 | 451 |
| Non-financial public enterprises | 392 | 354 | 293 | 398 | 333 | 142 | 228 | 83 | 114 | 168 | 166 | 279 | 133 |
| Municipal governments | 103 | 98 | 120 | 113 | 130 | 185 | 208 | 246 | 262 | 327 | 315 | 151 | 287 |
| Others | 221 | 43 | 52 | 50 | 63 | 58 | 25 | 29 | 35 | 79 | 25 | 50 | 42 |
| Other capital | 59 | 77 | 143 | 134 | 3 | 9 | 16 | 12 | 188 | 117 | 19 | 61 | 84 |
| **Balance** | -14 | 80 | -154 | -414 | -347 | -795 | -604 | 237 | 64 | 110 | 212 | -463 | 156 |
| Discrepancy 2/ | 0 | 0 | 34 | 22 | 0 | 60 | 156 | 10 | 4 | 0 | 85 | 54 | 25 |
| **Overall Balance** | -85 | -27 | -188 | -436 | -347 | -855 | -760 | 227 | 60 | 110 | 297 | -517 | 173 |
| **Primary Balance** | 513 | 508 | 403 | 173 | 335 | -153 | 340 | 1280 | 853 | 729 | 834 | 220 | 924 |
| Percent change | | | | | | | | | | | | | |

# TABLE A2: NON-FINANCIAL PUBLIC SECTOR (CONTINUED)

(Real, Growth)

| | 1993 | 1994 | 1995 | 1996 | 1997 | 1998 | 1999 | 2000 | 2001 | 2002 | 2003 | Average 1995–99 | Average 2000–03 |
|---|---|---|---|---|---|---|---|---|---|---|---|---|---|
| **Total Revenues** | | 0.0 | 6.2 | -1.6 | -5.2 | -11.3 | 14.1 | 26.3 | -4.8 | 13.6 | 1.3 | 0.4 | 9.1 |
| Petroleum | | -15.1 | 4.1 | 15.2 | -24.5 | -25.4 | 50.1 | 49.8 | -26.2 | -8.1 | 10.2 | 3.9 | 6.4 |
| Non Petroleum | | 5.3 | 9.2 | -6.7 | 12.6 | 2.5 | -1.5 | 16.0 | 10.0 | 20.7 | -0.2 | 3.2 | 11.6 |
| o/w VAT | | 6.2 | 3.3 | -0.8 | 15.3 | 10.7 | -7.1 | 62.7 | 29.9 | 2.2 | -4.1 | 4.3 | 22.7 |
| Operating surplus on the non-financial public enterprises | | 21.7 | -2.2 | -16.5 | -38.9 | -93.9 | 850.7 | 21.6 | -43.6 | 57.9 | -24.0 | 139.8 | 3.0 |
| **Total Expenditures 1/** | | -2.9 | 13.7 | 5.7 | -6.4 | 2.3 | 5.8 | 0.5 | -0.6 | 12.7 | -1.0 | 4.2 | 2.9 |
| Current Expenditures | | -3.0 | 17.7 | 1.5 | -1.5 | 4.3 | 3.7 | 5.2 | -11.0 | 17.3 | 3.9 | 5.1 | 3.8 |
| Interest | | -10.3 | 10.4 | 2.9 | 12.0 | 3.0 | 56.7 | -4.3 | -24.6 | -22.0 | -13.3 | 17.0 | -16.0 |
| External | | -10.0 | 6.2 | -4.2 | 6.8 | 3.5 | 46.0 | 9.7 | -27.3 | -23.8 | -12.2 | 11.7 | -13.4 |
| Domestic | | -12.3 | 42.5 | 43.7 | 32.0 | 1.3 | 90.3 | -38.1 | -13.1 | -15.7 | -16.7 | 42.0 | -20.9 |
| Salaries | | 3.0 | 8.6 | 1.1 | -2.6 | 13.8 | -23.4 | -17.4 | 21.7 | 35.4 | 19.5 | -0.5 | 14.8 |
| Goods and Services | | -23.2 | -22.9 | 69.9 | 5.4 | -1.6 | -8.8 | 11.1 | 12.5 | 39.0 | -3.2 | 8.4 | 14.9 |
| Others | | 11.4 | 68.4 | -18.0 | -15.8 | -7.3 | 4.4 | 57.7 | -34.3 | 24.9 | -2.1 | 6.3 | 11.6 |
| Capital Expenditures | | -2.6 | 3.2 | 18.6 | -19.2 | -4.1 | 13.1 | -14.5 | 40.0 | 1.2 | -15.0 | 2.3 | 2.9 |
| Fixed capital formation | | -4.9 | -4.8 | 23.3 | -7.8 | -4.8 | 12.3 | -14.3 | 18.2 | 9.1 | -7.1 | 3.6 | 1.5 |
| Central government | | 159.3 | -2.4 | 27.1 | -10.1 | 30.6 | 5.4 | -5.9 | 21.0 | -15.3 | -0.6 | 10.1 | -0.2 |
| Non-financial public enterprises | | -9.8 | -17.4 | 36.0 | -16.3 | -57.5 | 61.0 | -63.7 | 37.4 | 47.7 | -1.3 | 1.2 | 5.0 |
| Municipal governments | | -4.4 | 21.6 | -5.6 | 14.9 | 42.2 | 12.8 | 18.0 | 6.6 | 24.8 | -3.7 | 17.2 | 11.4 |
| Others | | -80.8 | 21.5 | -2.6 | 24.4 | -7.3 | -56.3 | 15.1 | 21.1 | 122.8 | -68.7 | -4.1 | 22.6 |
| Other capital | | 31.1 | 85.0 | -6.1 | -97.9 | 201.5 | 89.6 | -25.2 | 1426.0 | -37.5 | -83.7 | 54.4 | 319.9 |
| **Balance** | | -683.6 | -292.0 | 168.8 | -16.2 | 129.2 | -24.0 | -139.3 | -73.1 | 72.0 | 93.0 | -6.8 | -11.8 |
| **Overall Balance** | | -67.6 | 587.5 | 131.7 | -20.4 | 146.4 | -11.1 | -129.9 | -73.7 | 83.5 | 170.7 | 166.8 | 12.7 |
| **Primary Balance** | | -0.8 | -20.6 | -57.1 | 93.6 | -145.7 | -322.3 | 276.4 | -33.3 | -14.6 | 14.4 | -90.4 | 60.7 |
| Note: GDP Deflator (2000 = 1) | 1.06 | 1.24 | 1.33 | 1.37 | 1.46 | 1.41 | 1.08 | 1.00 | 1.26 | 1.40 | 1.53 | | |

Source: BCE

1/ Expenditures on accrued basis.
2/ Includes reduction of personnel and costs of strengthening the private financial system.

## TABLE A3: CENTRAL GOVERNMENT
### (Nominal, % GDP, %NFPS)

| | 1995 | 1996 | 1997 | 1998 | 1999 | 2000 | 2001 | 2002 | 2003 | Average 1995–99 | Average 2000–03 |
|---|---|---|---|---|---|---|---|---|---|---|---|
| **Millions of US$** | | | | | | | | | | | |
| **Total Revenues** | 3129 | 3222 | 3448 | 3227 | 2688 | 3250 | 3839 | 4572 | 4771 | | |
| Petroleum | 1200 | 1480 | 1206 | 888 | 994 | 1397 | 1280 | 1363 | 1561 | | |
| Non Petroleum | 1929 | 1742 | 2242 | 2339 | 1694 | 1853 | 2559 | 3210 | 3210 | | |
| Tax | 1434 | 1407 | 1887 | 1998 | 1482 | 1623 | 2370 | 2748 | 2790 | | |
| Non Tax | 340 | 212 | 230 | 178 | 138 | 237 | 139 | 340 | 375 | | |
| Transfers | 156 | 124 | 125 | 164 | 75 | −7 | 50 | 122 | 45 | | |
| **Total Expenditures** | 3419 | 3726 | 3726 | 4186 | 3163 | 3230 | 3994 | 4757 | 5010 | | |
| Current Expenditures | 2696 | 2843 | 2947 | 3141 | 2427 | 2572 | 2555 | 3531 | 3693 | | |
| Interest | 622 | 772 | 939 | 941 | 1121 | 1009 | 938 | 823 | 827 | | |
| External | 505 | 604 | 703 | 708 | 781 | 812 | 728 | 621 | 614 | | |
| Domestic | 117 | 168 | 237 | 233 | 341 | 197 | 210 | 202 | 213 | | |
| Salaries | 1252 | 1317 | 1369 | 1510 | 898 | 707 | 1088 | 1672 | 1864 | | |
| Goods and Services | 81 | 202 | 209 | 197 | 123 | 175 | 122 | 318 | 329 | | |
| Others | 527 | 276 | 9 | 65 | 206 | 542 | 300 | 351 | 257 | | |
| Transfers | 214 | 275 | 421 | 428 | 79 | 140 | 107 | 366 | 416 | | |
| Capital Expenditures | 723 | 883 | 779 | 1045 | 736 | 659 | 1439 | 1227 | 1317 | | |
| Fixed capital formation | 381 | 498 | 478 | 602 | 485 | 425 | 645 | 611 | 660 | | |
| Others | | | | | | | 233 | −3 | 15 | | |
| Transfers | 173 | 232 | 301 | 443 | 251 | 234 | 562 | 618 | 642 | | |
| **CG Balance** | −289 | −505 | −278 | −959 | −476 | 19 | −155 | −185 | −239 | | |
| **CG Primary Balance** | 332 | 268 | 661 | −18 | 646 | 1029 | 782 | 638 | 588 | | |
| **Percent of GDP** | | | | | | | | | | | |
| **Total Revenues** | 15.5 | 15.1 | 14.6 | 13.9 | 16.1 | 20.4 | 18.3 | 18.8 | 17.7 | 15.0 | 18.8 |
| Petroleum | 5.9 | 7.0 | 5.1 | 3.8 | 6.0 | 8.8 | 6.1 | 5.6 | 5.8 | 5.6 | 6.6 |
| Non Petroleum | 9.6 | 8.2 | 9.5 | 10.1 | 10.2 | 11.6 | 12.2 | 13.2 | 11.9 | 9.5 | 12.2 |
| Tax | 7.1 | 6.6 | 8.0 | 8.6 | 8.9 | 10.2 | 11.3 | 11.3 | 10.4 | 7.8 | 10.8 |
| Non Tax | 1.7 | 1.0 | 1.0 | 0.8 | 0.8 | 1.5 | 0.7 | 1.4 | 1.4 | 1.0 | 1.2 |
| Transfers | 0.8 | 0.6 | 0.5 | 0.7 | 0.4 | 0.0 | 0.2 | 0.5 | 0.2 | 0.6 | 0.2 |

## TABLE A3: CENTRAL GOVERNMENT (CONTINUED)
(Nominal, % GDP, %NFPS)

| | 1995 | 1996 | 1997 | 1998 | 1999 | 2000 | 2001 | 2002 | 2003 | Average 1995–99 | Average 2000–03 |
|---|---|---|---|---|---|---|---|---|---|---|---|
| **Total Expenditures** | 16.9 | 17.5 | 15.8 | 18.0 | 19.0 | 20.3 | 19.0 | 19.6 | 18.6 | 17.4 | 19.4 |
| Current Expenditures | 13.3 | 13.4 | 12.5 | 13.5 | 14.6 | 16.1 | 12.2 | 14.5 | 13.7 | 13.4 | 14.1 |
| Interest | 3.1 | 3.6 | 4.0 | 4.0 | 6.7 | 6.3 | 4.5 | 3.4 | 3.1 | 4.3 | 4.3 |
| External | 2.5 | 2.8 | 3.0 | 3.0 | 4.7 | 5.1 | 3.5 | 2.6 | 2.3 | 3.2 | 3.3 |
| Domestic | 0.6 | 0.8 | 1.0 | 1.0 | 2.0 | 1.2 | 1.0 | 0.8 | 0.8 | 1.1 | 1.0 |
| Salaries | 6.2 | 6.2 | 5.8 | 6.5 | 5.4 | 4.4 | 5.2 | 6.9 | 6.9 | 6.0 | 5.9 |
| Goods and Services | 0.4 | 1.0 | 0.9 | 0.8 | 0.7 | 1.1 | 0.6 | 1.3 | 1.2 | 0.8 | 1.1 |
| Others | 2.6 | 1.3 | 0.0 | 0.3 | 1.2 | 3.4 | 1.4 | 1.4 | 1.0 | 1.1 | 1.8 |
| Transfers | 1.1 | 1.3 | 1.8 | 1.8 | 0.5 | 0.9 | 0.5 | 1.5 | 1.5 | 1.3 | 1.1 |
| Capital Expenditures | 3.6 | 4.2 | 3.3 | 4.5 | 4.4 | 4.1 | 6.8 | 5.0 | 4.9 | 4.0 | 5.2 |
| Fixed capital formation | 1.9 | 2.3 | 2.0 | 2.6 | 2.9 | 2.7 | 3.1 | 2.5 | 2.5 | 2.4 | 2.7 |
| Others | 0.0 | 0.0 | 0.0 | 0.0 | 0.0 | 0.0 | 1.1 | 0.0 | 0.1 | 0.0 | 0.3 |
| Transfers | 0.9 | 1.1 | 1.3 | 1.9 | 1.5 | 1.5 | 2.7 | 2.5 | 2.4 | 1.3 | 2.3 |
| **CG Balance** | -1.4 | -2.4 | -1.2 | -4.1 | -2.9 | 0.1 | -0.7 | -0.8 | -0.9 | -2.4 | -0.6 |
| **CG Primary Balance** | 1.6 | 1.3 | 2.8 | -0.1 | 3.9 | 6.5 | 3.7 | 2.6 | 2.2 | 1.9 | 3.7 |
| **Percent of NFPS** | | | | | | | | | | | |
| Total Revenues | 68.0 | 69.2 | 73.2 | 80.1 | 76.5 | 78.8 | 77.8 | 72.9 | 69.1 | 73.4 | 74.6 |
| Total Expenditures | 71.2 | 71.4 | 71.4 | 81.4 | 76.0 | 83.1 | 82.3 | 77.8 | 76.1 | 74.2 | 79.8 |
| Current Expenditures | 74.6 | 75.4 | 74.2 | 78.7 | 76.7 | 83.1 | 73.9 | 77.8 | 72.1 | 75.9 | 76.7 |
| Interest | 79.1 | 92.9 | 94.4 | 95.4 | 94.8 | 95.9 | 94.1 | 94.6 | 100.9 | 91.3 | 96.4 |
| External | 75.5 | 91.7 | 93.5 | 94.5 | 93.2 | 95.2 | 93.4 | 93.5 | 96.9 | 89.7 | 94.7 |
| Domestic | 100.0 | 97.4 | 97.3 | 98.2 | 98.5 | 99.0 | 96.7 | 98.4 | 114.6 | 98.3 | 102.2 |
| Salaries | 87.8 | 88.9 | 88.8 | 89.3 | 90.6 | 92.9 | 93.6 | 95.0 | 81.5 | 89.1 | 90.7 |
| Goods and Services | 26.7 | 38.0 | 34.8 | 34.6 | 30.9 | 42.6 | 21.0 | 35.3 | 34.7 | 33.0 | 33.4 |
| Others | 47.9 | 29.8 | 1.1 | 8.7 | 34.6 | 62.2 | 41.8 | 35.0 | 24.1 | 24.4 | 40.7 |
| Capital Expenditures | 72.4 | 69.8 | 62.5 | 91.5 | 75.0 | 84.2 | 124.0 | 86.6 | 92.0 | 74.3 | 96.7 |
| CG Balance | 115.9 | 84.8 | 54.9 | 79.8 | 58.2 | 8.5 | -206.8 | -120.1 | 100.0 | 78.7 | -54.6 |
| CG Primary Balance | 62.0 | 113.4 | 135.4 | 8.3 | 176.6 | 80.4 | 73.0 | 62.3 | 5.8 | 99.1 | 55.4 |
| Non transfer expenditures/ NFPS expenditures | 63.1 | 61.6 | 57.6 | 64.4 | 68.0 | 73.5 | 68.5 | 61.7 | 60.0 | 63.0 | 65.9 |

Source: BCE, MEF, and own calculations

## TABLE A3b: CENTRAL GOVERNMENT
### (Real, % GDP, %NFPS)

| Millions of 2000 US$ | 1995 | 1996 | 1997 | 1998 | 1999 | 2000 | 2001 | 2002 | 2003 | Average 1995–99 | Average 2000–03 |
|---|---|---|---|---|---|---|---|---|---|---|---|
| **Total Revenues** | 2356 | 2358 | 2363 | 2295 | 2498 | 3250 | 3058 | 3255 | 3125 | 2374 | 3172 |
| Petroleum | 903 | 1083 | 826 | 631 | 924 | 1397 | 1020 | 970 | 1023 | 874 | 1102 |
| Non Petroleum | 1452 | 1275 | 1537 | 1664 | 1575 | 1853 | 2039 | 2285 | 2102 | 1501 | 2070 |
| Tax | 1079 | 1030 | 1293 | 1421 | 1377 | 1623 | 1888 | 1956 | 1827 | 1240 | 1824 |
| Non Tax | 256 | 155 | 158 | 126 | 128 | 237 | 111 | 242 | 246 | 165 | 209 |
| Transfers | 117 | 90 | 86 | 117 | 69 | -7 | 40 | 87 | 30 | 96 | 37 |
| **Total Expenditures** | 2573 | 2728 | 2554 | 2977 | 2940 | 3230 | 3182 | 3387 | 3282 | 2755 | 3270 |
| Current Expenditures | 2029 | 2081 | 2020 | 2234 | 2256 | 2572 | 2035 | 2514 | 2419 | 2124 | 2385 |
| Interest | 468 | 565 | 644 | 670 | 1042 | 1009 | 747 | 586 | 542 | 678 | 721 |
| External | 380 | 442 | 481 | 504 | 725 | 812 | 580 | 442 | 402 | 507 | 559 |
| Domestic | 88 | 123 | 162 | 166 | 317 | 197 | 167 | 143 | 139 | 171 | 162 |
| Salaries | 942 | 964 | 938 | 1074 | 835 | 707 | 867 | 1191 | 1221 | 951 | 996 |
| Goods and Services | 61 | 148 | 143 | 140 | 114 | 175 | 97 | 226 | 216 | 121 | 178 |
| Others | 397 | 202 | 6 | 46 | 191 | 542 | 239 | 250 | 169 | 168 | 300 |
| Transfers | 161 | 202 | 288 | 304 | 74 | 140 | 86 | 261 | 272 | 206 | 190 |
| Capital Expenditures | 544 | 646 | 534 | 744 | 684 | 659 | 1146 | 873 | 863 | 630 | 885 |
| Fixed capital formation | 287 | 365 | 328 | 428 | 451 | 425 | 514 | 435 | 432 | 372 | 451 |
| Others | 0 | 0 | 0 | 0 | 0 | 0 | 185 | -2 | 10 | 0 | 48 |
| Transfers | 130 | 170 | 206 | 315 | 233 | 234 | 447 | 440 | 421 | 211 | 386 |
| **CG Balance** | -218 | -369 | -191 | -682 | -442 | 19 | -124 | -132 | -156 | -380 | -98 |
| **CG Primary Balance** | 250 | 196 | 453 | -13 | 600 | 1029 | 623 | 454 | 385 | 297 | 623 |
| **Fiscal Law Indicators** | | | | | | | | | | | |
| Primary Expenditures | 2106 | 2162 | 1910 | 2308 | 1898 | 2221 | 2435 | 2801 | 2740 | 2077 | 2549 |
| Percent change | | | | | | | | | | | |

## TABLE A3b: CENTRAL GOVERNMENT (CONTINUED)
### (Real, % GDP, %NFPS)

| | 1995 | 1996 | 1997 | 1998 | 1999 | 2000 | 2001 | 2002 | 2003 | Average 1995–99 | Average 2000–03 |
|---|---|---|---|---|---|---|---|---|---|---|---|
| **Total Revenues** | | 0.1 | 0.2 | −2.9 | 8.9 | 30.1 | −5.9 | 6.4 | −4.0 | 1.6 | 6.7 |
| Petroleum | | 19.9 | −23.7 | −23.6 | 46.3 | 51.2 | −27.0 | −4.9 | 5.4 | 4.7 | 6.2 |
| Non Petroleum | | −12.2 | 20.5 | 8.3 | −5.4 | 17.7 | 10.0 | 12.1 | −8.0 | 2.8 | 7.9 |
| Tax | | −4.6 | 25.6 | 9.9 | −3.1 | 17.8 | 16.3 | 3.6 | −6.6 | 7.0 | 7.8 |
| Non Tax | | −39.4 | 1.8 | −20.0 | 1.2 | 85.1 | −53.3 | 118.9 | 1.4 | −14.1 | 38.0 |
| Transfers | | −23.0 | −5.0 | 35.7 | −40.4 | −110.1 | −672.5 | 116.2 | −65.9 | −8.2 | −183.1 |
| **Total Expenditures** | | 6.0 | −6.4 | 16.6 | −1.2 | 9.9 | −1.5 | 6.4 | −3.1 | 3.7 | 2.9 |
| Current Expenditures | | 2.6 | −2.9 | 10.6 | 1.0 | 14.0 | −20.9 | 23.5 | −3.8 | 2.8 | 3.2 |
| Interest | | 20.8 | 13.9 | 4.0 | 55.7 | −3.2 | −26.0 | −21.6 | −7.5 | 23.6 | −14.6 |
| External | | 16.4 | 8.8 | 4.6 | 44.0 | 12.0 | −28.6 | −23.7 | −9.0 | 18.5 | −12.3 |
| Domestic | | 39.9 | 31.9 | 2.2 | 91.0 | −37.8 | −15.1 | −14.2 | −3.0 | 41.3 | −17.5 |
| Salaries | | 2.3 | −2.7 | 14.5 | −22.3 | −15.3 | 22.6 | 37.4 | 2.5 | −2.0 | 11.8 |
| Goods and Services | | 142.0 | −3.4 | −2.1 | −18.5 | 52.9 | −44.4 | 133.5 | −4.8 | 29.5 | 34.3 |
| Others | | −49.1 | −96.9 | 631.0 | 314.6 | 183.3 | −55.8 | 4.5 | −32.6 | 199.9 | 24.9 |
| Transfers | | 25.1 | 43.1 | 5.5 | −75.7 | 89.0 | −38.7 | 204.9 | 4.4 | −0.5 | 64.9 |
| Capital Expenditures | | 18.8 | −17.4 | 39.3 | −8.0 | −3.8 | 74.1 | −23.8 | −1.2 | 8.2 | 11.3 |
| Fixed capital formation | | 27.1 | −10.1 | 30.6 | 5.4 | −5.9 | 21.0 | −15.3 | −0.6 | 13.2 | −0.2 |
| Others | | −101.0 | −644.7 | ... | −372.8 | | | | | | |
| Transfers | | 30.6 | 21.1 | 53.1 | −26.1 | 0.4 | 91.2 | −1.6 | −4.4 | 19.7 | 21.4 |
| **CG Balance** | | 69.5 | −48.4 | 258.0 | −35.2 | −104.4 | −740.2 | 6.5 | 18.9 | 61.0 | −204.8 |
| **CG Primary Balance** | | −21.6 | 131.2 | −102.8 | −4814.0 | 71.4 | −39.4 | −27.2 | −15.2 | −1201.8 | −2.6 |
| **Fiscal Law Indicators** | | | | | | | | | | | |
| **Primary Expenditures** | | 2.7 | −11.7 | 20.8 | −17.8 | 17.0 | 9.6 | 15.0 | −2.2 | −1.5 | 9.9 |

Source: BCE, MEF, and own calculations

## TABLE A4: REST OF GENERAL GOVERNMENT
### (Nominal, GDP, Percent of NFPS)

| | 1995 | 1996 | 1997 | 1998 | 1999 | 2000 | 2001 | 2002 | 2003 | Average 1995–99 | Average 2000–03 |
|---|---|---|---|---|---|---|---|---|---|---|---|
| **Millions of US$** | | | | | | | | | | | |
| **Total Revenues** | 1283 | 1375 | 1424 | 1503 | 978 | 989 | 1615 | 2422 | 2870 | | |
| Oil-related revenues | 127 | 94 | 63 | 25 | 55 | 64 | 72 | 27 | 22 | | |
| Non oil revenues | 1155 | 1281 | 1361 | 1478 | 923 | 925 | 1545 | 2395 | 2848 | | |
| Contributions to Social Security | 506 | 450 | 455 | 451 | 230 | 228 | 455 | 767 | 916 | | |
| Interests and gains | 85 | 149 | 102 | 92 | 123 | 62 | 91 | 158 | 209 | | |
| Others | 274 | 318 | 364 | 310 | 319 | 311 | 337 | 539 | 706 | | |
| Transfers | 291 | 363 | 439 | 625 | 251 | 324 | 663 | 931 | 1018 | | |
| **Total Expenditures** | 1186 | 1264 | 1391 | 1449 | 977 | 814 | 1281 | 1992 | 2289 | | |
| Current | 937 | 1010 | 1106 | 1096 | 708 | 527 | 905 | 1255 | 1704 | | |
| Wages | 312 | 310 | 335 | 379 | 215 | 160 | 263 | 335 | 425 | | |
| Goods and services | 224 | 331 | 391 | 372 | 274 | 235 | 457 | 583 | 619 | | |
| Interest | 70 | 10 | 11 | 11 | 27 | 12 | 21 | 20 | 9 | | |
| External | 70 | 10 | 11 | 11 | 27 | 12 | 14 | 17 | 6 | | |
| Internal | 0 | 0 | 0 | 0 | 0 | 0 | 6 | 3 | 3 | | |
| Transfers | 322 | 359 | 369 | 334 | 191 | 120 | 164 | 317 | 651 | | |
| To public sector | 0 | 0 | 0 | 0 | 0 | 0 | 0 | 0 | 62 | | |
| To private sector | 322 | 359 | 369 | 334 | 191 | 120 | 164 | 317 | 589 | | |
| Others | 9 | 0 | 0 | 0 | 0 | 0 | 0 | 0 | 0 | | |
| Capital Expenditures | 250 | 254 | 285 | 353 | 269 | 287 | 376 | 737 | 585 | | |
| Fixed investments | 228 | 223 | 281 | 341 | 251 | 275 | 373 | 570 | 561 | | |
| Net lending concessions | –1 | 0 | –8 | 1 | 11 | –10 | –1 | 159 | 11 | | |
| Others | 23 | 32 | 13 | 11 | 7 | 22 | 3 | 9 | 14 | | |
| **Balance** | 97 | 111 | 33 | 54 | 1 | 175 | 335 | 430 | 581 | | |
| **Percent of GDP** | | | | | | | | | | | |

# TABLE A4: REST OF GENERAL GOVERNMENT (CONTINUED)
## (Nominal, GDP, Percent of NFPS)

| | 1995 | 1996 | 1997 | 1998 | 1999 | 2000 | 2001 | 2002 | 2003 | Average 1995–99 | Average 2000–03 |
|---|---|---|---|---|---|---|---|---|---|---|---|
| **Total Revenues** | 6.4 | 6.5 | 6.0 | 6.5 | 5.9 | 6.2 | 7.7 | 10.0 | 10.7 | 6.2 | 8.6 |
| Oil-related revenues | 0.6 | 0.4 | 0.3 | 0.1 | 0.3 | 0.4 | 0.3 | 0.1 | 0.1 | 0.4 | 0.2 |
| Non oil revenues | 5.7 | 6.0 | 5.8 | 6.4 | 5.5 | 5.8 | 7.4 | 9.9 | 10.6 | 5.9 | 8.4 |
| Contributions to Social Security | 2.5 | 2.1 | 1.9 | 1.9 | 1.4 | 1.4 | 2.2 | 3.2 | 3.4 | 2.0 | 2.5 |
| Interests and gains | 0.4 | 0.7 | 0.4 | 0.4 | 0.7 | 0.4 | 0.4 | 0.6 | 0.8 | 0.5 | 0.6 |
| Others | 1.4 | 1.5 | 1.5 | 1.3 | 1.9 | 2.0 | 1.6 | 2.2 | 2.6 | 1.5 | 2.1 |
| Transfers | 1.4 | 1.7 | 1.9 | 2.7 | 1.5 | 2.0 | 3.2 | 3.8 | 3.8 | 1.8 | 3.2 |
| **Total Expenditures** | 5.9 | 5.9 | 5.9 | 6.2 | 5.9 | 5.1 | 6.1 | 8.2 | 8.5 | 6.0 | 7.0 |
| Current | 4.6 | 4.7 | 4.7 | 4.7 | 4.2 | 3.3 | 4.3 | 5.2 | 6.3 | 4.6 | 4.8 |
| Wages | 1.5 | 1.5 | 1.4 | 1.6 | 1.3 | 1.0 | 1.3 | 1.4 | 1.6 | 1.5 | 1.3 |
| Goods and services | 1.1 | 1.6 | 1.7 | 1.6 | 1.6 | 1.5 | 2.2 | 2.4 | 2.3 | 1.5 | 2.1 |
| Interest | 0.3 | 0.0 | 0.0 | 0.0 | 0.2 | 0.1 | 0.1 | 0.1 | 0.0 | 0.1 | 0.1 |
| External | 0.3 | 0.0 | 0.0 | 0.0 | 0.2 | 0.1 | 0.1 | 0.1 | 0.0 | 0.1 | 0.1 |
| Internal | 0.0 | 0.0 | 0.0 | 0.0 | 0.0 | 0.0 | 0.0 | 0.0 | 0.0 | 0.0 | 0.0 |
| Transfers | 1.6 | 1.7 | 1.6 | 1.4 | 1.1 | 0.8 | 0.8 | 1.3 | 2.4 | 1.5 | 1.3 |
| To public sector | 0.0 | 0.0 | 0.0 | 0.0 | 0.0 | 0.0 | 0.0 | 0.0 | 0.2 | 0.0 | 0.1 |
| To private sector | 1.6 | 1.7 | 1.6 | 1.4 | 1.1 | 0.8 | 0.8 | 1.3 | 2.2 | 1.5 | 1.3 |
| Others | 0.0 | 0.0 | 0.0 | 0.0 | 0.0 | 0.0 | 0.0 | 0.0 | 0.0 | 0.0 | 0.0 |
| Capital Expenditures | 1.2 | 1.2 | 1.2 | 1.5 | 1.6 | 1.8 | 1.8 | 3.0 | 2.2 | 1.4 | 2.2 |
| Fixed investments | 1.1 | 1.0 | 1.2 | 1.5 | 1.5 | 1.7 | 1.8 | 2.3 | 2.1 | 1.3 | 2.0 |
| Net lending concessions | 0.0 | 0.0 | 0.0 | 0.0 | 0.1 | −0.1 | 0.0 | 0.7 | 0.0 | 0.0 | 0.2 |
| Others | 0.1 | 0.1 | 0.0 | 0.0 | 0.0 | 0.1 | 0.0 | 0.0 | 0.1 | 0.1 | 0.1 |
| **Balance** | 0.5 | 0.5 | 0.1 | 0.2 | 0.0 | 1.1 | 1.6 | 1.8 | 2.2 | 0.3 | 1.7 |
| Non transfer expenditures/ NFPS expenditures | 18.0 | 17.3 | 19.6 | 21.7 | 18.9 | 17.9 | 23.0 | 27.4 | 24.9 | 19.1 | 23.3 |

Source: BCE

## TABLE A5: NON-FINANCIAL PUBLIC ENTERPRISES
### (Nominal, GDP, Percent of NFPS)

| | 1995 | 1996 | 1997 | 1998 | 1999 | 2000 | 2001 | 2002 | 2003 | Average 1995–99 | Average 2000–03 |
|---|---|---|---|---|---|---|---|---|---|---|---|
| **Millions of US$** | | | | | | | | | | | |
| Operating Revenues | 1645 | 1692 | 1628 | 974 | 618 | 639 | 746 | 937 | 1718 | | |
| Operating Expenditures | 1092 | 1218 | 1319 | 956 | 486 | 490 | 640 | 750 | 1627 | | |
| Salaries | 179 | 190 | 217 | 166 | 90 | 69 | 100 | 129 | 161 | | |
| Contributions to social security | 24 | 23 | 24 | 17 | 10 | 9 | 9 | 14 | 16 | | |
| Goods and Services | 889 | 1005 | 1078 | 773 | 386 | 412 | 531 | 608 | 1451 | | |
| Operating Balance | 553 | 475 | 310 | 18 | 132 | 150 | 106 | 187 | 91 | | |
| Non-operating Revenues | 145 | 133 | 239 | 170 | 46 | 57 | 47 | 77 | 176 | | |
| Non-operating Expenditures | 321 | 235 | 323 | 202 | 108 | 81 | 109 | 119 | 85 | | |
| Interest | 94 | 49 | 44 | 34 | 35 | 31 | 38 | 27 | 14 | | |
| External | 94 | 45 | 38 | 30 | 30 | 29 | 37 | 27 | 14 | | |
| Domestic | | 5 | 7 | 4 | 5 | 2 | 1 | 1 | 0 | | |
| Transfers to public sector | 131 | 93 | 39 | 40 | 38 | 9 | 5 | 2 | 0 | | |
| Other | 96 | 93 | 240 | 128 | 35 | 41 | 66 | 90 | 68 | | |
| Capital Expenditures | 389 | 544 | 486 | 199 | 245 | 83 | 143 | 236 | 210 | | |
| Balance | −12 | −172 | −261 | −213 | −175 | 43 | −100 | −91 | −28 | | |
| **Percent of GDP** | | | | | | | | | | | |
| Operating Revenues | 8.1 | 8.0 | 6.9 | 4.2 | 3.7 | 4.0 | 3.5 | 3.9 | 6.4 | 6.2 | 4.4 |
| Operating Expenditures | 5.4 | 5.7 | 5.6 | 4.1 | 2.9 | 3.1 | 3.0 | 3.1 | 6.0 | 4.7 | 3.8 |
| Salaries | 0.9 | 0.9 | 0.9 | 0.7 | 0.5 | 0.4 | 0.5 | 0.5 | 0.6 | 0.8 | 0.5 |
| Contributions to social security | 0.1 | 0.1 | 0.1 | 0.1 | 0.1 | 0.1 | 0.0 | 0.1 | 0.1 | 0.1 | 0.1 |
| Goods and Services | 4.4 | 4.7 | 4.6 | 3.3 | 2.3 | 2.6 | 2.5 | 2.5 | 5.4 | 3.9 | 3.2 |
| Operating Balance | 2.7 | 2.2 | 1.3 | 0.1 | 0.8 | 0.9 | 0.5 | 0.8 | 0.3 | 1.4 | 0.6 |
| Non-operating Revenues | 0.7 | 0.6 | 1.0 | 0.7 | 0.3 | 0.4 | 0.2 | 0.3 | 0.7 | 0.7 | 0.4 |

## TABLE A5: NON-FINANCIAL PUBLIC ENTERPRISES (*CONTINUED*)
(Nominal, GDP, Percent of NFPS)

| | 1995 | 1996 | 1997 | 1998 | 1999 | 2000 | 2001 | 2002 | 2003 | Average 1995–99 | Average 2000–03 |
|---|---|---|---|---|---|---|---|---|---|---|---|
| Non-operating Expenditures | 1.6 | 1.1 | 1.4 | 0.9 | 0.6 | 0.5 | 0.5 | 0.5 | 0.3 | 1.1 | 0.5 |
| Interest | 0.5 | 0.2 | 0.2 | 0.1 | 0.2 | 0.2 | 0.2 | 0.1 | 0.1 | 0.2 | 0.1 |
| External | 0.5 | 0.2 | 0.2 | 0.1 | 0.2 | 0.2 | 0.2 | 0.1 | 0.1 | 0.2 | 0.1 |
| Domestic | 0.0 | 0.0 | 0.0 | 0.0 | 0.0 | 0.0 | 0.0 | 0.0 | 0.0 | 0.0 | 0.0 |
| Transfers to public sector | 0.6 | 0.4 | 0.2 | 0.2 | 0.2 | 0.1 | 0.0 | 0.0 | 0.0 | 0.3 | 0.0 |
| Other | 0.5 | 0.4 | 1.0 | 0.5 | 0.2 | 0.3 | 0.3 | 0.4 | 0.3 | 0.5 | 0.3 |
| Capital Expenditures | 1.9 | 2.6 | 2.1 | 0.9 | 1.5 | 0.5 | 0.7 | 1.0 | 0.8 | 1.8 | 0.7 |
| Balance | −0.1 | −0.8 | −1.1 | −0.9 | −1.0 | 0.3 | −0.5 | −0.4 | −0.1 | −0.8 | −0.2 |
| | | | | | | | | | | | |
| Non-transfer non-operating expenditures/NFPS expenditures | 12.0 | 13.1 | 14.8 | 7.0 | 7.6 | 4.0 | 5.1 | 5.8 | 4.4 | | |

*Source*: BCE and own calculations

## Table A6: Central Government by Sectoral Classification

| | 1995 | 1996 | 1997 | 1998 | 1999 | 2000 | 2001 | 2002 |
|---|---|---|---|---|---|---|---|---|
| | (In millions of US dollars) | | | | | | | |
| General Administration | 101 | 117 | 50 | 40 | 14 | 34 | 24 | 47 |
| Defense | 499 | 483 | 588 | 622 | 311 | 340 | 443 | 669 |
| Public Order | 317 | 362 | 350 | 291 | 161 | 179 | 253 | 440 |
| Education | 586 | 676 | 605 | 707 | 391 | 357 | 568 | 920 |
| Health and Social Welfare | 275 | 345 | 278 | 256 | 196 | 198 | 364 | 444 |
| Productive Activities | 169 | 235 | 213 | 109 | 227 | 56 | 304 | 210 |
| Infrastructure | 272 | 311 | 354 | 435 | 242 | 163 | 408 | 402 |
| Other Economic Services | 919 | 905 | 844 | 1048 | 1263 | 1509 | 1721 | 1195 |
| Others | 281 | 293 | 444 | 676 | 358 | 349 | 308 | 431 |
| Total | 3419 | 3726 | 3726 | 4186 | 3163 | 3185 | 4394 | 4757 |
| | (In percent of GDP) | | | | | | | |
| General Administration | 0.5 | 0.6 | 0.2 | 0.2 | 0.1 | 0.2 | 0.1 | 0.2 |
| Defense | 2.5 | 2.3 | 2.5 | 2.7 | 1.9 | 2.1 | 2.1 | 2.8 |
| Public Order | 1.6 | 1.7 | 1.5 | 1.3 | 1.0 | 1.1 | 1.2 | 1.8 |
| Education | 2.9 | 3.2 | 2.6 | 3.0 | 2.3 | 2.2 | 2.7 | 3.8 |
| Health and Social Welfare | 1.4 | 1.6 | 1.2 | 1.1 | 1.2 | 1.2 | 1.7 | 1.8 |
| Productive Activities | 0.8 | 1.1 | 0.9 | 0.5 | 1.4 | 0.3 | 1.4 | 0.9 |
| Infrastructure | 1.3 | 1.5 | 1.5 | 1.9 | 1.5 | 1.0 | 1.9 | 1.7 |
| Other Economic Services | 4.6 | 4.3 | 3.6 | 4.5 | 7.6 | 9.5 | 8.2 | 4.9 |
| Others | 1.4 | 1.4 | 1.9 | 2.9 | 2.1 | 2.2 | 1.5 | 1.8 |
| **Total Central Government** | **16.9** | **17.5** | **15.8** | **18.0** | **19.0** | **20.0** | **20.9** | **19.6** |
| | (in percent of total) | | | | | | | |
| General Administration | 2.9 | 3.2 | 1.3 | 1.0 | 0.5 | 1.1 | 0.5 | 1.0 |
| Defense | 14.6 | 13.0 | 15.8 | 14.9 | 9.8 | 10.7 | 10.1 | 14.1 |
| Public Order | 9.3 | 9.7 | 9.4 | 7.0 | 5.1 | 5.6 | 5.8 | 9.3 |
| Education | 17.1 | 18.1 | 16.2 | 16.9 | 12.4 | 11.2 | 12.9 | 19.3 |
| Health and Social Welfare | 8.0 | 9.2 | 7.4 | 6.1 | 6.2 | 6.2 | 8.3 | 9.3 |
| Productive Activities | 5.0 | 6.3 | 5.7 | 2.6 | 7.2 | 1.7 | 6.9 | 4.4 |
| Infrastructure | 8.0 | 8.3 | 9.5 | 10.4 | 7.7 | 5.1 | 9.3 | 8.4 |
| Other Economic Services | 26.9 | 24.3 | 22.6 | 25.0 | 39.9 | 47.4 | 39.2 | 25.1 |
| Others | 8.2 | 7.9 | 11.9 | 16.1 | 11.3 | 10.9 | 7.0 | 9.1 |
| **Total Central Government** | **100.0** | **100.0** | **100.0** | **100.0** | **100.0** | **100.0** | **100.0** | **100.0** |

## TABLE A6: CENTRAL GOVERNMENT BY SECTORAL CLASSIFICATION (CONTINUED)

| | 1995 | 1996 | 1997 | 1998 | 1999 | 2000 | 2001 | 2002 |
|---|---|---|---|---|---|---|---|---|
| | | | | (real percent change) | | | | |
| General Administration | | 13.4 | −59.9 | −16.6 | −53.2 | 155.7 | −44.2 | 75.0 |
| Defense | | −6.0 | 14.0 | 9.8 | −34.6 | 17.7 | 3.6 | 35.1 |
| Public Order | | 11.1 | −9.5 | −13.6 | −28.0 | 19.7 | 13.0 | 55.3 |
| Education | | 12.3 | −16.2 | 21.2 | −27.7 | −1.6 | 26.6 | 44.6 |
| Health and Social Welfare | | 22.0 | −24.6 | −4.3 | 0.1 | 8.7 | 46.1 | 9.0 |
| Productive Activities | | 34.8 | −14.8 | −46.8 | 170.7 | −73.6 | 335.9 | −38.4 |
| Infrastructure | | 11.1 | 6.6 | 27.7 | −27.3 | −27.8 | 99.9 | −12.0 |
| Other Economic Services | | −4.3 | −12.7 | 28.9 | 57.4 | 28.5 | −9.1 | −38.0 |
| Others | | 1.3 | 41.9 | 58.1 | −30.7 | 4.7 | −29.6 | 24.9 |
| | | | | | | | | |
| Total Central Government | | 6.0 | −6.4 | 16.6 | −1.2 | 8.3 | 9.9 | −3.2 |

Source: MEF

| **Real** | 1995 | 1996 | 1997 | 1998 | 1999 | 2000 | 2001 | 2002 |
|---|---|---|---|---|---|---|---|---|
| General Administration | 75.8 | 86.0 | 34.4 | 28.7 | 13.4 | 34.4 | 19.2 | 33.6 |
| Defense | 376.0 | 353.5 | 402.9 | 442.6 | 289.3 | 340.4 | 352.5 | 476.3 |
| Public Order | 238.5 | 265.1 | 239.9 | 207.3 | 149.2 | 178.6 | 201.9 | 313.5 |
| Education | 440.8 | 494.8 | 414.9 | 502.7 | 363.2 | 357.4 | 452.7 | 654.7 |
| Health and Social Welfare | 206.8 | 252.3 | 190.2 | 182.1 | 182.4 | 198.3 | 289.8 | 315.9 |
| Productive Activities | 127.4 | 171.7 | 146.3 | 77.9 | 210.8 | 55.6 | 242.5 | 149.4 |
| Infrastructure | 204.6 | 227.4 | 242.5 | 309.7 | 225.1 | 162.6 | 325.0 | 286.0 |
| Other Economic Services | 691.8 | 662.4 | 578.4 | 745.7 | 1174.0 | 1509.1 | 1371.1 | 850.7 |
| Others | 211.6 | 214.3 | 304.0 | 480.8 | 333.0 | 348.7 | 245.6 | 306.8 |
| | | | | | | | | |
| Total Central Government | 2573.4 | 2727.5 | 2553.7 | 2977.4 | 2940.4 | 3185.2 | 3500.3 | 3386.8 |

## TABLE A7: WAGES AND SALARIES OF THE CENTRAL GOVERNMENT BY SECTORAL CLASSIFICATION

| | 1995 | 1996 | 1997 | 1998 | 1999 | 2000 | 2001 | 2002 |
|---|---|---|---|---|---|---|---|---|
| | | | | (In millions of US dollars) | | | | |
| General Administration | 14 | 10 | 11 | 17 | 2 | 1 | 2 | 3 |
| Defense | 373 | 379 | 437 | 491 | 270 | 200 | 266 | 356 |
| Public Order | 173 | 163 | 193 | 214 | 118 | 91 | 131 | 200 |
| Education | 335 | 456 | 450 | 499 | 308 | 297 | 458 | 722 |
| Health and Social Welfare | 214 | 167 | 163 | 137 | 83 | 70 | 97 | 190 |
| Productive Activities | 49 | 36 | 31 | 28 | 14 | 10 | 16 | 23 |
| Infrastructure | 54 | 42 | 34 | 35 | 20 | 17 | 21 | 58 |
| Other Economic Services | 39 | 24 | 25 | 66 | 6 | 4 | 6 | 13 |
| Others | 2 | 41 | 24 | 21 | 77 | 16 | 90 | 107 |
| **Total CG Wages and Salaries** | **1252** | **1317** | **1369** | **1510** | **898** | **707** | **1088** | **1672** |

| | 1995 | 1996 | 1997 | 1998 | 1999 | 2000 | 2001 | 2002 |
|---|---|---|---|---|---|---|---|---|
| | | | | (In percent of GDP) | | | | |
| General Administration | 0.1 | 0.0 | 0.0 | 0.1 | 0.0 | 0.0 | 0.0 | 0.0 |
| Defense | 1.8 | 1.8 | 1.8 | 2.1 | 1.6 | 1.3 | 1.3 | 1.5 |
| Public Order | 0.9 | 0.8 | 0.8 | 0.9 | 0.7 | 0.6 | 0.6 | 0.8 |
| Education | 1.7 | 2.1 | 1.9 | 2.1 | 1.8 | 1.9 | 2.2 | 3.0 |
| Health and Social Welfare | 1.1 | 0.8 | 0.7 | 0.6 | 0.5 | 0.4 | 0.5 | 0.8 |
| Productive Activities | 0.2 | 0.2 | 0.1 | 0.1 | 0.1 | 0.1 | 0.1 | 0.1 |
| Infrastructure | 0.3 | 0.2 | 0.1 | 0.2 | 0.1 | 0.1 | 0.1 | 0.2 |
| Other Economic Services | 0.2 | 0.1 | 0.1 | 0.3 | 0.0 | 0.0 | 0.0 | 0.1 |
| Others | 0.0 | 0.2 | 0.1 | 0.1 | 0.5 | 0.1 | 0.4 | 0.4 |
| **Total CG Wages and Salaries** | **6.2** | **6.2** | **5.8** | **6.5** | **5.4** | **4.4** | **5.2** | **6.9** |

| | 1995 | 1996 | 1997 | 1998 | 1999 | 2000 | 2001 | 2002 |
|---|---|---|---|---|---|---|---|---|
| | | | | (in percent of total CG wages and salaries) | | | | |
| General Administration | 1.1 | 0.8 | 0.8 | 1.2 | 0.2 | 0.2 | 0.2 | 0.2 |
| Defense | 29.8 | 28.8 | 31.9 | 32.5 | 30.1 | 28.4 | 24.5 | 21.3 |
| Public Order | 13.8 | 12.4 | 14.1 | 14.2 | 13.1 | 12.9 | 12.0 | 12.0 |
| Education | 26.7 | 34.6 | 32.9 | 33.1 | 34.3 | 42.0 | 42.1 | 43.2 |
| Health and Social Welfare | 17.1 | 12.7 | 11.9 | 9.1 | 9.2 | 9.9 | 8.9 | 11.4 |
| Productive Activities | 3.9 | 2.7 | 2.3 | 1.9 | 1.5 | 1.5 | 1.5 | 1.3 |
| Infrastructure | 4.3 | 3.2 | 2.5 | 2.3 | 2.3 | 2.4 | 1.9 | 3.5 |
| Other Economic Services | 3.1 | 1.9 | 1.9 | 4.4 | 0.6 | 0.6 | 0.6 | 0.8 |
| Others | 0.2 | 3.1 | 1.8 | 1.4 | 8.6 | 2.2 | 8.3 | 6.4 |
| **Total CG Wages and Salaries** | **100.0** | **100.0** | **100.0** | **100.0** | **100.0** | **100.0** | **100.0** | **100.0** |

## TABLE A7: WAGES AND SALARIES OF THE CENTRAL GOVERNMENT BY SECTORAL CLASSIFICATION (CONTINUED)

| | 1995 | 1996 | 1997 | 1998 | 1999 | 2000 | 2001 | 2002 |
|---|---|---|---|---|---|---|---|---|
| | | | | (real percent change) | | | | |
| General Administration | | −31.4 | −0.3 | 71.4 | −85.2 | −20.7 | 34.7 | 14.0 |
| Defense | | −1.2 | 8.0 | 16.6 | −28.2 | −20.1 | 5.9 | 19.5 |
| Public Order | | −8.3 | 11.0 | 15.2 | −28.1 | −16.9 | 14.6 | 36.6 |
| Education | | 32.4 | −7.6 | 15.2 | −19.3 | 3.6 | 23.1 | 40.7 |
| Health and Social Welfare | | −24.0 | −8.4 | −12.7 | −21.1 | −9.1 | 9.8 | 75.9 |
| Productive Activities | | −29.3 | −19.2 | −5.0 | −36.0 | −20.2 | 24.0 | 26.0 |
| Infrastructure | | −24.9 | −22.7 | 6.2 | −24.8 | −9.4 | −2.4 | 150.4 |
| Other Economic Services | | −38.8 | −2.7 | 169.3 | −88.6 | −21.7 | 20.2 | 81.2 |
| Others | | 1998.4 | −44.5 | −10.0 | 376.9 | −78.2 | 358.0 | 6.1 |
| **Total CG Wages and Salaries** | | **2.3** | **−2.7** | **14.5** | **−22.3** | **−15.3** | **22.6** | **37.4** |

Source: MEF

| **Real** | 1995 | 1996 | 1997 | 1998 | 1999 | 2000 | 2001 | 2002 |
|---|---|---|---|---|---|---|---|---|
| General Administration | 10.6 | 7.3 | 7.2 | 12.4 | 1.8 | 1.5 | 2.0 | 2.2 |
| Defense | 280.8 | 277.5 | 299.6 | 349.3 | 250.9 | 200.4 | 212.3 | 253.7 |
| Public Order | 129.9 | 119.1 | 132.3 | 152.4 | 109.6 | 91.1 | 104.4 | 142.7 |
| Education | 251.9 | 333.5 | 308.3 | 355.0 | 286.5 | 296.7 | 365.3 | 513.9 |
| Health and Social Welfare | 160.8 | 122.2 | 112.0 | 97.7 | 77.1 | 70.1 | 77.0 | 135.4 |
| Productive Activities | 37.0 | 26.2 | 21.2 | 20.1 | 12.9 | 10.3 | 12.7 | 16.0 |
| Infrastructure | 40.5 | 30.4 | 23.5 | 25.0 | 18.8 | 17.0 | 16.6 | 41.6 |
| Other Economic Services | 29.2 | 17.9 | 17.4 | 46.8 | 5.3 | 4.2 | 5.0 | 9.1 |
| Others | 1.4 | 30.1 | 16.7 | 15.0 | 71.8 | 15.6 | 71.5 | 75.9 |
| Total Central Government | 942.3 | 964.3 | 938.2 | 1073.8 | 834.7 | 706.9 | 866.8 | 1190.5 |

## TABLE A8: GOODS AND SERVICES OF THE CENTRAL GOVERNMENT BY SECTORAL CLASSIFICATION

| | 1995 | 1996 | 1997 | 1998 | 1999 | 2000 | 2001 | 2002 |
|---|---|---|---|---|---|---|---|---|
| | | | | (In millions of US dollars) | | | | |
| General Administration | 9.0 | 12.1 | 10.1 | 9.8 | 4.6 | 9.4 | 5.0 | 8.9 |
| Defense | 0.4 | 46.6 | 41.4 | 41.7 | 17.0 | 47.8 | 22.5 | 103.7 |
| Public Order | 11.8 | 41.1 | 44.3 | 36.3 | 21.0 | 20.2 | 17.9 | 43.2 |
| Education | 4.4 | 18.6 | 15.6 | 14.4 | 15.3 | 12.1 | 12.0 | 18.7 |
| Health and Social Welfare | 26.4 | 35.6 | 42.4 | 51.7 | 24.7 | 48.8 | 23.0 | 54.4 |
| Productive Activities | 8.9 | 15.4 | 14.5 | 8.3 | 5.9 | 1.9 | 5.5 | 7.3 |
| Infrastructure | 6.7 | 11.6 | 10.9 | 6.3 | 4.5 | 1.5 | 4.2 | 5.5 |
| Other Economic Services | 4.8 | 6.1 | 8.4 | 8.5 | 15.0 | 18.5 | 7.5 | 15.2 |
| Others | 9.1 | 15.2 | 21.2 | 19.9 | 14.8 | 14.2 | 24.1 | 61.2 |
| **Total CG Goods and Services** | **81.3** | **202.3** | **208.8** | **197.0** | **122.8** | **174.5** | **121.7** | **318.0** |

| | 1995 | 1996 | 1997 | 1998 | 1999 | 2000 | 2001 | 2002 |
|---|---|---|---|---|---|---|---|---|
| | | | | (In percent of GDP) | | | | |
| General Administration | 0.0 | 0.1 | 0.0 | 0.0 | 0.0 | 0.1 | 0.0 | 0.0 |
| Defense | 0.0 | 0.2 | 0.2 | 0.2 | 0.1 | 0.3 | 0.1 | 0.4 |
| Public Order | 0.1 | 0.2 | 0.2 | 0.2 | 0.1 | 0.1 | 0.1 | 0.2 |
| Education | 0.0 | 0.1 | 0.1 | 0.1 | 0.1 | 0.1 | 0.1 | 0.1 |
| Health and Social Welfare | 0.1 | 0.2 | 0.2 | 0.2 | 0.1 | 0.3 | 0.1 | 0.2 |
| Productive Activities | 0.0 | 0.1 | 0.1 | 0.0 | 0.0 | 0.0 | 0.0 | 0.0 |
| Infrastructure | 0.0 | 0.1 | 0.0 | 0.0 | 0.0 | 0.0 | 0.0 | 0.0 |
| Other Economic Services | 0.0 | 0.0 | 0.0 | 0.0 | 0.1 | 0.1 | 0.0 | 0.1 |
| Others | 0.0 | 0.1 | 0.1 | 0.1 | 0.1 | 0.1 | 0.1 | 0.3 |
| **Total CG Goods and Services** | **0.4** | **1.0** | **0.9** | **0.8** | **0.7** | **1.1** | **0.6** | **1.3** |

| | 1995 | 1996 | 1997 | 1998 | 1999 | 2000 | 2001 | 2002 |
|---|---|---|---|---|---|---|---|---|
| | | | | (in percent of total CG goods and services) | | | | |
| General Administration | 11.1 | 6.0 | 4.8 | 5.0 | 3.7 | 5.4 | 4.1 | 2.8 |
| Defense | 0.5 | 23.1 | 19.8 | 21.1 | 13.8 | 27.4 | 18.5 | 32.6 |
| Public Order | 14.5 | 20.3 | 21.2 | 18.5 | 17.1 | 11.6 | 14.7 | 13.6 |
| Education | 5.4 | 9.2 | 7.5 | 7.3 | 12.5 | 7.0 | 9.9 | 5.9 |
| Health and Social Welfare | 32.4 | 17.6 | 20.3 | 26.3 | 20.1 | 28.0 | 18.9 | 17.1 |
| Productive Activities | 10.9 | 7.6 | 6.9 | 4.2 | 4.8 | 1.1 | 4.6 | 2.3 |
| Infrastructure | 8.2 | 5.7 | 5.2 | 3.2 | 3.6 | 0.8 | 3.4 | 1.7 |
| Other Economic Services | 5.9 | 3.0 | 4.0 | 4.3 | 12.2 | 10.6 | 6.1 | 4.8 |
| Others | 11.2 | 7.5 | 10.2 | 10.1 | 12.1 | 8.1 | 19.8 | 19.2 |
| **Total CG Goods and Services** | **100.0** | **100.0** | **100.0** | **100.0** | **100.0** | **100.0** | **100.0** | **100.0** |

## TABLE A8: GOODS AND SERVICES OF THE CENTRAL GOVERNMENT BY SECTORAL CLASSIFICATION (CONTINUED)

| | 1995 | 1996 | 1997 | 1998 | 1999 | 2000 | 2001 | 2002 |
|---|---|---|---|---|---|---|---|---|
| | | | | (real percent change) | | | | |
| General Administration | | 30.8 | −22.0 | 0.8 | −39.1 | 122.2 | −57.7 | 59.4 |
| Defense | | 10616.3 | −16.9 | 4.5 | −46.6 | 202.3 | −62.5 | 312.0 |
| Public Order | | 239.9 | 0.9 | −14.8 | −24.4 | 3.5 | −29.5 | 115.6 |
| Education | | 310.3 | −21.3 | −4.1 | 38.5 | −14.6 | −21.1 | 38.8 |
| Health and Social Welfare | | 31.2 | 11.5 | 26.6 | −37.6 | 112.6 | −62.4 | 111.1 |
| Productive Activities | | 69.3 | −11.9 | −40.3 | −7.3 | −64.9 | 129.2 | 17.0 |
| Infrastructure | | 69.3 | −11.9 | −40.3 | −7.3 | −64.9 | 129.2 | 17.0 |
| Other Economic Services | | 24.6 | 28.4 | 5.7 | 130.3 | 32.8 | −67.9 | 81.8 |
| Others | | 62.6 | 31.0 | −2.7 | −2.7 | 3.1 | 34.9 | 127.2 |
| **Total CG Wages and Salaries** | | **142.0** | **−3.4** | **−2.1** | **−18.5** | **52.9** | **−44.4** | **133.5** |

Source: MEF

**Nominal**

| | 1995 | 1996 | 1997 | 1998 | 1999 | 2000 | 2001 | 2002 |
|---|---|---|---|---|---|---|---|---|
| Total Central Government | 81.3 | 202.3 | 208.8 | 197.0 | 122.8 | 174.5 | 121.7 | 318.0 |

**Real**

| | 1995 | 1996 | 1997 | 1998 | 1999 | 2000 | 2001 | 2002 |
|---|---|---|---|---|---|---|---|---|
| General Administration | 6.8 | 8.9 | 6.9 | 7.0 | 4.2 | 9.4 | 4.0 | 6.4 |
| Defense | 0.3 | 34.1 | 28.4 | 29.6 | 15.8 | 47.8 | 17.9 | 73.8 |
| Public Order | 8.8 | 30.1 | 30.3 | 25.9 | 19.5 | 20.2 | 14.3 | 30.8 |
| Education | 3.3 | 13.6 | 10.7 | 10.3 | 14.2 | 12.1 | 9.6 | 13.3 |
| Health and Social Welfare | 19.9 | 26.1 | 29.1 | 36.8 | 23.0 | 48.8 | 18.3 | 38.7 |
| Productive Activities | 6.7 | 11.3 | 9.9 | 5.9 | 5.5 | 1.9 | 4.4 | 5.2 |
| Infrastructure | 5.0 | 8.5 | 7.5 | 4.5 | 4.1 | 1.5 | 3.3 | 3.9 |
| Other Economic Services | 3.6 | 4.5 | 5.7 | 6.1 | 14.0 | 18.5 | 5.9 | 10.8 |
| Others | 6.8 | 11.1 | 14.6 | 14.2 | 13.8 | 14.2 | 19.2 | 43.6 |
| Total Central Government | 61.2 | 148.1 | 143.1 | 140.1 | 114.1 | 174.5 | 97.0 | 226.4 |

## TABLE A9: FIXED INVESTMENT OF THE CENTRAL GOVERNMENT BY SECTORAL CLASSIFICATION

| | 1995 | 1996 | 1997 | 1998 | 1999 | 2000 | 2001 | 2002 |
|---|---|---|---|---|---|---|---|---|
| | | | | (In millions of US dollars) | | | | |
| General Administration | 0 | 0 | 2 | 2 | 8 | 3 | 10 | 10 |
| Defense | 0 | 12 | 36 | 3 | 0 | 1 | 2 | 43 |
| Public Order | 4 | 9 | 18 | 8 | 6 | 47 | 32 | 79 |
| Education | 18 | 15 | 15 | 19 | 8 | 11 | 9 | 30 |
| Health and Social Welfare | 7 | 14 | 18 | 11 | 55 | 29 | 67 | 54 |
| Productive Activities | 102 | 71 | 106 | 66 | 195 | 33 | 246 | 146 |
| Infrastructure | 157 | 234 | 234 | 305 | 186 | 140 | 251 | 202 |
| Other Economic Services | 88 | 71 | 1 | 0 | 0 | 1 | 10 | 25 |
| Others | 5 | 72 | 48 | 187 | 28 | 205 | 18 | 21 |
| **Total CG Fixed Investment** | **381** | **498** | **478** | **602** | **485** | **470** | **645** | **611** |

| | 1995 | 1996 | 1997 | 1998 | 1999 | 2000 | 2001 | 2002 |
|---|---|---|---|---|---|---|---|---|
| | | | | (In percent of GDP) | | | | |
| General Administration | 0.0 | 0.0 | 0.0 | 0.0 | 0.0 | 0.0 | 0.0 | 0.0 |
| Defense | 0.0 | 0.1 | 0.2 | 0.0 | 0.0 | 0.0 | 0.0 | 0.2 |
| Public Order | 0.0 | 0.0 | 0.1 | 0.0 | 0.0 | 0.3 | 0.2 | 0.3 |
| Education | 0.1 | 0.1 | 0.1 | 0.1 | 0.0 | 0.1 | 0.0 | 0.1 |
| Health and Social Welfare | 0.0 | 0.1 | 0.1 | 0.0 | 0.3 | 0.2 | 0.3 | 0.2 |
| Productive Activities | 0.5 | 0.3 | 0.4 | 0.3 | 1.2 | 0.2 | 1.2 | 0.6 |
| Infrastructure | 0.8 | 1.1 | 1.0 | 1.3 | 1.1 | 0.9 | 1.2 | 0.8 |
| Other Economic Services | 0.4 | 0.3 | 0.0 | 0.0 | 0.0 | 0.0 | 0.0 | 0.1 |
| Others | 0.0 | 0.3 | 0.2 | 0.8 | 0.2 | 1.3 | 0.1 | 0.1 |
| **Total CG Fixed Investment** | **1.9** | **2.3** | **2.0** | **2.6** | **2.9** | **2.9** | **3.1** | **2.5** |

| | 1995 | 1996 | 1997 | 1998 | 1999 | 2000 | 2001 | 2002 |
|---|---|---|---|---|---|---|---|---|
| | | | | (in percent of total CG fixed investments) | | | | |
| General Administration | 0.0 | 0.1 | 0.4 | 0.4 | 1.6 | 0.6 | 1.5 | 1.7 |
| Defense | 0.0 | 2.5 | 7.6 | 0.6 | 0.0 | 0.2 | 0.3 | 7.0 |
| Public Order | 0.9 | 1.7 | 3.7 | 1.3 | 1.3 | 10.0 | 5.0 | 12.9 |
| Education | 4.6 | 3.0 | 3.2 | 3.1 | 1.5 | 2.4 | 1.4 | 4.9 |
| Health and Social Welfare | 1.9 | 2.8 | 3.8 | 1.8 | 11.3 | 6.2 | 10.4 | 8.8 |
| Productive Activities | 26.9 | 14.3 | 22.2 | 11.0 | 40.2 | 7.0 | 38.2 | 23.9 |
| Infrastructure | 41.1 | 46.9 | 48.8 | 50.7 | 38.3 | 29.8 | 38.9 | 33.1 |
| Other Economic Services | 23.1 | 14.3 | 0.2 | 0.1 | 0.0 | 0.1 | 1.6 | 4.2 |
| Others | 1.4 | 14.5 | 10.1 | 31.1 | 5.8 | 43.7 | 2.7 | 3.4 |
| **Total CG Fixed Investment** | **100.0** | **100.0** | **100.0** | **100.0** | **100.0** | **100.0** | **100.0** | **100.0** |

## TABLE A9: FIXED INVESTMENT OF THE CENTRAL GOVERNMENT BY SECTORAL CLASSIFICATION (CONTINUED)

| | 1995 | 1996 | 1997 | 1998 | 1999 | 2000 | 2001 | 2002 |
|---|---|---|---|---|---|---|---|---|
| | | | | (real percent change) | | | | |
| General Administration | | ... | 358.7 | 43.2 | 315.3 | −61.0 | 165.3 | −1.7 |
| Defense | | 6938.4 | 172.4 | −90.4 | −100.0 | .. | 90.9 | 1662.7 |
| Public Order | | 129.0 | 93.7 | −53.5 | 7.4 | 678.0 | −45.4 | 119.8 |
| Education | | −19.0 | −2.7 | 27.2 | −47.7 | 62.1 | −35.8 | 192.8 |
| Health and Social Welfare | | 92.2 | 22.0 | −39.9 | 578.3 | −43.2 | 83.8 | −28.2 |
| Productive Activities | | −32.3 | 39.5 | −35.4 | 285.3 | −81.9 | 497.9 | −46.9 |
| Infrastructure | | 44.9 | −6.4 | 35.6 | −20.5 | −18.9 | 42.8 | −27.9 |
| Other Economic Services | | −21.6 | −98.5 | −57.7 | −83.3 | 955.6 | 1310.5 | 120.4 |
| Others | | 1189.9 | −37.2 | 301.9 | −80.5 | 690.3 | −93.1 | 4.5 |
| **Total CG Fixed Investment** | | **27.1** | **−10.1** | **30.6** | **5.4** | **4.1** | **9.4** | **−15.3** |

Source: MEF

| **Real** | 1995 | 1996 | 1997 | 1998 | 1999 | 2000 | 2001 | 2002 |
|---|---|---|---|---|---|---|---|---|
| General Administration | 0.0 | 0.3 | 1.2 | 1.8 | 7.3 | 2.9 | 7.6 | 7.5 |
| Defense | 0.1 | 9.1 | 24.8 | 2.4 | 0.0 | 0.9 | 1.7 | 30.5 |
| Public Order | 2.7 | 6.2 | 12.1 | 5.6 | 6.0 | 46.9 | 25.6 | 56.3 |
| Education | 13.3 | 10.8 | 10.5 | 13.3 | 7.0 | 11.3 | 7.3 | 21.3 |
| Health and Social Welfare | 5.3 | 10.2 | 12.5 | 7.5 | 50.9 | 28.9 | 53.2 | 38.2 |
| Productive Activities | 77.1 | 52.2 | 72.8 | 47.1 | 181.3 | 32.8 | 196.0 | 104.0 |
| Infrastructure | 118.1 | 171.1 | 160.1 | 217.1 | 172.6 | 139.9 | 199.8 | 144.1 |
| Other Economic Services | 66.3 | 52.0 | 0.8 | 0.3 | 0.1 | 0.6 | 8.2 | 18.1 |
| Others | 4.1 | 52.8 | 33.1 | 133.2 | 26.0 | 205.3 | 14.1 | 14.7 |
| Total Central Government | 287.0 | 364.7 | 327.9 | 428.3 | 451.2 | 469.5 | 513.5 | 434.7 |

## Table A10: Transfers of the Central Government by Sectoral Classification

| | 1995 | 1996 | 1997 | 1998 | 1999 | 2000 | 2001 | 2002 |
|---|---|---|---|---|---|---|---|---|
| | (In millions of US dollars) | | | | | | | |
| General Administration | 46 | 49 | 15 | 4 | 0 | 0 | 2 | 2 |
| Defense | 106 | 19 | 45 | 12 | 5 | 43 | 124 | 86 |
| Public Order | 100 | 76 | 58 | 4 | 5 | 20 | 57 | 101 |
| Education | 209 | 94 | 90 | 73 | 13 | 12 | 13 | 19 |
| Health and Social Welfare | 27 | 66 | 35 | 18 | 15 | 46 | 132 | 62 |
| Productive Activities | 9 | 73 | 58 | 2 | 1 | 9 | 9 | 20 |
| Infrastructure | 54 | 23 | 72 | 85 | 15 | 1 | 10 | 11 |
| Other Economic Services | 21 | 30 | 10 | 72 | 108 | 521 | 381 | 323 |
| Others | 171 | 122 | 226 | 268 | 125 | 29 | 80 | 93 |
| **Total CG Fixed Investment** | **741** | **551** | **609** | **538** | **285** | **681** | **808** | **718** |
| | (In percent of GDP) | | | | | | | |
| General Administration | 0.2 | 0.2 | 0.1 | 0.0 | 0.0 | 0.0 | 0.0 | 0.0 |
| Defense | 0.5 | 0.1 | 0.2 | 0.1 | 0.0 | 0.3 | 0.6 | 0.4 |
| Public Order | 0.5 | 0.4 | 0.2 | 0.0 | 0.0 | 0.1 | 0.3 | 0.4 |
| Education | 1.0 | 0.4 | 0.4 | 0.3 | 0.1 | 0.1 | 0.1 | 0.1 |
| Health and Social Welfare | 0.1 | 0.3 | 0.1 | 0.1 | 0.1 | 0.3 | 0.6 | 0.3 |
| Productive Activities | 0.0 | 0.3 | 0.2 | 0.0 | 0.0 | 0.1 | 0.0 | 0.1 |
| Infrastructure | 0.3 | 0.1 | 0.3 | 0.4 | 0.1 | 0.0 | 0.0 | 0.0 |
| Other Economic Services | 0.1 | 0.1 | 0.0 | 0.3 | 0.6 | 3.3 | 1.8 | 1.3 |
| Others | 0.8 | 0.6 | 1.0 | 1.2 | 0.8 | 0.2 | 0.4 | 0.4 |
| **Total CG Fixed Investment** | **3.7** | **2.6** | **2.6** | **2.3** | **1.7** | **4.3** | **3.8** | **3.0** |
| | (in percent of total CG transfers) | | | | | | | |
| General Administration | 6.1 | 8.9 | 2.5 | 0.7 | 0.0 | 0.0 | 0.2 | 0.3 |
| Defense | 14.3 | 3.4 | 7.4 | 2.2 | 1.6 | 6.3 | 15.4 | 12.0 |
| Public Order | 13.5 | 13.7 | 9.4 | 0.7 | 1.6 | 2.9 | 7.0 | 14.1 |
| Education | 28.1 | 17.1 | 14.8 | 13.5 | 4.5 | 1.7 | 1.6 | 2.6 |
| Health and Social Welfare | 3.7 | 12.0 | 5.8 | 3.3 | 5.1 | 6.8 | 16.3 | 8.7 |
| Productive Activities | 1.2 | 13.3 | 9.5 | 0.4 | 0.3 | 1.3 | 1.1 | 2.8 |
| Infrastructure | 7.3 | 4.1 | 11.8 | 15.9 | 5.1 | 0.2 | 1.2 | 1.6 |
| Other Economic Services | 2.8 | 5.4 | 1.7 | 13.4 | 37.8 | 76.5 | 47.1 | 45.0 |
| Others | 23.0 | 22.1 | 37.0 | 49.8 | 43.9 | 4.3 | 9.9 | 12.9 |
| **Total CG Fixed Investment** | **100.0** | **100.0** | **100.0** | **100.0** | **100.0** | **100.0** | **100.0** | **100.0** |

**TABLE A10: TRANSFERS OF THE CENTRAL GOVERNMENT BY SECTORAL CLASSIFICATION (CONTINUED)**

| | 1995 | 1996 | 1997 | 1998 | 1999 | 2000 | 2001 | 2002 |
|---|---|---|---|---|---|---|---|---|
| | | | | (real percent change) | | | | |
| General Administration | | ... | −71.1 | −73.3 | −97.5 | 186.9 | 658.5 | −10.2 |
| Defense | | −82.9 | 125.8 | −72.2 | −49.4 | .. | 131.9 | −38.4 |
| Public Order | | −26.3 | −28.9 | −93.1 | 56.8 | 359.7 | 130.2 | 59.4 |
| Education | | −56.1 | −10.3 | −16.3 | −77.0 | −1.9 | −10.4 | 29.2 |
| Health and Social Welfare | | 134.8 | −49.8 | −48.0 | 7.7 | 242.6 | 126.1 | −57.7 |
| Productive Activities | | 723.7 | −25.8 | −96.4 | −42.6 | 1014.7 | −20.6 | 97.8 |
| Infrastructure | | −59.1 | 197.1 | 23.3 | −77.8 | −90.3 | 493.7 | 1.8 |
| Other Economic Services | | 40.7 | −68.2 | 641.8 | 95.4 | 420.5 | −41.8 | −24.2 |
| Others | | −30.5 | 73.1 | 23.2 | −38.9 | −75.1 | 120.1 | 3.8 |
| **Total CG Fixed Investment** | | **−27.7** | **3.5** | **−8.4** | **−30.7** | **157.1** | **−5.5** | **−20.6** |

*Source:* MEF

| **Real** | | | | | | | | |
|---|---|---|---|---|---|---|---|---|
| General Administration | 34.3 | 35.8 | 10.3 | 2.8 | 0.1 | 0.2 | 1.5 | 1.4 |
| Defense | 79.9 | 13.7 | 30.9 | 8.6 | 4.3 | 42.7 | 99.1 | 61.1 |
| Public Order | 75.2 | 55.4 | 39.4 | 2.7 | 4.3 | 19.7 | 45.3 | 72.1 |
| Education | 157.0 | 69.0 | 61.9 | 51.8 | 11.9 | 11.7 | 10.4 | 13.5 |
| Health and Social Welfare | 20.5 | 48.2 | 24.2 | 12.6 | 13.6 | 46.5 | 105.0 | 44.5 |
| Productive Activities | 6.5 | 53.7 | 39.8 | 1.4 | 0.8 | 9.2 | 7.3 | 14.4 |
| Infrastructure | 40.6 | 16.6 | 49.3 | 60.8 | 13.5 | 1.3 | 7.8 | 7.9 |
| Other Economic Services | 15.4 | 21.7 | 6.9 | 51.2 | 100.1 | 520.8 | 303.4 | 230.0 |
| Others | 128.5 | 89.3 | 154.6 | 190.4 | 116.4 | 29.0 | 63.8 | 66.2 |
| Total Central Government | 557.9 | 403.4 | 417.4 | 382.3 | 264.9 | 681.0 | 643.5 | 511.0 |

## TABLE A11: ECONOMIC CLASSIFICATION OF DEFENSE EXPENDITURE
### (Nominal, GDP)

| | 1995 | 1996 | 1997 | 1998 | 1999 | 2000 | 2001 | Prel. 2002 | Average 1995–99 | Average 2000–02 |
|---|---|---|---|---|---|---|---|---|---|---|
| | | | | | (In millions of US dollars) | | | | | |
| Total expenditures | 499 | 483 | 588 | 622 | 311 | 340 | 443 | 669 | | |
| Current | 480 | 444 | 524 | 545 | 292 | 291 | 413 | 546 | | |
| Wages and salaries | 373 | 379 | 437 | 491 | 270 | 200 | 266 | 356 | | |
| Goods and services | 0 | 47 | 41 | 42 | 17 | 48 | 22 | 104 | | |
| Interest payments | ... | ... | ... | ... | ... | ... | ... | ... | | |
| Transfers | 106 | 19 | 45 | 12 | 5 | 43 | 124 | 86 | | |
| Capital | 20 | 38 | 64 | 77 | 20 | 49 | 29 | 123 | | |
| Fixed capital formation | 0 | 12 | 36 | 3 | 0 | 1 | 2 | 43 | | |
| Capital transfers | 20 | 26 | 28 | 74 | 20 | 49 | 27 | 80 | | |
| | | | | | (In percent of GDP) | | | | | |
| Total expenditures | 2.5 | 2.3 | 2.5 | 2.7 | 1.9 | 2.1 | 2.1 | 2.8 | 2.5 | 2.2 |
| Current | 2.4 | 2.1 | 2.2 | 2.3 | 1.7 | 1.8 | 2.0 | 2.2 | 2.3 | 1.9 |
| Wages and salaries | 1.8 | 1.8 | 1.8 | 2.1 | 1.6 | 1.3 | 1.3 | 1.5 | 1.9 | 1.4 |
| Goods and services | 0.0 | 0.2 | 0.2 | 0.2 | 0.1 | 0.3 | 0.1 | 0.4 | 0.1 | 0.2 |
| Interest payments | ... | ... | ... | ... | ... | ... | ... | ... | | |
| Transfers | 0.5 | 0.1 | 0.2 | 0.1 | 0.0 | 0.3 | 0.6 | 0.4 | 0.2 | 0.3 |
| Capital | 0.1 | 0.2 | 0.3 | 0.3 | 0.1 | 0.3 | 0.1 | 0.5 | 0.2 | 0.3 |
| Fixed capital formation | 0.0 | 0.1 | 0.2 | 0.0 | 0.0 | 0.0 | 0.0 | 0.2 | 0.1 | 0.0 |
| Capital transfers | 0.1 | 0.1 | 0.1 | 0.3 | 0.1 | 0.3 | 0.1 | 0.3 | 0.2 | 0.2 |

Sources: MEF; and BCE

## TABLE A12: ECONOMIC CLASSIFICATION OF EDUCATION EXPENDITURE
### (Nominal, GDP)

| | 1995 | 1996 | 1997 | 1998 | 1999 | 2000 | 2001 | 2002 (p) |
|---|---|---|---|---|---|---|---|---|
| | (In millions of US dollars) | | | | | | | |
| Total expenditures | 586 | 676 | 605 | 707 | 391 | 357 | 568 | 920 |
| Current | 548 | 568 | 556 | 586 | 336 | 321 | 484 | 759 |
| Wages and salaries | 335 | 456 | 450 | 499 | 308 | 297 | 458 | 722 |
| Goods and services | 4 | 19 | 16 | 14 | 15 | 12 | 12 | 19 |
| Interest payments | ... | ... | ... | ... | ... | ... | ... | ... |
| Transfers | 209 | 94 | 90 | 73 | 13 | 12 | 13 | 19 |
| Capital | 38 | 108 | 50 | 120 | 54 | 37 | 85 | 160 |
| Fixed capital formation | 18 | 15 | 15 | 19 | 8 | 11 | 9 | 30 |
| Capital transfers | 20 | 93 | 34 | 102 | 47 | 26 | 75 | 130 |
| | (In percent of GDP) | | | | | | | |
| Total expenditures | 2.9 | 3.2 | 2.6 | 3.0 | 2.3 | 2.2 | 2.7 | 3.8 |
| Current | 2.7 | 2.7 | 2.4 | 2.5 | 2.0 | 2.0 | 2.3 | 3.1 |
| Wages and salaries | 1.7 | 2.1 | 1.9 | 2.1 | 1.8 | 1.9 | 2.2 | 3.0 |
| Goods and services | 0.0 | 0.1 | 0.1 | 0.1 | 0.1 | 0.1 | 0.1 | 0.1 |
| Interest payments | ... | ... | ... | ... | ... | ... | ... | ... |
| Transfers | 1.0 | 0.4 | 0.4 | 0.3 | 0.1 | 0.1 | 0.1 | 0.1 |
| Capital | 0.2 | 0.5 | 0.2 | 0.5 | 0.3 | 0.2 | 0.4 | 0.7 |
| Fixed capital formation | 0.1 | 0.1 | 0.1 | 0.1 | 0.0 | 0.1 | 0.0 | 0.1 |
| Capital transfers | 0.1 | 0.4 | 0.1 | 0.4 | 0.3 | 0.2 | 0.4 | 0.5 |

Sources: MEF; and BCE

## TABLE A13: ECONOMIC CLASSIFICATION OF HEALTH AND SOCIAL WELFARE EXPENDITURE
### (Nominal, GDP)

| | 1995 | 1996 | 1997 | 1998 | 1999 | 2000 | 2001 | 2002 (p) | Average 1995–99 | Average 2000–02 |
|---|---|---|---|---|---|---|---|---|---|---|
| | (In millions of US dollars) | | | | | | | | | |
| Total expenditures | 274.8 | 344.6 | 277.6 | 256.0 | 196.2 | 198.3 | 363.7 | 443.7 | | |
| Current | 267.3 | 268.4 | 241.1 | 206.8 | 122.2 | 165.3 | 251.5 | 307.0 | | |
| Wages and salaries | 213.7 | 167.0 | 163.4 | 137.4 | 82.9 | 70.1 | 96.6 | 190.2 | | |
| Goods and services | 26.4 | 35.6 | 42.4 | 51.7 | 24.7 | 48.8 | 23.0 | 54.4 | | |
| Interest payments | ... | ... | ... | ... | ... | ... | ... | ... | | |
| Transfers | 27.3 | 65.9 | 35.3 | 17.7 | 14.6 | 46.5 | 131.8 | 62.4 | | |
| Capital | 7.5 | 76.2 | 36.4 | 49.3 | 74.0 | 33.0 | 112.3 | 136.7 | | |
| Fixed capital formation | 7.1 | 14.0 | 18.2 | 10.6 | 54.8 | 28.9 | 66.7 | 53.6 | | |
| Capital transfers | 0.4 | 62.2 | 18.2 | 38.7 | 19.2 | 4.0 | 45.5 | 83.1 | | |
| | (In percent of GDP) | | | | | | | | | |
| Total expenditures | 1.4 | 1.6 | 1.2 | 1.1 | 1.2 | 1.2 | 1.7 | 1.8 | 1.3 | 1.5 |
| Current | 1.3 | 1.3 | 1.0 | 0.9 | 0.7 | 1.0 | 1.2 | 1.3 | 1.1 | 1.1 |
| Wages and salaries | 1.1 | 0.8 | 0.7 | 0.6 | 0.5 | 0.4 | 0.5 | 0.8 | 0.8 | 0.5 |
| Goods and services | 0.1 | 0.2 | 0.2 | 0.2 | 0.1 | 0.3 | 0.1 | 0.2 | 0.2 | 0.2 |
| Interest payments | ... | ... | ... | ... | ... | ... | ... | ... | ... | ... |
| Transfers | 0.1 | 0.3 | 0.1 | 0.1 | 0.1 | 0.3 | 0.6 | 0.3 | 0.2 | 0.3 |
| Capital | 0.0 | 0.4 | 0.2 | 0.2 | 0.4 | 0.2 | 0.5 | 0.6 | 0.2 | 0.4 |
| Fixed capital formation | 0.0 | 0.1 | 0.1 | 0.0 | 0.3 | 0.2 | 0.3 | 0.2 | 0.1 | 0.3 |
| Capital transfers | 0.0 | 0.3 | 0.1 | 0.2 | 0.1 | 0.0 | 0.2 | 0.3 | 0.1 | 0.2 |

Sources: MEF; and BCE

## TABLE A14: NUMBER OF ASCRIBED INSTITUTIOS TO LINE MINISTRIES

|  | 1995 | 1996 | 1997 | 1998 | 1999 | 2000 | 2001 | 2002 |
|---|---|---|---|---|---|---|---|---|
| Number of institutions | 65 | 54 | 51 | 51 | 46 | 42 | 41 | 46 |
| Administration and Planning | 6 | 6 | 6 | 6 | 1 | 1 | 1 | 1 |
| Environment | 1 | 1 | 1 | 1 | 1 | 1 | 1 | 2 |
| Justice | 5 | 6 | 6 | 6 | 6 | 6 | 6 | 6 |
| National Defense | 1 | 1 | 1 | 1 | 1 | 1 | 1 | 1 |
| External Relations | 0 | 0 | 0 | 0 | 0 | 0 | 0 | 1 |
| Education and Culture | 10 | 10 | 10 | 10 | 10 | 8 | 8 | 8 |
| Human Development | 3 | 2 | 2 | 2 | 2 | 2 | 2 | 5 |
| Work and Human Resources | 3 | 2 | 2 | 2 | 2 | 1 | 1 | 1 |
| Health | 3 | 3 | 3 | 3 | 3 | 2 | 2 | 2 |
| Agriculture | 23 | 16 | 14 | 14 | 14 | 14 | 14 | 13 |
| Energy and Mining | 4 | 3 | 3 | 3 | 3 | 3 | 2 | 2 |
| Industry | 5 | 4 | 3 | 3 | 3 | 3 | 3 | 3 |
| Information and Tourism | 1 | 0 | 0 | 0 | 0 | 0 | 0 | 0 |
| Public Works and Communication | 0 | 0 | 0 | 0 | 0 | 0 | 0 | 1 |
| Housing and Urban Development | 0 | 0 | 0 | 0 | 0 | 0 | 0 | 0 |

*Source:* MEF.

## TABLE A15: EXPENDITURES OF ASCRIBED INSTITUTIONS TO LINE MINISTRIES
### (In percent of the sector's total expenditures)

|  | 1995 | 1996 | 1997 | 1998 | 1999 | 2000 | 2001 | 2002 |
|---|---|---|---|---|---|---|---|---|
| Administration and Planning | 20.3 | 21.0 | 48.3 | 58.5 | 42.3 | 6.8 | 29.1 | 12.7 |
| Environment | 100.0 | 100.0 | 59.5 | 41.7 | 17.7 | 25.1 | 4.2 | 19.6 |
| Justice | 50.1 | 59.9 | 64.7 | 94.7 | 94.6 | 89.0 | 95.3 | 93.1 |
| National Defense | 0.6 | 1.0 | 6.0 | 0.6 | 0.5 | 0.4 | 0.6 | 0.8 |
| External Relations | 0.0 | 0.0 | 0.0 | 0.0 | 0.0 | 0.0 | 0.0 | 11.7 |
| Education and Culture | 3.5 | 2.1 | 2.7 | 2.1 | 2.1 | 1.2 | 0.9 | 0.5 |
| Human Development | 2.9 | 0.8 | 0.9 | 2.8 | 5.8 | 18.3 | 13.0 | 14.4 |
| Work and Human Resources | 54.9 | 63.0 | 65.7 | 63.2 | 64.6 | 7.6 | 58.9 | 51.3 |
| Health | 8.3 | 8.7 | 5.0 | 6.0 | 4.1 | 2.0 | 3.7 | 4.5 |
| Agriculture | 88.5 | 74.1 | 90.0 | 83.2 | 91.5 | 71.6 | 78.9 | 77.9 |
| Energy and Mining | 19.1 | 12.3 | 3.0 | 1.5 | 5.4 | 16.5 | 10.1 | 10.0 |
| Industry | 37.4 | 31.3 | 36.4 | 33.8 | 19.4 | 11.6 | 16.5 | 8.5 |
| Information and Tourism | 50.3 | 0.0 | 0.0 | 0.0 | 0.0 | 0.0 | 0.0 | 0.0 |
| Public Works and Communication | 0.0 | 0.0 | 0.0 | 0.0 | 0.0 | 0.0 | 0.0 | 19.2 |
| Total | 16.1 | 17.2 | 20.1 | 15.5 | 21.0 | 11.2 | 19.4 | 19.5 |

*Source:* MEF.

## TABLE A16: OPERATIONS OF MUNICIPAL & PROVINCIAL COUNCILS

| | 2001 Auth. | 2002 Proj. | 2003 Proj. | 2004 |
|---|---|---|---|---|
| | | (In millions of US$) | | |
| **Revenue** | 814 | 1032 | 1079 | 1125 |
| Current revenue | 137 | 251 | 274 | 293 |
| Interest and profits[1] | 54 | 40 | 60 | 63 |
| Other | 83 | 211 | 214 | 229 |
| Transfers | 678 | 782 | 805 | 832 |
| Capital transfers from budgetary operations | 562 | 618 | 642 | 635 |
| 25% income tax sharing | | 30 | 38 | 54 |
| Fondo Salvamiento Cultural | 24 | 24 | 27 | 30 |
| From the rest of public sector | 92 | 110 | 98 | 114 |
| From **FODESEC** | 39 | 73 | 80 | 90 |
| *From others* | *53* | *37* | *18* | *24* |
| | | | | |
| **Expenditure** | 706 | 982 | 1102 | 1160 |
| Current | 376 | 495 | 621 | 644 |
| Wages and salaries | 108 | 137 | 169 | 171 |
| Purchases of goods and services | 261 | 345 | 352 | 367 |
| Interest payments | 2 | 2 | 3 | 2 |
| External | 2 | 2 | 3 | 2 |
| Current transfers | 5 | 12 | 97 | 104 |
| To IESS | 4 | 7 | 10 | 11 |
| To other public sector | 0 | 3 | 27 | 29 |
| To private sector | 0 | 2 | 60 | 64 |
| Capital | 329 | 487 | 480 | 516 |
| | | | | |
| Overall surplus or deficit (−) | 109 | 50 | −23 | −35 |

*Source:* MEF; and IMF staff estimates and projections

## TABLE A17: ORGANIZATION RECEIVING EARMARKED REVENUES

| Concept | % Central Government Budget | Income Tax | Road Tax | Value-added Tax (VAT) | Excise Tax | Tariffs on the CIF Value | Credit Operations Tax | Interest on Late Taxes | Tax Penalties | Non Tax Non Specific |
|---|---|---|---|---|---|---|---|---|---|---|
| Hydralic Sources Board for Jipijapa Pajan y Puerto Lopez | | | | | | 3% of the tariffs payment calculated over the CIF value | | | | |
| Guayas Transit Committee | | 6% of the Income Tax to Guayas province | | | | | | | | |
| Manabi Rehabilitation Center | | 6% of the Income Tax to Manabi province | | | | | 12.5% of credit operations tax | | | |
| Sectional Development Fund FODESEC | | 10% of Income Tax | | | | $22,800 monthly + $14,000 for non-collected coffee and cocoa tax | 27.5% of credit operations tax (55% of the 50% total) (l) | | | |
| Internal Income Service | | 1.5% of Income Tax | 1.5% of Road Tax | 1.5% of VAT | 1.5% of Excise Tax | | | 1.5% of the revenue | 1.5% of the revenue | 1.5% of the revenue |
| Official Universities | | 10% of Income Tax | | | | | | | | |
| Private Universities | | 1% of Income Tax | | | | | | | | |
| Permanent fund of university development FOPEDEUPO | | | | 10% of VAT | | | | | | |
| Agricultural Universities | | | | 0.5% of VAT | | | | | | |
| Cultural Patrimony Rescue Fund | | 6% of the Income Tax in the respective municipality (except Guayas and Manabi) | | | | | | | | |
| Loja Province Highway Administration Fund | | | 1% on the purchase of used vehicles | | | | | | | |
| Manta Port Authority | | | | | | | | | | |

(continued)

# TABLE A17: ORGANIZATION RECEIVING EARMARKED REVENUES (CONTINUED)

| Concept | % Central Government Budget | Income Tax | Road Tax | Value-added Tax (VAT) | Excise Tax | Tariffs on the CIF Value | Credit Operations Tax | Interest on Late Taxes | Tax Penaltes | Non Tax Non Specific |
|---|---|---|---|---|---|---|---|---|---|---|
| Supplies Equipment Program and Hospital maintenance | | | | | 10% of Excise Tax | | | | | |
| Free Maternity Services | | | | | 3% of the total Excise Tax of Group I without telecommunications | | | | | |
| Oswaldo Loor Moreira Foundation | | | | | 2% of the total Excise Tax on alcohol | | | | | |
| Sectional Utility Corporation | | | | | 2/3 of Excise tax on telecomunication and radioelectrical services less the IRS share. | | | | | |
| National Secretary of Sports SENADER | | | | | 1/3 of Excise tax on telecomunication and radioelectrical services less the IRS share | | | | | |
| Ecuadorian Customs Corporation | | | | | | 3% of the tariffs payment calculated over the CIF value | | | | |
| Society for Fight against Cancer | | | | | | | 50% of credit operations tax | | | |
| PREDESUR | | | | | | | 25% of credit operations tax | | | |
| Municipalities and Provincial Counsels | 15% of the central government budget (2) | | | | | | | | | |

(1) 55% distributed as: 7.5% Development Fund for the Province of Bolivar; 5% FONDORO; 12.5% Fund for Agricultural Workers in the Chimborazo Province; 15% Development Fund of Pichincha, 15% Development Fund of CarchiXX.

(2) Except for the income from internal and external credits of investment projects that benefit of municipalities and provincial counsels

Source: MEF.

## TABLE A18: INSTITUTIONS RECEIVING EARMARKED REVENUES

| Institution | 15% Law of General Budget of the State | Other Special Laws: Law 47, FODESEC, FONDEPRO, FIM-Bank of Development | Highway Administration Fund of Loja | Cultural Patrimony Rescue Fund-FONSAL Tax | Rental Tax Donations | 10% of the Taxes for Special Consumptions (ICE) on the tele-communication services and radio-electronics for water provision | Petroleum participation: Law 10, reformed with ECORAE law-Amazon Subnational governments and Law 120 Corpecuador | Budgetary assignments for investments-capital transfers | Interinstitutional Conventions for Project Investments |
|---|---|---|---|---|---|---|---|---|---|
| Sectional Organizations | | | | | | | | | |
| Municipality | x | x | x | x | x | x | x | x | |
| Provincial Counsel | x | x | x | x | | x | | x | |
| Regional Development Organizations | | | | | | | | | |
| Economic Retrofitting Center of Austro (CREA) | | | | | | | | | |
| Rehabilitation Center of Manabi | | x | | | | | | x | |
| Commission of Development Studies Cuenca Rio Guayas (CEDEGE) | | | | | | | | x | |
| Subcom. Ecua. Des. Of Cuencas of Los Rios Puyango-Tumbez (PREDESUR) | | x | | | | | | x | |
| Regional Corporation of the Sierra Centro (CORSICEN) | | | | | | | | x | |

(continued)

## TABLE A18: INSTITUTIONS RECEIVING EARMARKED REVENUES (CONTINUED)

| Institution | 15% Law of General Budget of the State | Other Special Laws: Law 47, FODESEC, FONDEPRO, FIM-Bank of Development | Highway Administration Fund of Loja | Cultural Patrimony Rescue Fund-FONSAL Tax | Rental Tax Donations | 10% of the Taxes for Special Consumptions (ICE) on the tele-communication services and radio-electronics for water provision | Petroleum participation: Law 10, reformed with ECORAE law-Amazon Subnational governments and Law 120 Corpecuador | Budgetary assignments for investments-capital transfers | Interinstitutional Conventions for Project Investments |
|---|---|---|---|---|---|---|---|---|---|
| Regional Corporation of the Sierra Norte (CORSINOR) | | | | | | | | | |
| Regional Development Corporation of El Oro (CODELORO) | | | | | | | | x | |
| Regional Development Corporation of Chimborazo (CODERECH) | | | | | | | | x | |
| Regional Development Corporation of Cotopaxi (CODERECO) | | | | | | | | x | |
| Galapagos National Institute (INGALA) | | x | | | | | | x | |
| Corporation of Afroecuadorian Development (CODAE) | | | | | | | | x | |
| North Development Unit (UDENOR) | | | | | | | | x | |
| Development Counsel of Ecuadorian Nationalities and Towns (CODENPE) | | | | | | | | x | |

CREATING FISCAL SPACE FOR POVERTY REDUCTION IN ECUADOR    175

## TABLE A18: INSTITUTIONS RECEIVING EARMARKED REVENUES (CONTINUED)

| Institution | 15% Law of General Budget of the State | Other Special Laws: Law 47, FODESEC, FONDEPRO, FIM-Bank of Development | Highway Administration Fund of Loja | Cultural Patrimony Rescue Fund-FONSAL Tax | Rental Tax Donations | 10% of the Taxes for Special Consumptions (ICE) on the tele-communication services and radio-electronics for water provision | Petroleum participation: Law 10, reformed with ECORAE law-Amazon Subnational governments and Law 120 Corpecuador | Budgetary assignments for investments-capital transfers | Interinstitutional Conventions for Project Investments |
|---|---|---|---|---|---|---|---|---|---|
| Development Counsel of the Pueblo Montubio and Subtropical Zones of the Region Litoral (CODEPMOC) | | | | | | | | x | |
| Free Standing Entities | | | | | | | | x | |
| Corpecuador | | | | | x | x | | x | |
| Executive Corporation for the Reconstruction of the Zones Affected by the El Niño Phenomenon (COPEFEN) | | | | | | | | | |
| Eco-Development Institute for the Amazon Region (ECORAE) | | | | | | | x | x | |
| Galapagos National Park | | x | | | | | | x | |
| Hydraulics Promotion Resources Board and Development of the Contones Jipijapa and Pajan and Puerto Lopez | x | | | | | | | | |

*Source:* MEF.

## TABLE A19: SOCIAL EXPENDITURES AS PERCENT OF CENTRAL GOVERNMENT BUDGET

| Transfers to the Social Sector | 1994 | 1995 | 1996 | 1997 | 1998 | 1999 | 2000 | 2001 |
|---|---|---|---|---|---|---|---|---|
| *Mlns US$* | | | | | | | | |
| Education | 464.5 | 562.1 | 624.2 | 563.3 | 638.0 | 368.2 | 310.7 | 492.8 |
| Social Welfare | 83.5 | 70.4 | 118.8 | 70.9 | 59.4 | 69.4 | 76.2 | 126.8 |
| Work | 4.6 | 7.0 | 10.3 | 9.8 | 9.0 | 5.4 | 6.3 | 5.6 |
| Health | 127.3 | 194.8 | 204.3 | 191.4 | 186.0 | 110.1 | 121.2 | 188.6 |
| Urban Development | 99.0 | 67.3 | 47.7 | 50.8 | 54.0 | 11.5 | 31.7 | 134.9 |
| **Total Social Budget** | 779.0 | 901.6 | 1005.4 | 886.3 | 946.5 | 564.5 | 546.2 | 948.7 |
| | | | | | | | | |
| *Percent of CG Budget* | | | | | | | | |
| Education | 19% | 17% | 18% | 16% | 19% | 15% | 11% | 12% |
| Social Welfare | 3% | 2% | 3% | 2% | 2% | 3% | 3% | 3% |
| Work | 0% | 0% | 0% | 0% | 0% | 0% | 0% | 0% |
| Health | 5% | 6% | 6% | 5% | 5% | 4% | 4% | 4% |
| Urban Development | 4% | 2% | 1% | 1% | 2% | 0% | 1% | 3% |
| **Total Social Budget** | 31% | 27% | 29% | 25% | 28% | 22% | 19% | 23% |
| | | | | | | | | |
| *Notes:* | | | | | | | | |
| Public Debt Interest / Social Budget | 53% | 90% | 61% | 89% | 78% | 120% | 158% | 193% |
| Total Central Government Budget | 2487.2 | 3311.3 | 3408.6 | 3595.3 | 3400.2 | 2532.9 | 2831.7 | 4196.5 |

*Source:* MEF.

## TABLE A20: PERSONNEL EXPENDITURES IN EDUCATION
### (in US$)

|  | 1995 | 1996 | 1997 | 1998 | 1999 | 2000 |
|---|---|---|---|---|---|---|
| Ministry of Education and Culture | 204,160,433 | 422,769,422 | 350,793,654 | 454,234,986 | 308,753,551 | 245,079,025 |
| National Inst. of Cultural Patrimony | 584,828 | 426,704 | 382,182 | 399,948 | 240,455 | 206,772 |
| Ecuad. Museum Natural C. | 76,066 | 87,020 | 65,206 | 55,971 | 29,722 | 24,769 |
| National Unit of Dance | 54,931 | 66,205 | 58,310 | 50,872 | 27,912 | 25,928 |
| National System of Archives and National Archive | 53,197 | 60,663 | 54,356 | 56,433 | 38,230 | 22,579 |
| National System of Libraries | 6,434 | 11,419 | 10,185 | 10,255 | 4,763 | 2,216 |
| National Council of Culture | 117,490 | 99,004 | 108,032 | 87,105 | 48,580 | 37,872 |
| SENACYT |  | 39,679 | 32,364 | 256,860 | 10,847 |  |
| National Council of Sports | 46,189 | 73,219 | 83,876 | 73,858 | 51,654 | 38,900 |
| DINACE | 1,055,843 | 1,160,315 | 1,040,912 | 1,081,383 | 320,680 | 549,625 |
| DINADER | 440,283 | 352,657 | 419,547 | 451,652 | 290,598 | 3,215 |
| **TOTAL** | **206,597,690** | **425,148,303** | **353,050,621** | **456,761,321** | **309,818,992** | **245,992,900** |
| TOTAL EDUCATION SECTOR | 560,208,644 | 608,816,064 | 525,640,347 | 623,952,767 | 370,794,090 | 283,509,503 |
| New series total (UNICEF) | **523,584,971** | **604,390,865** | **550,140,576** | **596,302,775** | **400,819,048** | **329,276,625** |
| New series MINEF | **562** | **624** | **563** | **638** | **368** | **311** |
| **% TOTAL EDUCATION EXPENDITURE** | 36.9% | 69.8% | 67.2% | 73.2% | 83.6% | 86.8% |
| % of UNICEF total | 39.5% | 70.3% | 64.2% | 76.6% | 77.3% | 74.7% |
| % of MINEF total | 36.8% | 68.1% | 62.7% | 71.6% | 84.1% | 79.2% |

Source: Ministerio de Economía y Finanzas, 1995–2000

## TABLE A21: EXPENDITURES IN EDUCATION BY LEVEL (IN MLN US$)

| | 1995 | 1996 | 1997 | 1998 | 1999 | 2000 | 2001 | 2002 |
|---|---|---|---|---|---|---|---|---|
| Basic Hispanic Education | 193.9 | 212.7 | 191.7 | 225.9 | 145.7 | 117.7 | 155.0 | 284.5 |
| Bilingual Basic Education | 7.9 | 9.8 | 9.5 | 11.8 | 7.7 | 6.8 | 9.3 | 16.0 |
| Intermediate Education | 194.0 | 249.6 | 203.9 | 227.7 | 154.1 | 118.6 | 159.3 | 304.1 |
| Advanced Education | 127.8 | 132.3 | 145.1 | 130.9 | 17.7 | 11.2 | nd | nd |
| TOTAL | 523.6 | 604.4 | 550.1 | 596.3 | 325.1 | 254.3 | 323.6 | 604.6 |
| *Share* | | | | | | | | |
| Basic Hispanic Education | #DIV/0! | #DIV/0! | #DIV/0! | #DIV/0! | #DIV/0! | #DIV/0! | #DIV/0! | #DIV/0! |
| Bilingual Basic Education | #DIV/0! | #DIV/0! | #DIV/0! | #DIV/0! | #DIV/0! | #DIV/0! | #DIV/0! | #DIV/0! |
| Intermediate Education | #DIV/0! | #DIV/0! | #DIV/0! | #DIV/0! | #DIV/0! | #DIV/0! | #DIV/0! | #DIV/0! |
| Advanced Education | t#DIV/0! | #DIV/0! | #DIV/0! | #DIV/0! | #DIV/0! | #DIV/0! | | |
| TOTAL | #DIV/0! | #DIV/0! | #DIV/0! | #DIV/0! | #DIV/0! | #DIV/0! | #DIV/0! | #DIV/0! |

*Source:* Ministerio de Economía y Finanzas, 1995–2002

## TABLE A22: BUDGET ISSUED FOR EDUCATION (US $)

| | 1999 |
|---|---|
| Personel Expenses | 309,816,993 |
| Services | 5,092,129 |
| Subministries and Materials | 7,978,724 |
| Furniture | 247,366 |
| Public Works | 22,532,916 |
| Transfers | 25,125,959 |
| **TOTAL** | 370,794,088 |
| Salaries (%) | 84% |

## TABLE A23: FINANCING SOURCES FOR EDUCATION, 2003
(in US$)

| Sector | Financing Source | | | | Distribution by Financing Source | | | |
|---|---|---|---|---|---|---|---|---|
| | Fiscal | Own Resources | External Credit | Domestic Credit | TOTAL | Fiscal | Own Resources | External Credit | Domestic Credit |
| Ministry of Education and Culture | 760.2 | 23.7 | 15.3 | 31.3 | 830.5 | 91.5 | 2.9 | 1.8 | 3.8 |
| National Inst. of Cultural Patrimony | 1.2 | 1.2 | 0.0 | 0.0 | 2.3 | 49.8 | 50.2 | 0.0 | 0.0 |
| Ecuad. Museum Natural C. | 0.2 | 0.0 | 0.0 | 0.0 | 0.2 | 93.8 | 6.3 | 0.0 | 0.0 |
| National Unit of Dance | 0.1 | 0.0 | 0.0 | 0.0 | 0.1 | 97.2 | 2.8 | 0.0 | 0.0 |
| National System of Archives and National Archive | 0.3 | 0.0 | 0.0 | 0.0 | 0.3 | 96.3 | 3.7 | 0.0 | 0.0 |
| National System of Libraries | 0.1 | 0.0 | 0.0 | 0.0 | 0.1 | 81.8 | 18.2 | 0.0 | 0.0 |
| National Council of Culture | 0.2 | 0.5 | 0.0 | 0.0 | 0.6 | 23.4 | 76.6 | 0.0 | 0.0 |
| SENACYT | 0.0 | 0.2 | 0.0 | 0.2 | 0.4 | 0.0 | 53.5 | 0.0 | 46.5 |
| **TOTAL** | **762.1** | **25.7** | **15.3** | **31.5** | **834.5** | **91.3** | **3.1** | **1.8** | **3.8** |

Source: MEF.

## TABLE A24: SUPPLY OF PUBLIC AND PRIVATE HEALTH CENTERS, 1975–2000

| | Public | Total Private | Total | In-patient care Public | Private | Sub-total | Only out-patient Public | Private | Sub-total |
|---|---|---|---|---|---|---|---|---|---|
| **Establishments per 100,000 inhabitants** | | | | | | | | | |
| 1975 | | | 17.1 | | | 3.2 | | | 13.9 |
| 1980 | 19.5 | 2.7 | 22.2 | 1.8 | 1.6 | 3.4 | 17.7 | 1.1 | 18.8 |
| 1990 | 24.7 | 3.5 | 28.2 | 1.6 | 2.3 | 3.9 | 23 | 1.2 | 24.2 |
| 2000 | 24.6 | 4.5 | 29.1 | 1.4 | 3.3 | 4.7 | 23.2 | 1.2 | 24.4 |
| **Number of establishments** | | | | | | | | | |
| 1975 | | | 1,182 | | | 224 | | | 958 |
| 1980 | 1,550 | 216 | 1,766 | 144 | 128 | 272 | 1,406 | 88 | 1,494 |
| 1990 | 2,533 | 359 | 2,892 | 169 | 235 | 404 | 2,364 | 124 | 2,488 |
| 2000 | 3,027 | 555 | 3,582 | 178 | 405 | 583 | 2,849 | 150 | 2,999 |

Source: INEC, *Anuario de recursos y actividades de salud*, various years.

# TABLE A25: PREASSIGNED SPENDING IN THE 2004 CENTRAL GOVERNMENT PROFORMA
(in Thous US $)

| I. PREASSIGNED REVENUES—TAXES | Percent assigned | Percent of total revenues | US$ |
|---|---|---|---|
| Income | 100.0% | 12.4% | 892,107,109 |
| Donations | | 0.7% | 53,615,010 |
| Net Income | | 11.7% | 838,492,099 |
| SRI | 1.5% | 0.2% | 12,577,381 |
| State Universities | 10.0% | 1.2% | 83,849,210 |
| Universities | 1.0% | 0.1% | 8,384,921 |
| FODESEC | 10.0% | 1.2% | 83,849,210 |
| FONSAL | 5.9% | 0.5% | 34,881,580 |
| CRM | 0.1% | 0.0% | 857,016 |
| Transit Commission Guayas | 0.0% | 0.2% | 14,570,930 |
| Central Government | 71.5% | 8.3% | 599,521,851 |
| Value Added Tax | 100.0% | 30.3% | 2,179,015,795 |
| VAT Refund | | 1.6% | 116,721,684 |
| Net Value Added Tax | | 28.7% | 2,062,294,111 |
| SRI | 1.5% | 0.5% | 32,685,237 |
| FOPEDEUPO | 10.0% | 3.0% | 217901579.5 |
| Agriculture Universities | 0.5% | 0.2% | 10895078.98 |
| Central Government | 88% | 25.0% | 1,800,812,216 |

| II. PREASSIGNED REVENUES—PETROLEUM | Percent of petrol revenues | Percent of total revenues | US$ |
|---|---|---|---|
| Highway Administration Law of Agropecuaria | 0.0% | 0.0% | 145,833 |
| 70% MOP | | 0.0% | 102,083 |
| 25% MIDUVI | | 0.0% | 36,458 |
| 5% MIN AMBIENT | | 0.0% | 7,292 |
| Armed Forces | 0.3% | 0.2% | 11,097,541 |
| ISSFA (Law 169) | | 0.0% | 286,652 |
| DEFENSE GROUP | | 0.2% | 10,810,889 |
| Universities | 0.0% | 0.0% | 999,815 |
| State | | 0.0% | 908,872 |
| Particular | | 0.0% | 90,943 |
| FERUM | 0.0% | 0.0% | 109,771 |
| Subnational Organizations | 2.8% | 1.3% | 90,682,426 |
| Provincial Counsels (Law 72) | | 0.0% | 2,277,196 |
| Esmeralda Development (Doc.1137 and Doc.1678) | | 0.0% | 7,012 |
| Amazonic Eco-Development Fund (Law 10, Law 20) | | 1.2% | 86,222,961 |
| Municipios Esmeraldas, Napo, Sucumbios Participación Law 40 | | 0.0% | 2,136,571 |
| Napo, Sucumbios, Pastaza, M. Santiago, Z. Chinchipe y Orellana Participación Municipalities Law 122 | | 0.0% | 28,758 |
| ExConsortium Exports (FODESEC) | | 0.0% | 9,929 |

(continued)

# TABLE A25: PREASSIGNED SPENDING IN THE 2004 CENTRAL GOVERNMENT PROFORMA (CONTINUED)
(in Thous US $)

| | | | | | | | |
|---|---|---|---|---|---|---|---|
| **Tariffs on Imports** | 100% | 6.7% | **480,522,899** | **Others** | | 2.3% | **73,378,270** |
| Group of Hydraulic Resources | 3% | 0.2% | 14,415,687 | State Bank | | 0.0% | 23,052 |
| Customs | 3 % | 0.2% | 14,415,687 | BEV | | 0.0% | 2,363 |
| Port Authority of Manta | 1% | 0.0% | 325,902 | Banco Central | | 0.0% | 17 |
| FODESEC (Fixed annual quota) | 0% | 0.0% | 273,600 | Banco de Fomento | | 0.2% | 12,054,511 |
| FODESEC Fixed quota | 0% | 0.0% | 14,000 | IECE | | 0.0% | 93 |
| Central Government | 94% | 6.3% | 451,078,023 | INNFA | | 0.0% | 590 |
| **Special Consumption (ICE)** | 100% | 4.3% | **311,536,543** | CORPEI | | 0.0% | 399,378 |
| Telecommunications | | 1.5% | 106,842,301 | CORPECUADOR | | 0.2% | 12,054,511 |
| Hospital Equipment 10% total | 10% | 0.3% | 20,306,720 | TARIFA OCP | | 0.7% | 48,843,754 |
| Free Maternity Care 3% ICE Group 1 | 3.0% | 0.1% | 4,816,369 | **FEIREP** | 9.2% | 4.1% | **292,135,933** |
| Fund. Oswaldo Loor 2% ICE Pr. Alcoh | 2.0% | 0.0% | 459,339 | 70% Financial Investments | | 2.8% | 204,495,153 |
| SRI | 1.5% | 0.1% | 4,673,048 | 20% Petroleum Investments Establishings | | 0.8% | 58,427,187 |
| Promoting Athletics | | 1.0% | 71,263,815 | 10% Human Development Programs | | 0.4% | 29,213,593 |
| Potable Water Enterprises | | 0.5% | 35,578,486 | | | | |
| Central Government | | 2.4% | 174,438,765 | **TOTAL PETROLEUM REVENUES** | 100.0% | 44.3% | **3,188,002,741** |
| **Credit Operations** | 100.0% | 0.6% | **42,893,490** | PETROECUADOR 2/ | 45.9% | 20.3% | 1,461,734,907 |
| SOLCA 50% | 50.0% | 0.3% | 21,446,745 | **CENTRAL GOVERNMENT** | 39.5% | 17.5% | 1,257,718,244 |
| PREDESUR | 25.0% | 0.1% | 5,361,686 | **PREASSIGNED** | 14.7% | 6.5% | 468,549,590 |
| FONDORO | 5.0% | 0.0% | 1,072,337 | % of Petroleum revenues | | 14.7% | |
| Provincial Fund Chimborazo | 12.5% | 0.0% | 2,680,843 | | | | |

## TABLE A25: PREASSIGNED SPENDING IN THE 2004 CENTRAL GOVERNMENT PROFORMA (CONTINUED)
(in Thous US $)

| Item | % | | Amount | % |
|---|---|---|---|---|
| Provincial Fund Bolívar | 7.5% | | 1,608,506 | 0.0% |
| CRM | 12.5% | | 2,680,843 | 0.0% |
| Provincial Fund Pichincha | 15.0% | | 3,217,012 | 0.0% |
| Provincial Fund Carchi | 15.0% | | 3,217,012 | 0.0% |
| CEDEM | 0.1% | | 27,881 | 0.0% |
| Central Government | 7.5% | | 1,580,625 | 0.0% |
| Vehicle Registration | 100.0% | | 57,424,383 | 0.8% |
| SRI | 1.5% | | 861,366 | 0.0% |
| Central Government | 98.5% | | 56,563,017 | 0.8% |
| Modernización y Ampliación Ferrocarriles | 20.0% | | | 0.0% |
| Ley Gratuidad combatientes Cenepa | 30.0% | | | 0.0% |
| Impuesto a la propiedad de Unidades de Transporte Suntuario | | | | 0.0% |
| SRI | 0 | | | 0.0% |
| Gobierno Central | 1 | | | 0.0% |
| Other Taxes | | | 80,244,636 | 1.1% |
| SRI (only of tax fines) | 1.5% | | 491,467 | 0.0% |
| Customs | | | 225,090 | 0.0% |
| Central Government | 98.5% | | 79,528,079 | 1.1% |
| Loja Highway Administration Fund | 0.1% | | 5,872,599 | 0.1% |
| Univ. of Guayaquil Hospital Fund | 0.0% | | 2,609,541 | 0.0% |

| III. PREASSIGNED EXPENDITURES | % | Amount |
|---|---|---|
| 15% SUBNATIONAL GOVERNMENTS | 9.2% | 664,402,495 |
| FODESEC | 0.1% | 5,922,000 |
| FONDEPRO | 0.1% | 5,922,000 |
| COTOPAXI CULTURE FUND | 0.0% | 325,060 |
| FINES ON PROTESTED CHECKS | 0.3% | 23,623,960 |
| POLICE FINES | 0.0% | 3,000 |
| 1% PUBLIC CONTRACTING | 0.0% | 1,958,000 |
| MINISTRY OF ECONOMICS | 0.0% | 457,790 |
| SENACYT (1% Public contracts) | 0.0% | 1,500,000 |
| MOP | 0.0% | 3,294,502 |
| MIDUVI | 0.1% | 6,034,279 |
| TOTAL PREASSIGNED EXPENDITURES | 9.9% | 713,443,086 |
| % of Total revenues | | 10% |

(continued)

## TABLE A25: PREASSIGNED SPENDING IN THE 2004 CENTRAL GOVERNMENT PROFORMA (CONTINUED)
### (in Thous US $)

| | | |
|---|---|---|
| Tax (Law 67 Income to P. Galápagos) | 0.1% | 8,487,855 |
| TRADITIONAL REVENUES 1/ | 54.9% | 3,949,016,108 |
| CENTRAL GOVERNMENT | 35.6% | 2,564,000,725 |
| PREASSIGNED | 10.1% | 726,855,579 |
| % Traditional revenues | | 18.4% |

| IV. SUMMARY | | |
|---|---|---|
| TOTAL REVENUES (inlcudes transfers) | 100% | 7,192,866,071 |
| Total Preassigned | 27% | 1,908,848,254 |
| Preassigned Revenues | 17% | 1,195,405,169 |
| Traditional | 10% | 726,855,579 |
| Petroleum | 7% | 468,549,590 |
| Preassigned Expenditures | 10% | 713,443,086 |

Source: Ministry of Finance
1/ Includes an additonal $658 mln.
2/ Petroecuador income doesn't include IVA

## TABLE A26: EXPENDITURES MANAGED BY THE REGIONAL DEVELOPMENT ORGANIZATIONS, 2003

| Institutions | Mlns US$ |
|---|---|
| **Central Government Entities** | **171.29** |
| Center for Economic Reconversion of Austro (CREA) | 3.95 |
| Rehabilitation Center of Manabi (CRM) | 38.47 |
| Development Commission Cuenca Rio Guayas (CEDEGE) | 39.36 |
| Subcom. Ecua.Des.Cuencas Puyango-Tumbez (PREDESUR) | 20.56 |
| Regional Corporation of the Sierra Centro (CORSICEN) | 3.81 |
| Regional Corporation of the Sierra Norte (CORSINOR) | 2.53 |
| Regional Development Corporation of El Oro (CODELORO) | 7.09 |
| Regional Development Corporation of Chimborazo (CODERECH) | 1.30 |
| Regional Development Corporation of Cotopaxi (CODERECO) | 2.36 |
| National Institute of Galapagos (INGALA) | 1.61 |
| Afroecuadorian Development Corporation | 1.93 |
| North Development Unit (UDENOR) | 39.11 |
| Ecuador National and Town Development Council | 8.71 |
| Pueblo Montubio and Subtropical Zones Development Council (CODEPMOC) | 0.50 |
| **Autonomous Entities** | **75.46** |
| Executive Corporation for the Reconstruction of El Niño Affected Zones | 47.24 |
| Eco-Development Institute of the Amazonic Region (ECORAE) | 6.09 |
| Galapagos National Park | 7.21 |
| Group of Hydraulic Resources Jipijapa, Pajan Puerto Lopez | 14.92 |
| **TOTAL** | **246.75** |

## TABLE A27: MILITARY EXPENDITURES

|  | 1998 | 1999 | 2000 | 2001 | 2002 |
|---|---|---|---|---|---|
| *Percent of Government Expenditures* | | | | | |
| **Ecuador** | **9.5** | **7.5** | **7.6** | **12.4** | |
| Bolivia | 6.0 | 6.2 | 5.3 | 4.8 | |
| Chile | 17.9 | 16.4 | 17.2 | 15.7 | |
| Colombia | 9.0 | 9.0 | 8.5 | 11.5 | |
| Peru | 8.8 | 8.4 | 8.0 | 8.3 | |
| LAC mean | 6.0 | 5.8 | 5.4 | 5.7 | |
| Developed economies | 6.1 | 6.0 | 6.1 | 6.3 | |
| Africa | 14.0 | 14.2 | 13.4 | 10.4 | |
| *Percent of GDP* | | | | | |
| **Ecuador** | **2.3** | **2.0** | **2.0** | **3.0** | **3.0** |
| Bolivia | 1.8 | 1.8 | 1.6 | 1.6 | 1.6 |
| Chile | 3.8 | 3.7 | 3.9 | 3.6 | 4.1 |
| Colombia | 2.5 | 2.7 | 2.6 | 3.7 | 3.7 |
| Peru | 1.7 | 1.8 | 1.7 | 1.7 | 1.6 |
| LAC mean | 1.5 | 1.6 | 1.5 | 1.6 | na |
| Developed economies | 2.3 | 2.2 | 2.2 | 2.4 | na |
| Africa | 3.5 | 3.5 | 3.5 | 2.8 | na |

*Source:* International Institute for Strategic Studies (IISS) Yearbook 1997–2003

# TABLE A28: SALARY TABLES OF THE NON-FINANCIAL PUBLIC SECTOR, 2002–2004

| SECTOR | 2002* | | | | 2003** | | | | 2004** | | | |
|---|---|---|---|---|---|---|---|---|---|---|---|---|
| | No. of Civil Servants | Salary Table | Annual Cost/person | Monthly Cost/person | No. of Civil Servants | Salary Table | Annual Cost/person | Monthly Cost/person | No. of Civil Servants | Salary Table | Annual Cost/person | Monthly Cost/person |
| 00 TESORO NACIONAL | 0 | 0 | 0 | 0 | 0 | 33,000,000 | 0 | 0 | | | | |
| 01 LEGISLATIVO | 1,669 | 23,969,803 | 14,362 | 1,197 | 1,669 | 24,582,766 | 14,729 | 1,227 | 1,683 | 27,453,593 | 16,312 | 1,359 |
| 02 JURISDICCIONAL | 4,633 | 84,798,376 | 18,303 | 1,525 | 4,631 | 119,466,138 | 25,797 | 2,150 | 4,914 | 133,113,877 | 27,089 | 2,257 |
| 03 ADMINISTRATIVO | 411 | 3,144,569 | 7,651 | 638 | 389 | 3,723,916 | 9,573 | 798 | 392 | 5,884,134 | 15,011 | 1,251 |
| 04 MEDIO AMBIENTE | 647 | 3,858,449 | 5,964 | 497 | 299 | 5,076,886 | 16,980 | 1,415 | 650 | 5,555,485 | 8,547 | 712 |
| 05 ASUNTOS INTERNOS | 33,379 | 196,383,065 | 5,883 | 490 | 40,590 | 272,116,860 | 6,704 | 559 | 43,857 | 293,484,815 | 6,692 | 558 |
| 06 DEFENSA NACIONAL | 56,517 | 339,510,580 | 6,007 | 501 | 56,581 | 397,705,959 | 7,029 | 586 | 66,517 | 421,781,001 | 6,341 | 528 |
| 07 ASUNTOS DEL EXTERIOR | 796 | 31,660,525 | 39,775 | 3,315 | 796 | 29,602,084 | 37,189 | 3,099 | 647 | 34,467,888 | 53,273 | 4,439 |
| 08 FINANZAS | 893 | 12,754,746 | 14,283 | 1,190 | 1,005 | 16,822,193 | 16,739 | 1,395 | 983 | 16,487,051 | 16,772 | 1,398 |
| 09 EDUCACION | 130,994 | 606,527,649 | 4,630 | 386 | 131,001 | 623,219,146 | 4,757 | 396 | 131,033 | 732,612,169 | 5,591 | 466 |
| 10 BIENESTAR SOCIAL | 1,604 | 12,308,855 | 7,674 | 639 | 1,606 | 17,876,389 | 11,131 | 928 | 1,074 | 14,429,102 | 13,435 | 1,120 |
| 11 TRABAJO | 837 | 5,148,547 | 6,151 | 513 | 426 | 4,693,651 | 11,018 | 918 | 682 | 5,593,569 | 8,202 | 683 |
| 12 SALUD | 33,686 | 183,351,473 | 5,443 | 454 | 35,112 | 226,954,284 | 6,464 | 539 | 35,111 | 217,345,799 | 6,190 | 516 |
| 13 AGROPECUARIO | 4,338 | 22,761,244 | 5,247 | 437 | 3,836 | 22,149,260 | 5,774 | 481 | 3,792 | 26,279,218 | 6,930 | 578 |
| 14 RECURSOS NATURALES | 710 | 7,142,005 | 10,059 | 838 | 489 | 5,188,162 | 10,610 | 884 | 489 | 7,835,179 | 16,023 | 1,335 |
| 15 INDUSTRIAS Y COMERCIO | 521 | 3,901,819 | 7,489 | 624 | 324 | 3,707,210 | 11,442 | 954 | 419 | 4,082,838 | 9,744 | 812 |
| 16 TURISMO | 162 | 1,102,127 | 6,803 | 567 | 161 | 1,252,866 | 7,782 | 648 | 161 | 1,300,688 | 8,079 | 673 |
| 17 COMUNICACIONES | 6,022 | 41,477,265 | 6,888 | 574 | 5,968 | 44,607,379 | 7,474 | 623 | 5,810 | 50,509,809 | 8,694 | 724 |
| 18 DESARROLLO URBANO Y VIVIENDA | 820 | 7,060,423 | 8,610 | 718 | 819 | 7,314,609 | 8,931 | 744 | 817 | 7,326,199 | 8,967 | 747 |
| 19 OTROS ORGANISMOS DEL ESTADO | 662 | 13,007,387 | 19,649 | 1,637 | 676 | 11,723,350 | 17,342 | 1,445 | 697 | 21,963,364 | 31,511 | 2,626 |
| **GOBIERNO CENTRAL** | **279,301** | **1,599,868,906** | **5,728** | **477** | **286,378** | **1,870,783,108** | **6,533** | **544** | **299,728** | **2,027,505,779** | **6,764** | **564** |
| ENTIDADES AUTONOMAS | 8,149 | 137,176,677 | 16,834 | 1,403 | 7,870 | 195,499,174 | 24,841 | 2,070 | | | | |
| SEGURIDAD SOCIAL | 15,068 | 33,690,513 | 2,236 | 186 | 15,068 | 30,444,099 | 2,020 | 168 | | | | |
| PETROECUADOR | 3,981 | 98,600,000 | 24,768 | 2,064 | 3,984 | 113,500,000 | 28,489 | 2,374 | | | | |
| PORTUARIAS | 235 | 6,884,107 | 29,294 | 2,441 | 235 | 11,072,114 | 47,115 | 3,926 | | | | |
| UNIVERSIDADES | 24,320 | 122,270,864 | 5,028 | 419 | 24,320 | 128,313,579 | 5,276 | 440 | | | | |
| BEDE | 0 | | | | 833 | 5,000,000 | 0 | 0 | | | | |
| GOBIERNOS SECCIONALES | 0 | 0 | 0 | 0 | 25,000 | 151,000,000 | 6,040 | 503 | | | | |
| **TOTAL SECTOR PUBLICO NO FINANCIERO** | **331,054** | **1,998,491,068** | **6,037** | **503** | **363,688** | **2,505,612,075** | **6,889** | **574** | | | | |

(*) Corresponde presupuesto codificado
(**) Corresponde presupuesto inicial

Source: MEF.

## TABLE A29: DIRECT SUBSIDIES TO WATER AND SANITATION SECTOR

| | 2001 | 2002 | 2003 |
|---|---|---|---|
| **Subsidies from Central Government** | | | |
| A. MIDUVI | 64,000 | 17,743 | 22,490 |
| B. I.C.E. | 50,000 | 46,000 | 45,000 |
| | | | |
| Sub-total subsidies from Central Government: | 114,000 | 63,743 | 67,490 |
| | | | |
| Subsidies from Municipalities | 32,000 | N.A. | N.A. |
| TOTAL c/ | 146,000 | 63,743 | 67,490 |

*Source:* MIDUVI - SAPYSB, Estado de Ejecuccion presupuestaria, 2002 y 2003, and Ecuador Infrastructure Policy Notes, World Bank 2003

## TABLE A.30: ILLITERACY RATE AND YEARS OF SCHOOLING OF ADULT POPULATION (25 YRS AND OLDER), 1990–2001

| | ILLITERACY RATE | | YEARS OF SCHOOLING | |
| | 1990 | 2001 | 1990 | 2001 |
|---|---|---|---|---|
| **BY PROVINCE** | | | | |
| Azuay | 13.8 | 8.8 | 5.9 | 6.9 |
| Bol'var | 22.1 | 17.5 | 4.4 | 5.4 |
| Cañar | 20.8 | 15.4 | 4.4 | 5.3 |
| Carchi | 10.1 | 7.2 | 5.4 | 6.3 |
| Chimborazo | 27.0 | 19.0 | 4.6 | 5.8 |
| Cotopaxi | 23.7 | 17.6 | 4.4 | 5.4 |
| El Oro | 5.9 | 5.5 | 7.1 | 7.5 |
| Esmeraldas | 14.5 | 11.6 | 5.7 | 6.2 |
| Galápagos | 2.9 | 2.7 | 9.2 | 9.5 |
| Guayas | 7.4 | 7.1 | 7.7 | 7.8 |
| Imbabura | 18.4 | 13.4 | 5.3 | 6.2 |
| Loja | 10.7 | 7.9 | 5.9 | 6.9 |
| Los R'os | 15.8 | 11.7 | 5.3 | 6.1 |
| Manab' | 15.5 | 12.5 | 5.3 | 6.1 |
| Morona Santiago | 12.3 | 10.0 | 5.3 | 5.8 |
| Napo | 15.7 | 10.5 | 5.3 | 6.4 |
| Orellana | 13.5 | 9.2 | 4.9 | 5.9 |
| Pastaza | 14.3 | 10.1 | 6.1 | 7.1 |
| Pichincha | 7.3 | 5.5 | 8.5 | 8.9 |
| Sucumb'os | 10.9 | 8.5 | 5.2 | 6.0 |
| Tungurahua | 14.0 | 10.0 | 5.9 | 6.8 |
| Zamora Chinchipe | 9.9 | 8.2 | 5.5 | 6.2 |
| Non-delimited areas | 15.8 | 12.4 | 4.5 | 5.1 |
| **BY GENDER** | | | | |
| Men | 9.5 | 7.7 | 7.1 | 7.5 |
| Women | 13.8 | 10.3 | 6.3 | 7.1 |
| **BY AREA** | | | | |
| Rural | 20.8 | 15.5 | 4.0 | 4.9 |
| Urban | 6.1 | 5.3 | 8.3 | 8.7 |
| **BY ETHNIC GROUP** | | | | |
| Indigenous | n.a. | 28.2 | n.a. | 3.3 |
| Blacks | n.a. | 11.6 | n.a. | 5.9 |
| Other | n.a. | 7.4 | n.a. | 7.6 |
| **NATIONAL AVERAGE** | **11.7** | **9.0** | **6.7** | **7.3** |

Source: Population Census, 1990 and 2001.

## TABLE A.31: ECUADOR: POPULATION (25 YEARS AND OLDER) BY COMPLETED EDUCATION LEVEL (PERCENT OF TOTAL)

| | COMPLETED PRIMARY | | COMPLETED SECUNDARY | | COMPLETED TERTIARY | |
|---|---|---|---|---|---|---|
| | 1990 | 2001 | 1990 | 2001 | 1990 | 2001 |
| **BY PROVINCE** | | | | | | |
| Azuay | 62.6 | 61.4 | 21.5 | 21.3 | 11.5 | 16.5 |
| Bolívar | 51.8 | 47.9 | 13.2 | 13.5 | 6.4 | 10.9 |
| Cañar | 54.5 | 49.1 | 12.5 | 12.0 | 5.6 | 8.9 |
| Carchi | 60.4 | 57.8 | 15.4 | 13.9 | 7.3 | 11.0 |
| Chimborazo | 53.6 | 52.9 | 16.9 | 18.6 | 9.4 | 14.6 |
| Cotopaxi | 54.0 | 50.7 | 14.4 | 13.3 | 6.8 | 10.1 |
| El Oro | 74.3 | 71.2 | 23.1 | 20.6 | 12.3 | 16.2 |
| Esmeraldas | 53.6 | 56.1 | 17.3 | 18.3 | 11.1 | 14.7 |
| Galápagos | 86.4 | 85.6 | 35.4 | 34.0 | 20.9 | 29.5 |
| Guayas | 73.9 | 71.5 | 27.0 | 24.8 | 16.8 | 19.6 |
| Imbabura | 58.2 | 55.3 | 18.3 | 18.0 | 9.8 | 14.9 |
| Loja | 64.8 | 63.1 | 18.5 | 20.8 | 11.7 | 17.2 |
| Los Ríos | 56.6 | 57.1 | 14.3 | 14.8 | 9.0 | 11.4 |
| Manabí | 54.1 | 54.0 | 16.6 | 17.1 | 10.0 | 13.4 |
| Morona Santiago | 63.1 | 54.6 | 14.1 | 12.1 | 5.7 | 10.4 |
| Napo | 62.3 | 65.0 | 15.0 | 15.6 | 6.7 | 12.6 |
| Orellana | 58.1 | 58.9 | 10.8 | 10.7 | 4.3 | 8.7 |
| Pastaza | 67.2 | 65.7 | 23.2 | 19.1 | 10.1 | 16.4 |
| Pichincha | 78.7 | 77.9 | 36.2 | 32.6 | 22.6 | 26.9 |
| Sucumbíos | 59.0 | 58.8 | 11.6 | 12.6 | 5.6 | 9.9 |
| Tungurahua | 66.0 | 61.6 | 19.8 | 19.1 | 11.3 | 15.7 |
| Zamora Chinchipe | 66.2 | 62.1 | 13.4 | 13.8 | 7.1 | 11.7 |
| Non-delimited areas | 51.0 | 48.1 | 9.6 | 9.0 | 4.4 | 6.2 |
| **BY GENDER** | | | | | | |
| Men | 69.0 | 66.6 | 24.4 | 22.7 | 15.9 | 18.7 |
| Women | 64.8 | 64.8 | 22.9 | 22.5 | 12.5 | 17.5 |
| **BY AREA** | | | | | | |
| Rural | 48.8 | 45.4 | 8.3 | 8.7 | 4 | 6.3 |
| Urban | 78.3 | 77.7 | 33.0 | 30.5 | 20.4 | 24.8 |
| **BY ETHNIC GROUP** | | | | | | |
| Indigenous | n.a. | 31.5 | n.a. | 4.7 | n.a. | 3.4 |
| Blacks | n.a. | 55.6 | n.a. | 13.4 | n.a. | 10.6 |
| Other | n.a. | 69.0 | n.a. | 24.7 | n.a. | 20.2 |
| **NATIONAL AVERAGE** | **66.8** | **66.8** | **23.6** | **22.6** | **14.2** | **18.1** |

Source: Population Census, 1990 and 2001.

## TABLE A.32: ECUADOR: NET ENROLMENT RATES BY EDUCATIONAL LEVEL, 1990 AND 2001

| | NET ENROLMENT RATES | | | | | |
| | PRIMARY | | SECONDARY | | TERTIARY | |
| | 1990 | 2001 | 1990 | 2001 | 1990 | 2001 |
|---|---|---|---|---|---|---|
| **BY PROVINCE** | | | | | | |
| Pichincha | 92.3 | 93.0 | 58.3 | 55.3 | 17.6 | 18.3 |
| Azuay | 90.9 | 92.7 | 37.3 | 43.3 | 11.8 | 16.5 |
| Loja | 89.7 | 92.4 | 36.3 | 42.3 | 11.8 | 15.2 |
| Chimborazo | 88.3 | 90.4 | 36.6 | 41.5 | 11.0 | 14.9 |
| Tungurahua | 92.6 | 93.6 | 43.4 | 45.2 | 11.0 | 13.4 |
| Guayas | 90.9 | 90.2 | 49.7 | 47.3 | 12.0 | 11.3 |
| Imbabura | 89.7 | 90.8 | 40.9 | 39.8 | 12.0 | 10.6 |
| El Oro | 91.6 | 92.9 | 47.8 | 50.8 | 8.5 | 9.3 |
| Cotopaxi | 88.7 | 88.9 | 34.1 | 36.5 | 7.4 | 9.0 |
| Manabí | 82.8 | 86.5 | 32.0 | 36.8 | 6.8 | 8.9 |
| Cañar | 89.0 | 91.1 | 30.7 | 34.9 | 6.3 | 7.8 |
| Bolívar | 84.2 | 89.1 | 31.2 | 39.4 | 5.0 | 7.7 |
| Pastaza | 87.0 | 90.6 | 42.1 | 46.2 | 3.1 | 7.3 |
| Carchi | 90.9 | 91.6 | 38.2 | 44.9 | 6.4 | 6.4 |
| Galápagos | 94.4 | 95.0 | 48.9 | 61.1 | 2.5 | 5.6 |
| Los Ríos | 85.0 | 85.8 | 34.6 | 36.2 | 6.0 | 5.4 |
| Zamora Chinchipe | 86.9 | 90.7 | 26.3 | 39.1 | 2.9 | 5.3 |
| Napo | 87.8 | 91.9 | 35.4 | 27.0 | 1.8 | 4.5 |
| Esmeraldas | 81.0 | 83.0 | 32.6 | 35.8 | 4.3 | 4.5 |
| Morona Santiago | 88.3 | 88.1 | 32.7 | 30.9 | 1.5 | 2.5 |
| Sucumbíos | 84.5 | 86.6 | 21.8 | 35.3 | 0.5 | 2.4 |
| Non-delimited areas | 79.7 | 81.0 | 24.2 | 40.3 | 1.3 | 2.2 |
| Orellana | 85.6 | 87.3 | 17.9 | 31.5 | 0.4 | 1.5 |
| **BY GENDER** | | | | | | |
| Men | 88.6 | 89.9 | 42.0 | 43.9 | 10.3 | 11.1 |
| Women | 89.2 | 90.4 | 44.1 | 45.4 | 11.3 | 12.6 |
| **BY AREA** | | | | | | |
| Rural | 84.4 | 86.7 | 23.2 | 28.8 | 3.2 | 4.3 |
| Urban | 92.5 | 92.7 | 57.7 | 55.7 | 15.4 | 16.2 |
| **BY ETHNIC GROUP** | | | | | | |
| Indigenous | n.a. | 86.2 | n.a. | 22.6 | n.a. | 2.4 |
| Blacks | n.a. | 84.4 | n.a. | 32.3 | n.a. | 4.5 |
| Other | n.a. | 89.8 | n.a. | 43.2 | n.a. | 10.9 |
| **NATIONAL AVERAGE** | **88.9** | **90.1** | **43.1** | **44.6** | **10.9** | **11.9** |

Source: Population Census, 1990 and 2001.

**TABLE A.33: ECUADOR: YEARS OF SCHOOLING BY CONSUMPTION QUINTILES AND GENDER, 1995 AND 1999**

| Quintiles | Sex | 1995 | 1999 |
|---|---|---|---|
| Poorest 20 percent | Females | 3.5 | 3.2 |
| | Males | 4.1 | 4.1 |
| | Total | 3.8 | 3.7 |
| Second Quintile | Females | 4.7 | 5.0 |
| | Males | 5.6 | 5.6 |
| | Total | 5.1 | 5.3 |
| Third Quintile | Females | 6.3 | 6.7 |
| | Males | 6.5 | 7.0 |
| | Total | 6.4 | 6.8 |
| Fourth Quintile | Females | 7.9 | 8.2 |
| | Males | 8.0 | 8.4 |
| | Total | 7.9 | 8.3 |
| Richest 20 percent | Females | 10.2 | 10.8 |
| | Males | 10.7 | 11.6 |
| | Total | 10.4 | 11.2 |
| **Total** | **Females** | **7.0** | **7.3** |
| | Males | 7.4 | 7.8 |
| | **Total** | **7.2** | **7.5** |

*Source:* Calculations based on LSMS (ECV) surveys for 1995 and 1999.

**TABLE A.34: ECUADOR: YEARS OF SCHOOLING BY CONSUMPTION QUINTILES AND AREA, 1995 AND 1999**

| Quintiles | Area | 1995 | 1999 |
|---|---|---|---|
| Poorest 20 percent | Rural | 3.2 | 3.1 |
| | Urban | 5.2 | 5.3 |
| | Total | 3.8 | 3.7 |
| Second Quintile | Rural | 4.3 | 4.2 |
| | Urban | 6.2 | 6.5 |
| | Total | 5.1 | 5.3 |
| Third Quintile | Rural | 4.4 | 5.1 |
| | Urban | 7.6 | 8.0 |
| | Total | 6.4 | 6.8 |
| Fourth Quintile | Rural | 5.7 | 6.5 |
| | Urban | 8.8 | 9.0 |
| | Total | 7.9 | 8.3 |
| Richest 20 percent | Rural | 6.2 | 7.8 |
| | Urban | 11.1 | 11.8 |
| | Total | 10.4 | 11.2 |
| **Total** | Rural | 4.4 | 4.8 |
| | Urban | 8.8 | 9.2 |
| | Total | 7.2 | 7.5 |

*Source:* Calculations based on LSMS (ECV) surveys for 1995 and 1999.

**TABLE A.35: ECUADOR: NET ENROLMENT RATES BY EDUCATIONAL LEVEL AND QUINTILES OF P.C. CONSUMPTION**

| Quintiles | Sex | Primary | | Secondary | | University | |
|---|---|---|---|---|---|---|---|
| | | 1995 | 1999 | 1995 | 1999 | 1995 | 1999 |
| Poorest 20 percent | Females | 85.7 | 82.4 | 22.4 | 16.9 | 1.9 | 0.5 |
| | Males | 81.7 | 83.4 | 15.1 | 21.0 | 1.7 | 2.8 |
| | Total | 83.7 | 82.9 | 18.6 | 19.0 | 1.8 | 1.6 |
| Second Quintile | Females | 92.6 | 92.3 | 44.7 | 43.6 | 5.5 | 5.2 |
| | Males | 88.0 | 88.0 | 36.5 | 43.0 | 6.2 | 5.0 |
| | Total | 90.1 | 90.0 | 40.5 | 43.3 | 5.8 | 5.1 |
| Third Quintile | Females | 89.4 | 92.5 | 56.5 | 57.4 | 8.2 | 9.2 |
| | Males | 92.3 | 94.8 | 52.1 | 54.1 | 4.2 | 6.1 |
| | Total | 90.9 | 93.7 | 54.3 | 55.8 | 6.3 | 7.6 |
| Fourth Quintile | Females | 92.3 | 95.6 | 69.4 | 66.6 | 15.7 | 16.4 |
| | Males | 91.5 | 93.4 | 64.9 | 73.0 | 8.6 | 18.9 |
| | Total | 91.9 | 94.4 | 67.1 | 69.7 | 12.3 | 17.7 |
| Richest 20 percent | Females | 91.9 | 92.4 | 74.2 | 77.3 | 20.3 | 36.3 |
| | Males | 88.8 | 92.4 | 73.8 | 79.1 | 26.4 | 38.9 |
| | Total | 90.4 | 92.4 | 74.0 | 78.1 | 22.9 | 37.6 |
| Total | Females | 90.0 | 90.3 | 52.8 | 51.6 | 11.2 | 14.2 |
| | Males | 88.1 | 90.2 | 46.4 | 51.4 | 9.5 | 15.4 |
| | Total | 89.0 | 90.3 | 49.6 | 51.5 | 10.4 | 14.8 |

Source: Calculations based on LSMS (ECV) surveys for 1995 and 1999.

## TABLE A.36: ECUADOR: TEST SCORES FOR LANGUAGE AND MATHEMATICS SKILLS, BY GENDER, REGION AND AREA

| BY GENDER | 1996 | |
|---|---|---|
| | Boys | Girls |
| **Second grade** | | |
| Spanish language skills | 10.26 | 10.64 |
| Mathematics | 9.43 | 9.14 |
| **Sixth grade** | | |
| Spanish language skills | 10.74 | 11.59 |
| Mathematics | 7.35 | 6.98 |
| **Ninth grade** | | |
| Spanish language skills | 12.54 | 13.16 |
| Mathematics | 7.53 | 7.07 |

| BY REGION | 1996 | | 1997 | | 2000 | |
|---|---|---|---|---|---|---|
| | Costa | Sierra | Costa | Sierra | Costa | Sierra |
| **Second grade** | | | | | | |
| Spanish language skills | 10.00 | 10.74 | 7.57 | 9.25 | 8.97 | 10.15 |
| Mathematics | 8.74 | 9.75 | 6.59 | 8.14 | 8.03 | 9.15 |
| **Sixth grade** | | | | | | |
| Spanish language skills | 10.65 | 11.51 | 8.38 | 10.48 | 9.58 | 10.09 |
| Mathematics | 6.60 | 7.57 | 4.11 | 5.80 | 5.74 | 6.45 |
| **Ninth grade** | | | | | | |
| Spanish language skills | 11.81 | 13.73 | 10.21 | 12.45 | 11.81 | 11.47 |
| Mathematics | 6.60 | 7.86 | 4.56 | 6.41 | 6.00 | 6.02 |

| BY AREA and PUBLIC/PRIVATE | 1996 | | | 1997 | | |
|---|---|---|---|---|---|---|
| | Urban private | Urban Public | Rural | Urban private | Urban Public | Rural |
| **Second grade** | | | | | | |
| Spanish language skills | 12.36 | 10.21 | 8.73 | 10.65 | 8.36 | 7.04 |
| Mathematics | 10.96 | 9.04 | 8.12 | 8.88 | 7.29 | 6.38 |
| **Sixth grade** | | | | | | |
| Spanish language skills | 13.37 | 10.73 | 9.41 | 11.98 | 9.43 | 7.51 |
| Mathematics | 8.27 | 6.95 | 6.29 | 6.37 | 4.88 | 3.92 |
| **Ninth grade** | | | | | | |
| Spanish language skills | 14.29 | 12.22 | 11.95 | 12.83 | 10.64 | 10.50 |
| Mathematics | 8.55 | 6.68 | 6.66 | 6.80 | 4.91 | 4.70 |

*Notes:* Test scores are on a scale of 20 with 13 considered as the pass grade. Ninth grade refers to third year of secondary school. Data have not been processed by the APRENDO program for all years at the given levels of disaggregation. As indicated in the text, the national test score program was discontinued after 2000.

*Source:* APRENDO.

## TABLE A.37: ECUADOR: INTERNAL EFFICIENCY INDICATORS FOR PRIMARY EDUCATION, 1995 AND 2001

| | Retention rate (%) (5th grade) | | Years to complete school | | Efficiency indicador (%) (5th grade) | |
|---|---|---|---|---|---|---|
| | 1995 | 2001 | 1995 | 2001 | 1995 | 2001 |
| **BY PROVINCE** | | | | | | |
| Azuay | 92.68 | 96.27 | 6.46 | 6.56 | 92.83 | 91.49 |
| Bolivar | 82.04 | 75.14 | 7.14 | 7.10 | 83.98 | 84.47 |
| Cañar | 86.66 | 83.34 | 7.21 | 7.13 | 83.24 | 84.18 |
| Carchi | 92.18 | 71.41 | 6.74 | 7.78 | 89.04 | 77.09 |
| Cotopaxi | 84.24 | 81.40 | 7.04 | 6.88 | 85.19 | 87.26 |
| Chimborazo | 80.70 | 82.96 | 7.28 | 6.97 | 82.44 | 86.08 |
| El Oro | 88.44 | 91.27 | 6.96 | 6.72 | 86.18 | 89.24 |
| Esmeraldas | 52.27 | 80.38 | 8.58 | 6.63 | 69.96 | 90.54 |
| Guayas | 79.81 | 74.57 | 6.69 | 6.93 | 89.70 | 86.53 |
| Imbabura | 93.32 | 86.60 | 6.82 | 6.84 | 88.02 | 87.66 |
| Loja | 87.35 | 55.55 | 6.70 | 9.25 | 89.58 | 64.89 |
| Los Ríos | 71.74 | 69.96 | 7.40 | 7.61 | 81.50 | 78.88 |
| Manabí | 87.89 | 71.42 | 6.38 | 7.22 | 94.02 | 83.11 |
| Pichincha | 90.46 | 94.77 | 6.61 | 6.40 | 90.71 | 93.69 |
| Tungurahua | 98.51 | 87.65 | 6.43 | 6.64 | 93.37 | 90.35 |
| **BY GENDER** | | | | | | |
| Men | 84.13 | 81.50 | 6.75 | 6.84 | 88.90 | 87.74 |
| Women | 84.29 | 81.37 | 6.79 | 6.86 | 88.36 | 87.43 |
| **BY AREA** | | | | | | |
| Urban | 87.69 | 84.58 | 6.56 | 6.68 | 91.41 | 89.78 |
| Rural | 76.34 | 74.16 | 7.32 | 7.30 | 81.95 | 82.14 |
| **National average** | 84.22 | 81.44 | 6.77 | 6.85 | 88.63 | 87.59 |

*Note:* Efficiency indicator as defined by UNESCO stands for the ratio of the number of students of a particular cohort which completed a given level of education with respect to the 'ideal' number of students that would have reached that level with zero repetition and desertion.

*Source:* SINEC data base.

## TABLE A.38:  LATIN AMERICA: INTERNAL EFFICIENCY INDICATORS FOR PRIMARY EDUCATION, 1990s

| | Primary education efficiency indicator (percent) | | |
|---|---|---|---|
| *Andean countries* | | | |
| Bolivia (1995–99) | 81.5 | 84.5 | 83.0 |
| Colombia (1991–95) | 75.6 | 70.4 | 73.0 |
| **Ecuador (WB, 1995–99)** | **79.4** | **76.4** | **77.8** |
| Ecuador (SINEC, 1997–2001) | 87.4 | 87.7 | 87.6 |
| Peru (1994–98) | 87.6 | 88.2 | 87.8 |
| Venezuela (1994–98) | 94.3 | 87.6 | 90.8 |
| *Other Latin American countries* | | | |
| Argentina (1995–99) | 90.5 | 90.1 | 90.3 |
| Costa Rica (1995–99) | 84.2 | 76.7 | 80.2 |
| Dominican Republic (1994–98) | 79.1 | 71.4 | 75.1 |
| Mexico (1995–99) | 89.5 | 87.5 | 88.5 |
| Uruguay (1994–98) | 88.4 | 93.2 | 90.8 |

*Note:* Efficiency indicator as defined by UNESCO stands for the ratio of the number of students of a particular cohort which completed a given level of education with respect to the 'ideal' number of students that would have reached that level with zero repetition and desertion.

*Source:* World Bank, World Development Indicators (2003). Second estimates for Ecuador are from SINEC data base.

## TABLE A.39:  ECUADOR: DIFFERENTIAL VERSUS AVERAGE UNIT COSTS IN ESTIMATION THE PUBLIC EXPENDITURE INCIDENCE IN EDUCATION, 1999

| unit cost estimation: | Public Primary | | Public Secondary | | Public Tertiary | | Private Tertiary | |
|---|---|---|---|---|---|---|---|---|
| | differential | average | differential | average | differential | average | differential | average |
| Poorest 20 percent | 35% | 30% | 15% | 10% | 3% | 2% | 0% | 0% |
| Second quintile | 26% | 26% | 23% | 22% | 12% | 8% | 1% | 1% |
| Third Quintile | 20% | 21% | 26% | 26% | 16% | 13% | 6% | 5% |
| Fourth Quintile | 13% | 16% | 22% | 27% | 28% | 35% | 22% | 14% |
| Richest 20 percent | 6% | 7% | 14% | 15% | 40% | 42% | 70% | 79% |

*Source:* INEC, *Encuesta de Condiciones de Vida* (ECV), 1999 and education expenditure data.

## TABLE A.40: ECUADOR: "MARGINAL" EXPENDITURE INCIDENCE IN EDUCATION, 1995 AND 1999

| Deciles | Primary | | Secondary | | Public Tertiary | | Private University | | Total Education | | Per capita consumption | |
|---|---|---|---|---|---|---|---|---|---|---|---|---|
| | 1995 | 1999 | 1995 | 1999 | 1995 | 1999 | 1995 | 1999 | 1995 | 1999 | 1995 | 1999 |
| 1 | 17.9% | 15.8% | 3.9% | 3.3% | 0.0% | 0.0% | 0.0% | 0.0% | 8.0% | 6.1% | 2.2% | 1.9% |
| 2 | 14.2% | 14.3% | 6.1% | 6.3% | 3.0% | 2.4% | 0.8% | 0.0% | 8.2% | 7.2% | 3.5% | 3.1% |
| 3 | 14.2% | 12.3% | 9.6% | 10.7% | 4.2% | 3.3% | 4.0% | 1.2% | 10.1% | 8.4% | 4.6% | 4.0% |
| 4 | 11.9% | 13.7% | 11.9% | 11.1% | 4.6% | 5.0% | 2.8% | 0.3% | 10.3% | 9.3% | 5.6% | 4.9% |
| 5 | 11.3% | 11.1% | 13.0% | 12.7% | 6.0% | 8.0% | 4.5% | 0.6% | 10.9% | 9.7% | 6.6% | 5.9% |
| 6 | 9.7% | 10.1% | 13.1% | 13.6% | 11.3% | 4.8% | 2.0% | 4.5% | 11.0% | 9.5% | 7.9% | 7.1% |
| 7 | 7.4% | 8.3% | 13.1% | 13.2% | 12.1% | 15.7% | 5.3% | 3.4% | 10.5% | 11.0% | 9.6% | 8.8% |
| 8 | 6.6% | 7.2% | 13.8% | 14.3% | 17.4% | 19.3% | 5.2% | 11.0% | 11.3% | 12.8% | 11.9% | 11.2% |
| 9 | 4.1% | 4.5% | 9.4% | 9.4% | 18.4% | 20.4% | 24.5% | 29.1% | 9.8% | 12.6% | 15.9% | 15.7% |
| 10 | 2.7% | 2.6% | 6.0% | 5.5% | 22.9% | 21.2% | 50.8% | 50.0% | 9.9% | 13.4% | 32.1% | 37.3% |
| Total | 100.0% | 100.0% | 100.0% | 100.0% | 100.0% | 100.0% | 100.0% | 100.0% | 100.0% | 100.0% | 100.0% | 100.0% |

*Note:* Data refer to benefit incidence in each year using average unit costs. The difference between the two years might be interpreted as the "marginal" effect.

*Source:* INEC, *Encuesta de Condiciones de Vida* (ECV), 1995 and 1999 and education expenditure data.

## TABLE A.41: ECUADOR: COST-EFFECTIVENESS MODEL ESTIMATES FOR NET ENROLMENT IN PRIMARY EDUCATION

(linear multinomial logit specification)

| | Poor | | | Non-poor | | |
|---|---|---|---|---|---|---|
| | Coefficient | ey/ex | Significance | Coefficient | ey/ex | Significance |
| **Public primary schools** | | | | | | |
| Education costs | − 0.000027 | − 0.1917 | 0.0000 | − 0.000001 | − 2.5837 | 0.7130 |
| Sex | − 0.5967 | 0.0114 | 0.2160 | − 0.3778 | − 0.0749 | 0.3980 |
| Age | 2.2607 | − 0.3932 | 0.1510 | − 0.7220 | 2.7793 | 0.4450 |
| Age squared | − 0.1155 | 0.2491 | 0.2460 | 0.0569 | − 1.1970 | 0.2630 |
| Education level father | − 0.0941 | − 0.1189 | 0.1270 | − 0.0618 | − 0.5482 | 0.4080 |
| Education level mother | 0.3205 | 0.1282 | 0.0000 | 0.1544 | − 0.2880 | 0.2100 |
| Location: Quito = 1 | 1.0787 | 0.0366 | 0.0320 | 1.1219 | 0.1464 | 0.1580 |
| Region (Costa = 1) | − 1.1744 | − 0.1365 | 0.0580 | 3.9791 | − 0.3372 | 0.0020 |
| Students per classroom | 0.1237 | 0.1130 | 0.0180 | − 0.0106 | − 0.7235 | 0.9350 |
| Percentage of teachers with teaching qualification | 6.0027 | 0.0806 | 0.0290 | 17.8841 | 1.6331 | 0.0000 |
| Percentage of teachers with university degree | − 0.5159 | 0.0190 | 0.8410 | − 14.9457 | − 0.3393 | 0.0000 |
| Percentage of teachers appointed by MoE | − 0.7781 | − 0.1414 | 0.7480 | − 13.6122 | − 0.3799 | 0.0000 |
| Constant | − 15.1981 | 0.0330 | 0.0907 | 0.9880 | | |
| **Private primary schools** | | | | | | |
| Education costs | 0.0000 | 1.3234 | 0.0010 | 0.0000 | 0.7400 | 0.0000 |
| Sex | − 0.9755 | − 0.1890 | 0.0210 | − 0.2050 | 0.0207 | 0.6650 |
| Age | 3.3550 | 8.9130 | 0.0010 | − 1.1540 | − 0.8189 | 0.2700 |
| Age squared | − 0.1804 | − 4.6386 | 0.0070 | 0.0785 | 0.3583 | 0.1700 |
| Education level father | 0.0442 | 0.8302 | 0.5750 | 0.0033 | 0.1547 | 0.9670 |
| Education level mother | 0.2249 | − 0.4937 | 0.0250 | 0.1910 | 0.0884 | 0.0770 |
| Location: Quito = 1 | − 0.3555 | − 0.2506 | 0.5340 | 0.2714 | − 0.0411 | 0.7480 |
| Region (Costa = 1) | 0.6222 | 0.9598 | 0.4920 | 4.7639 | 0.1050 | 0.0000 |
| Students per classroom | 0.1235 | 0.1054 | 0.0370 | 0.0208 | 0.2062 | 0.8740 |
| Percentage of teachers with teaching qualification | 6.8636 | 0.8397 | 0.0110 | 15.5642 | − 0.4099 | 0.0010 |
| Percentage of teachers with university degree | − 0.9919 | − 0.2450 | 0.7280 | − 14.2165 | 0.0665 | 0.0030 |
| Percentage of teachers appointed by MoE | 3.5209 | 1.1420 | 0.2750 | − 12.0046 | 0.0941 | 0.0010 |
| Constant | − 25.9500 | 0.0000 | − 1.1238 | 0.8740 | | |

Source: Model estimations based on 1999 LSMS survey. See Appendix A.2 in Vos (2004a) for model specification.

## TABLE A.42: DETERMINANTS OF YEARS OF SCHOOLING AND NET ENROLMENT IN PRIMARY AND SECONDARY EDUCATION AT THE DISTRICT (CANTONAL) LEVEL, 2001

**Dependent variable:**

| Years of schooling | Model 1 | Model 2 | Model 3 | Model 4 |
|---|---|---|---|---|
| Share of rural population | −0.040962* | −0.04001* | −0.035997* | |
| Share of indigenous population | | | −0.011259* | |
| Poverty incidence (UBN) | | | | −0.07831* |
| Regional dummy for Costa | −0.184024 | 0.048407 | −0.049981 | 0.74270* |
| Regional dummy for Oriente | 0.763725* | 0.754012* | 0.980182* | 0.91284* |
| Pupils per classroom (primary schools) | | −0.01281* | −0.012131** | −0.002955 |
| Pupils per classroom (secondary schools) | | 0.001271 | 0.0000025 | −0.000566 |
| Share of one-teacher (unidocente) schools | | −0.001820 | −0.004896 | 0.001853 |
| Teacher quality[1] | | | 0.077745*** | 0.050195 |
| Constant | 8.17978* | 8.516025 | 7.971077 | 10.8162* |
| $R^2$ | 0.5579 | 0.5579 | 0.588 | 0.7716 |

**Dependent variable:**
**Net enrolment in primary education**

| | Model 1 | Model 2 | Model 3 | Model 4 |
|---|---|---|---|---|
| Share of rural population | −0.085465* | −0.071468* | −0.043086* | |
| Share of indigenous population | −0.043853* | −0.052403* | −0.045286* | |
| Poverty incidence (UBN) | | | | −0.143479* |
| Regional dummy for Costa | −5.98924* | −5.08484* | −4.31605* | −2.79523* |
| Regional dummy for Oriente | 0.035547 | 0.746331 | 1.33866** | 0.702439 |
| Pupils per classroom (primary schools) | | −0.053048* | −0.058566** | −0.043853* |
| Share of one-teacher (unidocente) schools | | −0.051462* | −0.054299* | −0.030050 |
| Teacher quality[1] | | | 1.01943* | 0.876846* |
| Constant | 97.0141* | 99.68792* | 90.3573* | 97.0328* |
| $R^2$ | 0.4047 | 0.4379 | 0.5130 | 0.5713 |

**Dependent variable:**
**Net enrolment in secondary education**

| | Model 1 | Model 2 | Model 3 | Model 4 |
|---|---|---|---|---|
| Share of rural population | −0.313211* | −0.313126* | −0.26742* | |
| Share of indigenous population | −0.074687* | −0.074705* | −0.059888* | |
| Poverty incidence (UBN) | | | | −0.61184* |
| Regional dummy for Costa | −6.25430* | −6.26186* | −4.60912* | 1.96075** |
| Regional dummy for Oriente | 3.07857*** | 3.08184 | 3.92957* | 4.30481* |
| Pupils per classroom (secondary schools) | | 0.000542 | −0.03023 | −0.02551 |
| Teacher quality[1] | | | 1.86975* | 1.5099* |
| Constant | 57.7269* | 57.7091* | 41.2119* | 69.8136* |
| $R^2$ | 0.4392 | 0.4392 | 0.4884 | 0.7493 |

*Notes:* All estimates have been corrected for heteroscedacity. * Significant at 99 percent level; ** significant at 95 percent level and *** significant at 90 percent level.

1. Teacher quality proxied by average salary level of teachers in district. This variable correlates highly with alternative specifications such as the share of teachers with secondary or university level training and shares of teachers with 15–30 years of experience.

*Source:* INEC, Population census 2001; SINEC database.

**TABLE A.43: DETERMINANTS OF TEST SCORES FOR LANGUAGE AND MATHEMATICS AT PRIMARY (2ND AND 6TH GRADE) AND SECONDARY (10TH GRADE) LEVEL BY DISTRICTS (CANTONS), 2001**

| Test scores: Primary | Spanish 2nd grade | Mathematics 2nd grade | Spanish 6th grade | Mathematics 6th grade |
|---|---|---|---|---|
| Share of rural population | −0.013134 | −0.011256 | −0.011256 | −0.002711 |
| Share of indigenous population | 0.00291 | 0.012759 | 0.012759 | −0.01360 |
| Regional dummy for Costa | −1.04343 | −0.899487 | −0.899487 | −1.01049 |
| Regional dummy for Oriente | −0.94261 | −0.929692 | −0.929692 | 1.52098 |
| Pupils per classroom (primary schools) | −0.02082 | 0.008524 | 0.008524 | 0.01744 |
| Share of one-teacher (unidocente) schools | −0.00384 | −0.003536 | −0.003536 | −0.03992 |
| Teacher quality[1] | −0.28453 | −0.373924 | −0.37392 | −0.12737 |
| Average level of schooling | 0.38626 | 0.572619** | 0.572619** | 0.167951 |
| Constant | 11.0784* | 8.32515* | 8.32515* | 7.10771* |
| $R^2$ | 0.3183 | 0.3103 | 0.3619 | 0.4172 |

| Test scores: Secondary | Spanish 10th grade | Mathematics 10th grade |
|---|---|---|
| Share of rural population | −0.024371 | −0.009358 |
| Share of indigenous population | −0.024581 | 0.005553 |
| Regional dummy for Costa | −1.466913 | −0.713785 |
| Regional dummy for Oriente | 0.215342 | −0.640394 |
| Pupils per classroom (secondary schools) | −0.005824 | 0.006055 |
| Teacher quality[1] | −0.531906 | 0.015544 |
| Average level of schooling | 0.493665** | 0.282452 |
| Constant | 14.55702* | 4.160791*** |
| $R^2$ | 0.3869 | 0.2577 |

*Note:* All estimates have been corrected for heteroscedacity. * Significant at 99 percent level; ** significant at 95 percent level and *** significant at 90 percent level.

1. Teacher quality proxied by average salary level of teachers in district. This variable correlates highly with alternative specifications such as the share of teachers with secondary or university level training and shares of teachers with 15–30 years of experience.

*Source:* APRENDO and SINEC database.

## TABLE A.44: RETURNS TO EDUCATION FOR URBAN WORKERS, 1990–2002 (SPECIFICATION 1)

| Dependent variable: Log hourly labour income | 1990 | 1995 | 1999 | 2002 |
|---|---|---|---|---|
| Age | 0.04663* | 0.037823* | 0.035451* | 0.031806* |
| Age squared | −0.00044* | −0.00037* | −0.000304* | −0.000272* |
| Sex (female = 1) | −0.24029* | −0.219613* | −0.167533* | −0.191946* |
| Years of schooling | 0.060783* | 0.063502* | 0.075719* | 0.072984* |
| Dummy Employers | 0.159022** | 0.484643* | 0.477405* | 0.206899* |
| Dummy Self-employed | −0.080048 | 0.022223 | 0.061917 | −0.13599** |
| Dummy Public sector workers | −0.022409 | −0.089235 | −0.009430 | −0.02894 |
| Dummy Private sector workers | −0.125576*** | −0.151246 | −0.124045 | −0.28861* |
| Dummy Modern sector workers | 0.154993* | 0.275220* | 0.295771* | 0.284010* |
| Dummy Informal sector workers | −0.048390 | −0.139169* | −0.195299* | −0.041285 |
| Dummy Quito | 0.122607* | 0.259545* | 0.2513267* | 0.307813* |
| Dummy Guayaquil | 0.05215* | 0.089547* | 0.112876* | 0.066625* |
| Dummy Cuenca | 0.042701*** | 0.199734* | 0.099603* | 0.201051* |
| Constant | 4.38338* | 6.25446* | 7.123794* | −1.36919* |
| | | | | |
| **Heckman selection equation** | | | | |
| Age | 0.05313* | 0.062282* | 0.077416* | 0.115522* |
| Age squared | −0.00067* | −0.000775* | −0.000956* | −0.001381* |
| Sex (female = 1) | 0.237919* | 0.249121* | 0.104719* | −0.458433* |
| Years of schooling | −0.02426* | −0.019044* | −0.010509* | −0.031387* |
| Dummy Employers | 3.381763* | 3.164547* | 3.004328* | 1.927083* |
| Dummy Self-employed | 3.349655* | 3.146664* | 2.878786* | 1.821808* |
| Dummy Public sector workers | 3.549583* | 3.588317* | 3.58531* | 2.261496* |
| Dummy Private sector workers | 3.285143* | 3.479024* | 3.143168* | 2.002983* |
| Dummy Modern sector workers | −0.54169* | −0.865282* | −1.172938* | −0.093226 |
| Dummy Informal sector workers | −0.17838* | −0.196854* | −0.168075* | 0.694701* |
| Dummy Quito | −0.13566* | 0.1811485* | 0.1330385* | −0.07867** |
| Dummy Guayaquil | 0.13424* | 0.141310* | 0.0541961 | −0.018018 |
| Dummy Cuenca | 0.13178* | −0.279711* | 0.0454622 | −0.066061 |
| Number of children 0–5 years | 0.05309* | 0.037097** | 0.0203716 | −0.00404*** |
| Number of children 6–10 years | −0.04046** | −0.048430** | −0.056745* | −0.00148 |
| Dummy head of household | 0.375907* | 0.420933* | 0.311681* | 0.619840* |
| Constant | −2.647381* | −2.78977* | −2.81467* | −2.49129* |
| /athrho | −0.47782* | −0.447623* | −0.428941* | −0.320253* |
| /lnsigma | −0.317001* | −0.332464* | −0.239392* | −0.237471* |
| Wald test of indep.eqns (prob chi 2) | 0.0000 | 0.0000 | 0.0000 | 0.0000 |

* significant at 99 percent, ** significant at 95 percent, *** significant at 90 percent
*Estimates have been corrected for heteroscedasticity and for Heckman selection bias.

*Source:* Vos (2004a).

## TABLE A.45: RETURNS TO EDUCATION FOR URBAN WORKERS, 1990–2002 (SPECIFICATION 2)

| Dependent variable: Log hourly labour income | 1990 | 1995 | 1999 | 2002 |
|---|---|---|---|---|
| Age | 0.048161* | 0.039633* | 0.037307* | 0.036810* |
| Age squared | −0.000460* | −0.000394* | −0.00033* | −0.000340* |
| Sex (female = 1) | −0.236599* | −0.216669* | −0.171522* | −0.200075* |
| Dummy Primary | 0.286526* | 0.273503* | 0.263963* | 0.187704* |
| Dummy Secondary | 0.577270* | 0.580138* | 0.563814* | 0.484728* |
| Dummy Tertiary | 0.944181* | 0.975027* | 1.148927* | 0.995283* |
| Dummy Employers | 0.193955** | 0.494273* | 0.499188* | 0.258925* |
| Dummy Self-employed | −0.070897 | 0.008055 | 0.065918 | −0.111301 |
| Dummy Public sector workers | −0.00368 | −0.089786 | 0.013894 | 0.014428 |
| Dummy Private sector workers | −0.122936*** | −0.167746*** | −0.115617 | −0.253482* |
| Dummy Modern sector workers | 0.194408* | 0.31137* | 0.328558* | 0.318270* |
| Dummy Informal sector workers | −0.037836 | −0.127038* | −0.160156* | −0.012676 |
| Dummy Quito | 0.125470* | 0.262345* | 0.257789* | 0.320304* |
| Dummy Guayaquil | 0.047675* | 0.087757* | 0.120849* | 0.070033* |
| Dummy Cuenca | 0.050948** | 0.205858* | 0.101773* | 0.207237* |
| Constant | 4.360915* | 6.285155* | 7.22305* | −1.29527* |

| Heckman selection equation | | | | |
|---|---|---|---|---|
| Age | 0.059702* | 0.068339* | 0.083218* | 0.119148* |
| Age squared | −0.000746* | −0.000846* | −0.001028* | −0.001432* |
| Sex (female = 1) | 0.227881* | 0.240854* | 0.097601* | −0.463672* |
| Dummy Primary | 0.109432*** | 0.095117 | 0.153950*** | 0.0620591 |
| Dummy Secondary | −0.103152 | −0.154748** | −0.094921 | −0.338876* |
| Dummy Tertiary | −0.13227*** | −0.13398*** | −0.000510 | −0.360222* |
| Dummy Employers | 3.360116* | 3.154139* | 3.002508* | 1.918642* |
| Dummy Self-employed | 3.349083* | 3.146859* | 2.884234* | 1.831032* |
| Dummy Public sector workers | 3.530839* | 3.576834* | 3.587225* | 2.265916* |
| Dummy Private sector workers | 3.298993* | 3.493261* | 3.164747* | 2.029496* |
| Dummy Modern sector workers | −0.568170* | −0.870465* | −1.17843* | −0.105790*** |
| Dummy Informal sector workers | −0.181692* | −0.184898* | −0.15662* | 0.708992* |
| Dummy Quito | −0.144294* | 0.178434* | 0.13487* | −0.07571*** |
| Dummy Guayaquil | 0.1295324* | 0.143907* | 0.05934*** | −0.008542 |
| Dummy Cuenca | 0.1236273* | −0.290042* | 0.04078 | −0.066344 |
| Number of children 0–5 years | 0.039160** | 0.0232076 | 0.00871 | −0.00394*** |
| Number of children 6–10 years | −0.032906*** | −0.047958** | −0.05848* | −0.00133 |
| Dummy head of household | 0.352657* | 0.396010* | 0.290610* | 0.60817* |
| Constant | −2.93900* | −3.00897* | −3.02183* | −2.64863* |
| /athrho | −0.473026* | −0.456165* | −0.419226* | −0.29488* |
| /lnsigma | −0.311069* | −0.326662* | −0.237280* | −0.230680* |
| Wald test of ind. Eqs. Prob chi2 | 0.0000 | 0.0000 | 0.0000 | 0.0000 |

* significant at 99 percent, ** significant at 95 percent, *** significant at 90 percent
*Estimates have been corrected for heteroscedasticity and for Heckman selection bias
Source: INEC, Urban Household (Labour Force) Surveys, 1990–2002.

## TABLE A.46: PROFILE OF MALNUTRITION, EDUCATION, WATER AND SANITATION CONDITIONS, 2000 AND 2003

| | Stunting (low height for age) (% of children age 0–5) | Under-weight (low weight for height) (% children 0–5) | Education women 15–49 yrs (years of schooling) | Access to safe water (% of population) | Access to sewerage (% of population) | Housing overcrow-dedness (% of population) | Population shares (households) | Population shares (0–5 year olds) | Population shares (women 15–49 years) |
|---|---|---|---|---|---|---|---|---|---|
| **Ethnicity by language of household head** | | | | | | | | | |
| Non-indigenous | 23.7% | 11.5% | 9.4 | 83.2% | 83.9% | 34.7% | 90.0% | 81.9% | 91.8% |
| Indigenous | 35.1% | 11.9% | 6.5 | 77.1% | 59.6% | 48.9% | 10.0% | 18.1% | 8.2% |
| Total | 25.8% | 11.6% | 9.2 | 82.6% | 81.4% | 36.1% | 100.0% | 100.0% | 100.0% |
| **Ethnicity by self-definition of household head** | | | | | | | | | |
| Indigenous | 49.9% | 15.5% | 5.2 | 75.5% | 52.1% | 53.0% | 8.5% | 8.2% | 7.1% |
| Black (Afro) | 15.8% | 8.2% | 8.5 | 76.9% | 78.2% | 50.0% | 4.4% | 9.8% | 4.0% |
| Mestizo | 25.0% | 12.0% | 9.4 | 83.2% | 84.1% | 34.2% | 78.6% | 69.0% | 80.5% |
| Caucasian | 22.5% | 9.9% | 10.3 | 87.5% | 87.8% | 29.6% | 8.2% | 11.9% | 8.2% |
| Other | 21.8% | 1.8% | 9.9 | 92.0% | 91.5% | 37.0% | 0.3% | 1.1% | 0.2% |
| Total | 25.8% | 11.6% | 9.2 | 82.6% | 81.4% | 36.1% | 100.0% | 100.0% | 100.0% |
| **Sex of household head** | | | | | | | | | |
| Male | 27.2% | 11.1% | | 81.5% | 81.3% | 36.8% | 81.8% | 52.2% | |
| Female | 24.2% | 12.1% | | 87.6% | 82.1% | 33.2% | 18.2% | 47.8% | |
| Total | 25.8% | 11.6% | | 82.6% | 81.4% | 36.1% | 100.0% | 100.0% | |
| **Area of residence** | | | | | | | | | |
| Urban | 18.5% | 8.9% | 10.3 | 95.1% | 93.7% | 31.0% | 66.0% | 58.7% | 70.1% |
| Rural | 36.0% | 15.3% | 6.4 | 58.4% | 57.7% | 46.2% | 34.0% | 41.3% | 29.9% |
| Total | 25.8% | 11.6% | 9.2 | 82.6% | 81.4% | 36.1% | 100.0% | 100.0% | 100.0% |

## TABLE A.46: PROFILE OF MALNUTRITION, EDUCATION, WATER AND SANITATION CONDITIONS, 2000 AND 2003 (CONTINUED)

| | Stunting (low height for age) (% of children age 0–5) | Under-weight (low weight for height) (% children 0–5) | Education women 15–49 yrs (years of schooling) | Access to safe water (% of population) | Access to sewerage (% of population) | Housing overcrow-dedness (% of population) | Population shares (households) | Population shares (0–5 year olds) | Population shares (women 15–49 years) |
|---|---|---|---|---|---|---|---|---|---|
| **Income deciles** | | | | | | | | | |
| 10% poorest | 33.4% | 16.1% | 6.2 | 65.9% | 54.8% | 62.8% | 9.7% | 15.9% | 8.0% |
| 2 | 35.2% | 15.3% | 6.6 | 69.8% | 65.1% | 57.9% | 10.1% | 13.6% | 9.1% |
| 3 | 34.6% | 18.6% | 7.3 | 73.2% | 72.0% | 53.1% | 10.2% | 12.0% | 9.2% |
| 4 | 23.6% | 10.3% | 7.7 | 78.2% | 77.0% | 47.8% | 10.0% | 11.7% | 9.5% |
| 5 | 24.8% | 10.3% | 8.3 | 80.8% | 82.7% | 40.5% | 10.1% | 8.7% | 10.3% |
| 6 | 22.6% | 9.2% | 8.6 | 84.9% | 84.6% | 36.2% | 9.9% | 10.4% | 10.0% |
| 7 | 18.0% | 8.1% | 9.6 | 89.1% | 90.4% | 29.7% | 9.8% | 7.2% | 10.3% |
| 8 | 19.7% | 6.5% | 10.2 | 91.6% | 92.5% | 17.8% | 10.3% | 8.0% | 11.1% |
| 9 | 13.2% | 4.0% | 11.6 | 95.0% | 96.8% | 12.3% | 9.9% | 7.9% | 10.7% |
| 10% richest | 8.9% | 6.6% | 13.3 | 97.7% | 98.7% | 4.4% | 10.0% | 4.7% | 11.9% |
| Total | 25.8% | 11.7% | 9.2 | 82.6% | 81.5% | 36.2% | 100.0% | 100.0% | 100.0% |
| **Region** | | | | | | | | | |
| Costa | 20.2% | 10.4% | | | | | | 53.7% | |
| Sierra | 32.4% | 13.3% | | | | | | 38.8% | |
| Amazonã | 31.2% | 10.7% | | | | | | 7.6% | |
| Total | 25.8% | 11.6% | | | | | | 100.0% | |

Source: INEC, EMEDINHO (special module of household survey), 2000 for malnutrition indicators; INEC, Sistema Integrado de Encuestas de Hogares (SIEH), special module on access to social services, December 2003, for other indicators.

## TABLE A.47: PROFILE OF KNOWLEDGE OF FAMILY PLANNING AND SEXUALLY TRANSMITTED DISEASES, 1999 AND 2000

| | Women that know about family planning methods | Women that do not use family planning methods | Population that knows HIV/AIDS can be transmitted to child at birth | Knowledge of how to protect against HIV/AIDS during sex | Population shares (Women 15–45 years) | Population shares (15 years and older) |
|---|---|---|---|---|---|---|
| **Ethnicity by language of household head** | | | | | | |
| Non-indigenous | 85.8% | 41.1% | 74.0% | 59.1% | 94.9% | 81.9% |
| Indigenous | 33.8% | 82.1% | 54.0% | 44.6% | 5.1% | 18.1% |
| Total | 83.2% | 43.4% | 71.4% | 57.2% | 100.0% | 100.0% |
| **Ethnicity by self-definition of household head** | | | | | | |
| Indigenous | | | 31.5% | 24.0% | | 8.2% |
| Black (Afro) | | | 72.2% | 52.8% | | 9.8% |
| Mestizo | | | 73.9% | 59.1% | | 69.0% |
| Caucasian | | | 75.6% | 62.1% | | 11.9% |
| Other | | | 63.1% | 64.0% | | 1.1% |
| Total | | | 71.5% | 57.3% | | 100.0% |
| **Sex of household head** | | | | | | |
| Male | 72.4% | 58.3% | 0.0% | 52.2% | | |
| Female | 83.2% | 43.4% | 70.5% | 56.1% | 99.9% | 47.8% |
| Total | 83.2% | 43.4% | 71.4% | 57.2% | 100.0% | 100.0% |
| **Area of residence** | | | | | | |
| Urban | 91.8% | 36.5% | 79.4% | 62.7% | 64.9% | 58.7% |
| Rural | 67.1% | 55.7% | 55.7% | 46.3% | 35.1% | 41.3% |
| Total | 83.2% | 43.4% | 71.4% | 57.2% | 100.0% | 100.0% |
| **Income deciles** | | | | | | |
| 10% poorest | 48.0% | 71.2% | 58.1% | 46.1% | 7.8% | 15.9% |
| 2 | 67.9% | 61.4% | 59.6% | 45.7% | 8.8% | 13.6% |
| 3 | 79.3% | 49.1% | 67.7% | 53.1% | 9.4% | 12.0% |
| 4 | 80.5% | 38.4% | 68.9% | 56.2% | 8.7% | 11.7% |
| 5 | 85.9% | 40.6% | 69.7% | 54.4% | 10.0% | 8.7% |
| 6 | 85.8% | 41.5% | 72.9% | 60.8% | 10.4% | 10.4% |
| 7 | 90.4% | 40.4% | 74.3% | 58.3% | 10.9% | 7.2% |
| 8 | 92.8% | 34.7% | 77.2% | 59.9% | 11.4% | 8.0% |
| 9 | 92.8% | 37.0% | 80.2% | 66.0% | 10.9% | 7.9% |
| 10% richest | 93.0% | 32.1% | 79.3% | 65.4% | 11.7% | 4.7% |
| Total | 83.1% | 43.4% | 71.6% | 57.4% | 100.0% | 100.0% |

*Source:* INEC, ECV (LSMS) 1999 for family planning indicators and INEC, EMEDINHO (special module of household survey), 2000 for HIV/SIDA indicators.

## TABLE A.48: PROFILE OF ACCESS TO SERVICES OF CHILDREN AGE 0–5, 1999

| | Prevalence of diarrhoea | Medical assistance for diarrhoea | Repiratory diseases | Medical assistance for respiratory diseases | Population shares (children 0–5 years) |
|---|---|---|---|---|---|
| **Ethnicity by language of household head** | | | | | |
| Non-indigenous | 26.2% | 32.4% | 58.7% | 29.7% | 90.6% |
| Indigenous | 25.4% | 23.2% | 47.2% | 10.8% | 9.4% |
| Total | 26.1% | 31.6% | 57.6% | 28.3% | 100.0% |
| **Ethnicity by self-definition of household head** | | | | | |
| Indigenous | | | | | |
| Black (Afro) | | | | | |
| Mestizo | | | | | |
| Caucasian | | | | | |
| Other | | | | | |
| Total | | | | | |
| **Sex of household head** | | | | | |
| Male | 26.2% | 31.8% | 57.3% | 30.8% | 51.3% |
| Female | 26.0% | 31.4% | 58.0% | 25.7% | 48.7% |
| Total | 26.1% | 31.6% | 57.6% | 28.3% | 100.0% |
| **Area of residence** | | | | | |
| Urban | 26.2% | 33.7% | 59.5% | 34.8% | 53.4% |
| Rural | 26.0% | 29.2% | 55.6% | 20.3% | 46.6% |
| Total | 26.1% | 31.6% | 57.6% | 28.3% | 100.0% |
| **Income deciles** | | | | | |
| 10% poorest | 25.5% | 15.7% | 50.0% | 12.3% | 14.1% |
| 2 | 31.6% | 28.3% | 55.8% | 13.1% | 13.2% |
| 3 | 29.8% | 34.3% | 62.6% | 23.7% | 12.3% |
| 4 | 26.8% | 32.3% | 53.7% | 36.6% | 11.1% |
| 5 | 26.1% | 40.0% | 63.9% | 27.1% | 11.1% |
| 6 | 26.1% | 29.9% | 54.9% | 31.7% | 10.0% |
| 7 | 25.3% | 35.7% | 65.1% | 25.8% | 8.7% |
| 8 | 21.6% | 41.3% | 59.8% | 51.9% | 7.4% |
| 9 | 24.7% | 40.7% | 60.1% | 37.7% | 6.1% |
| 10% richest | 14.2% | 32.7% | 53.3% | 51.9% | 5.9% |
| Total | 26.1% | 31.6% | 57.6% | 28.3% | 100.0% |

*Source:* INEC, ECV (LSMS), 1999.

## TABLE A.49: PROFILE OF ACCESS TO HEALTH SERVICES PREGNANT WOMEN, 2003

| | Birth delivery in hospital or health centre | Birth delivery in public hospital or health centre | Birth delivery in private hospital or health centre | Birth delivery without professional medical assistance | Coverage vaccination against tetanus | Five or more pre-natal medical controls | Population shares of women of 12 years and older who are pregnant or breast feeding | Population shares of women of 12 years and older who are breast feeding |
|---|---|---|---|---|---|---|---|---|
| **Ethnicity by language of household head** | | | | | | | | |
| Non-indigenous | 86.6% | 66.3% | 20.4% | 13.4% | 71.8% | 58.1% | 89.2% | 88.3% |
| Indigenous | 64.8% | 54.4% | 10.5% | 35.2% | 63.7% | 25.6% | 10.8% | 11.7% |
| Total | 84.3% | 65.0% | 19.3% | 15.7% | 71.0% | 54.3% | 100.0% | 100.0% |
| **Ethnicity by self-definition of household head** | | | | | | | | |
| Indigenous | 59.3% | 51.2% | 8.1% | 40.7% | 60.6% | 23.5% | 10.6% | 11.8% |
| Black (Afro) | 82.2% | 76.2% | 6.0% | 17.8% | 74.2% | 44.3% | 4.7% | 4.4% |
| Mestizo | 87.7% | 66.6% | 21.1% | 12.3% | 72.5% | 59.6% | 76.9% | 76.9% |
| Caucasian | 85.6% | 61.2% | 24.4% | 14.4% | 68.5% | 51.5% | 7.6% | 6.7% |
| Other | 81.0% | 81.0% | 0.0% | 19.0% | 81.0% | 86.4% | 0.2% | 0.3% |
| Total | 84.2% | 65.0% | 19.2% | 15.8% | 71.1% | 54.2% | 100.0% | 100.0% |
| **Sex of household head** | | | | | | | | |
| Male | | | | | | | 0.0% | 0.0% |
| Female | 84.3% | 65.0% | 19.3% | 15.7% | 71.0% | 54.3% | 100.0% | 100.0% |
| Total | 84.3% | 65.0% | 19.3% | 15.7% | 71.0% | 54.3% | 100.0% | 100.0% |
| **Area of residence** | | | | | | | | |
| Urban | 90.0% | 66.6% | 23.4% | 10.0% | 70.9% | 66.5% | 59.5% | 58.5% |
| Rural | 75.9% | 62.7% | 13.2% | 24.1% | 71.1% | 37.1% | 40.5% | 41.5% |
| Total | 84.3% | 65.0% | 19.3% | 15.7% | 71.0% | 54.3% | 100.0% | 100.0% |

## TABLE A.49: PROFILE OF ACCESS TO HEALTH SERVICES PREGNANT WOMEN, 2003 (CONTINUED)

| Income deciles | Birth delivery in hospital or health centre | Birth delivery in public hospital or health centre | Birth delivery in private hospital or health centre | Birth delivery without professional medical assistance | Coverage vaccination against tetanus | Five or more pre-natal medical controls | Population shares of women of 12 years and older who are pregnant or breast feeding | Population shares of women of 12 years and older who are breast feeding |
|---|---|---|---|---|---|---|---|---|
| 10% poorest | 77.2% | 69.3% | 7.9% | 22.8% | 76.8% | 34.6% | 13.8% | 15.9% |
| 2 | 80.5% | 71.4% | 9.1% | 19.5% | 72.7% | 49.1% | 12.6% | 14.1% |
| 3 | 80.9% | 65.7% | 15.1% | 19.1% | 65.9% | 48.5% | 13.1% | 12.6% |
| 4 | 87.3% | 72.0% | 15.3% | 12.7% | 72.2% | 51.1% | 10.2% | 10.9% |
| 5 | 85.6% | 66.3% | 19.3% | 14.4% | 65.7% | 55.9% | 9.9% | 9.6% |
| 6 | 86.3% | 65.9% | 20.4% | 13.7% | 73.9% | 55.9% | 10.6% | 10.2% |
| 7 | 82.5% | 62.6% | 19.9% | 17.5% | 71.6% | 62.3% | 8.3% | 7.8% |
| 8 | 86.6% | 61.4% | 25.2% | 13.4% | 71.4% | 71.5% | 8.4% | 7.1% |
| 9 | 89.8% | 49.6% | 40.2% | 10.2% | 67.9% | 78.4% | 7.2% | 6.2% |
| 10% richest | 96.7% | 46.9% | 49.8% | 3.3% | 66.4% | 79.9% | 5.8% | 5.5% |
| Total | 84.2% | 64.8% | 19.4% | 15.8% | 70.8% | 54.4% | 100.0% | 100.0% |

*Source:* INEC, Sistema Integrado de Encuestas de Hogares (SIEH), special module on access to social services, December 2003.

### TABLE A.50: PROFILE OF VACCINATIONS OF 2–5 YEAR OLDS, 2003

| | Has vaccination card | Has complete doses of all vaccinations | BCG | DPT | Population shares (children 2–5 years) |
|---|---|---|---|---|---|
| **Ethnicity by language of household head** | | | | | |
| Non-indigenous | 87.2% | 43.6% | 98.4% | 68.6% | 89.3% |
| Indigenous | 87.1% | 43.7% | 96.9% | 70.9% | 10.7% |
| Total | 87.2% | 43.7% | 98.2% | 68.9% | 100.0% |
| **Ethnicity by self-definition of household head** | | | | | |
| Indigenous | 86.8% | 45.4% | 97.7% | 73.5% | 9.6% |
| Black (Afro) | 89.3% | 45.8% | 98.7% | 66.9% | 5.7% |
| Mestizo | 87.4% | 43.5% | 98.2% | 68.3% | 76.7% |
| Caucasian | 84.1% | 40.4% | 99.1% | 69.9% | 7.7% |
| Other | 90.1% | 71.3% | 100.0% | 86.4% | 0.3% |
| Total | 87.2% | 43.7% | 98.2% | 68.9% | 100.0% |
| **Sex of household head** | | | | | |
| Male | 87.1% | 42.7% | 98.0% | 67.9% | 50.7% |
| Female | 87.3% | 44.6% | 98.5% | 69.9% | 49.3% |
| Total | 87.2% | 43.7% | 98.2% | 68.9% | 100.0% |
| **Area of residence** | | | | | |
| Urban | 87.2% | 42.1% | 98.9% | 66.7% | 63.1% |
| Rural | 87.3% | 46.3% | 97.1% | 72.7% | 36.9% |
| Total | 87.2% | 43.7% | 98.2% | 68.9% | 100.0% |
| **Income deciles** | | | | | |
| 10% poorest | 84.6% | 44.0% | 97.7% | 71.3% | 13.4% |
| 2 | 87.2% | 43.2% | 97.1% | 69.4% | 13.1% |
| 3 | 85.0% | 38.1% | 98.4% | 65.2% | 12.6% |
| 4 | 86.8% | 41.8% | 97.9% | 69.5% | 11.1% |
| 5 | 88.9% | 44.2% | 97.6% | 73.6% | 11.0% |
| 6 | 88.6% | 46.3% | 99.1% | 67.2% | 9.7% |
| 7 | 88.7% | 44.1% | 98.2% | 68.5% | 8.8% |
| 8 | 86.6% | 44.8% | 99.4% | 71.4% | 7.6% |
| 9 | 85.9% | 51.1% | 99.6% | 68.8% | 7.6% |
| 10% richest | 94.5% | 40.5% | 99.2% | 57.6% | 5.2% |
| Total | 87.2% | 43.6% | 98.2% | 68.8% | 100.0% |

*Source:* INEC, Sistema Integrado de Encuestas de Hogares (SIEH), special module on access to social services, December 2003.

## TABLE A.51. PROFILE OF ACCESS TO NUTRITION AND HEALTH RELATED SOCIAL ASSISTANCE PROGRAMS 2003

| | Mi Papilla (1) | Mi Bebida (2) | Knows about Maternidad Gratuita (3) | BDH (4) | PAE (5) | Early Childhood programs (6) | Children aged 6–24 months (1) | Women aged 12–49 years (2) | Women aged 15–49 years (3) | Women older than 15 years and old aged (4) | Population 5–14 years (5) | Population 0–5 years (6) |
|---|---|---|---|---|---|---|---|---|---|---|---|---|
| **Ethnicity by language of household head** | | | | | | | | | | | | |
| Non-indigenous | 32.0% | 25.2% | 31.0% | 17.4% | 19.2% | 11.4% | 89.3% | 89.2% | 91.8% | 91.5% | 91.3% | 89.2% |
| Indigenous | 36.6% | 28.8% | 19.4% | 26.4% | 30.6% | 20.8% | 10.7% | 10.8% | 8.2% | 8.5% | 8.7% | 10.8% |
| Total | 32.5% | 25.6% | 30.1% | 18.1% | 20.2% | 12.4% | 100.0% | 100.0% | 100.0% | 100.0% | 100.0% | 100.0% |
| **Ethnicity by self-definition of household head** | | | | | | | | | | | | |
| Indigenous | 35.4% | 26.5% | 15.5% | 27.7% | 30.7% | 19.6% | 10.4% | 10.6% | 7.1% | 7.6% | 10.7% | 10.0% |
| Black (Afro) | 36.8% | 37.8% | 25.5% | 21.8% | 23.8% | 14.5% | 5.1% | 4.7% | 4.0% | 3.8% | 4.7% | 5.5% |
| Mestizo | 31.9% | 24.1% | 31.1% | 17.6% | 18.6% | 11.3% | 76.5% | 76.9% | 80.5% | 79.9% | 76.5% | 76.5% |
| Caucasian | 30.3% | 30.7% | 35.6% | 13.1% | 19.0% | 12.2% | 7.9% | 7.6% | 8.2% | 8.4% | 7.9% | 7.8% |
| Other | 62.7% | 51.1% | 19.8% | 28.6% | 15.5% | 14.2% | 0.2% | 0.2% | 0.2% | 0.2% | 0.3% | 0.2% |
| Total | 32.5% | 25.6% | 30.1% | 18.1% | 20.2% | 12.4% | 100.0% | 100.0% | 100.0% | 100.0% | 100.0% | 100.0% |
| **Sex of household head** | | | | | | | | | | | | |
| Male | 32.6% | | | 16.0% | 20.3% | 13.1% | 50.1% | 0.0% | 0.0% | 8.6% | 51.4% | 50.6% |
| Female | 32.3% | 25.6% | 30.1% | 18.3% | 20.1% | 11.7% | 49.9% | 100.0% | 100.0% | 91.4% | 48.6% | 49.4% |
| Total | 32.5% | 25.6% | 30.1% | 18.1% | 20.2% | 12.4% | 100.0% | 100.0% | 100.0% | 100.0% | 100.0% | 100.0% |
| **Area of residence** | | | | | | | | | | | | |
| Urban | 27.2% | 21.4% | 34.8% | 14.1% | 12.2% | 12.5% | 63.0% | 59.5% | 70.1% | 67.8% | 61.6% | 62.8% |
| Rural | 41.3% | 31.7% | 19.0% | 26.7% | 33.0% | 12.3% | 37.0% | 40.5% | 29.9% | 32.2% | 38.4% | 37.2% |
| Total | 32.5% | 25.6% | 30.1% | 18.1% | 20.2% | 12.4% | 100.0% | 100.0% | 100.0% | 100.0% | 100.0% | 100.0% |

(continued)

# TABLE A.51. PROFILE OF ACCESS TO NUTRITION AND HEALTH RELATED SOCIAL ASSISTANCE PROGRAMS 2003 (CONTINUED)

| | Mi Papilla (1) | Mi Bebida (2) | Knows about Maternidad Gratuita (3) | BDH (4) | PAE (5) | Early Childhood programs (6) | Children aged 6–24 months (1) | Women aged 12–49 years (2) | Women aged 15–49 years (3) | Women older than 15 years and old aged (4) | Population 5–14 years (5) | Population 0–5 years (6) |
|---|---|---|---|---|---|---|---|---|---|---|---|---|
| **Income deciles** | | | | | | | | | | | | |
| 10% poorest | 43.8% | 37.8% | 22.1% | 34.7% | 32.9% | 12.3% | 13.3% | 13.8% | 8.0% | 8.6% | 12.8% | 13.5% |
| 2 | 41.3% | 26.9% | 20.6% | 32.3% | 25.9% | 11.3% | 13.6% | 12.6% | 9.1% | 9.1% | 13.2% | 13.2% |
| 3 | 35.0% | 27.7% | 21.1% | 30.9% | 24.2% | 12.1% | 12.8% | 13.1% | 9.2% | 9.1% | 12.7% | 12.8% |
| 4 | 36.1% | 32.4% | 24.1% | 25.9% | 23.8% | 9.6% | 11.4% | 10.2% | 9.5% | 9.5% | 11.2% | 11.1% |
| 5 | 33.2% | 24.0% | 23.7% | 24.3% | 19.9% | 11.4% | 10.2% | 9.9% | 10.3% | 9.8% | 11.1% | 10.7% |
| 6 | 30.5% | 24.4% | 29.2% | 19.5% | 18.9% | 10.4% | 10.3% | 10.6% | 10.0% | 9.9% | 10.0% | 9.7% |
| 7 | 29.0% | 23.6% | 34.6% | 12.6% | 14.3% | 15.2% | 8.0% | 8.3% | 10.3% | 10.3% | 8.5% | 8.7% |
| 8 | 21.2% | 14.0% | 33.4% | 8.8% | 9.3% | 11.0% | 8.7% | 8.4% | 11.1% | 11.2% | 8.0% | 7.8% |
| 9 | 14.8% | 12.5% | 39.2% | 4.9% | 6.3% | 15.1% | 6.5% | 7.2% | 10.7% | 10.9% | 6.7% | 7.2% |
| 10% richest | 14.5% | 13.7% | 46.7% | 1.2% | 6.0% | 20.9% | 5.2% | 5.8% | 11.9% | 11.8% | 5.9% | 5.3% |
| Total | 32.4% | 25.4% | 30.2% | 18.4% | 20.2% | 12.4% | 100.0% | 100.0% | 100.0% | 100.0% | 100.0% | 100.0% |

Note: Data in shaded columns refer to population shares for respective groups of the population.

Source: INEC, Sistema Integrado de Encuestas de Hogares (SIEH), special module on access to social services, December 2003.

## TABLE A.52: PROFILE OF COVERAGE OF HEALTH INSURANCE, 2003 (% OF POPULATION)

| | Any form of health insurance | Private health insurance | Public social health insurance (IESS) | Farmers Health Insurance (Seguro Social Campesino) | Other health insurance | Population shares (total) |
|---|---|---|---|---|---|---|
| **Ethnicity by language of household head** | | | | | | |
| Non-indigenous | 18.8% | 2.0% | 11.3% | 4.1% | 1.4% | 91.5% |
| Indigenous | 15.6% | 1.2% | 5.9% | 7.6% | 0.9% | 8.5% |
| Total | 18.5% | 1.9% | 10.9% | 4.4% | 1.3% | 100.0% |
| **Ethnicity by self-definition of household head** | | | | | | |
| Indigenous | 14.4% | 0.8% | 5.7% | 7.3% | 0.6% | 7.5% |
| Black (Afro) | 18.6% | 1.4% | 9.1% | 6.9% | 1.2% | 3.9% |
| Mestizo | 22.5% | 1.9% | 15.2% | 4.0% | 1.4% | 80.2% |
| Caucasian | 27.4% | 4.0% | 18.6% | 3.3% | 1.5% | 8.1% |
| Other | 16.4% | 1.0% | 8.2% | 7.2% | 0.0% | 0.3% |
| Total | 22.1% | 2.0% | 14.5% | 4.3% | 1.4% | 100.0% |
| **Sex of household head** | | | | | | |
| Male | 19.3% | 2.0% | 11.3% | 4.4% | 1.6% | 50.0% |
| Female | 15.2% | 1.8% | 8.2% | 4.1% | 1.0% | 50.0% |
| Total | 17.2% | 1.9% | 9.7% | 4.3% | 1.3% | 100.0% |
| **Area of residence** | | | | | | |
| Urban | 18.5% | 2.6% | 13.3% | 0.8% | 1.8% | 66.0% |
| Rural | 14.8% | 0.4% | 2.8% | 11.1% | 0.4% | 34.0% |
| Total | 17.2% | 1.9% | 9.7% | 4.3% | 1.3% | 100.0% |
| **Income deciles** | | | | | | |
| 10% poorest | 9.7% | 0.1% | 1.1% | 8.4% | 0.1% | 9.7% |
| 2 | 8.8% | 0.4% | 1.5% | 6.8% | 0.1% | 10.1% |
| 3 | 9.4% | 0.2% | 1.9% | 6.9% | 0.3% | 10.2% |
| 4 | 9.4% | 0.4% | 3.8% | 4.8% | 0.3% | 10.0% |
| 5 | 9.8% | 0.5% | 4.3% | 4.0% | 1.0% | 10.1% |
| 6 | 12.7% | 1.1% | 6.9% | 3.8% | 0.9% | 9.9% |
| 7 | 15.9% | 1.2% | 9.8% | 3.6% | 1.3% | 9.8% |
| 8 | 20.0% | 1.2% | 14.3% | 2.1% | 2.4% | 10.3% |
| 9 | 29.6% | 2.6% | 23.2% | 1.3% | 2.6% | 9.9% |
| 10% richest | 47.4% | 10.9% | 30.9% | 1.1% | 4.5% | 10.0% |
| Total | 17.3% | 1.9% | 9.8% | 4.3% | 1.3% | 100.0% |

*Source:* INEC, Sistema Integrado de Encuestas de Hogares (SIEH), special module on access to social services, December 2003.

## TABLE A.53: PROFILE OF LIFESTYLE HABITS, 1999

| | Share of population that smokes daily | Share of population consuming alcohol regularly | Share of population practicing sports | Population shares (15 years and older) |
|---|---|---|---|---|
| **Ethnicity by language of household head** | | | | |
| Non-indigenous | 8.6% | 24.6% | 29.4% | 94.3% |
| Indigenous | 1.0% | 20.8% | 20.4% | 5.7% |
| Total | 8.2% | 24.3% | 28.9% | 100.0% |
| **Ethnicity by self-definition of household head** | | | | |
| Indigenous | | | | |
| Black (Afro) | | | | |
| Mestizo | | | | |
| Caucasian | | | | |
| Other | | | | |
| Total | | | | |
| **Sex of household head** | | | | |
| Male | 13.8% | 42.5% | 46.0% | 48.9% |
| Female | 2.7% | 7.0% | 12.5% | 51.1% |
| Total | 8.2% | 24.3% | 28.9% | 100.0% |
| **Area of residence** | | | | |
| Urban | 9.1% | 25.1% | 32.3% | 61.6% |
| Rural | 6.7% | 23.1% | 23.4% | 38.4% |
| Total | 8.2% | 24.3% | 28.9% | 100.0% |
| **Income deciles** | | | | |
| 10% poorest | 3.4% | 19.8% | 19.5% | 7.9% |
| 2 | 5.4% | 19.3% | 22.1% | 8.6% |
| 3 | 7.7% | 21.4% | 25.5% | 9.1% |
| 4 | 6.4% | 22.4% | 26.8% | 9.4% |
| 5 | 6.4% | 27.0% | 27.0% | 9.9% |
| 6 | 7.7% | 21.7% | 25.4% | 10.0% |
| 7 | 9.0% | 24.8% | 29.1% | 10.7% |
| 8 | 8.2% | 25.8% | 32.5% | 10.7% |
| 9 | 10.3% | 28.4% | 35.5% | 11.8% |
| 10% richest | 13.4% | 28.0% | 38.6% | 11.9% |
| Total | 8.1% | 24.2% | 28.9% | 100.0% |

*Source:* INEC, ECV (LSMS) 1999.

**TABLE A.54: TARGETING EFFICIENCY OF SCHOOL MEALS PROGRAM (PAE), CHILD AND MATERNAL NUTRITION SUPPORT (PANN) AND CASH TRANSFER PROGRAM (BDH), DECEMBER 2003**

*Targeting errors if eligible population is income poor*

| Indicator | PAE | BDH | Papilla-PANN | Bebida-PANN |
|---|---|---|---|---|
| Efficiency | 65.4% | 59.6% | 61.2% | 62.3% |
| Leakage effect | 34.6% | 40.4% | 38.8% | 37.7% |
| Undercoverage | 30.9% | 37.9% | 38.9% | 32.5% |
| Exclusion error | 32.7% | 23.4% | 31.2% | 36.0% |
| Inclusion error | 7.7% | 9.7% | 12.6% | 10.5% |

*Targeting errors if eligible population is poor according to SELBEN index*

| Indicator | PAE | BDH | Papilla-PANN | Bebida-PANN |
|---|---|---|---|---|
| Efficiency | 74.4% | 68.8% | 77.5% | 78.0% |
| Leakage effect | 25.6% | 31.2% | 22.5% | 22.0% |
| Undercoverage | 32.7% | 42.1% | 38.4% | 31.7% |
| Exclusion error | 34.2% | 22.2% | 40.5% | 47.1% |
| Inclusion error | 5.7% | 7.3% | 7.3% | 6.2% |

*Source:* INEC, SIEH survey, December 2003.

## TABLE A.54a: ECONOMETRIC RESULTS OF ACCESS TO HEALTH SERVICES MODEL (1)

**Multinomial Logistic Regression**

Log pseudo-likelihood = −7436.9461

Number of obs = 8734
Wald chi2(28) = 2111.08
Prob > chi2 = 0.0000
Pseudo R2 = 0.2122

| child delivery | Coef. | Robust Std. Err. | z | P>\|z\| | [95% Conf. Interval] | |
|---|---|---|---|---|---|---|
| **Public medical assistance during child delivery** | | | | | | |
| motherage | −.0497466 | .0335403 | −1.48 | 0.138 | −.1154844 | .0159913 |
| motheragesq | .0009839 | .0006055 | 1.63 | 0.104 | −.0002028 | .0021706 |
| ethnic | −1.114562 | .1541768 | −7.23 | 0.000 | −1.416743 | −.8123808 |
| motherschool | .1091593 | .0123994 | 8.80 | 0.000 | .084857 | .1334616 |
| segiess | .4543054 | .1762758 | 2.58 | 0.010 | .1088112 | .7997997 |
| segother | −.4090823 | .1039085 | −3.94 | 0.000 | −.6127393 | −.2054253 |
| premature | .4569984 | .169017 | 2.70 | 0.007 | .1257312 | .7882656 |
| prenatal | .9960061 | .0755828 | 13.18 | 0.000 | .8478666 | 1.144146 |
| tasin99 | 3.447864 | .6209034 | 5.55 | 0.000 | 2.230916 | 4.664812 |
| tasper99 | .0193296 | .0075508 | 2.56 | 0.010 | .0045303 | .034129 |
| urban | .480766 | .0746713 | 6.44 | 0.000 | .3344129 | .6271191 |
| coast | .5514504 | .1165911 | 4.73 | 0.000 | .3229361 | .7799647 |
| sierra | .7181279 | .1048154 | 6.85 | 0.000 | .5126934 | .9235624 |
| logcons | .8418111 | .069812 | 12.06 | 0.000 | .704982 | .9786402 |
| cons | −11.85295 | .9525744 | −12.44 | 0.000 | −13.71996 | −9.985937 |
| **Private medical assistance during child delivery** | | | | | | |
| motherage | −.0796691 | .0433046 | −1.84 | 0.066 | −.1645447 | .0052064 |
| motheragesq | .0016382 | .0007851 | 2.09 | 0.037 | .0000994 | .003177 |
| ethnic | −1.560406 | .325238 | −4.80 | 0.000 | −2.197861 | −.922951 |
| motherschool | .140571 | .0143748 | 9.78 | 0.000 | .1123968 | .1687451 |
| segiess | −.4449881 | .2005398 | −2.22 | 0.026 | −.8380388 | −.0519374 |
| segother | −.1710756 | .137003 | −1.25 | 0.212 | −.4395965 | .0974453 |
| premature | .5367914 | .193296 | 2.78 | 0.005 | .1579382 | .9156445 |
| prenatal | .8463122 | .1058596 | 7.99 | 0.000 | .6388311 | 1.053793 |
| tasin99 | −1.439944 | .8779082 | −1.64 | 0.101 | −3.160613 | .2807242 |
| tasper99 | .0038656 | .0086115 | 0.45 | 0.654 | −.0130126 | .0207439 |
| urban | .9210909 | .0914131 | 10.08 | 0.000 | .7419245 | 1.100257 |
| coast | 2.168203 | .1626961 | 13.33 | 0.000 | 1.849324 | 2.487081 |
| sierra | .955125 | .155626 | 6.14 | 0.000 | .6501036 | 1.260146 |
| logcons | 1.605723 | .0891111 | 18.02 | 0.000 | 1.431069 | 1.780378 |
| _cons | −22.71929 | 1.219182 | −18.63 | 0.000 | −25.10885 | −20.32974 |

## TABLE A.54a: ECONOMETRIC RESULTS OF ACCESS TO HEALTH SERVICES MODEL (1) (CONTINUED)

### Multinomial Logistic Regression

|  |  |  |  |  |  |
|---|---|---|---|---|---|
| | | | Number of obs | = | 8734 |
| | | | Wald chi2(28) | = | 2111.08 |
| | | | Prob > chi2 | = | 0.0000 |
| Log pseudo-likelihood = −7436.9461 | | | Pseudo R2 | = | 0.2122 |

| child delivery | Coef. | Robust Std. Err. | z | P>\|z\| | [95% Conf. Interval] |
|---|---|---|---|---|---|

**Marginal effects on the probability of public medical assistance during child delivery**
Predicted probability = .5163273

| variable | dy/dx | X |
|---|---|---|
| motherage | −.0022378 | 25.5921 |
| motheragesq | .0000363 | 696.126 |
| ethnic* | −.141728 | .036849 |
| escolam | .009289 | 8.17529 |
| segiess* | .1593452 | .081466 |
| segother* | −.0808517 | .093355 |
| premature* | .0375999 | .061837 |
| prenatal* | .1527258 | .818675 |
| tasin99 | 1.045141 | .045511 |
| tasper99 | .004333 | .915242 |
| urban* | .0049252 | .549393 |
| coast* | −.1513633 | .448091 |
| sierra* | .0563149 | .483088 |
| logcons | .0049399 | 12.4698 |

(*) dy/dx is for discrete change of dummy variable from 0 to 1

**Marginal effects on the probability of private medical assistance during child delivery**
Predicted probability = .24761028

| variable | dy/dx | X |
|---|---|---|
| motherage | −.0084823 | 25.5921 |
| motheragesq | .0001794 | 696.126 |
| ethnic* | −.1352754 | .036849 |
| motherschool | .0122325 | 8.17529 |
| segiess* | −.1203158 | .081466 |
| segother* | .0179069 | .093355 |
| premature* | .0397861 | .061837 |
| prenatal* | .0420164 | .818675 |
| tasin99 | −.7090631 | .045511 |
| tasper99 | −.0017511 | .915242 |
| urban* | .1085097 | .549393 |
| coast* | .3389076 | .448091 |
| sierra* | .085662 | .483088 |
| logcons | .1915215 | 12.4698 |

(*) dy/dx is for discrete change of dummy variable from 0 to 1

(continued)

## TABLE A.54a:   ECONOMETRIC RESULTS OF ACCESS TO HEALTH SERVICES MODEL (1) (CONTINUED)

### Multinomial Logistic Regression

| | | | | | |
|---|---|---|---|---|---|
| Log pseudo-likelihood = −7436.9461 | | | Number of obs | = 8734 | |
| | | | Wald chi2(28) | = 2111.08 | |
| | | | Prob > chi2 | = 0.0000 | |
| | | | Pseudo R2 | = 0.2122 | |

| child delivery | Coef. | Robust Std. Err. | z | P>|z| | [95% Conf. Interval] |
|---|---|---|---|---|---|

**Marginal effects on the probability of no professional medical assistance during child delivery**
Predicted probability = .23606242

| variable | dy/dx | X |
|---|---|---|
| motherage | .0107202 | 25.5921 |
| motheragesq | −.0002157 | 696.126 |
| ethnic* | .2770034 | .036849 |
| motherschool | −.0215215 | 8.17529 |
| segiess* | −.0390294 | .081466 |
| segother* | .0629448 | .093355 |
| premature* | −.077386 | .061837 |
| prenatal* | −.1947422 | .818675 |
| tasin99 | −.3360777 | .045511 |
| tasper99 | −.002582 | .915242 |
| urban* | −.1134349 | .549393 |
| coast* | −.1875442 | .448091 |
| sierra* | −.1419769 | .483088 |
| logcons | −.1964615 | 12.4698 |

(*) dy/dx is for discrete change of dummy variable from 0 to 1

*Source:* Vos et al. (2004b)

**TABLE A.54b: ECONOMETRIC RESULTS OF ACCESS TO HEALTH SERVICES MODEL (2) (DIFFERENTIATING FOR POVERTY STATUS)**

**Multinomial Logistic Regression**

Number of obs = 8789
Wald chi2(30) = 2149.62
Prob > chi2 = 0.0000
Pseudo R2 = 0.2051

Log pseudo-likelihood = −7552.6731

| child delivery | Coef. | Robust Std. Err. | z | P>\|z\| | [95% Conf. Interval] | |
|---|---|---|---|---|---|---|
| **Private medical assistance during child delivery** | | | | | | |
| motherage | −.027721 | .0378811 | −0.73 | 0.464 | −.1019666 | .0465247 |
| motheragesq | .0006387 | .0006903 | 0.93 | 0.355 | −.0007142 | .0019916 |
| ethnic | −.5256076 | .3373288 | −1.56 | 0.119 | −1.18676 | .1355447 |
| motherschool | .0531941 | .0140692 | 3.78 | 0.000 | .025619 | .0807691 |
| segiess | −.8448353 | .1197283 | −7.06 | 0.000 | −1.079498 | −.6101723 |
| segother | .3265989 | .127186 | 2.57 | 0.010 | .0773189 | .5758788 |
| premature | .1015231 | .1219678 | 0.83 | 0.405 | −.1375294 | .3405755 |
| prenatal | −.1265036 | .1085864 | −1.17 | 0.244 | −.3393291 | .086322 |
| tasin99 | −4.569829 | .7523565 | −6.07 | 0.000 | −6.044421 | −3.095237 |
| tasper99 | −.0168079 | .0053851 | −3.12 | 0.002 | −.0273625 | −.0062533 |
| urban | .4594418 | .0807476 | 5.69 | 0.000 | .3011794 | .6177041 |
| coast | 1.543108 | .1513095 | 10.20 | 0.000 | 1.246546 | 1.839669 |
| sierra | .228362 | .1448796 | 1.58 | 0.115 | −.0555967 | .5123207 |
| povertycons | .3165306 | .2297867 | 1.38 | 0.168 | −.1338431 | .7669042 |
| nopovertycons | .3338368 | .2164033 | 1.54 | 0.123 | −.0903059 | .7579795 |
| _cons | −5.597298 | 2.734849 | −2.05 | 0.041 | −10.9575 | −.2370924 |
| **No professional medical assistance during child delivery** | | | | | | |
| motherage | .0492707 | .033322 | 1.48 | 0.139 | −.0160393 | .1145807 |
| motheragesq | −.0009394 | .0006006 | −1.56 | 0.118 | −.0021166 | .0002378 |
| ethnic | 1.124449 | .1522932 | 7.38 | 0.000 | .8259601 | 1.422939 |
| motherschool | −.121411 | .0120753 | −10.05 | 0.000 | −.145078 | −.0977439 |
| segiess | −.5581175 | .1777254 | −3.14 | 0.002 | −.906453 | −.2097821 |
| segother | .4649545 | .1022941 | 4.55 | 0.000 | .2644617 | .6654473 |
| premature | −.4936718 | .1652666 | −2.99 | 0.003 | −.8175885 | −.1697552 |
| prenatal | −1.02866 | .0749116 | −13.73 | 0.000 | −1.175484 | −.8818358 |
| tasin99 | −3.655743 | .6276646 | −5.82 | 0.000 | −4.885943 | −2.425543 |
| tasper99 | −.01861 | .0075802 | −2.46 | 0.014 | −.0334669 | −.0037531 |
| urban | −.5872361 | .0733392 | −8.01 | 0.000 | −.7309782 | −.4434939 |
| coast | −.4207808 | .1177154 | −3.57 | 0.000 | −.6514988 | −.1900628 |
| sierra | −.6049926 | .1063183 | −5.69 | 0.000 | −.8133728 | −.3966125 |
| povertycons | −.084268 | .027974 | −3.01 | 0.003 | −.1390961 | −.0294399 |
| nopovertycons | −.1419281 | .0261029 | −5.44 | 0.000 | −.1930887 | −.0907674 |
| _cons | 2.874505 | .5638197 | 5.10 | 0.000 | 1.769438 | 3.979571 |

Outcome delivery = Public medical assistance during child delivery is the comparator group

(continued)

**Table A.54b: Econometric Results of Access to Health Services Model (2) (Differentiating for Poverty Status) (Continued)**

**Multinomial Logistic Regression**

| | | | | | | Number of obs = 8789 |
|---|---|---|---|---|---|---|
| | | | | | | Wald chi2(30) = 2149.62 |
| | | | | | | Prob > chi2 = 0.0000 |
| Log pseudo-likelihood = −7552.6731 | | | | | | Pseudo R2 = 0.2051 |

| child delivery | Coef. | Robust Std. Err. | z | P>\|z\| | [95% Conf. Interval] | |
|---|---|---|---|---|---|---|

**Marginal effects on the probability of public medical assistance during child delivery**
Predicted probability = .51150358

| variable | dy/dx | X |
|---|---|---|
| motherage | −.0024683 | 25.6036 |
| motheragesq | .000033 | 696.765 |
| ethnic* | −.1396402 | .037478 |
| motherschool | .0080147 | 8.17574 |
| segiess* | .1676768 | .081904 |
| segother* | −.0983826 | .094395 |
| premature* | .0376237 | .061826 |
| prenatal* | .1552804 | .818107 |
| tasin99 | 1.030311 | .045518 |
| tasper99 | .0044197 | .914973 |
| urban* | .0162211 | .54821 |
| coast* | −.1559971 | .445701 |
| sierra* | .0440194 | .485221 |
| povertycons | −.0301833 | 5.64377 |
| nopovertycons | −.0253598 | 6.7481 |

(*) dy/dx is for discrete change of dummy variable from 0 to 1

**Marginal effects on the probability of public medical assistance during child delivery**
Predicted probability = .24993506

| variable | dy/dx | X |
|---|---|---|
| motherage | −.0081345 | 25.6036 |
| motheragesq | .0001758 | 696.765 |
| ethnic* | −.1458584 | .037478 |
| motherschool | .0172113 | 8.17574 |
| segiess* | −.1107326 | .081904 |
| segother2* | .0306878 | .094395 |
| premature* | .0466071 | .061826 |
| prenatal* | .0496072 | .818107 |
| tasin99 | −.6387214 | .045518 |
| tasper99 | −.0020413 | .914973 |
| urban* | .1192334 | .54821 |
| coast* | .3204807 | .445701 |
| sierra* | .0785841 | .485221 |
| povertycons | .0643637 | 5.64377 |
| nopovertycons | .071046 | 6.7481 |

(*) dy/dx is for discrete change of dummy variable from 0 to 1

**TABLE A.54b: ECONOMETRIC RESULTS OF ACCESS TO HEALTH SERVICES MODEL (2) (DIFFERENTIATING FOR POVERTY STATUS) (CONTINUED)**

**Multinomial Logistic Regression**

Number of obs  = 8789
Wald chi2(30)  = 2149.62
Prob > chi2   = 0.0000
Pseudo R2    = 0.2051

Log pseudo-likelihood = −7552.6731

| child delivery | Coef. | Robust Std. Err. | z | P>\|z\| | [95% Conf. Interval] |
|---|---|---|---|---|---|

**Marginal effects on the probability of no professional medical assistance during child delivery**
Predicted probability = .23856136

| variable | dy/dx | X |
|---|---|---|
| motherage | .0106029 | 25.6036 |
| motheragesq | −.0002087 | 696.765 |
| ethnic* | .2854987 | .037478 |
| motherschool | −.025226 | 8.17574 |
| segiess* | −.0569442 | .081904 |
| segother* | .0676949 | .094395 |
| premature* | −.0842307 | .061826 |
| prenatal* | −.2048876 | .818107 |
| tasin99 | −.3915898 | .045518 |
| tasper99 | −.0023783 | .914973 |
| urban* | −.1354545 | .54821 |
| coast* | −.1644836 | .445701 |
| sierra* | −.1226036 | .485221 |
| povertycons | −.0341803 | 5.64377 |
| nopovertycons | −.0456862 | 6.7481 |

(*) dy/dx is for discrete change of dummy variable from 0 to 1

*Source:* Vos et al. (2004b)

## TABLE A.55: Econometric Results of Infant Mortality (CPH) Model
### COX Proportional Hazard Regression—Breslow method for ties

Failure condition is death before 12 months and analysis time is age in months of the child.

No. of subjects = 8333.41  
No. of failures = 229.71  
Time at risk = 267638.22  
Log pseudo-likelihood = − 1828.0596

Number of obs = 8654

Wald chi2(26) = 1302.98  
Prob > chi2 = 0.0000

| age-months | Coef. | Std. Err. | z | P>\|z\| | [95% Conf. Interval] | |
|---|---|---|---|---|---|---|
| sexh | .3300083 | .1345469 | 2.45 | 0.014 | .0663012 | .5937155 |
| etnia | .0797408 | .2957927 | 0.27 | 0.787 | −.5000022 | .6594838 |
| multi | .4165362 | .2798836 | 1.49 | 0.137 | −.1320256 | .9650979 |
| prematu | 1.200407 | .1628445 | 7.37 | 0.000 | .881238 | 1.519576 |
| primo | −.5664898 | .1736109 | −3.26 | 0.001 | −.9067609 | −.2262187 |
| private | −.7020839 | .226774 | −3.10 | 0.002 | −1.146553 | −.2576149 |
| public | −.2783172 | .1586849 | −1.75 | 0.079 | −.5893338 | .0326994 |
| prenatal | −.4767503 | .1670435 | −2.85 | 0.004 | −.8041495 | −.149351 |
| breast | −3.133959 | .145596 | −21.53 | 0.000 | −3.419322 | −2.848597 |
| anticon | −.0029464 | .1610362 | −0.02 | 0.985 | −.3185715 | .3126787 |
| motherage | −.0279377 | .071583 | −0.39 | 0.696 | −.1682378 | .1123625 |
| motheragesq | .0005065 | .0012899 | 0.39 | 0.695 | −.0020217 | .0030346 |
| motherschool | −.0561199 | .0226313 | −2.48 | 0.013 | −.1004765 | −.0117633 |
| hhsize | −.1832374 | .0449701 | −4.07 | 0.000 | −.2713771 | −.0950977 |
| poverty | .271631 | .1768258 | 1.54 | 0.125 | −.0749411 | .6182031 |
| water | .1937337 | .1763515 | 1.10 | 0.272 | −.1519088 | .5393762 |
| sanitation | .28795 | .2100322 | 1.37 | 0.170 | −.1237055 | .6996055 |
| urban | .0771543 | .1791172 | 0.43 | 0.667 | −.273909 | .4282176 |
| coast | −.3148814 | .2365184 | −1.33 | 0.183 | −.7784489 | .1486861 |
| sierra | −.3915519 | .2206265 | −1.77 | 0.076 | −.8239719 | .0408681 |
| immune | −2.032153 | .6001818 | −3.39 | 0.001 | −3.208488 | −.8558186 |
| b1994 | −.2984598 | .3192781 | −0.93 | 0.350 | −.9242334 | .3273137 |
| b1995 | −.3734531 | .3146699 | −1.19 | 0.235 | −.9901948 | .2432886 |
| b1996 | .0829271 | .282448 | 0.29 | 0.769 | −.4706609 | .6365151 |
| b1997 | −.2489747 | .2956106 | −0.84 | 0.400 | −.8283609 | .3304114 |
| b1998 | .0116956 | .2905883 | 0.04 | 0.968 | −.557847 | .5812382 |

## TABLE A.55: ECONOMETRIC RESULTS OF INFANT MORTALITY (CPH) MODEL (CONTINUED)

### COX Proportional Hazard Regression—Breslow method for ties

Failure condition is death before 12 months and analysis time is age in months of the child.

No. of subjects     = 8333.41
No. of failures     = 229.71
Time at risk        = 267638.22
Log pseudo-likelihood = − 1828.0596

Number of obs = 8654

Wald chi2(26)  = 1302.98
Prob > chi2    = 0.0000

**Marginal effects on the probability of infant mortality after COX**
Predicted probability = .00154343

| variable | dy/dx | X |
|---|---|---|
| sexh* | .0005103 | .507978 |
| breast* | − .0297797 | .958641 |
| hhsize | − .0002828 | 5.41863 |
| etnia* | .0001278 | .035386 |
| primo* | − .0007875 | .29172 |
| motherage | − .0000431 | 25.5714 |
| motheragesq | 7.82e-07 | 695.004 |
| multi* | .0007935 | .012168 |
| prenatal* | − .0008658 | .821355 |
| water* | .000287 | .718845 |
| urban* | .0001186 | .552542 |
| coast* | − .0004805 | .450579 |
| sierra* | − .0006038 | .481283 |
| sanitation* | .0004018 | .862462 |
| private* | − .0009509 | .284827 |
| public* | − .0004221 | .425276 |
| prematu* | .0033264 | .061897 |
| immune | − .0031365 | .542454 |
| anticon* | − 4.55e-06 | .810469 |
| poverty* | .0004236 | .472818 |
| motherschool | − .0000866 | 8.20421 |
| b1994* | − .0004209 | .184845 |
| b1995* | − .0005145 | .180456 |
| b1996* | .0001314 | .188627 |
| b1997* | − .0003566 | .18946 |
| b1998* | .0000181 | .183673 |

(*) dy/dx is for discrete change of dummy variable from 0 to 1.

*Source:* Vos et al. (2004b)

## TABLE A.56: UNIT COST ESTIMATES FOR PUBLIC HEALTH SERVICES (IN US$)

| in US dollars | Unit | Comment | Beneficiaries in 2003 | Estimated unit costs 2002 | 2003 |
|---|---|---|---|---|---|
| **General medical services** | | | | | |
| –Personnel cost IESS | | | | | |
| Nurses | per worker/month | | | 414.93 | 665.25 |
| Auxiliary personnel | per worker/month | | | 338.26 | 542.33 |
| Medical doctors (4 hour shift) | per worker/month | | | 457.29 | 733.17 |
| Medical doctors (6 hour shift) | per worker/month | | | 582.36 | 933.69 |
| Dentists | per worker/month | | | 393.47 | 630.84 |
| –Personnel cost MoH | | | | | |
| Resident doctor assistant | per worker/month | | | 324.00 | 519.46 |
| Doctor (tratante 15) (8 hr) | per worker/month | | | 702.00 | 1,125.51 |
| Doctor (tratante 15) (6 hr) | per worker/month | | | 527.00 | 844.93 |
| Doctor (tratante 1) (8hr) | per worker/month | | | 379.00 | 607.64 |
| Nurse (2) (6 hr) | per worker/month | | | 251.00 | 402.42 |
| Mean auxiliary health worker (8 hr) | per worker/month | | | 204.00 | 327.07 |
| **Construction cost of health centres** | | | | | |
| Municipal hospital | unit | 250 m2 construction, equipment and furniture | | | 325,000 |
| Health centre | unit | 150 m2 construction, equipment and furniture | | | 169,500 |
| Clinic | unit | 200 m2 construction, equipment and furniture | | | 236,000 |
| **Maintenance and operation cost health centres** | | | | | |
| Hospitals and clinics | per health unit | Own estimate | | | 135,079 |
| Health centres | per health unit | Own estimate | | | 20,404 |
| **Special programs** | | | | | |
| –Bono Desarrollo Humano (Bono Solidario) | person/year | Includes administrative overhead and targeting costs | 1,273,346 | | 186.92 |
| –Maternidad gratuita | beneficiary/year | Includes administrative overhead and cost medical personnel | 1,999,867 | | 14.94 |
| –Immunization program (PAI) | beneficiary/year | Budget divided by vaccinated children | 948,049 | | 10.97 |
| –Mobile health units | per health unit/year | Operating cost | | | 29,300.00 |
| | per beneficiary/consult | Per medical consult | 182,562 | | 5.09 |
| –Subsidies on health insurance premium targeted at poor | per beneficiary/month | Assumption by authors | | | 1.00 |
| –Subsidies on health insurance premium for non-poor | per beneficiary/month | Assumption by authors | | | 1.00 |
| –Subsidies on health insurance premium for indigenous population | per beneficiary/month | Assumption by authors | | | 1.00 |

Source: Vos et al. (2004b) and SIISE, based on budget data.

## TABLE A.57: ECUADOR: BUDGET EXECUTION OF INSTITUTIONAL WAGES, CENTRAL GOVERNMENT[1]

| Sector | 1995 | 1996 | 1997 | 1998 | 1999 | 2000 | 2001 | 2002 | 1995-2002 | 1995-1999 | 2000-2002 |
|---|---|---|---|---|---|---|---|---|---|---|---|
| Legislative | ... | ... | ... | ... | 1.42 | 0.94 | 1.15 | 1.14 | 1.16 | 1.42 | 1.08 |
| Judiciary | 1.22 | 1.37 | 1.30 | 1.00 | 1.02 | 0.82 | 1.24 | 0.90 | 1.11 | 1.18 | 0.98 |
| Administration | 1.35 | 1.42 | 1.36 | 1.91 | 1.17 | 0.93 | 1.61 | 1.23 | 1.37 | 1.44 | 1.26 |
| o/w Office of the President | 1.27 | 1.70 | 1.82 | 1.32 | 1.04 | 0.87 | 1.61 | 1.21 | 1.35 | 1.43 | 1.23 |
| National Security Council (Cosena) | 1.53 | 1.31 | 1.35 | 1.03 | 1.16 | 0.87 | 1.45 | 1.17 | 1.23 | 1.28 | 1.16 |
| Staff Development Service (Senda) | 1.35 | 1.37 | 1.25 | 3.27 | ... | ... | ... | ... | 1.81 | 1.81 | ... |
| CONAM | 5.00 | 5.19 | 10.28 | 6.00 | 6.84 | 4.37 | 6.16 | 4.64 | 6.06 | 6.66 | 5.06 |
| Planning | 1.30 | 1.27 | 1.15 | 2.04 | ... | ... | ... | ... | 1.44 | 1.44 | ... |
| Environment | ... | ... | ... | ... | 0.99 | 0.27 | 1.08 | 0.84 | 0.80 | 0.99 | 0.73 |
| Interior | 1.24 | 1.24 | 1.24 | 1.20 | 1.07 | 0.91 | 1.11 | 1.07 | 1.13 | 1.20 | 1.03 |
| o/w Police | 1.24 | 1.22 | 1.23 | 1.22 | 1.11 | 0.97 | 1.07 | 0.98 | 1.13 | 1.20 | 1.01 |
| Defense | 0.98 | 1.14 | 1.22 | 1.25 | 1.02 | 0.98 | 1.10 | 1.02 | 1.09 | 1.12 | 1.03 |
| External Affairs | 1.06 | 1.07 | 1.00 | 1.14 | 1.86 | 0.98 | 0.91 | 1.04 | 1.13 | 1.23 | 0.97 |
| Finance and economic services | 1.38 | 1.45 | 1.30 | 2.97 | 0.16 | 0.05 | 1.18 | 1.48 | 1.25 | 1.45 | 0.91 |
| Social Sectors | 1.36 | 1.98 | 1.11 | 1.03 | 1.27 | 0.88 | 1.25 | 1.26 | 1.27 | 1.35 | 1.13 |
| o/w Education | 1.20 | 2.52 | 1.04 | 1.06 | 1.32 | 0.88 | 1.22 | 1.27 | 1.31 | 1.43 | 1.13 |
| Social Welfare | 2.08 | 1.28 | 1.22 | 1.06 | 1.18 | 1.10 | 1.13 | 1.42 | 1.31 | 1.37 | 1.22 |
| Health | 1.64 | 1.24 | 1.36 | 0.93 | 1.10 | 0.87 | 1.36 | 1.21 | 1.21 | 1.25 | 1.15 |
| Labor | 1.21 | 1.37 | 1.23 | 1.02 | 1.15 | 0.75 | 1.22 | 2.92 | 1.36 | 1.20 | 1.63 |
| o/w Professional Training Service | ... | ... | ... | ... | ... | ... | ... | 2.03 | 2.03 | ... | 2.03 |
| Agriculture, Fishing and Livestock | 1.33 | 1.46 | 1.27 | 1.36 | 1.17 | 0.86 | 1.34 | 0.95 | 1.22 | 1.32 | 1.05 |
| Energy | 1.56 | 1.20 | 1.16 | 1.24 | 1.12 | 0.99 | 1.16 | 1.08 | 1.19 | 1.26 | 1.08 |
| Industry | 1.06 | 1.24 | 1.30 | 1.07 | 1.37 | 0.86 | 1.60 | 1.03 | 1.19 | 1.21 | 1.16 |
| Tourism | 0.73 | 0.20 | 1.02 | 1.01 | 0.11 | 0.04 | 2.38 | 1.26 | 0.84 | 0.61 | 1.23 |
| Transport and Communications | 1.27 | 1.20 | 1.30 | 1.07 | 1.08 | 0.88 | 1.27 | 1.08 | 1.14 | 1.18 | 1.08 |
| o/w Directorate of Civil Aviation | ... | ... | ... | ... | ... | ... | ... | 1.11 | 1.11 | ... | 1.11 |
| Housing and Urban Development | 1.81 | 1.97 | 1.28 | 1.04 | 1.01 | 1.16 | 0.83 | 0.84 | 1.24 | 1.42 | 0.94 |
| Others General Services[2] | 1.88 | 0.99 | 4.58 | 0.18 | 1.34 | 1.63 | 1.62 | 1.14 | 1.67 | 1.79 | 1.46 |
| TOTAL | 1.20 | 1.47 | 1.18 | 1.15 | 1.11 | 0.83 | 1.17 | 1.14 | 1.16 | 1.22 | 1.05 |

Notes:
[1] Refers to the ratio of devengado to the initial planned budget. Shaded areas indicate overspending/underspending above 15%.
[2] Include the Electoral and Constitutional Courts.

Source: Ministry of Finance.

## TABLE A.58: ACTIVITIES AND COMPONENTS OF SOCIAL PROGRAMS BY PRIORITY FUNCTION

| Sector | EDU | DIS | CIS | HOU | DPC | OTH |
|---|---|---|---|---|---|---|
| *Education* | | | | | | |
| 1 Mejoramiento de la educacion intercultural bilingue | X | | | | | |
| 2 Desarrollo e implementacion de la educacion basica | X | | | | | |
| 3 Desarrollo e implementacion del bachillerato | X | | | | | |
| 4 Descentralizacion y desconcentracion del MEC | X | | | | | |
| 5 Ecuador Educa | X | | | | | |
| 6 Programa nacional de educacion pre-escolar (PRONEPE) | X | | | | | |
| 7 Programa de Ailmentacion Escolar (PAE) | | | X | | | |
| 8 Redes amigas | X | | | | | |
| *Social Welfare* | | | | | | |
| 9 Bono de Desarrollo Humano | | X | | | | X |
| 10 Credito Productivo Solidario | | | | | | X |
| 11 Direccion de proteccion de menores | | | X | | | |
| 12 Direccion Nacional de Discapacitados | | X | | | | |
| 13 Fondo de desarrollo de la juventud | | | X | | | |
| 14 Fondo de Inversion Social de Emergencia (FISE) | | | | | | X |
| 15 Comision Nacional de Discapacitados | | X | | | | |
| 16 Programa de Alimentacion y Desarrollo Comunitario (PRADEC) | | | X | | | |
| 17 Gerontologia | | X | | | | |
| 18 Nuestros Niños | | | X | | | |
| 19 Operacion de rescate infantil (ORI) | | | X | | | |
| 20 PROLOCAL | | | | | | X |
| 21 PRODEPINE | | | | | | X |
| 22 SELBEN | | | | | | X |
| *Health* | | | | | | |
| 23 Control de Malaria | | | | | X | |
| 24 Dengue | | | | | X | |
| 25 Tuberculosis | | | | | X | |
| 26 Cuidado Materno Infantil | | | X | | X | |
| 27 Programa de Alimentacion y Nutricion Nacional (PANN) | | | X | X | | |
| 28 Plan Ampliado de Inmunizaciones (PAI) | | | | | X | |
| 29 Programa de micronutrientes | | | X | | | |
| 30 Medicamentos Genericos | | | X | | | |
| 31 Aseguramiento social basico | | | | | | X |
| 32 Unidades moviles | | | | | | X |
| *Housing and urban development* | | | | | | |
| 33 Agua potable y saneamiento ambiental (PRAGUAS) | | | | X | | |
| 34 Mejoramiento de barrios | | | | X | | |
| 35 Programa de agua potable y saneamiento ambiental | | | | X | | |
| 36 Programa de construccion y rehabilitacion de agua y saneamiento | | | | X | | |
| 37 Vivienda Bono Solidario | | | | X | | |
| 38 Vivienda Campesina | | | | X | | |
| 39 Vivienda Urbana SIV | | | | X | | |
| 40 Vivienda urbano marginal | | | | X | | |

## TABLE A.58: ACTIVITIES AND COMPONENTS OF SOCIAL PROGRAMS BY PRIORITY FUNCTION (CONTINUED)

| Sector | EDU | DIS | CIS | HOU | DPC | OTH |
|---|---|---|---|---|---|---|
| 41 Capacitacion laboral | | | | | | X |
| 42 Compras estatales | | | | | | X |
| 43 Mediacion laboral | | | | | | X |
| 44 Erradicacion del trabajo infantil | | | X | | | |
| 45 Perfiles profesionales | | | | | | X |

*Notes:* EDU = Education reform; DIS = Welfare aid to disabled and aging people; CIS = Child and infant support (food and development); HOU = Low-cost housing; DPC = Disease prevention and control; OTH = Aid to rural and indigenous households, and other general purpose aid.

*Source:* Secretaria Tecnica del Frente Social (STFS).

## TABLE A.59: NUMBER OF BENEFICIARIES PER PRIORITY SOCIAL PROGRAM, 2003

| Program/Goal and targeted beneficiaries | Outcome |
|---|---|
| **Bono de Desarrollo Humano (BDH)** To transfer a cash stipend to 1,280,000 poor people as recorded by SELBEN (1,025,882 mothers, 244,234 elderly people, and 9,884 disabled people) | Cash stipends were provided to 1,043,826 mothers, 226,848 elderly people, and 8,840 disabled people |
| **Programa de Alimentación Escolar (PAE)** To provide free breakfast and lunch to 1,450,000 children in school age (between 5 and 14 years old), for 160 days | In the region Sierra, lunch was provided to 520,000 children for 120 days whereas in the Coast, lunch was provided to 751,710 children and breakfast to 371,821 children, for 40 days. |
| Programa de Alimentación y Desarrollo Comunitario (PRADEC) To feed 118,221 children ages between 2 and 6 years old and 87,963 middle and high schoolers ages between 7 and 14 years old, to feed 207,536 elderly people and 30,000 disabled people, and train 60,000 people in the development of community projects | Feeding was provided to 160,125 children in primary school age and 87,963 middle and high schoolers, and to 149,135 elderly people and 28,729 disabled people. A total of 43,087 small entrepreneurs were trained in community development projects. |
| Programa de Maternidad Gratuita y Atencion a la Infancia (LMG) To provide maternal care and delivery services to 4,613,515 pregnant and fertile women and primary health care services to infants ages below 5 years old | Services were provided to 4,315,215 pregnant and fertile women |
| Plan Ampliado de Inmunizaciones (PAI) To apply 5,264,991 vaccines to vulnerable children, infants, and pregnant women. Vaccines to prevent polio, diphtheria, measles, tetanus, and yellow fever, among others. | 5.1 million vaccines were applied to the targeted population groups. By type of vaccines, services were provided as follows: 355,000 doses of BCG, 522,349 DTP, 657,110 pentavelante, 1'382,750 OPV, 90,558 SRP, 518,332 DT children, and 1'085,912 DT women, and 157,882 doses for preventing yellow fever. |

*Source:* STFS.

## TABLE A.60: PROVISION OF LMG SERVICES TO INFANTS AND PREGNANT WOMEN, 2003

| | Projected Population | Number of beneficiaries | Coverage |
|---|---|---|---|
| Pre-birth controls | | | |
| First pre-birth control | 371379 | 318471 | 86% |
| Subsequent controls | 568210 | 529029 | 93% |
| Dental care to pregnant women | 371379 | 209528 | 56% |
| VIH tests in pregnant women | 371379 | 18198 | 5% |
| Normal labor | 371379 | 102201 | 28% |
| Cesareas | 371379 | 30376 | 8% |
| Obstetric emergencies | | | |
| Toxemia | 371379 | 4888 | 1% |
| Hemorrage of first half of pregnancy | 371379 | 23135 | 6% |
| Hemorrage of second half of pregnancy | 371379 | 2024 | 1% |
| Hemorrage of labor and puerperio | 371379 | 2764 | 1% |
| Sepsis | 371379 | 660 | 0% |
| Post partum | | | |
| Postbirth control | 371379 | 112731 | 30% |
| Family counseling | | | |
| Counseling and prevention | 3990840 | 660154 | 17% |
| Sterilization | 2770464 | 15694 | 1% |
| Vasectomy | 500 | 147 | 29% |
| Early detection of cervical uterino cancer | 1757110 | 156344 | 9% |
| Sexual transmission diseases | | | |
| Siphilis | 4249006 | 2219 | 0% |
| Gonorrea | 4249006 | 2360 | 0% |
| Genital herpes | 4249006 | 807 | 0% |
| HPV | 4249006 | 1090 | 0% |
| Newborn babies care | | | |
| Newborn babies care, normal | 378807 | 117007 | 31% |
| Newborn babies care, pathological | | | |
| Intermediate care | 259427 | 11479 | 4% |
| Intensive care | 259427 | 2749 | 1% |
| Care to infants ages < 5 years old | | | |
| Infants < 1 year old | n/a | 1097323 | n/a |
| Infants between 1 and 5 years | n/a | 1451253 | n/a |
| Hospital complications | n/a | 30324 | n/a |
| Blood and hemoderivatives | | | |
| Blood components | 371379 | 9412 | 3% |
| Total blood | 371379 | 8699 | 2% |
| Total | | | 16% |

Source: Programa de Maternidad Gratuita y Atencion a la Infancia/MPH.

## TABLE A61: BUDGET REVISION AND EXECUTION OF SOCIAL INSTITUTIONS, 2000–2002

(In millions of US dollars)

|  | Initial Budget | Revised budget | Devengado |
|---|---|---|---|
| **2000** | | | |
| Education | 356.4 | 307.5 | 283.7 |
| Social Welfare | 248.9 | 87.7 | 54.2 |
| Health | 125.8 | 115.5 | 103.2 |
| Total | 731.1 | 510.7 | 441.1 |
| **2001** | | | |
| Education | 456.2 | 519.5 | 492.8 |
| Social Welfare | 187.7 | 151.7 | 126.8 |
| Health | 151.8 | 191.6 | 188.6 |
| Total | 795.7 | 862.8 | 808.2 |
| **2002** | | | |
| Education | 601.8 | 733.5 | 694.3 |
| Social Welfare | 217.6 | 115.2 | 76.0 |
| Health | 311.1 | 314.6 | 259.0 |
| Total | 1,130.5 | 1,163.3 | 1,029.3 |

*Source:* Ministry of Finance.


## TABLE A62: PRIORITY SOCIAL PROGRAMS BUDGET AND EXECUTION, 2003

(In millions of US dollars, except otherwise noted)

| Sector/Program | Programmed | | | Executed | |
|---|---|---|---|---|---|
|  | Approved budget | Revised budget | Change % | Devengado | Transferred |
| **Ministry of Social Welfare** | | | | | |
| Bono de Desarrollo Humano[1] | 203.1 | 164.6 | −19% | 161.8 | 161.8 |
| PAE | 30.7 | 17.0 | −45% | 14.2 | 15.2 |
| PRADEC | 12.2 | 10.0 | −18% | 7.0 | 7.0 |
| **Ministry of Health** | | | | | |
| PANN 2000 | 5.7 | 5.7 | −1% | 5.7 | 5.7 |
| PAI | 10.0 | 9.0 | −10% | 9.1 | 9.1 |
| Ley de Maternidad Gratuita | 19.9 | 25.5 | 28% | 23.9 | 22.1 |
| **Ministry of Education** | | | | | |
| Investment expenditure[2] | 90.8 | 98.4 | 8% | 26.0 | 26.1 |
| **I. TOTAL** | | | | | |
|  | 372.4 | 330.2 | −11% | 247.7 | 247.0 |

*Notes:*
[1] Includes Beca Escolar.
[2] Includes Secretaria Nacional de Deportes.

*Source:* Ministry of Finance

## TABLE A63:  TRACK OF TREASURY TRANSFERS TO SOCIAL PROGRAMS, 2003
### (In million of US$)

| Program | Treasury transfer to Ministry | Ministry transfer to Program | Ministry owes to Program |
|---|---|---|---|
| Bono de Desarrollo Humano[1] | 162.2 | 161.8 | 0.4 |
| PAE | 17.2 | 14.2 | 3.0 |
| PRADEC | 8.6 | 7.0 | 1.6 |
| | | | |
| PANN 2000 | 1.4 | 1.4 | 0.0 |
| PAI | 11.1 | 9.1 | 2.0 |
| Ley de Maternidad Gratuita[2] | 7.1 | 7.1 | 0.0 |
| | | | |
| | 207.6 | 200.6 | 7.0 |

*Sources:* MEF and STFS.

## A64: TRANSFERS AND PAYMENTS OF THE "15 PERCENT LAW" TO MUNICIPALITIES, 2002

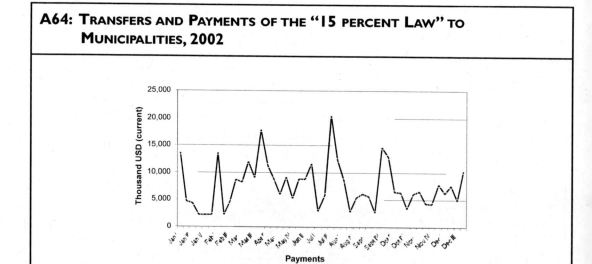

*Source:* Based on information provided by MEF (2004).

**A65: TRANSFERS AND PAYMENTS OF THE "15 PERCENT LAW" TO MUNICIPALITIES, 2001**

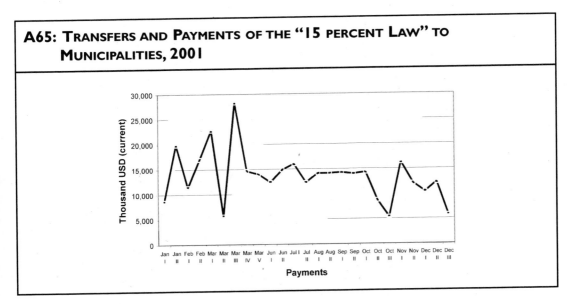

*Note:* No payments were executed in months of April and May.
*Source:* Based on information provided by MEF (2004).

**A66: TRANSFERS OF 15 PERCENT LAW AND IMPLICATIONS FOR CASH-MANAGEMENT OF THE CENTRAL GOVERNMENT BUDGET, 2002**

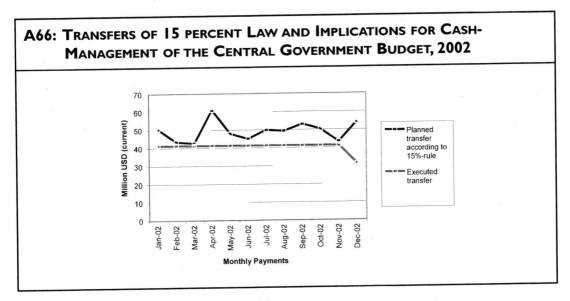

*Source:* Based on information provided by MEF (2004).

**A67: TRANSFERS OF 15 PERCENT LAW AND IMPLICATIONS FOR CASH-MANAGEMENT OF THE CENTRAL BUDGET, 2001**

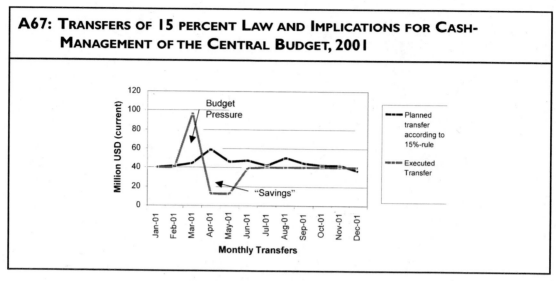

*Source:* Based on information provided by MEF (2004).

**A68: REVENUE BASE FOR 15 PERCENT-LAW WITH AND WITHOUT PETROLEUM REVENUE, 2002**

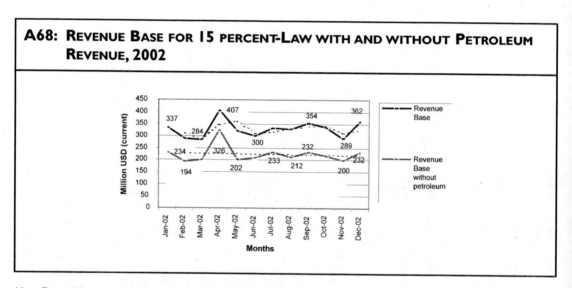

*Note:* Dotted line represents trend-line (moving average).
*Source:* Based on information provided by MEF (2004).

**A69: REVENUE BASE FOR 15 PERCENT-LAW WIITH AND WITHOUT PETROLEUM REVENUE, 2001**

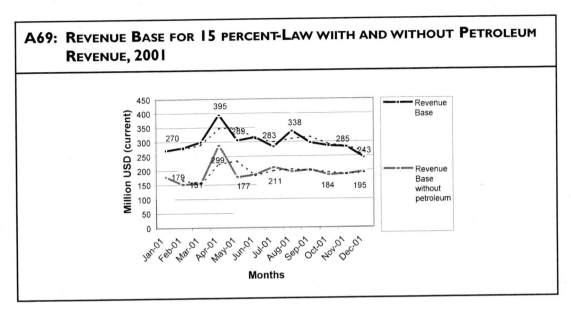

Note: Dotted line represents trend-line (moving average).
Source: Based on information provided by MEF (2004).

**A70: TOTAL PER CAPITA INVESTMENT OF MUNICIPALITIES AND PROVINCIAL COUNCILS (in USD), 2002**

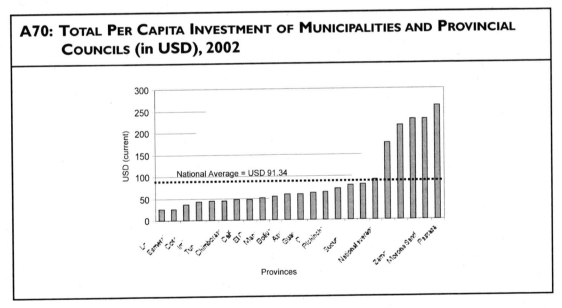

Source: Based on information provided by MEF (2004) and INEC (2001 population data).

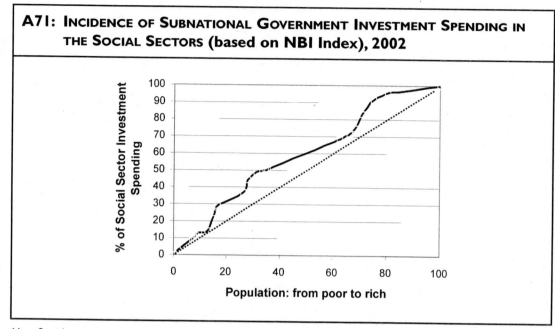

**A71: INCIDENCE OF SUBNATIONAL GOVERNMENT INVESTMENT SPENDING IN THE SOCIAL SECTORS (based on NBI Index), 2002**

*Note:* Social sector investment spending includes: health and education expenditures.
*Source:* Based on expenditure data provided by MEF (2004); the Unsatisfied Needs Indicator (*Necesidades Básicas Insatisfechas,* NBI) based on SIISE (2001); population data from INEC, based on the 2002 Census.

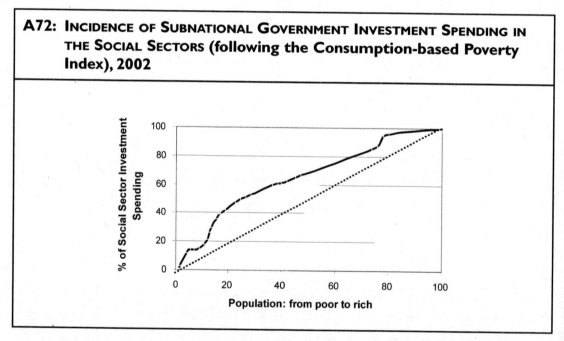

**A72: INCIDENCE OF SUBNATIONAL GOVERNMENT INVESTMENT SPENDING IN THE SOCIAL SECTORS (following the Consumption-based Poverty Index), 2002**

*Note:* Social sector investment spending includes: health and education expenditures. Subnational government includes both municipalities and provincial councils. No Consumption-based Poverty Index is available for the Morona Santiago, Napo, Pastaza, Zamora Chinchipe, Sucumbíos, and Orellana provinces and hence they are not included in this analysis.
*Source:* Based on expenditure data provided by MEF (2004); the consumption-based Poverty Index developed by Caolina Sánchez-Páamo (World Bank, Ecuador Poverty Assessment 2004); and population data from INEC, based on the 2002 Census.

## TABLE A73: OWN REVENUE AND EXPENDITURES PER LEVEL OF GOVERNMENT (IN PERCENT), 1997 AND 2002

|  | 1997 | | 2002 | |
| --- | --- | --- | --- | --- |
|  | Own Revenue | Expenditures | Own Revenue | Expenditures |
| Central government | 95.03 | 86.01 | 99.92 | 88.08 |
| Provincial Councils | 0.32 | 2.87 | 0.00 | 4.13 |
| Municipalities | 4.65 | 11.12 | 0.08 | 7.79 |
| Total | 100 | 100 | 100 | 100 |

Source: Based on information provided by Ministry of Economy and Finance (2004) and Central Bank (2002).

## TABLE A74: PER CAPITA INVESTMENT OF MUNICIPALITIES AND PROVINCIAL COUNCILS (IN USD), 2002

| Region | Province | Per capita investment in health | Per capita investment in education | Total per capita investment |
| --- | --- | --- | --- | --- |
| Costa |  | 0.04 | 0.11 | 19.80 |
|  | El Oro | 0.18 | 0.03 | 8.92 |
|  | Esmeraldas | 0.00 | 0.03 | 3.53 |
|  | Guayas | 0.00 | 0.07 | 25.74 |
|  | Los Rios | 0.01 | 0.13 | 12.21 |
|  | Manabi | 0.02 | 0.06 | 17.77 |
|  | Galapagos | 0.00 | 0.00 | 42.24 |
| Oriente |  | 0.03 | 0.18 | 37.34 |
|  | Francisco de Orellana | 0.00 | 0.00 | 7.55 |
|  | Morona Santiago | 0.12 | 0.33 | 39.09 |
|  | Napo | 0.00 | 0.13 | 54.12 |
|  | Pastaza | 0.00 | 0.13 | 35.60 |
|  | Sucumbios | 0.05 | 0.20 | 25.98 |
|  | Zamora Chinchipe | 0.00 | 0.28 | 71.56 |
| Sierra |  | 0.09 | 0.10 | 8.81 |
|  | Azuay | 0.03 | 0.06 | 23.33 |
|  | Bolivar | 0.04 | 0.06 | 11.15 |
|  | Canar | 0.25 | 0.25 | 6.77 |
|  | Carchi | 0.00 | 0.21 | 8.69 |
|  | Chimborazo | 0.00 | 0.02 | 4.93 |
|  | Cotopaxi | 0.33 | 0.08 | 3.46 |
|  | Imbabura | 0.22 | 0.10 | 13.49 |
|  | Loja | 0.07 | 0.08 | 19.60 |
|  | Pichincha | 0.00 | 0.02 | 3.38 |
|  | Tungurahua | 0.02 | 0.06 | 12.76 |
| National average |  | 0.05 | 0.13 | 15.62 |

Source: Based on information provided by MEF (2004) and INEC (2001 population data).

# TABLE A75: INTERGOVERNMENTAL TRANSFERS TO MUNICIPALITIES AND PROVINCIAL COUNCILS

| Ley | No. | R.O. | Fecha | Monto/% | Fuente | Criterios | Uso |
|---|---|---|---|---|---|---|---|
| Fondo de Salvamento del Patrimonio Cultural | 82 | 838 | 23/dic/87 | 0.03 | Localidades espectáculos públicos | | Restauración, conservación y protección de bienes históricos, artísticos y culturales |
| | | | | 0.1 | Presupuesto del Fondo de Emergencias Nacionales (FONEN) | | Inversiones |
| Fondo de Desarrollo Provincial de Bol'var | 46 | 281 | 22/sep/89 | 7.5% | 1% de transacciones de operaciones de crédito en moneda nacional | 20% Consejo Provincial 16% Guaranda 16% Chillanes 16% Chimbo 16% San Miguel 16% Echeand'a | Saneamiento ambiental Alcantarillado Desarrollo urbano |
| Decreto legislativo de asignaciones a favor de las provincias de Azuay, Cañar y Morona Santiago | 47 | 281 | 22/sep/89 | 5% | Facturas de energía de INECEL a empresas eléctricas por generación de centrales de Pisayambo, Paute y Agoyán | 60% municipios de Azuay, Cañar y Morona Santiago | 100% para infraestructura |
| | | | | | | 40% CREA | 80% ejecucióon de obras 20% forestación |
| Fondo de Saneamiento Ambiental, Vialidad y Riego de la Provincia de El Oro (FONDORO) | 57 | 344 | 28/dic/89 | 10% | Ingresos Autoridad Portuaria Puerto Bol'var | 20% Consejo Provincial | Riego, drenaje y vialidad |
| | | | | 5% | 1% de operaciones en moneda nacional | 60% municipios 20% municipios en función de población | Saneamiento y vialidad |
| Fondo de Desarrollo Provincial (FONDEPRO) | 65 | 395 | 14/mar/90 | 2% | Ingresos corrientes totales del presupuesto | 47.5% aporte al capital del BdE | Respaldar créditos del BdE |
| | | | | | | 47.5% Consejos provinciales e INGALA: 25% por población y 75% equitativo | Obras de desarrollo |
| | | | | | | 0.5% CONCOPE | CONCOPE |

## TABLE A75: INTERGOVERNMENTAL TRANSFERS TO MUNICIPALITIES AND PROVINCIAL COUNCILS (CONTINUED)

| | | | | | | | |
|---|---|---|---|---|---|---|---|
| Fondo de Desarrollo Seccional (FODESEC) | 72 | 441 | 21/may/90 | 2% distribuido: 2% | Ingresos corrientes netos del presupuesto | Municipios capitales de provincia: 25% Quito, 25% Guayaquil, 50% otros equitativamente | |
| | | | | 98% | | 20% consejos provinciales (60% población, 20% NBI, 20% Eficiencia administrativa y eficacia fiscal) | 70% gasto corriente/inversión 30% inversión zona rural |
| | | | | | | 75% municipios: 60% municipios (60% población, 30% NBI, 10 eficiencia administrativa y eficacia fiscal; 40% BdE | 40% BdE: Fondo de inversión |
| | | | | | | 5% emergencias | Organismos seccionales |
| Programa de Vialidad Rural de la Provincia de Manab' | 75 | 455 | 11/jun/90 | 3,000 millones | Previo a distribución de ingresos petroleros que recibe el Estado | | |
| | | | | 10,000 millones hasta 2002 | Presupuesto General del Estado | Contraparte créditos BdE | Fideicomiso créditos BdE |
| | | | | Otras asignaciones presupuesta-rias | | | |
| Fondo de Riego de la Provincia de Cotopaxi | 93 | 501 | 16/ago/90 | 1,000 millones desde 1991 | Presupuesto General del Estado | 30% Consejo Provincial | Plan provincial de riego |
| Fondo para el Sector Agropecuario de la Provincia de Chimborazo | 115 | 612 | 28/ene/91 | 12.5% | 1% operaciones de crédito en moneda nacional | 30% Consejo Provincial | Caminos vecinales, irrigación, forestación |
| | | | | | | 20% municipio de Riobamba | Mercado zonal y saneamiento ambiental |
| | | | | | | 50% equitativo entre resto de cantones | Centros de acopio y saneamiento ambiental |

*(continued)*

## TABLE A75: INTERGOVERNMENTAL TRANSFERS TO MUNICIPALITIES AND PROVINCIAL COUNCILS (CONTINUED)

| | | | | | | | |
|---|---|---|---|---|---|---|---|
| Fondos de Desarrollo de las Provincias de la Región Amazónica | 122 | 676 | 3/may/91 | 2.5% | Facturación por servicios petroleros a Petroecuador de las empresas nacionales | 50% Consejo Provincial 20% capital de provincia 30% equitativo entre consejos provinciales restantes | Obras de infraestructura urbana y rural de Sucumb'os, Napo, Pastaza, Morona Santiago, Zamora Chinchipe y Orellana |
| | | | | 4.5% | Facturación por servicios petroleros a Petroecuador de empresas extranjeras | | |
| | 40 | S. 248 | 7/ago/89 | US$ 5 ctvs. | Por barril de petróleo transportado por el oleoducto | Equitativo para Napo, Esmeraldas y Sucumb'os | 50% obras de infraestructura de los municipios 50% obras de infraestructura de los consejos provinciales |
| | 10 | 30 | 21/sep/92 | US$ 10 ctvs. | Por barril de petróleo producido en la región amazónica | BdE reparte 30% consejos provinciales 60% municipios (55% equitativo, 45% población) 10% Fondo regional | 80% proyectos de vialidad y saneamiento ambiental 20% gasto corriente |
| Fondo de Desarrollo de la Provincia de Pichincha | 145 | 899 | 23/mar/92 | 15% | 1% operaciones de crédito en moneda nacional | 25% Consejo Provincial 25% Quito 50% equitativo entre el resto de cantones | Estudios, construcción, mejoramiento de caminos vecinales y obras de infraestructura en parroquias urbanas y rurales |
| Fondo de Desarrollo de la Provincia de Carchi | 146 | 899 | 23/mar/92 | 15% | Diferencial cambiario de transacciones semanales del BCE | 20% Consejo Provincial 27.5% Tulcán 16.5% Montúfar 11% Espejo 9% Bolívar 9% Mira 7% Dacha | Obras de vialidad e infraestructura urbana y rural |
| | | | | 15% | 1% operaciones de crédito en moneda nacional | | |
| Distribución del 15% del Presupuesto del Gobierno Central | s/n | 27 | 20/mar/97 | 15% | Ingresos del presupuesto del gobierno central con excepción de los provenientes de créditos internos y externos | 70% municipios (50% NBI, 40% población, 10% equitativo) 30% consejos provinciales (50% NBI, 40% población, 10% superficie) | Planes de desarrollo económico, social y cultural |

## TABLE A75: INTERGOVERNMENTAL TRANSFERS TO MUNICIPALITIES AND PROVINCIAL COUNCILS (CONTINUED)

| | | | | | | | |
|---|---|---|---|---|---|---|---|
| Sustitutiva de la ley que crea el Fondo de Vialidad de la Provincia de Loja (FONDVIAL) | 92 | 335 | 9/jun/98 | 100% | Impuesto del 1% a compra-venta de vehículos usados | 70% municipios 30% consejo provincial | Obras de vialidad Equipo caminero |
| Creación de CORPECUADOR | 10 | S. 378 | 7/ago/98 | 100% 25% | Peaje vías rehabilitadas Renta líquida anual del Fondo de solidaridad. Donaciones y subvenciones | | Reconstrucción de zonas afectadas por el Fenómeno de El Niño Inversión proporcional al daño por el fenómeno de El Niño |
| | | | | 10% | Participación del Estado en incremento de exportaciones petroleras | | |
| | | | | 0.7% | Exportaciones de banano | | |
| | | | | | Prestamos a nombre del Estado | | |
| | | | | | Préstamos a nombre de Corpecuador | | |
| | | | | | Asignaciones presupuestarias | | |

*Source:* CONAM (2000): Nuevo Modelo de Gestión para el Ecuador.

## TABLE A76: INTEREST PAYMENT SAVINGS FROM ADDITIONAL DEBT REPURCHASE

|  | 2003 | 2004 | 2005 | 2006 |
|---|---|---|---|---|
| *In US$ millions* | | | | |
| Additional debt repurchase | 77 | 266 | 165 | 199 |
| Interest payments | 815 | 811 | 848 | 844 |
| Scheduled interest payments | 815 | 843 | 900 | 920 |
| Reduced interest payments | | 32 | 52 | 76 |
| *In percent of GDP* | | | | |
| Interest payments | 3.0% | 2.8% | 2.8% | 2.6% |
| Scheduled interest payments | 3.0% | 2.9% | 2.9% | 2.8% |
| Reduced interest payments | | 0.1% | 0.2% | 0.2% |
|  | 4.7% | 5.0% | 5.0% | 4.8% |

*Note:* NFPS Primary balance

# BIBLIOGRAPHY

Antinolfi, Gaetano and Todd Keister. 2001. "Dollarization as a Monetary Arrangement for Emerging Market Economies." *Review.* Federal Reserve Bank of St. Louis, November/December, Volume 83, No. 6:29–39.

Artana Daniel, Ricardo López Murphy, and Fernando Navajas. 2003. "A Fiscal Policy Agenda" in Pedro Pablo Kuckzynski and John Williamson, Editors. *After the Washington Consensus. Restarting Growth and Reform in Latin America.* Institute for International Economics, Washington D.C.

Banco Central del Ecuador 2003. Quarterly Report, Quito.

Beckerman, Paul. 2002. "Longer-Term Origins of Ecuador 'Predollarization' Crisis." in Paul Beckerman and Andrés Solimano eds., *Crisis and Dollarization in Ecuador. Stability, Growth and Social Equity.* The World Bank, Washington, D.C.

Berg, Andrew and Eduardo Borensztein. 2000. "The Pros and Cons of Full Dollarization." IMF Working Paper WP/00/50. Research Department, International Monetary Fund, March, Washington, D.C.

Braconier, Henrik and Tomas Forsfält. 2004. "A New Method for Constructing a Cyclically Adjusted Budget Balance: The Case of Sweden." The National Institute of Economic Research, Working Paper No. 90, Stockholm.

Calvo, Guillermo. 1999. "On Dollarization," University of Maryland, April 20, College Park, MD.

Chang, Roberto (2000). "Dollarization: A Scorecard." Economic Review. Federal Reserve Bank of Atlanta, Third Quarter, Vol. 92, No. 1, pp. 1-11.

Collier, Paul and Anke Hoeffler. 2002. "Military Expenditure: Threats, Aid, and Arms Races." World Bank Policy Research Working Paper No. 2927. Washington, D.C.

Conaghan, Catherine M. 1994. "Loose Parties, 'Floating' Politicians, and Institutional Stress: Presidentialism in Ecuador, 1979-1988," in Juan J. Linz and Arturo Valenzuela, Editors, *The Failure of Presidential Democracy.* Baltimore, Maryland: The Johns Hopkins University Press.

Conaghan, Catherine M. 1995. "Politicians Against Parties: Discord and Disconnection in Ecuador's Party System." in Scott Mainwaring and Timothy R. Scully, Editors, *Building Democratic Institution: Party Systems in Latin America*. Stanford, California: Stanford University Press.

Coppedge, Michael. 1997. "A Classification of Latin American Political Parties," Working Paper No. 244, South Bend, Indiana: Kellogg Institute for International Studies, University of Notre Dame.

Cuentas Nacionales de Salud. 1997.

De la Torre, Augusto, Roberto García-Saltos, and Yira Mascaró. 2001. "Banking, Currency, and Debt Meltdown: Ecuador Crisis in the late 1990s." October mimeo.

Donders, Jan and Caroline Kollau. 2002. "The Cyclically Adjusted Budget Balance: The Brussels' Methodology." CPB Report, 4.

Eifert, Benn, Alan Gelb, and Nils Borje Tallroth. 2002. "The Political Economy of Fiscal Policy and Economic Management in Oil Exporting Countries." World Bank Policy Research Working Paper No. 2899. World Bank , Washington, D.C.

Fierro-Renoy, Virginia and Mariana Naranjo (2003). Ecuador: sostenibilidad fiscal y desarrollo humano, 1970-2001. Quito: UNDP/UNICEF.

Frank, Jonas. 2004. "Revenue Trends in Ecuador," Contribution to Ecuador Public Expenditure Review. The World Bank. Washington D.C.

Fretes-Cibils, Vicente, Marcel M. Giugale, and José Roberto López-Cálix, Editors. 2003. Ecuador—An Economic and Social Agenda in the New Millennium. The World Bank, Washington, D.C.

Gelb, Alan and Jorge Marshall-Silva 1988. " Ecuador: Windfalls of a New Exporter," in Alan Gelb and Associates. *Oil Windfalls: Blessing or Curse?* New York: Oxford University Press.

Gómez, Carlos R. and Eloy Vidal. 2004. "Telecom." Background Paper for *Ecuador—Creating Fiscal Space for Poverty Reduction—A Fiscal Management and Public Expenditure Review* (Volume II)

Hagemann, Robert. 1999. "The Structural Budget Balance: The IMF's Methodology," IMF Working Paper No. 99/95. Washington, D.C.

Hodrick, Robert, and Edward Prescott. 1997. "Postwar U.S. Business Cycles." *Journal of Money, Credit and Banking*, 29(1): 1-16.

International Monetary Fund 2000. *Ecuador. Selected Issues and Statistical Annex*, Western Hemisphere Department, August 18, Washington, D.C.

International Monetary Fund 2003a. *Ecuador: 2003 Article IV Consultation, Request for a Stand-By Arrangement and Approval of an Exchange Restriction*. IMF Country Report No. 03/90. Western Hemisphere Department and Policy Development and Review Department, March 14, Washington, D.C.

International Monetary Fund 2003b. *Ecuador. First Review Under the Stand-By Arrangement and Requests for Modifications and Waiver of Non-Observance and Applicability of Performance Criteria*. IMF Country Report No. 03/248. Western Hemisphere Department, July 23, Washington, D.C.

International Monetary Fund, 2003. "Informes sobre la Observancia de Códigos y Normas. Módulo de Transparencia Fiscal." Report elaborated by Julio Viñuela, Jan Singh and Esteban Vesperoni. IMF. Washington D.C.

International Monetary Fund, 2003b. Country Report No. 03/233. Trinidad and Tobago: Selected Issues and Statistical Appendix. Washington D.C., July.

Izquierdo, Alejandro 2002. "Sudden Stops in Capital Flows: Ecuador's Performance and Options," Research Department, Inter-American Development Bank, October 11, Washington, D.C.

Jácome, Luis I. 2004. "The Late 1990s Financial Crisis in Ecuador: Institutional Weaknesses, Fiscal Rigidities, and Financial Dollarization at Work". IMF Working Paper WP/04/12, Monetary and Financial Systems Department, January, Washington, D.C.

Jones, Mark P. 1995. *Electoral Laws and the Survival of Presidential Democracies.* University of Notre Dame Press, Notre Dame.

Judge, Lindsay and Jeni Klugman, 2003. "The Budget process in Bolivia," Contribution to Bolivia Public Expenditure Review, Mimeo, The World Bank, Washington D.C.

Kaufmann, Daniel, Aart Kraay, and Pablo Zoido-Lobatón. 2002. "Governance Matters II: Updated Governance Indicators for 2000/01." Policy Research Working Paper Series No. 2772, World Bank, Washington, D.C.

Kopits, George, E.Haindl, E. Ley and J. Toro, 1999. Ecuador, Modernization of the Tax System. International Monetary Fund, Dept. of Public Finances, November, Washington D.C.

Latin American Index of Budgetary Transparency, 2003. "Annual Report," Coordinated by Poder Ciudadano, Quito.

Lecaros, Fernando. 2004. "Electricity." Background Paper for *Ecuador—Creating Fiscal Space for Poverty Reduction—A Fiscal Management and Public Expenditure Review* (Volume II)

López-Cálix, José R. 2003. "Maintaining Stability with Fiscal Discipline and Competitiveness," in Fretes-Cibils, Vicente, Marcelo M. Giugale, and José R. López-Cálix. *Ecuador: An Economic and Social Agenda in the New Millennium.* The World Bank, Washington, D.C.

LSMS. 1994. *Ecuador Living Standard Measurement Survey,* The World Bank, Washington D.C.

Mainwaring, Scott and Matthew Soberg Shugart, eds., 1997. *Presidentialism and Democracy in Latin America.* New York: Cambridge University Press.

Marcel, M., M. Tokman, R. Valdés, and P. Benavides. 2001. "Structural budget balance: methodology and estimation for the Chilean Central Government 1987–2001." Cepal. Serie Seminarios y Conferencias. Santiago.

Mejía-Acosta, Andrés 1999. "Explaining '*Camisetazos*': The Logic of Party-Switching in the Ecuadorian Congress 1979-1996." Paper prepared for the 57th Annual Meeting of the Midwest Political Science Association, Chicago, Illinois, April 15-17.

Melo, Alberto 2003. *La Competitividad de Ecuador en la Era de la Dolarización: Diagnóstico y Propuestas.* Working Paper No. C-101, Competitiveness Studies Series, Research Department and Regional Operations Department 3, July, Washington, D.C.

Pachano, Simón, María Caridad Araujo, Andrés Mejía Acosta, Aníbal Pérez-Linán y Sebastián Saiegh 2004. Political Institutions, Policymaking processes, and Policy Outcomes in Ecuador. FLACSO. Latin American Research Network, Inter-American Development Bank, first draft, January.

PAHO. 1994. Annual Report, Geneva. PanAmerican Health Organization

PAHO. 2002. Health Report, Geneva. PanAmerican Health Organization.

Powell, Andrew (2002). "Ensuring a Sound and Financial System in a Dollarized Economy. Assessment and Prescriptions for Ecuador." Paper submitted to IDB seminar on "Dollarization in Ecuador. Policies to Ensure Success." Mimeo. Washington, DC.

Reis. 2003. "Ecuador Post-Dolarizacion, Recomendaciones de Política Fiscal." Report to proyecto SALTO/USAID, Mimeo, Quito.

Rofman, Rafael P. 2004. "Pensions." Background Paper for *Ecuador—Creating Fiscal Space for Poverty Reduction—A Fiscal Management and Public Expenditure Review* (Volume II)

Rogers, Halsey, José López-Cálix, Nancy Córdoba, Nazmul Chaudhury, Jeffrey Hammer, Michael Kremer and Karthik Muralidhharan, 2004. "Teachers Absence, Incentives, and Service Delivery in Ecuadorian Primary Education: results from a National Survey," World Bank, CEDATOS and Harvard University, Mimeo. Washington D.C.

Salazar, 2004. "Informe del Gasto Público en Ecuador." Report delivered to the PER misión. Quito.

SALTO/AID, 2003. "Medición del Gasto Tributario en Ecuador. Paper by Jerónimo Roca and Hugo Vallarino, Mimeo, Quito.

Schenone, Osvaldo. 2003. Tax Policy and Administration in Fretes-Cibils, Vicente, Marcelo M. Giugale, and José R. López-Cálix, editors. *Ecuador: An Economic and Social Agenda in the New Millennium.* The World Bank, Washington, D.C.

Schick, Allen, 1998. "A Contemporary Approach to Public Expenditure Management," The World Bank Institute, Washington. D.C.

Shepherd, Jorge A. 2004a. "Ecuador: Public Expenditure Structure and Trends, 1995-2003." Background paper for Ecuador's Public Expenditure Review, March 9, Washington, D.C.

Shepherd, Jorge. 2004b. "Social Sectors Spending in Ecuador," Report to Ecuador Public Expenditure Review, Mimeo, Washington D.C.

Sistema de Información Municipal, 2001. Cuantas de Gobiernos Seccionales. Mimeo. Quito

Sotomayor, Maria Angelica. 2004. "Water and Sanitation." Background Paper for Ecuador—Creating Fiscal Space for Poverty Reduction—A Fiscal Management and Public Expenditure Review (Volume II)

STFS—Secretaria Tecnica del Frente Social. Several documents.

Traa, Bob 2003. "The Balance Sheet as an Indicator of Sustainable Fiscal Policies," in International Monetary Fund. Ecuador: Selected Issues and Statistical Appendix. IMF Country Report No. 03/91, Western Hemisphere Department, April, Washington, D.C.

United Nations Devopment Programme/UNICE, 2003. Ecuador: Sostenibilidad Fiscal y Desarrollo Humano, 1970-2010. Quito

Vos, Rob, Juan Ponce, Mauricio León, Jose Cuesta y Wladymir Brborich, 2003. "Quien se Beneficia del Gasto Social en Ecuador?" Estudios e Informes del SIISE-STFS No.4, Secretaría Técnica del Frente Social, Quito.

Vos, Rob and Juan Ponce. 2004. "Education." Background Paper for Ecuador—Creating Fiscal Space for Poverty Reduction—A Fiscal Management and Public Expenditure Review (Volume II)

Vos, Rob, Jose Cuesta, Lucio León, and Mauricio Rosero. 2004. "Health." Background Paper for Ecuador—Creating Fiscal Space for Poverty Reduction—A Fiscal Management and Public Expenditure Review (Volume II)

World Bank 1984. Ecuador: An Agenda for Recovery and Sustained Growth. Country Study, PUB-5094, Washington, D.C.

World Bank 1991. Ecuador: Public Sector Reforms for Growth in the Era of Declining Oil Output. Country Study 9596, Washington, D.C.

World Bank 1993. Ecuador. Public Expenditure Review: Changing the Role of the State. Report No. 10541-EC, August 13, Latin America and the Caribbean Regional Office, Washington, D.C.

World Bank, 1996. Ecuador Poverty Report. The World Bank. Washington D.C.

World Bank. 1998. Public Expenditure Management Handbook, The World Bank, Washington D.C.

World Bank. 2001. "Honduras, Improving Access, Efficiency and Quality of Care in the Health Sector." The World Bank, Washington D.C.

World Bank 2003a. Implementation Completion Report on a Loan in the Amount of US $151.52 Million to the Republic of Ecuador for a Structural Adjustment Program. Report No. 27471, Latin America and the Caribbean Region, December 29, Washington, D.C.

World Bank. 2003b. "Ecuador, Fiscal Consolidation and Competitive Growth," Loan Document. The World Bank, Washington D.C.

World Bank, 2003c. "Country Assessment and Action Plan for HIPC," Mimeo, Washington D.C.

World Bank 2004a. Ecuador. Development Policy Review. Sustainable Growth, Social Inclusion and Governance: The Road Ahead. Report No. 27443, The Latin American and Caribbean Region, March 5, Washington, D.C.

World Bank. 2004b. Ecuador Poverty Assessment. Green Cover Mimeo. The World Bank. Washington D.C.

World Bank. 2004c. Making Services Work for Poor People. The World Bank. Washington. D.C.

World Bank, 2004d. World Development Indicators. 2003. The World Bank, Washington D.C.

World Bank and Inter-American Development Bank 1997, Honduras, Public Expenditure Management for Poverty Reduction and Fiscal Sustainability. Report No.22070. The World Bank. Washington D.C.

World Bank and Inter-American Development Bank 2002. *Peru. Restoring Fiscal Discipline for Poverty Reduction. A Public Expenditure Review.* Report No. 24286-PE, October 24, Washington, D.C.

World Bank and Inter-American Development Bank 2003, Peru, Restoring Fiscal Discipline for Poverty Reduction: A Public Expenditure Review. The World Bank. Washington D.C.

World Bank and Inter-American Development Bank 2004. "CFAA Report on Ecuador," Paper Submitted to ROSC, CFA and PER meeting, Quito, May 20-21.

World Bank and Inter-American Development Bank, 2004. Ecuador Country Financial Arrangements Assesment. The World Bank. Washington. D.C.

World Bank and Inter-American Development Bank 2004. *República del Ecuador. Prácticas y Sistemas de Administración Financiera Gubernamental.* Technical Background Document for Ecuador's Country Financial Accountability Assessment, April, Washington, D.C.

World Economic Forum. 2001. *The Global Competitiveness Report 2001–02.* New York: Oxford University Press.

WHO, 2003. *World Health Report.* World Health Organization Geneve.

Yepes, Gomez, and Maria Carvajal, 2002. "Plan Nacional de Desarrollo del Sector Agua Potable y Saneamiento Básico." Quito